DEVIL

D0880101

FLIGHT FROM THE DEVIL

SIX SLAVE NARRATIVES

COMPILED AND WITH AN INTRODUCTION

BY

WILLIAM LOREN KATZ

Africa World Press, Inc.

P.O. Box 1892
Trenton, NJ 08607

P.O. Box 48
Asmara, ERITREA

Africa World Press, Inc.

P.O. Box 1892
Trenton, NJ 08607

P.O. Box 48
Asmara, ERITREA

Copyright © 1996, Introduction by William Loren Katz
Ethrac Publications, Inc.

First Printing 1996

Book and Cover Design: Jonathan Gullery

Library of Congress Cataloging-in-Publication Data

Flight from the devil : six slave narratives / compiled and with an
    introduction by William Loren Katz.
          p.   cm.
        Includes bibliographical references.
        ISBN 0-86543-413-1. –ISBN 0-86543-414-X (pbk.)
          1. Slaves–United States–Biography. 2. Slaves–United States-
    -Social conditions. I. Katz, William Loren.
    E444.F58   1996
    973'.08'625–dc20

                                                          95-26718
                                                              CIP

Contents

INTRODUCTION

Southern Views of the "Peculiar Institution"

A Study in Black and White

PART 1:
SLAVERY AND TRUTH

The slaves are all well fed, well clad, have plenty of fuel, and are happy. They have no dread of the future—no fear of want. [The slaveholder] is the least selfish of men. . . . The institution of slavery gives full development and full play to the affections.

— George Fitzhugh, Virginia planter, 1850[1]

So galling was our bondage, that to escape from it, we suffered the loss of all things, and braved every peril, and endured every hardship. Some of us left parents, some wives, some children. Some of us were wounded with guns and dogs, as we fled. Some of us secreted ourselves in the suffocating holds of ships. Nothing was so dreadful to us as slavery ....

— New York Convention of fugitive slaves, 1850[2]

HISTORY HAS USUALLY CONSISTED OF TALES told by the victors. Dictated by conscience, and thus often displaying more self-justification than truth, for the original losers it has usually amounted to insult being heaped upon injury. Those who have been the victims of oppression have suffered again when their story is told by their oppressors. Perhaps the cruelest joke has been that the victims have been accused of lacking the detachment of those who have merely profited from their misery. This has long been the approach of historians to African American slavery.

Although the slave system in the United States has been studied as thoroughly as any institution of modern times, until recently few scholars have examined the testimony of its black victims. Presumably they were considered too unobservant, too subjective, and their views too poorly expressed to be of much value to the historian or sociologist. For the longest time the intellectual arbiters of the slave system were those who profited from it, their friends and relatives. The picture they painted was surrounded by nostalgia and based securely on myth: Africans brought from a savage land, achieved educational, religious and cultural advantages from their enslavement; therefore they cooperated with and remained loyal to their "white folks" and so found the slave experience suited to their mental capacities, limited skills and goals in life. Southern white observations of life and truth have always been colored by this myth.

Thus the early accounts of slavery sought to demonstrate the value of the institution to Black and white, Northerner and Southerner. Senator John C. Calhoun maintained that slavery made Africans "so civilized and so improved, not only physically, but morally and intellectually."[3] Virginia planter and slavery apologist George Fitzbugh found that slaves "love their master and his family, and the attachment is reciprocated.... Southern slavery has become a benign and protective institution, and our negroes are confessedly better off than any free laboring population in the world."[4] Inevitably, those who so arrogantly spoke for those they exploited soon recommended that Northern factory owners enslave their employees.

The pro-slavery argument rested on the basic assumption of racial inferiority and to support this conclusion history was rewritten and science distorted. Dr. Samuel Cartwright of the University of Louisiana was one of many Southern medical men who discovered biological reasons for slavery's value to both master and slave. Africans, noted Dr. Cartwright, "consume less oxygen than the white" and this fact "thus makes it a mercy and a blessing to negroes to have persons in authority set over them, to provide and take care of them." Among the eminent doctor's other conclusions, widely-circulated and respected in the antebellum South, were the following:

To expect to civilize or Christianize the negro without the intervention of slavery is to expect an impossibility.

* * *

The plantation laws . . . are gradually and silently converting the African barbarian into a moral, rational and civilized being.

* * *

The African will starve rather than engage in a regular system of agricultural labor, unless impelled by the stronger will of the white man.

* * *

They [Blacks] are dishonest when in the abnormal condition without a master.

* * *

. . . the obedience of the Nigritian to the Caucasian is spontaneous because it is normal for the weaker to yield obedience to
the stronger.[5]

Dr. Cartwright further argued that since the African's natural condition was slavery, he never raised any opposition to this condition.

All forms of African resistance to bondage were classified as
"Negro diseases." Thus, Dr. Cartwright found that slaves who fled
their masters suffered from "Draptomania, or the Disease Causing
Negroes to Run Away;" those who sabotaged tools and crops or pit-
ted masters against overseers suffered from "Dysthesia Aethiopica,
or Herbitude of the Mind and Obtuse Sensibility of Body;"[6] when
slaves carried out rebellions, such as the successful one in Haiti in
the 1790's, Dr. Cartwright simply maintained:

There never has been an insurrection of the prognathous
[Negro] race against their masters; and from the nature of the
ethnical elements of that race, there never can be. Hayti was no
exception . . . when the true history of the so-called insurrection
of that island is written.[7]

Out of such facts and documentation the theories of African inferiority and white racism were spun. Basic to the class of men who
kept others in bondage, they were taught to white and black alike,
and broadcast from pulpit, press, school room, lecture hall, and
even the floor of Congress. They were the *sine qua non* of Southern
society, "must" knowledge for the rest of the white community who
assisted in the enslavement of Africans. Wrote ex-slave Frederick
Douglass:

The slaveholders are the South.... They are the only active
power there. They rule the States entirely and tolerate no policy which in the least degree endangers their power.... The six
millions of free nonslaveholding whites are but freight cars,
full of cattle, attached to the three hundred and fifty thousand
slaveholding locomotives. Where the locomotives go, the train
must follow.[8]

The acceptance of racism had its impact on both Southern law and custom. Judge Ruffin of North Carolina ruled in an 1829 case: "The power of the master must be absolute to render the submission of the slave perfect.... The slave, to remain a slave, must be made sensible that there is no appeal from his master."[9] Nonslaveholding whites, forced to serve in the nightly slave patrols for six cents an hour, took out their fury on slaves caught without passes from their masters. Men such as John Long of Lexington, Missouri proudly advertised his special service for slave owners: "I would respectfully inform the citizens of Missouri that I still have my Nigger Dogs, and that they are in prime training, and ready to attend to all calls of Hunting and Catching runaway Niggers, at the following rates. "[10] After the Denmark Vesey slave plot of 1822 a Charleston pamphleteer emphasized that "The celebration of the Fourth of July belongs *exclusively* to the white population of the United States." He added:

> It therefore seems to me improper to allow these people to be present on these occasions. In our speeches and orations, much, and sometimes more than is politically necessary, is said about personal liberty, which negro auditors know not how to apply, except by running the parallel with their own condition. They therefore imbibe false notions, and give reality in their minds to what has no real existence. The peculiar state of our community must be steadily kept in view.[11]

Individual slaveholders, of course, held widely divergent views of slavery's rationale. Untold numbers were deeply troubled by the moral questions raised by the sale and ownership of men, women and children. Patrick Henry was impaled on this dilemma:

> Every thinking honest man rejects slavery in Speculation, how few in practice? Would anyone believe that I am Master of slaves of my own purchase? I am drawn along by the general inconvenience of living without them; I will not, I cannot justify it.[12]

Other American patriots and slaveholders, including George Washington, Thomas Jefferson and George Mason, father of the Bill of Rights, sought to appease their consciences by advocating a number of proposals other than outright abolition. Many slaveholders joined the American Colonization Society that linked manumission of slaves to their removal from America, an idea as impractical as it was grandiose. [13]

Those who ruled the lives of black men and women, whether convinced racists or not, became enmeshed in duplicity and contradictions when they discussed their slaves. British reporter William Howard Russell observed this Southern phenomenon when he toured a Louisiana plantation:

> The first place I visited with the overseer was a new sugar-house, which negro carpenters and masons were engaged in erecting. It would have been amusing had not the subject been so grave, to hear the overseer's praises of the intelligence and skill of these workmen, and his boast that they did all the work, of skilled labourers on the estate, and then listen to him, in a few minutes . . . on the utter helplessness and ignorance of the black race, their incapacity to do any good, or even to take care of themselves.

Later Russell generalized on his Southern tour in these words:

> I have seen, within the short time I have been in this part of the world, several dreadful accounts of murder and violence, in which masters suffered at the hands of their slaves. There is something suspicious in the constant never-ending statement that "we are not afraid of our slaves." The curfew and the night-patrol in the streets, the prisons and watch-houses, and the police regulations, prove that strict supervision, at all times, is needed and necessary.[14]

Both slaveholders and those who followed in their footsteps have endeavored to classify slave resistance as crime, placing sabotage, rebellion and flight on a level with rape, theft and murder.

Most slaveholders maintained that they "understood" their slaves and were expert at interpreting their behavior. One of the most consistent forms of slave resistance was the slow-down, accomplished through pretended sickness, infirmity, old age or mental disorder. During the Civil War Frederick A. Eustis returned to his plantation on the Sea Islands and hired his former slaves as free laborers. He found how distant had been the minds of masters and slaves. He told a Congressional committee:

> I never knew, during forty years of plantation life, so little sickness. Formerly, every man had a fever of some kind, and now the veriest old cripple, who did nothing under secesh rule, will row a boat three nights in succession to Edisto [island], or will pick up the corn about the corn house. There are twenty people whom I know who were considered worn out and too old to work under the slave system, who are now working cotton, as well as their two acres of provisions; and their crops look very well. I

have an old woman who has taken six tasks (that is, an acre and a half), and last year [as a slave] shc would do nothing.[15]

A most daring type of slave resistance— mass nonviolent resistance—took place during the Union capture of these Sea Islands and was described by Union General Rufus Saxton:

> They tried to take their negroes with them, but they would not go. They shot down their negroes in many instances because they would not go with them. They tied them behind their wagons, and tried to drag them off; but the negroes would not go. The great majority of negroes [eighty per cent] remained behind, and came into our lines.[16]

To protect themselves from the meaning of slave resistance, masters clamped a lid of secrecy on its existence. Reported a Charleston lady by private letter to a friend in 1822:

> Last evening twenty-five hundred of our citizens were under arms to guard our property and lives. But it is a subject not to be mentioned; and unless you hear of it elsewhere, say nothing about it.[17]

Those Southerners who opposed slavery, particularly after the cotton gin made it so profitable, were forced into silence or exile. "I'll tell you why abolition is impossible," shouted a Carolina planter, "because every healthy negro can fetch a thousand dollars in the Charleston market at this moment." Thomas Jefferson began to confine his antislavery remarks to his private letters. Armed Vigilance Committees terrorized those who favored abolition and in Texas and Mississippi put "suspects" to death. A Columbia, South Carolina editor told his readers "Let us declare, through the public journals of our country, that the question of slavery is not and shall not be open to discussion—that the very moment any private individual attempts to lecture us upon its evils and immorality, in the same moment his tongue shall be cut out and cast upon the dunghill."[18]

White Southerners who wished to examine slavery with any degree of objectivity knew they were not welcome in their community. Hinton Helper, the North Carolina poor white who thoroughly documented his charge that slavery was injurious to the entire South, had to publish his best-seller, *The Impending Crisis*, after he moved to the North. His book was proscribed in the South.[19]

Frederick Law Olmstead, the Northern traveller who was the most perceptive white observer of the South's "peculiar institution," bemoaned the lack of reliable information about the region:

> Of the masses of the South, black and white, it is more difficult for one to obtain information than of those of any country in Europe. 1 saw much more of what I had not anticipated and less of what I had, in the Slave States, than with a somewhat extended traveling experience in any other country I ever visited.[20]

This lack of accurate information largely stemmed from the power of the slavholding eite, its control of the White House, the Congress, the Federal judiciary and its influence on the print media of the day. Between 1789 and 1861 slaveowers sat in the White House two thirds of the time. Two thirds of Speakers of the House, two thirds of Presidents of the U.S. Senate and 20 of the 35 Supreme Court Justices, were southerners. Most Northerners in high office, including Presidents of the United States, either accepted slavery or were afraid to challenge the slavocracy's power.

In 1836 Senator John C. Calhoun recommended and Congress voted, in violation of the First Amendment, to deny a hearing to anti-slavery petitions. It took an eight year legislative struggle led by Congressman (former President) John Quincy Adams to remove this unconstitutional "gag rule."

The slavocracy also imposed its world view on the press. Pastor Robert Trendel has documented the slaveowner's censorship of the educational, popular and religious publishers in the 1840's and 1850's:

> School books for children and readers for youth were especially vulnerable. Lyric poetry, including psalm and hymns for public worship, were purged of references to the slave and slavery. Novels, memoires, history books, devotional literature, religious tracts and magazines suffered various forms of expurgation, suppression and intimidation. The accommodation of Northerners to these practices was demonstrated by the publishing activities of religious societies such as the American Trace Society, the American Sunday School Union and the American Bible Society; of denominational publishing houses such as the Methodist Book Concern and the Presbyterian Board Of Publication; and of secular publishers like Harper and Brothers. Editors, compilers, revisers, abridgers and even authors showed themselves willing to respect the feelings of the South by removing anti-slavery sentiments. [21]

Despite efforts to hide the plantation system from public view, eyewitness accounts reached the outside world, for example, through visitors. One dramatic depiction of slavery came from Thomas Anburey, a British officer during the Revolution who surrendered to the Americans at Saratoga in 1777. During his imprisonment in Virginia in 1779 he vividly detailed the slave labor system. His perceptions form a framework for and introduction to a discussion of slave narratives.

> The whole management of the plantation is left to the overseer, who as an encouragement to make the most of the crops, has a certain portion as his wages, but not having any interest in the negroes, any further than their labour, he drives and whips them about, and works them beyond their strength, and sometimes till they expire; he feels no loss in their death, he knows the plantation must be supplied, and his humanity is estimated by his interest, which rises always above the freezing point.

> It is the poor negroes who alone work hard, and I am sorry to say, fare hard. Incredible is the fatigue which the poor wretches undergo, and that nature should be able to support it; there certainly must be something in their constitutions, as well as their color, different from us, that enables them to endure it.

> They are called up at day break, and seldom allowed to swallow a mouthful of homminy, or hoe cake, but are drawn into the field immediately, where they continue at hard labor, without intermission, till noon, when they go to their dinners, and are seldom allowed an hour for that purpose . . . . After they have dined, they return to labour in the field, until dusk in the evening; here one naturally imagines the daily labour of these poor creatures was over, not so, they repair to the tobacco houses, where each has a task of stripping allotted which takes them up some hours, or else they have such a quantity of Indian corn to husk, and if they neglect it, are tied up in the morning, and receive a number of lashes from those unfeeling monsters, the overseers, whose masters suffer them to exercise their brutal authority without constraint. . . These poor creatures are all submission to injuries and insults, and are obliged to be passive, nor dare they resist or defend themselves if attacked, without the smallest provocation, by a white person, as the law directs the negroe's arm to be cut off who raises it against a white person, should it be only in defense against wanton barbarity and outrage. [22]

PART 2:
SLAVE NARRATIVES AND HISTORY

Where in the history of human slavery does there exist another literature of this ironic sort, consisting of the imaginative construction of human bondage narrated by hundreds of former chattel slaves? Moreover, where in the history of narration does there exist a literature that was propelled by the Enlightenment demand that a "race" place itself on the Great Chain of Being primarily through the exigencies of print?

— Henry Louis Gates, Jr, "Preface," *The Slave's Narrative*, 1984

The "slave narrative," which first made its appearance in 1705, seven decades before the Declaration of Independence, was the enslaved person's personal 1776 — his or her refutation of the master's moonlight and magnolias portrait of life in bondage. Each narrative was a declaration of independence and personal worth and a fiery blast at slaveholders. Explicitly or by implication, the narratives did not leave unscathed those who ruled the nation and its economic structure. And for this reason, these narratives won few friends among those in government and captains of the economic elite.

The narratives were a unique historical development. They constitute the world's first massive literature by people considered too ignorant, oppressed and inarticulate to think clearly and argue reasonably. These books were an irrefutable counterwieght to those who claimed Africans would never learn to read and never write a book. As political statement these books spoke for those fighting to be free, and proved their intelligence as well. In addition, for a slave to learn to read and write was a crime harshly punished, and anyone teaching a slave faced prison.

No one disputed that the oppressed had a record of brawl and rebellion against those in authority, society's premises and sometimes against one another. But this time the target was a wealthy enemy and the weapons were manly courage, command of language and the printing press. In America the slave narratives — along with early newspapers, polemical pamphlets, travel accounts and tales of Indian captivity — constituted the earliest forms of American popular reading.

The narratives dramatically blended autobiography, history and anti-slavery discourse. Their authors wrote for the millions who had no voice. They linked liberty to the literary, mastery of self to mastery of writing. They have also been welcomed and appreciated as early African American literature and have much in common with the spirituals that also flowered in slavery days. Scholar John F. Bayless compared the narratives not to the spirituals but to a latter day musical form, the blues, perhaps because they were created by free people and represent an individual lament about life.

Though moored in the individual's subjective reaction to slavery, and immediately seized on as arguments by the abolitionists, slave narratives have increasingly been seen as a field for scholarly study. Recent critics have uncovered several intertwined goals. Charles T. Davis and Henry Louis Gates, Jr. agree that the narratives focused on the evil slave system, but they also had wider aims. They tried to refute European charges of black inferiority commonly used to justify bondage and to deny citizenship rights to free people of color.

European racial theories ruled the day. Philosopher David Hume dismissed African people as uncivilized, lacking art and sciences and "naturally inferior to the whites." Immanuel Kant saw a self-evident correlation between "blackness" and "stupidity." [23] Uneducated classes, often egged on by the slaveholding elite, expressed such theories in cruder form and violent action. They often required little encouragement to attack people labelled racially inferior.

The narratives also represented something even more basic, state Davis and Gates, "the attempts of blacks to *write themselves into being*" and to disprove claims they could not write. [24] They cite slave Thomas Smallwood who described his 19th century neighbors "amazed at the fact that a black . . . could learn the Alphabet." A "walking curiousity," Smallwood was invited into homes where "the neighbors collected around to hear me say the Alphabet and to spell baker and cider, to their great surprise." The narratives established a link between reading and writing — and the right to legal freedom.[25]

Read as personal self-affirmation, stark drama or abolitionist tract, the slave narrative was a hard-hitting, sometimes electrifying, eyewitness account of human bondage by those on the receiving end of the whip. Many narratives included or ended with stories of relatives and loved ones who had to be left behind. Reverend Theodore Parker, an abolitionist speaker, in his oration, "The

American Scholar," saw them as a "wholly indigenous and original" literature "that could be written by none but Americans, and only here." Not in white novels, but in the narratives he found "all the original romance of Americans." [26] The autobiographies not only revealed feats of adaptation, resilience and fortitude by the oppressed, but provided the anti-slavery movement with irrefutable and persuasive eyewitness testimony. Slave narratives handed abolitionism some of its heaviest ammunition, in the words of one, "a monument more enduring than marble."

The narrative also put a black human face on the anonymous slave who had been represented by the master as a happy, quiet laborer accepting of his fate. Bronson Alcott said that the fugitive who stayed at his family's house "has given image and name to the entity of slavery."

Abolitionists seized on these Black contributions to refute charges that people of color lacked the ability or courage to compete in society as free men and women. In 1845 Wendell Phillips announced, "I am glad the time has come when the 'lions write history.' " Senator Charles Sumner said of the narrators:

> They are among the heroes of our age. Romance has no stories of more thrilling interest than theirs. Classical intiquity has preserved no examples of adventurous trial more worthy of renown.[27]

The enslavers justified themselves with the claim that among the races Africans were suited for bondage, and indeed clung to it with a docility and resignation no white man ever would. The narratives stood as a direct challenge to this assumption. Relying on the testimony of former slaves in the 1850s, abolitionist writer and activist Reverend Thomas W. Higginson, extolled the bravery of slave fugitives:

> These men and women, who have tested their courage in the lonely swamp, who have starved on the prairies, hidden in the holds, clung to locomotives, ridden hundreds of miles cramped in boxes, head downward, equally near to death if discovered or deserted — and who have then, after enduring all this, gone voluntarily back to risk it over again, for the sake of a wife or child — what are we pale faces, that we should claim a rival capacity with theirs for heroic deeds? [28]

Other white Christian abolitionists, unlike Higginson, preferred an image of the slave as a weepy, helpless victim fellow whites would find sympathetic and worthy of their charity. These biographies added a new and alarming note of activism. Largely written by runaways, they showed African Americans at war with slavery, wielding the sword of language and fighting to reunite with their enslaved families.

Written at a time when white posses, often led by Federal officers, roamed the land in search of runaways, the slave narratives have a startling immediacy. Since any citizen who aided fugitive slaves faced jail and fine under Federal law, narrators often withheld escape details and the names of those who risked so much to help them. For years some runaways hid the fact they were fugitives, even from their families. After passage of the stringent Fugitive Slave Law of 1850, some runaways, including Frederick Douglass and James Pennington, had to formally purchase their liberty to avoid seizure and return to slavery. To escape federal posses, other fugitives fled to Canada or Europe.

Should slave narratives, written during the debate that finally exploded into war, be seen as propaganda or history, special pleading or horrifying truth? Today scholars agree that the narrators were truthful and had something to say about the "peculiar institution" worth studying. Although some narrations were challenged at the time by slaveholders, they were not disproven. Gilbert Osofky's research found only one narrative, dictated in 1838 by James Williams of Alabama to poet John Greenleaf Whittier, to be false. Its author, a free man of color, had "picked up stories from neighbors and invented others." When his deception was uncovered, Williams fled to England. [29]

On the other hand, Osofsky subjected Josiah Henson's book to a line by line analysis, and found it "authentic when checked against other sources." [30] However, early historians, including foes of slavery, often remained skeptical about the credibility of slave narratives. This and a lack of data about the number of narratives produced kept many from using them as windows on the slave system.

Since most slaves could not read or write, they had to dictate their tales to white editors, including abolitionists. This has led to another charge — that editors, who had a reason to embellish the truth or inflate the tales with moralizing, took over the process. Actually, anti-slavery papers warned against accepting or publishing concocted tales. In his classic study, *The Slave Community*, [31] John W. Blassingame concludes: "Most of them have the ring of truth. Many of the writers, for instance, analyzed slavery in relatively dispassionate terms." He also found the narratives "peopled with the same range of heroes and villains, black and white, which one generally finds in the human race." [32]

Charles H. Nichols specifically examined the editors of the slave narratives for bias, and reached this conclusion:

> The slaves' amanuenses — Lydia Maria Child, John Greenleaf Whitter, Edmond Quincy, Samuel Eliot — were persons of proven integrity. They were well aware that their propaganda effort against slavery could not be advanced by fraud. [33]

Blassingame, who also carefully examined the editorial process that produced the autobiographies, found that most editors tried to write from, rather than embellish, the actual words of the narrators. "Former slaves were asked to submit evidence and some faced hours of interrogation on doubtful points. Generally, the editors of the ante-bellum narratives were an impressive group of people noted for integrity," he concluded. Many, Blassingame wrote, were lawyers, scientists, historians, ministers, physicians and journalists, whom he said

> had gained a great deal of prior experience in separating truth from fiction, applying rules of evidence, and accurately portraying men and events. Many of them were either antagonistic to or had little or no connection with professional abolitionists. [34]

For example, Henson's editor had been a mayor of Boston, and a Congressman who voted for the Fugitive Slave Law of 1850.

Before committing their words to print, many of the narrators had spent years recounting their stories from lecture platforms with a verve and style they carried into their books. Some former slaves had learned to read and write and needed no outside help in describing their lives — figures such as William Wells Brown, Frederick Douglass, Austin Steward, Richard Allen, John Thompson, Solomon Bayley, Noah Davis and G.W. Offley. [35]

As a test of the narratives' integrity, Nichols examined and weighed the internal evidence on their pages against known facts, and found them entirely credible. He also drew an interesting comparison between the pain of the narrators and that of figures in modern novels:

> It is noteworthy that the slave narrators (like the protagonists of modern fiction) relentlessly examine their own motives and psychological conflicts which their condition creates. Fear, hate, aggression and guilt stalk them all. And their moral and psychic

regeneration — their attainment of manhood — is achieved by immense effort and staunch devotion to the ideal of personal freedom in a just society. [36]

Some scholars have suggested that the narratives should be abandoned as a valid voice on the slave experience in favor of another and more modern collection, the massive interviews conducted with ex-slaves by government workers under the WPA in the 1930s. These, it has been argued, produced a broader, more representative and more reliable data base. The eight dozen or more pre-war slave narratives, some critics claim, were not a valid barometer of the plantation experience since they were the product of successful fugitives, mainly men who fled the upper south and in freedom had enjoyed abolitionist attention.

Blassingame compared the slave narratives with the WPA interviews and was left unconvinced the latter were superior to the former. First, the vast majority of WPA interviewers were southern whites — usually prejudiced — and not likely to be trusted by Black interviewees. Blassingame also discovered that some interviewers altered what they heard. He cited Peter Bruner who wrote his narrative in 1918. In a 1936 WPA interview, Blassingame found that Bruner concealed some earlier items from his white interviewer and forgot others. In addition to these distortions, wrote Blassingame, the interviewer had inaccurately transcribed Bruner's words. [37]

Some slave autobiographies, however, include stilted interjections that sound more like the evangelistic or puritan Christians who recorded them than the narrators whose lives they were. But even these edited versions, sprinkled as they were with moral or sentimental flourishes, still retain the sound and flavor of the men and women and their lives. Readers will have little difficulty separating the insights of the narrators from the transparent elaborations of editors.

In his essay on slave narratives, James Olney explains why dozens of these stories began with a simple declaration "I Was Born." Most often the pro-slavery media called into question the status of the author. In order to prove his or her existence, the published narratives invariably included a photograph, a signature and authenticating letters from prominent white figures. Historically, autobiographers might find their motives but not existence questioned. However, the slave had to establish his or her identity. Once the narrator's existence was clear, motives were obvious and not a matter of dispute. [38]

As intended, these autobiographies became part of the propaganda assault on bondage. The demand for liberty and equal justice for all reverberated in each book. Olney summarized the call for liberation found in the slave narratives:

> The theme is the reality of slavery and necessity of abolishing it; the content is a series of events and descriptions that will make the reader see and feel the realities of slavery; and the form is a chronological, episodic narrative beginning with the assertion of existence and surrounded by various testimonial evidences for that assertion. [39]

How effective were the narratives? In 1849 a white reviewer of Henry Bibb's *Narrative* said "narratives of slaves go right to the hearts of men" and were "destined to be a powerful lever." [40] *New York Times* journalist Frederich Law Olmsted regretted the fact that the narratives shaped the northern view of bondage.[41] Whether offered from lecture platforms or read in inexpensive autobiographies, the testimony of former slaves probably delivered the strongest possible messages about the slave system. The narrators gave whites who had been taught to turn away from Black pain a rare opportunity to identify with the narrators and their family members, and perhaps all held in bondage. Henry Bibb was able to bring white audiences to tears with his story of how his wife was stripped and beaten by a drunken slaveholder. From this testimony many Americans learned, often for the first time, that the millions in chains longed for liberty and were desperate to reunite with their families. In delivering blows to the ideological underpinnings of an oppressive system, the narratives also proved the humanity, intelligence and Christian piety of the victims.

In these plaintive tales the personal, the literary and the political were often inseparable. A reviewer of Frederick Douglass' *My Bondage and My Freedom* (1855) wrote:

> The mere fact that the member of an outcast and enslaved race should accomplish his freedom, and educate himself up to an equality of intellectual and moral vigor with the leaders of the race by which he was held in bondage, is, in itself, so remarkable that the story of the change cannot be otherwise than exciting.[42]

At about 25 cents a copy, slave narratives were often hawked at anti-slavery meetings and generally sold well. Authors sometimes ploughed profits back into projects aimed at spreading the abolitionist message. To "abolitionize" Ohio in the 1850s, Sojourner Truth piled 600 copies of her narrative into an old wagon, and crossed the state to lecture and sell copies. Some narrators used their profits to buy the freedom of relatives, and to begin a new life in the North, Canada or Europe. Others found their narratives had catapulted them into a high visibility role in the anti-slavery movement.

The autobiographies became popular reading in antebellum America. Benjamin Quarles believed virtually any former slave could get into print, a rare moment for African American authors. Moses Roper's story, first published in 1837, reached ten printings and was published in Celtic. Henson's story sold 6,000 copies in 1852, was translated into French and Dutch, and by 1878 had sold 100,000 copies. William Wells Brown's book had four printings in 1847 and sold 8,000 copies by 1849. By that year Douglass' narrative had gone through seven printings since 1845. Between 1853 and 1854 Solomon Northup sold 27,000 copies of his experience as a free New Yorker who was seized in Washington, D.C. and forced into slavery in Louisiana.[43]

If there was any exploitation involved in the production and sale of these autobiographies, it benefited both former slave authors and an American audience that needed this exposure to a pressing public issue. Douglass wrote his former master, "I intend to make full use of you as a weapon with which to assail the system of slavery."

Each work reminded readers that other human beings like the author and his family remained in chains. These tales were carried to a wider audience by abolitionist weeklys and this ex-slave literary output prepared the reading public for Harriet Beecher Stowe's *Uncle Tom's Cabin*, and one must add, for emancipation.[44]

In 1852 as her novel gripped the land, Mrs. Stowe arranged a nationwide tour of churches by former slave, Milly Edmundson, who was able to raise enough money in New Haven, New York, Boston, Brooklyn and Portland to purchase the liberty of her two children. However, Stowe chose to make her novel's hero, Uncle Tom, a weak, defenseless creature unable to stand up to any white person, unlike the real life runaway, Josiah Henson, who was her model.[45]

The autobiographies could be riveting reading. Abolitionist Lewis Tappan wrote about the impact of Douglass' book upon him and his wife: "Its contents will be laid up in our hearts." The slave narratives, wrote Benjamin Quarles, created "an adverse image of slavery that helped make possible the emergence of a Mrs. Stowe and an Abraham Lincoln."[46]

In recent decades critics who have examined the narratives have characterized them as useful biography, important history and increasingly as a compelling part of African American literature. Scholars have concluded the narratives form a distinct genre of American literature. Their reputation for accuracy has been steadily rising, and they have been judged a better data source on bondage and more influential in their time than previously believed.[47]

The six narrators in this compendium demonstrate an understandable rage against a system that held their lives and families in contempt and offered only family dislocation, pain and death. The authors uncover the shocking nature of enslavement, and direct some furious words at horrible practices and particularly vicious overseers and owners. Despite bitter experiences the narrators are remarkably free of gross exaggeration, anti-white animosity or a desire for vengeance. Almost always the enemy is the same — the inhuman slave system that debases all it touches.

The narratives provide important information about the day-to-day working of the "peculiar institution," its psychological complexities, economic underpinnings and the ever-so-human responses of its victims. Not intended as pleasant reading, they have the sting of personal anger and the bite of political declaration. Despite the limitations of each narrator to do more than report on his or her individual experiences, taken together, they add immeasurably to perceptions of a common history. Though depicting an institution rooted in a by-gone era and formally buried by the 13th Amendment to the Constitution, the narrators describe patterns of thought and behavior that survived the burial and still reverberate in the land.

In 1968 when *Five Slave Narratives* appeared, it was the first of its kind. Until then publishers in the 20th century had issued the classic autobiographies of Frederick Douglass and Booker T. Washington and ignored the others. A few collections of African American writing, such as *The Negro Caravan* (1941) did provide excerpts from other than these classic narratives.[48]

Five Slave Narratives was one book in the 146-volume Arno Press/*New York Times* reprint series, *The American Negro: History and Literature* in which I served as General Editor. The five autobiographies selected for the volume came from an African American book collection my father had started in the 1930s. The goal in publishing the five narratives under a single cover was to provide the reading public with testimonies about bondage written by lesser known figures than Douglass and Washington, and to provide students with a format that allowed for comparative studies.[49]

A year after *Five Slave Narratives* appeared, Benjamin Quarles' fine study, *Black Abolitionists*, documented the contribution of former slaves to the anti-slavery crusade and emphasized the role of the narratives as both evidence and propaganda in the struggle against bondage and for equality. And before the year ended such noted scholars as Arna Bontemps and Gilbert Osofsky each had selected three slave narratives for publication under one cover by a mainstream publisher.

In *Great Slave Narratives*, Bontemps reprinted the stories of Gustavus Vassa, James Pennington and Ellen and William Craft. In *Puttin' On Ole Massa*, Osofsky reissued the narratives of Henry Bibb, William Wells Brown and Solomon Northup. That same year *Many Thousand Gone*, Charles H. Nichols' study originally printed in 1963 in Leiden, Holland, and based on excerpts from narratives, appeared in an American paper edition.

In the next two decades significant studies of the narratives began to appear. In 1972 James W. Blassingame issued his pathbreaking *The Slave Community* which relied heavily on the narratives. That year George P. Rawick began the project of editing and publishing 41 volumes of slave testimonies, a daunting task that was completed in 1979.[50]

By the 1970s, feminist scholars led a search for the 12% of narratives written by enslaved women, whose oppression and indignities were multiplied when sex was added to race. A major break-through came in 1981 when Jean Fagan Yellin, a participant in the Arno Press series, was able to verify the authenticity of Harriet Jacobs' astounding narrative.[51]

This new research into the southern plantation system reversed a pattern of concealment and deception that stretched from the days of slavery into the 20th century. Between the Civil War and the 1960s most white Americans had come to assume that the enslaved left no record of their feelings. In 1939 historian John S. Kendall wrote that slaves' views of life were not only unknown but unknowable: "The slaves themselves never told. . . . [T]hey had no literary gift." Kendall's assessment appeared the same year as Hollywood's classic *Gone With the Wind*, which perpetuated the slaveholder's perception of bondage as benign and the master-slave relationship as endearing.[52]

As recently as 1966 Dwight Lowell Dumond's sympathetic study of the anti-slavery crusade marginalized black participation. Though he praised the slave narratives as showing "the very depths of depravity to which the slave system had sunk," he claimed that these autobiograhies began with Frederick Douglass and included only "four others." [53]

The narratives in this volume offer varied views of American slavery during its four final decades. Locales range from the Carolinas and Alabama to Maryland and Kentucky; occupations from blacksmiths and field hands to small entrepeneurs and forced concubines. In his life as a slave, for example, William Wells Brown worked as a field laborer, in a St. Louis doctor's office, in a saloon, for a printer, a tailor, a barber and on a steamboat that sailed the Mississippi from St. Louis to New Orleans.

After the Fugitive Slave Law of 1850, those who escaped could be legally seized by federal authorities anywhere in the United States and returned to their former masters. If a court hearing was required, the victims were denied the right to testify. The presiding judge received $10 if he ruled that a Black defendant was a slave, $5 if he did not.

Each narrative in this book has been reproduced in its original publishing form and includes all letters of endorsement standard for the genre, along with appropriate documents, such as slave bills of sale found in the orginal.

Who then are the six narrators? William Wells Brown was born to an enslaved woman in 1816 in Lexington, Kentucky. He wrote his life story in 1847 and soon became a leading African American intellectual and an abolitionist with an international reputation. He later wrote the first African American novel, several travel books and some early volumes on Black history.

Moses Grandy, born a slave in North Carolina never knew his year of birth. He dictated his poignant story to the noted British abolitionist George Thompson who preserved the "language of Moses himself." Grandy's direct, factual story ends with a chilling accounting sheet that details how much he paid for the freedom of each member of his family, and speaks of his hope to gain the liberty of his enslaved sister, Mary.

Lunsford Lane, born in 1803 on a North Carolina plantation

to a house slave, secretly learned to read and write. He then was able to pursue an entrepeneurial career denied other slaves. As a free man, he expanded his literary skills and had "the services of a friend" in writing his story. Like others, his book was part of a committed struggle to free loved ones. The same year his narrative was published, Lane addressed a meeting of the Liberty party in Boston and raised $33 toward the purchase of a relative still in chains.

James Pennington, born into slavery in Maryland, ran away at 21. In 1841, he wrote the first textbook history of African Americans, and in 1849 wrote his narrative. In 1856, as an ordained minister, he challenged segregation of passengers on New York City's 6th Avenue horse-drawn street cars with direct action. Pennington, said an eyewitness, was carried "backward through the car, the doctor apparently making all the resistance in his power." He sued in court, but not successfully.[54]

Jacob Stroyer, born in 1849 to an African father, was emancipated by Federal bayonets in April, 1865 in Columbia, South Carolina. He wrote his narrative more than a decade after the Civil War. By then he was a clergyman in Salem, Massachusetts. As the only one of the six volumes written after slavery was abolished, Stroyer's story may provide insights into how the issue of human liberty was viewed by one who no longer stood in danger of losing his.

Harriet Jacobs' narrative was not a part of the original *Five Slave Narratives* and was added to this edition for balance. Published originally in 1861, it remained out of print for more than a century. It has justifiably provoked a great deal of interest by women scholars. Jacobs' tale was one of the few by a woman and one that dared to openly discuss sexual exploitation under slavery. Under the name of Linda Brent, the author wrote, "Slavery is terrible for men, but it is far more terrible for women." At 28, Jacobs escaped from the sexual bondage of a white man, and waited a decade to write her story. She felt obliged to change names and hide details of her escape route. Her story is the longest and most thorough of the six in this volume.

Jacobs knew how to read and write and was fortunate in her editor, Lydia Marie Child, the noted children's writer, who took credit for such minor revisions as "condensation and orderly arrangement." In 1979 Blassingame questioned the autobiography's authenicity as "too orderly . . . too melodramatic." However, scholar Jean Fagin Yellin, who first accepted this assessement, established its veracity on all major points and many minor ones when she uncovered unpublished writings by Jacobs and pursued other research.[55]

These six autobiographies reveal the varied, deeply human responses of individuals who had to face the oppressive slave system. Together, they detail a painful chapter in America's past. And they represent a unique American genre that can be read as history, biography and literature.

The import and majesty of the slave narratives have not been lost on serious American writers. African American critic Arna Bontemps said slave narratives influenced Mark Twain, Herman Melville and "consciously or unconsciously" major African American authors who "reveal in their writing a debt to the narratives. . . ." [56] In our own day, Toni Morrison, Alice Walker and other significant writers of color have acknowledged their debt to these timeless, plaintive testaments to the African American spirit in chains.

— William Loren Katz, 1995

NOTES

1. George Fitzhugh, *Slavery Justified By A Southerner* (Fredericksburg, 1850).
2. "Letter to the American Slaves," *Anti-Slavery Bugle,* September 28, 1850, reprinted in *Common Ground,* VIII (Spring, 1947), 22.
3. *Congressional Globe,* 24th Congress, Second Session, 158.
4. George Fitzhugh, *Cannibals All!* (Richmond, 1857), 200.
5. S.A. Cartwright, "Slavery in the Light of Ethnology," 713-726, in E.N. Elliott (Ed.), *Cotton is King, and Pro-Slavery Arguments* (Savannah, 1860).
6. Dr. Cartwright of New Orleans, "1. Diseases and Peculiarities of the Negro Race," *De Bow's Review,* XII (September, 1851), 331-334.
7. S.A. Cartwright, *Op. Cit.*
8. *Frederick Douglass' Monthly,* April, 1861, 1.
9. William Goodell, *The American Slave Code* (New York, 1853), 172-173. Similar decisions for Alabama, Virginia and Louisiana appear on pages 92-93 and 322-323.
10. George W. Carlton (Ed.), *The Suppressed Book About Slavery!* (New York, 1864), 326-327.
11. Thomas Wentworth Higginson, "Denmark Vesey," *Atlantic Monthly* (June, 1861), 743.
12. Lydia Maria Child, *The Evils of Slavery, and The Cure of Slavery* (Newburyport, 1836), 3.
13. See James Forten letter, January 25, 1817 to Paul Cuffe, Paul Cuffe papers, New Bedford Library, in William Loren Katz, *Eyewitness: The Negro in American History* (New York, 1967), 147-148.

14. William Howard Russell, *My Diary North and South* (New York, 1863), 55, 105.

15. "Preliminary Report of the Freedmen's Inquiry Commission," June 30, 1863, *Official Records of the Union and Confederate Armies*, Series 3, III, 435.

16. *Report of the Joint Committee on the Conduct of the War*, 37th Congress, Third Session (No. 108, Washington, D.C., 1863), 327.

17. Harvey Wish, "American Slave Insurrections Before 1861," *Journal of Negro History*, XXI (July, 1939), 239.

18. Columbia, South Carolina *Telescope*, in Ralph Korngold, *Two Friends of Man* (Boston, 1950), 90.

19. Hinton Rowan Helper, *The Impending Crisis of the South* (New York, 1857) used statistics and documents to establish that slavery had ruined the lives of Southern whites as well as Blacks.

20. Frederick Law Olmstead, *A Journey in the Seaboard Slave States* (New York, 1856), 178-179.

21. Robert Trendel, "The Expurgation of Antislavery Materials by American Presses," *Journal of Negro History*, LVIII, 3, July, 1973, 271-275.

22. (Thomas Anburey), *Travels Through the Interior Parts of America by an Officer* (London, William Lane, 1889) II, Letter LXII, January 20, 1779, 330-334.

23. Charles T. Davis and Henry Louis Gates, Jr., *The Slave's Narrative* (New York, 1990), XXVI.

24. *Ibid*, XV, XXIII.

25. *Ibid*, XVII, XXIX.

26. *Ibid*, XXIII, XXI.

27. *Ibid*, XVI; *Liberator*, October 22, 1852 in Gilbert Osofsky (Ed.) *Puttin' On Ole Massa* (New York, 1969).

28. "Physical Courage," *Atlantic Monthly*, XIII (November,1858), 732.

29. Whittier wrote in the *Emancipator*, September 20, 1838: "Our cause needs no support of a doubtful character, and if the narrative in any essential particuliar is untrue, the slaveholders of Virginia and Alabama will confer a favor on us by immediately pronouncing testimony to that effect." Further, James Birney, a former Alabama slavemaster turned abolitionist, and later the Liberty party's Presidential candidate in 1840 and 1844, reassured Whittier that he found Williams' statements accorded with his knowledge. Birney is cited in Charles H. Nichols, *Many Thousand Gone*, (Leiden, Netherlands, 1963), XI.

30. Osofsky, *Op. Cit.*, 12-13.

31. John. W. Blassingame, *The Slave Community* (New York, 1979, revised and enlarged edition), 371; See also John W. Blassingame, "Using the Testimony of Ex-Slaves: Approaches and Problems," 78-97, in Davis and Gates, *Op. Cit.*

32. *Ibid*, 372.

33. Charles H. Nichols, *Many Thousand Gone*, (Leiden, Netherlands, 1963), XIII.

34. Blassingame, *Op. Cit.*, 79.

35. *Ibid.*, 83.

36. Charles A. Nichols, "The Slave Narrators and the Picaresque Mode: Archetypes for Modern Black Personae," in Davis and Gates, *Op. Cit.*, 285.

37. John W. Blassingame, *Op. Cit.*, 92. For an early collection of WPA ex-slave interviews see B.A. Botkin, *Lay My Burden Down* (Chicago,1946).

38. James Olney, "I was Born," in Gates and Davis, *Op. Cit.*,151-155.

39. *Ibid*, 156.

40. *The Anti-Slavery Bugle*, November 3, 1849, 1, cited in *Ibid.*, 29.

41. *A Journey in the Seaboard States*, I (New York, 1856), 198-199.

42. August Meier and Elliott Rudwick, *From Plantation to Ghetto* (Third Edition, New York, 1976), 146.

43. Charles Nichols, *Op. Cit.*, XII-XIII.

44. Arna Bontemps (Ed.), *Great Slave Narratives* (Boston, 1969), XI; Benjamin Quarles, *Black Abolitionists* (New York, 1969), 66-67.

45. Herbert Aptheker, *Abolitionism: A Revolutionary Movement* (Boston, 1989), 62. This study casts new light on the basic thrust of the anti-slavery vanguard. Henson was a conductor on the underground railroad and a strong anti-slavery voice during his life as a free man.

46. Benjamin Quarles, *Op. Cit.*, 66-67.

47. Sterling A. Brown, Arthur P. Davis and Ulysses Lee (Eds.), *The Negro Caravan,* (New York, 1941), 694-697; see also John W. Blassingame and Charles T. Davis (Eds.), *The Slave Narrative: Its Place In American History* (Washington, D.C.,1988), a reprinted edition of Marion Wilson Starling's 1946 dissertation, a seminal study of the genre.

48. *Ibid. The Negro Caravan's* thousand plus page compendium reprinted excerpts from a host of slave narratives on pages 703-745, critical comments and a spirited defense of their value as history and as the earliest example of African American autobiography, pages 694-697. This book was reissued in 1969 as part of the Times/Arno Press reprint series in which both Davis and Lee again served as editors, and appeared the following year in paperback.

49. *Five Slave Narratives* received one review, and that by noted critic Ernest Kaiser, who in *Freedomways* in 1970 referred to it as "poignant narratives . . . old but important nineteenth century works . . . a fine contribution to the series."

50. In 1977 John W. Blassingame edited another important volume, *Slave Testimony: Two Centuries of Letters, Speeches and Autobiographies.*

51. John W. Blassingame, "Using the Testimony of Ex-Slaves: Approaches and Problems," 83, in Davis and Gates, *Op. Cit.;* and Jean Fagin Yellin, "Texts and Contexts of Harriet Jacobs' Incidents in the Life of a Slave Girl: Written by Herself," 262-282, in Davis and Gates, *Op. Cit.*.

52. John W. Blassingame and Charles T. Davis, IX. In additon to the one hundred slave narratives available in various libraries, there also existed 10,000 pages of interviews with ex-slaves prepared in 1936-1938 by the Federal Writer's Project and available at the Library of Congress (some

later were in Botkin, *Op. Cit.*); and hundreds of interviews at Fisk University from 1929-1930 were also available to scholars. Writing in the *American Historical Review*, 1974, Vol. 79, 470-481, C. Vann Woodward found it still "rather a puzzle" that "historians have almost completely neglected these materials."

53. Dwight Lowell Dumond, *Antislavery, The Crusade for Freedom in America* (New York, 1966), 333-334, 338.

54. New York *Daily Tribune,* December 19, 1856,1.

55. John W. Blassingame, *The Slave Community,* 373; See Jean Fagan Yellin, "Texts and Contexts of Harriet Jacobs' Incidents in the Life of a Slave Girl: Written by Herself," in Davis and Gates, *Op. Cit.,* 262-282; also Jean Fagan Yellin (Ed.), *Harriet A. Jacobs, Incidents in the Life of a Slave Girl Written by Herself* (Cambridge, Massachusetts, 1987) which includes almost a hundred pages of notes. Yellin states that Jacobs' narrative "expresses the idea of struggle for freedom, her life empowers others" (VIII).

56. Arna Bontemps, *Op. Cit.,* XIX; Davis and Gates, *Op. Cit.,* XVIII-XIX, quotes Ralph Ellison denying his fictional *Invisible Man* was purposefully borrowed from slave narratives.

THE
NARRATIVE
OF
LUNSFORD
LANE

Formerly of Raleigh, NC

———

EMBRACING AN ACCOUNT OF HIS EARLY LIFE,
THE REDEMPTION BY PURCHASE OF HIMSELF AND FAMILY FROM SLAVERY,
AND HIS BANISHMENT FROM THE PLACE OF HIS BIRTH
FOR THE CRIME OF WEARING A COLORED SKIN.

PUBLISHED BY HIMSELF-1842

TO THE READER

I have been solicited by very many friends, to give my narrative to the public. Whatever my own judgement might be, I should yield to theirs. In compliance, therefore, with this general request, and in the hope that these pages may produce an impression favorable to my countrymen in bondage; also that I may realise something from the sale of my work towards the support of a numerous family, I have committed this publication to press. It might have been two or three or even six times larger, without diminishing from the interest of any one of its pages—indeed with an increased interest—but the want of the pecuniary means, and other considerations, have induced me to present it as here seen. should another edition be called for, and should my friends advise, the work will then be extended to a greater length.

I have not in this publication attempted or desired to argue anything. It is only a simple narration of such facts connected with my own case, as I thought would be most interesting and instructive to readers generally. The facts will, I think, cast some light upon the policy of a slaveholding community, and the effect on the minds of the more humane, and the *christian* portion of the southern people, of holding and trading in the bodies and souls of men.

I have said in the following pages, that my condition as a slave was comparatively a happy, indeed a highly favored one; and to this circumstance is it owing that I have been able to come up from bondage and relate the story to the public; and that my wife, my mother, and my seven children, are here with me to this day. If for any other thing this side the invisible world, I bless heaven, it is that I was not born a plantation slave, nor even a house servant under what is termed a hard and cruel master.

It has not been any part of my object to describe slavery generally, and in the narration of my own case I have dwelt as little as possible upon the dark side—have spoken mostly of the bright. In whatever I have been obliged to say unfavorable to others, I have endeavored not to overstate, but have chosen rather to come short of giving the full picture—omitting much which it did not seem important to my object to relate. And yet would not venture to say that this publication does not contain a single period which might be twisted to convey an idea more than should be expressed.

Those of whom I have had occasion to speak, are regarded, where they are known, as among the most kind men to their slaves. Mr. Smith, some of whose conduct will doubtless seem strange to the reader, is sometimes taunted with being an abolitionist, in consequence of the interest he manifests towards the colored people. If to any his character appear like a riddle, they should remember that men, like other things, have "two sides," and often a top and bottom in addition.

While in the South I succeeded by stealth in learning to read and write a little, and since I have been in the North I have learned more. But I need not say that I have been obliged to employ the services of a friend, in bringing this Narrative into shape for the public eye. And it should perhaps be said on the part of the writer, that it has been hastily compiled, with little regard to style, only to express the ideas accurately and in a manner to be understood.

NARRATIVE

The small city of Raleigh, North Carolina, it is known, is the capital of the state, situated in the interior and containing about thirty-six hundred inhabitants. Here lived Mr. Sherwood Haywood, a man of considerable respectability, a painter, and the cashier of a bank. He owned three plantations, at the distances respectively of seventy-five, thirty, and three miles from his residence in Raleigh. He owned in all about two hundred and fifty slaves, among the rest my mother, who was a house servant to her master, and of course a resident in the city. My father was a slave to a near neighbor. The apartment where I was born and where I spent my childhood and youth was called "the kitchen," situated some fifteen or twenty rods from the "great house." Here the house servants lodged and lived, and here the meals were prepared for the people in the mansion.

On the 30th of May, 1803, I was ushered into the world; but I did not begin to see the rising of its dark clouds, nor fancy how they might be broken and dispersed, until some time afterwards. My infancy was spent upon the floor, in a rough cradle, or sometimes in my mother's arms. My early boyhood in playing with the other boys and girls, colored and white, in the yard, and occasionally doing such little matters of labor as one of so young years could. I knew no difference between myself and the white children; nor did they seem to know any in turn. Sometimes my master would come out and give a biscuit to me, and another to one of his own white boys; but I did not perceive the difference between us. I had no brothers or sisters, but there were other colored families living in the same kitchen, and the children playing in the same yard, with me and my mother.

When I was ten or eleven years old, my master set me regularly to cutting wood, in the yard in the winter, and working in the garden in the summer. And when I was fifteen years of age, he gave me the care of the pleasure horses, and made me his carriage driver; but this did not exempt me from other labor, especially in the summer. Early in the morning I used to take his three horses to the plantation, and turn them into the pasture to graze, and myself into the cotton or cornfield, with a hoe in my hand, to work through the day; and after sunset I would take these horses back to the city, a distance of three miles, feed them, and then attend to any other business my master or any of his family had for me to do, until bed time, when with my blanket in my hand, I would go into the dining room to rest through the night. The next day the same round of labor would be repeated, unless some of the family wished to ride out, in which case I must be on hand with the horses to wait upon them, and in the meantime work about the yard. On Sunday I had to drive to Church twice, which with other things necessary to be done, took the whole day. So my life went wearily on from day to day, from night to night, and from week to week.

When I began to work, I discovered the difference between myself and my master's white children. They began to order me about, and were told to do so by my master and mistress. I found, too, that they had learned to read, while I was not permitted to have a book in my hand. To be in the possession of anything written or printed, was regarded as an offence. And then there was the fear that I might be sold away from those who were dear to me, and conveyed to the far South. I had learned that being a slave I was subject to this worst (to us) of all calamities; and I knew of others in similar situations to myself, thus sold away. My friends were not numerous; but in proportion as they were few they were dear; and the thought that I might be separated from them forever, was like that of having the heart wrenched from its socket; while the idea of being conveyed to the far South, seemed infinitely worse than the terrors of death. To know, also, that I was never to consult my own will, but was, while I lived, to be entirely under the control of another, was another state of mind hard for me to bear. Indeed all things now made me *feel,* what I had before known only in words, that *I was a slave.* Deep was this feeling, and it preyed upon my heart like a never-dying worm. I saw no prospect that my condition would ever be changed. Yet I used to plan in my mind from day to day, and from night to night, how I might be free.

One day, while I was in this state of mind, my father gave me a small basket of peaches. I sold them for thirty cents, which was the first money I ever had in my life. Afterwards I won some marbles, and sold them for sixty cents, and some weeks after Mr. Hog from Fayetteville, came to visit my master, and on leaving gave me one dollar. After that Mr. Bennahan from Orange county gave me a dollar, and a son of my master fifty cents. These sums, and the hope that then entered my mind of purchasing at some future time my freedom, made me long for money; and plans for money-making took the principal possession of my thoughts. At night I would steal away with my axe, get a load of wood to cut for twenty-five cents, and the next morning hardly escape a whipping for the offence. But I persevered until I had obtained twenty dollars. Now I began to think seriously of becoming able to buy myself; and cheered by this hope, I went on from one thing to another, laboring "at dead of night" after the long weary day's toil for my master was over, till I found I had collected one hundred dollars. This sum I kept hid, first in one place and then in another, as I dare not put it out, for fear I should lose it.

After this I lit upon a plan which proved of great advantage to me. My father suggested a mode of preparing smoking tobacco, different from any then or since employed. It had the double advantage of giving the tobacco a peculiarly pleasant flavor, and of enabling me to manufacture a good article out of a very indifferent material. I improved somewhat upon his suggestion, and commenced the manufacture, doing as I have before said, all my work in the night. The tobacco I put up in papers of about a quarter of a pound each, and sold them at fifteen cents. But the tobacco could not be smoked without a pipe, and as I had given the former a flavor peculiarly grateful, it occurred to me that I might so construct a pipe as to cool the smoke in passing through it, and thus meet the wishes of those who are more fond of smoke than heat. This I effected by means of a reed, which grows plentifully in that region; I made a passage through the reed with a hot wire, polished it, and attached a clay pipe to the end, so that the smoke should be cooled in flowing through the stem like whiskey or rum in passing from the boiler through the worm of the still. These pipes I sold at ten cents apiece. In the early part of the night I would sell my tobacco and pipes, and manufacture them in the latter part. As the Legislature sit in Raleigh every year, I sold these articles considerably to the members, so that I became known not only in the city, but in many parts of the State, as a *tobacconist*.

Perceiving that I was getting along so well, I began, slave as I was, to think about taking a wife. So I fixed my mind upon Miss Lucy Williams, a slave of Thomas Devereaux, Esq., an eminent lawyer in the place; but failed in my undertaking. Then I thought I never would marry; but at the end of two or three years my resolution began to slide away, till finding I could not keep it longer I set out once more in pursuit of a wife. So I fell in with her to whom I am now united, Miss Martha Curtis, and the bargain between *us* was completed. I next went to her master, Mr. Boylan, and asked him, according to the custom, if I might "marry his woman." His reply was, "Yes, if you will behave yourself." I told him I would. "And make her behave herself?" To this I also assented; and then proceeded to ask the approbation of my master, which was granted. So in May, 1828, I was bound as fast in wedlock as a slave can be. God may at any time sunder that band in a freeman; either master may do the same at pleasure in a slave. The bond is not recognized in law. But in my case it has never been broken; and now it cannot be, except by a higher power.

When we had been married nine months and one day, we were blessed with a son, and two years afterwards with a daughter. My wife also passed from the hands of Mr. Boylan into those of Mr. Benjamin B. Smith, a merchant, a member and class-leader in the Methodist church, and in much repute for his deep piety and devotion to religion. But grace (of course) had not wrought in the same *manner* upon the heart of Mr. Smith, as nature had done upon that of Mr. Boylan, who made no religious profession. This latter gentleman used to give my wife, who was a favorite slave, (her mother nursed every one of his own children,) sufficient food and clothing to render her comfortable, so that I had to spend for her but little, except to procure such small articles of extra comfort as I was prompted to from time to time. Indeed Mr. Boylan was regarded as a very kind master to all the slaves about him; that is, to his house servants; nor did he inflict much cruelty upon his field hands, except by proxy. The overseer on his nearest plantation (I know but little about the rest) was a very cruel man; in one instance, as it was said among the slaves, he whipped a man *to death;* but of course denied that the man died in consequence of the whipping. Still it was the choice of my wife to pass into the hands of Mr. Smith, as she had become attached to him in consequence of belonging to the same church, and receiving his religious instruction and counsel as her class-leader, and in consequence of the peculiar devotedness to the cause of religion for which he was noted, and which he always seemed to manifest.—But when she became his slave, he withheld both from her and her children, the needful food and clothing, while he exacted from them to the uttermost all the labor they were able to perform. Almost every article of clothing worn either by my wife or children, especially every article of much value, I had to purchase; while the food he furnished the family amounted to less than a meal a day, and that of the coarser kind. I have no remembrance that he ever gave us a blanket or any other article of bedding, although it is considered a rule at the South that the master shall furnish each of his slaves with one blanket a year. So that, both as to food and clothing, I had in fact to support both my wife and the children, while he claimed them as his property, and received all their labor. She was house servant to Mr. Smith, sometimes cooked the food for his family, and usually took it from the table, but her mistress was so particular in giving it out to be cooked, or so watched it, that she always knew whether it was all returned; and when the table was cleared away, the stern old lady would sit by and see that every dish (except the very little she would send into the kitchen) was put away, and then she would turn the key upon it, so as to be sure her slaves should not die of gluttony. This practice is common with some families in that region; but with others it is not. It was not so in that of her less pious master, Mr. Boylan, nor was it precisely so at my master's. We used to have corn bread enough, and some meat. When I was a boy, the pot-liquor, in which the meat was boiled for the "great house," together with some little corn-meal balls that had been thrown in just before the meat was done, was poured into a tray and set in the middle of the yard, and a clam shell or pewter spoon given to each of us children, who would fall upon the delicious fare as greedily as pigs. It was not generally so much as we wanted, consequently it was customary for some of the white persons who saw us from the piazza of the house where they were sitting, to order the more stout and greedy ones to eat slower, that those more young and feeble might have a chance. But it was not so with Mr. Smith: such luxuries were more than he could afford, kind and Christian man as he was considered to be. So that by the expense of providing for my wife and children, all the money I had earned and could earn by my night labor was consumed, till I found myself reduced to five dollars, and this I lost one day in going to the plantation. My light of hope now went out. My prop seemed to have given way from under me. Sunk in the very night of despair respecting my freedom, I discovered myself, as though I had never known it before, a husband, the father of two children, a family looking up to me for bread, and I a slave, penniless, and well watched by my master, his wife and his children, lest I should, perchance, catch the friendly light of the stars to make something in order to supply the cravings of nature in those with whom my soul was bound up; or lest some plan of freedom might lead me to trim the light of diligence after the day's labor was over, while the rest of the world were enjoying the hours in pleasure or sleep.

At this time an event occurred, which, while it cast a cloud over the prospects of some of my fellow slaves, was a rainbow over mine. My master died, and his widow, by the will, became sole executrix of his property. To the surprise of all, the bank of which he had been cashier presented a claim against the estate for forty thousand dollars. By a compromise, this sum was reduced to twenty thousand dollars; and my mistress, to meet the amount, sold some of her slaves, and hired out others. I hired my time of her,* for which I paid her a price varying from one hundred dollars to one hundred and twenty dollars per year. This was a privilege which comparatively few slaves at the South enjoy; and in this I felt truly blessed.

I commenced the manufacture of pipes and tobacco on an enlarged scale. I opened a regular place of business, labelled my tobacco in a conspicuous manner with the names of *"Edward and Lunsford Lane,"* and of some of the persons who sold it for me,— established agencies for the sale in various parts of the State, one at Fayetteville, one at Salisbury, one at Chapel Hill, and so on,—sold my articles from my place of business, and about town, also deposited them in stores on commission, and thus, after paying my mistress for my time, and rendering such support as necessary to my family, I found in the space of some six or eight years, that I had collected the sum of one thousand dollars. During this time I had found it politic to go shabbily dressed, and to appear to be very poor, but to pay my mistress for my services promptly. I kept my money hid, never venturing to put out a penny, nor to let any body but my wife know that I was making any. The thousand dollars was what I supposed my mistress would ask for me, and so I determined now what I would do.

I went to my mistress and inquired what was her price for me. She said a thousand dollars. I then told her that I wanted to be free, and asked her if she would sell me to be made free. She said she would; and accordingly I arranged with her, and with the master of my wife, Mr. Smith, already spoken of, for the latter to take my money * and buy of her my freedom, as I could not legally purchase it, and as the laws forbid emancipation except for "meritorious services." This done, Mr. Smith endeavored to emancipate me formally, and to get my manumission recorded; I tried also; but the court judged that I had done nothing "meritorious," and so I remained, nominally only, the slave of Mr. Smith for a year; when, feeling unsafe in that relation, I accompanied him to New York whither he was going to purchase goods, and was there regularly and formally made a freeman, and there my manumission was recorded. I returned to my family in Raleigh and endeavored to do by them as a freeman should. I had known what it was to be a slave, and I knew what it was to be free.

But I am going too rapidly over my story. When the money was paid to my mistress and the conveyance fairly made to Mr. Smith, I felt that I was free. And a queer and a joyous feeling it is to one who has been a slave. I cannot describe it, only it seemed as though I was in heaven. I used to lie awake whole nights thinking of it. And oh, the strange thoughts that passed through my soul, like so many

---

* It is contrary to the laws of the State for a slave to have command of his own time in this way, but in Raleigh it is sometimes winked at. I knew one slave-man who was *doing well for himself,* taken up by the public authorities and hired out for the public good, three times in succession for this offence. The time of hiring in such a case is one year. The master is subject to a fine. But generally, as I have said, if the slave is *orderly* and appears to be *making nothing,* neither he nor the master is interfered with.

* Legally, my money belonged to my mistress; and she could have taken it and refused to grant me any freedom. But she was a very kind woman for slave owner; and she would under the circumstances, scorn to do such a thing. I have known of slaves, however, served in this way.

rivers of light; deep and rich were their waves as they rolled;—these were more to me than sleep, more than soft slumber after long months of watching over the decaying, fading frame of a friend, and the loved one laid to rest in the dust. But I cannot describe my feelings to those who have never been slaves; then why should I attempt it? He who has passed from spiritual death to life, and received the witness within his soul that his sins are forgiven, may possibly form some distant idea, like the ray of the setting sun from the far off mountain top, of the emotions of an emancipated slave. That opens heaven. To break the bonds of slavery, opens up at once both earth and heaven. Neither can be truly seen by us while we are slaves.

And now will the reader take with me a brief review of the road I had trodden. I cannot here dwell upon its dark shades, though some of these were black as the pencilling of midnight, but upon the light that had followed my path from my infancy up, and had at length conducted me quite out of the deep abyss of bondage. There is a hymn opening with the following stanza, which very much expresses my feelings:

"When all thy mercies, Oh my God,
My rising soul surveys,
Transported with the view, I'm lost
In wonder, love, and praise."

I had endured what a freeman would indeed call hard fare; but my lot, on the whole, had been a favored one for a slave. It is known that there is a wide difference in the situations of what are termed house servants, and plantation hands. I, though sometimes employed upon the plantation, belonged to the former, which is the favored class. My master, too, was esteemed a kind and humane man; and altogether I fared quite differently from many poor fellows whom it makes my blood run chill to think of, confined to the plantation, with not enough of food and that little of the coarsest kind, to satisfy the gnawing of hunger,—compelled oftentimes, to hie away in the night-time, when worn down with work, and *steal*, (if it be stealing,) and privately devour such things as they can lay their hands upon,—made to feel the rigors of bondage with no cessation,—torn away sometimes from the few friends they love, friends doubly dear because they are few, and transported to a climate where in a few hard years they die,—or at best conducted heavily and sadly to their resting place under the sod, upon their old master's planta-tion,—sometimes, perhaps enlivening the air with merriment, but a forced merriment, that comes from a stagnant or a stupefied heart. Such as this is the fate of the plantation slaves generally, but such was not my lot. My way was comparatively light, and what is better, it conducted to freedom. And my wife and children were with me. After my master died, my mistress sold a number of her slaves from their families and friends—but not me. She sold several children from their parents—but my children were with me still. She sold two husbands from their wives—but I was still with mine. She sold one wife from her husband—but mine had not been sold from me. The master of my wife, Mr. Smith, had separated members of families by sale—but not of mine. with me and my house, the tenderer tendrils of the heart still clung to where the vine had entwined; pleasant was its shade and delicious its fruit to our taste, though we knew, and what is more, we *felt* that we were slaves. But all around I could see where the vine had been torn down, and its bleeding branches told of vanished joys, and of new wrought sorrows, such as, slave though I was, had never entered into my practical experience.

I never had been permitted to learn to read; but I used to attend church, and there I received instruction which I trust was of some benefit to me. I trusted, too, that I had experienced the renewing influences of the gospel; and after obtaining from my mis-tress a written *permit*, (a thing *always* required in such a case,) I had been baptized and received into fellowship with the Baptist denom-ination. So that in religious matters, I had been indulged in the exercise of my own conscience—a favor not always granted to slaves. Indeed I, with others, was often told by the minister how good God was in bringing us over to this country from dark and benighted Africa, and permitting us to listen to the sound of the gospel. To me, God also granted temporal freedom, which *man* without God's consent, had stolen away.

I often heard select portions of the scriptures read. And on the Sabbath there was one sermon preached expressly for the colored people which it was generally my privilege to hear. I became quite familiar with the texts, "Servant be obedient to your masters"—"Not with eye service as men pleasers"—"He that knoweth his mas-ter's will and doeth it not, shall be beaten with many stripes," and others of this class: for they formed the basis of most of these pub-lic instructions to us. The first commandment impressed upon our minds was to obey our masters, and the second was like unto it, namely, to do as much work when they or the overseers were not watching us as when they were. But connected with these instructions there was more or less that was truly excellent; though mixed up with much that would sound strangely in the ears of freedom. There was one very kindhearted Episcopal minister whom I often used to hear; he was very popular with the colored people. But after he had preached a sermon to us in which he argued from the Bible that it was the will of heaven from all eternity we should be slaves, and our masters be our owners, most of us left him; for like some of the faint hearted disciples in early times we said—"This is a hard saying, who can bear it?"

My manumission, as I call it; that is, the bill of sale conveying me to Mr. Smith, was dated Sept. 9, 1835. I continued in the tobacco and pipe business as already described, to which I added a small trade in a variety of articles; and some two years before I left Raleigh, I entered also into a considerable business in wood, which I used to purchase by the acre standing, cut it, haul it into the city, deposit it in a yard and sell it out as I advantageously could. Also I was employed about the office of the Governor as I shall hereafter relate. I used to keep one or two horses, and various vehicles, by which I did a variety of work at hauling about town. Of course I had to hire more or less help, to carry on my business.

In the manufacture of tobacco I met with considerable competition, but none that materially injured me. The method of preparing it having originated with me and my father, we found it necessary, in order to secure the advantage of the invention, to keep it to ourselves, and to decline, though often solicited, going into partnership with others. Those who undertook the manufacture could neither give the article a flavor so pleasant as ours, nor manufacture it so cheaply, so they either failed in it, or succeeded but poorly.

Not long after obtaining my own freedom, I began seriously to think about purchasing the freedom of my family. The first proposition was that I should buy my wife, and that we should jointly labor to obtain the freedom of the children afterwards as we were able. But that idea was abandoned, when her master, Mr. Smith, refused to sell her to me for less than one thousand dollars, a sum which then appeared too much for me to raise.

Afterwards, however, I conceived the idea of purchasing at once the entire family. I went to Mr. Smith to learn his price, which he put at three thousand dollars for my wife and six children, the number we then had. This seemed a large sum, both because it was a great deal for me to raise; and also because Mr. Smith, when he bought my wife and *two* children, had actually paid but five hundred and sixty dollars for them, and had received, ever since, their labor, while I had almost entirely supported them, as to food and clothing. Altogether, therefore, the case seemed a hard one, but as I was entirely in his power I must do the best I could. At length he concluded, perhaps partly of his own motion, and partly through the persuasion of a friend, to sell the family for $2,500, as I wished to free them, though he contended still that they were worth three thousand dollars. Perhaps they would at that time have brought this larger sum, if sold for the Southern market. The arrangement with Mr. Smith was made in December, 1838. I gave him five notes of five hundred dollars each, the first due in January, 1840, and one in January each succeeding year; for which he transferred my family into my own possession, with a *bond* to give me a bill of sale when I should pay the notes. With this arrangement, we found ourselves living in our own house—a house which I had previously purchased—in January, 1839.

After moving my family, my wife was for a short time sick, in consequence of her labor and the excitement in moving, and her excessive joy. I told her that it reminded me of a poor shoemaker in the neighborhood who purchased a ticket in a lottery; but not expecting to draw, the fact of his purchasing it had passed out of his mind. But one day as he was at work on his last, he was informed that his ticket had drawn the liberal prize of ten thousand dollars; and the poor man was so overjoyed, that he fell back on his seat, and immediately expired.

In this new and joyful situation, we found ourselves getting along very well, until September, 1840, when to my surprise, as I was passing the street one day, engaged in my business, the following note was handed to me. "Read it" said the officer, "or if you cannot read, get some white man to read it to you." Here it is, *verbatim:*

> To Lunsford Lane, a free man of Colour:
> Take notice that whereas complaint has been made to us two Justices of the Peace for the County of Wake and state of North Carolina that you are a free negro from another state who has migrated into this state contrary to the provisions of the act of assembly concerning free negroes and mulat-

toes now notice is given you that unless you leave and remove out of this state within twenty days that you will be proceeded against for the penalty porscribed by said act of assembly and be otherwise dealt with as the law directs given under our hands and seals this the 5th Sept 1840.

WILLIS SCOTT JP (Seal),
JORDAN WOMBEL JP (Seal).

This was a terrible blow to me; for it prostrated at once all my hopes in my cherished object of obtaining the freedom of my family, and led me to expect nothing but a separation from them forever.

In order that the reader may understand the full force of the foregoing notice, I will copy the Law of the State under which it was issued:

SEC 65. It shall not be lawful for any free negro or mulatto to migrate into this State: and if he or she shall do so, contrary to the provisions of this act, and being thereof infromed, shall not, within twenty days thereafter, remove out of the State, he or she being thereof convicted in the manner hereafter directed, shall be liable to a penalty of five hundred dollars; and upon failure to pay the same, within the time prescribed in the judgement awarded against such person or persons, he or she shall be liable to be held in servitude and at labor for a term of time not exceeding ten years, and in such manner and upon such terms as may be provided by the court awarding such sentence, and the proceedings arising therefrom shall be paid over to the county trustee for county purposes: Provided, that in case any free negro or mulatto shall pay the penalty of five hundred dollars, according to the provisions of this act, it shall be the duty of such free negro or mulatto to remove him or herself out of this State within twenty days thereafter, and for every such failure, he or she shall be subject to the like penalty, as is prescribed for a failure to remove in the first instance.—
Revised Statutes North Carolina, chap. III.

The next section provides that if the free person of color so notified, does not leave within the twenty days after receiving the notice, he may be arrested on a warrant from any Justice, and be held to bail for his appearance at the next county court, when he will be subject to the penalties specified above; or in case of his failure to give bonds, he may be sent to jail.

I made known my situation to my friends, and after taking legal counsel it was determined to endeavor to induce, if possible, the complainants to prosecute no farther at present, and then as the Legislature of the State was to sit in about two months, to petition that body for permission to remain in the State until I could complete the purchase of my family; after which I was willing, if necessary, to leave.

From January 1st, 1837, I had been employed as I have mentioned, in the office of the Governor of the State, principally under the direction of his private Secretary, in keeping the office in order, taking the letters to the Post Office, and doing such other duties of the sort as occurred from time to time. This circumstance, with the fact of the high standing in the city of the family of my former master, and of the former masters of my wife, had given me the friendship of the first people in the place generally, who from that time forward acted towards me the friendly part.

Mr. Battle, then private Secretary to Governor Dudley, addressed the following letter to the prosecuting attorney in my behalf:

> Raleigh, Nov. 3, 1840
> Dear Sir: — Lunsford Lane, a free man of color, has been in the employ of the State under me since my entering on my present situation. I understand that under a law of the State, he has been notified to leave, and that time is now at hand.
> In the discharge of the duties I had from him, I have found him prompt, obedient, and faithful. At this particular time, his absence to me would be much regretted, as I am now just fixing up my books and other papers in the new office, and I shall not have time to learn another what he can already do so well. With me the period of the Legislature is a very busy one, and I am compelled to have a servant who understands the business I want done, and one

I can trust. I would not wish to be an obstacle in the execution of any law, but the enforcing of the one against him, will be doing me a serious inconvenience, and the object of this letter is to ascertain whether I could not procure a suspension of the sentence till after the adjournment of the Legislature, say about 1st January, 1841.

I should feel no hesitation in giving my word that he will conduct himself orderly and obediently.

I am most respectfully,
Your obedient servant,
C. C. Battle

G. W. Haywood, Esq.
Attorney at Law, Raleigh, N. C.

To the above letter the following reply was made:

Raleigh, Nov. 3, 1840
My Dear Sir:—
I have no objection so far as I am concerned, that all further proceedings against Lunsford should be postponed until after the adjournment of the Legislature.

The process now out against him is one issued by two magistrates, Messrs. Willis Scott and Jordan Womble, over which I have no control. You had better see them today, and perhaps, at your request, they will delay further action on the subject.

Respectfully yours,
Geo. W. Haywood

Mr. Battle then enclosed the foregoing correspondence to Messrs. Scott and Womble, requesting their "favorable consideration." They returned the correspondence, but neglected to make any reply.

In consequence, however, of this action on the part of my friends, I was permitted to remain without further interruption, until the day the Legislature commenced its session. On that day a warrant was served upon me, to appear before the county court, to answer for the sin of having remained in the place of my birth for the space of twenty days and more after being warned out. I escaped going to jail through the kindness of Mr. Haywood, a son of my former master, and Mr. Smith, who jointly became security for my appearance at court.

This was on Monday; and on Wednesday I appeared before the court; but as my prosecutors were not ready for the trial, the case was laid over three months, to the next term.

I then proceeded to get a petition to the Legislature. It required much hard labor and persuasion on my part to start it; but after that, I readily obtained the signatures of the principal men in the place.— Then I went round to the members, many of whom were known to me, calling upon them at their homes, and urging them for my sake, for humanity's sake, for the sake of my wife and little ones, whose hopes had been excited by the idea that they were even now free; I appealed to them as husbands, fathers, brothers, sons, to vote in favor of my petition, and allow me to remain in the State long enough to purchase my family. I was doing well in business, and it would be but a short time before I could accomplish the object. Then, if it was desired, I and my wife and children, redeemed from bondage, would together seek a more friendly home, beyond the dominion of slavery. The following is the petition presented, endorsed as the reader will see:

> *To the Hon. General assembly of the State of North Carolina.*
> Gentlemen:— The petition of Lunsford Lane humbly shews—That about five years ago, he purchased his freedom from his mistress, Mrs. Sherwood Haywood, and by great economy and industry has paid the purchase money; that he has a wife and seven children whom he has agreed to purchase; and for whom he has paid a part of the purchase money; but not having paid in full, is not yet able to leave the State, without parting with his wife and children.
> Your petitioner prays your Honorable Body to pass a law, allowing him to remain a limited time within the State, until he can remove his family also. Your petitioner will give bond and good security for his good behaviour while he remains.

Your petitioner will ever pray, & c.
Lunsford Lane

The undersigned are well acquainted with Lunsford Lane, the petitioner, and join in his petition to the assembly for relief.

Charles Manly,	Drury Lacy,
R. W. Haywood,	Will. Peck,
Eleanor Haywood,	W. A. Stith,
Wm. Hill,	A. B. Stith,
R. Smith,	J. Brown,
Wm. Peace,	William White,
Jos. Peace,	Geo. Simpson,
Wm. M'Pheeters,	Jno. I. Christophers,
Wm. Boylan,	John Primrose,
Fabius J. Haywood,	Hugh M'Queen,
D. W. Stone,	Alex. J. Lawrence,
T. Meredith,	C. L. Hinton,
A. J. Battle,	

Lunsford Lane, the petitioner herein, has been servant to the Executive Office since the 1st of January, 1837, and it gives me pleasure to state that, during the whole time, without exception, I have found him faithful and obedient, in keeping every thing committed to his care in good condition. From what I have seen of his conduct and demeanor, I cheerfully join in the petition for his relief.
C. C. Battle
P. Secretary to Gov. Dudley.
Raleigh, Nov. 20, 1840.

The foregoing petition was presented to the Senate. It was there referred to a committee. I knew when the committee was to report, and watched about the State House that I might receive the earliest news of the fate of my petition. I should have gone within the senate chamber, but no colored man has that permission. I do not know why, unless for fear he may hear the name of *Liberty*. By and by a member came out, and as he passed me, said, "Well, Lunsford, *they have laid you out; the nigger bill is killed.*" I need not tell the reader that my feelings did not enter into the merriment of this honorable senator. To me, the fate of my petition was the last blow to my hopes. I had done all I could do, had said all I could say, laboring day and night, to obtain a favorable reception to my petition; but all in vain. Nothing appeared before me but I must leave the State, and leave my wife and children never to see them more. My friends had also done all they could for me.

And why must I be banished? Ever after I entertained the first idea of being free, I had endeavored so to conduct myself as not to become obnoxious to the white inhabitants, knowing as I did their power, and their hostility to the colored people. The two points necessary in such a case I had kept constantly in mind. First, I had made no display of the little property or money I possessed, but in every way I wore as much as possible the aspect of poverty. Second, I had never appeared to be even so intelligent as I really was. This all colored people at the south, free and slaves, find it peculiarly necessary to their own comfort and safety to observe.

I should, perhaps, have mentioned that on the same day I received the notice to leave Raleigh, similar notices were presented to two other free colored people, who had been slaves; were trying to purchase their families; and were otherwise in a like situation to myself. And they took the same course I did to endeavor to remain a limited time. Isaac Hunter, who had a family with five children, was one; and Waller Freeman, who had six children, was the other. Mr. Hunter's petition went before mine; and a bill of some sort passed the Senate, which was so cut down in the Commons, as to allow him only *twenty days* to remain in the State. He has since, however, obtained the freedom of his family, who are living with him now in Philadelphia.

Mr. Freeman's petition received no better fate than mine. His family were the property of Judge Badger, who was afterwards made a member of Mr. Harrison's cabinet. When Mr. Badger removed to Washington, he took with him among other slaves this family; and Freeman removed also to that city. After this, when Mr. B. resigned his office, with the other members of the cabinet under President Tyler, he entered into some sort of contract with Freeman, to sell him this family, which he left at Washington, while he took the rest of the slaves back to Raleigh. Freeman is now endeavoring to raise money to make the purchase.

It was now between two and three months to the next session of the court; and I knew that before or at that time I must leave the State. I was bound to appear before the court; but it had been arranged between my lawyer and the prosecuting attorney, that if I would leave the State, and pay the costs of the court, the case should be dropped, so that my bondsmen should not be involved. I therefore concluded to stay as long as I possibly could, and then leave. Determined to appeal to the kindness of the friends of the colored man in the North, for assistance, though I had but little hope of succeeding in this way. Yet it was the only course I could think of, by which I could see any possible hope of accomplishing the object.

I had paid Mr. Smith six hundred and twenty dollars; and had a house and lot worth $500, which he had promised to take when I should raise the balance. He gave me also a bill of sale of one of my children, Laura, in consideration of two hundred and fifty dollars of the money already paid; and her I determined to take with me to the North. The costs of the court which I had to meet, amounted to between thirty and forty dollars, besides the fee of my lawyer.

On the 18th of May, 1841, three days after the court commenced its session, I bid adieu to my friends in Raleigh, and set out for the city of New York. I took with me a letter of introduction and recommendation from Mr. John Primrose, a very estimable man, a recommendatory certificate from Mr. Battle, and a letter from the church of which I was a member, together with such papers are relating to the affair as I had in my possession. Also I received the following:

> Raleigh, N.C. May, 1841
> The bearer, Lunsford lane, a free man of color, for some time a resident in this place, being about to leave North Carolina in search of a more favorable location to pursue his trade, has desired us to give him a certificate of his good conduct heretofore. We take pleasure in saying that his habits are temperate and industrious, that his conduct has been orderly and proper, and that he has for these qualities been distinguished among his caste.
> Wm. Hill,   R. Smith,
> Weston R. Gates,   C. Dewey.
> C. L. Hinton.

The above was certified to officially in the usual form by the clerk of the court of Common Pleas and Quarter Sessions.

My success in New York was at first small; but at length I fell in with two friends who engaged to raise for me three hundred dollars, provided I should first obtain from other sources the balance of the sum required, which balance would be one thousand and eighty dollars. Thus encouraged, I proceeded to Boston; and in the city and vicinity the needful sum was contributed by about the 1st of April, 1842. My thanks I have endeavored to express in my poor way to the many friends who so kindly and liberally assisted me. I cannot reward them; I hope they will receive their reward in another world. If the limits of this publication would permit, I should like to record the names of many to whom I am very especially indebted for their kindness and aid, not only in contributing, but by introducing me and opening various ways of access to others.

On the 5th of February, 1842, finding that I should soon have in my possession the sum necessary to procure my family, and fearing that there might be danger in visiting Raleigh for that purpose, in consequence of the strong opposition of the many citizens against colored people, their opposition to me, and their previously persecuting me from the city, I wrote to Mr. Smith, requesting him to see the Governor and obtain under his hand a permit to visit the State for a sufficient time to accomplish this business. I requested Mr. Smith to publish the permit in one or two of the city papers, and then to enclose the original to me. This letter he answered, under date of Raleigh, 29th Feb. 1842, as follows:

> Lunsford:— Your letter of the 5th inst. came duly to hand, and in reply I have to inform you, that owing to the absence of Gov. Morehead, I cannot send you the permit you requested, but this will make no difference, for you can come home, and after your arrival you may obtain one to remain long enough to settle up your affairs. You ought of course to apply to the Governor immediately on your arrival, before any malicious person would have time to inform against you; I don't think by pursuing this course you need apprehend any danger.
>
> We are all alive at present in Raleigh on the subjects of temperance and religion. We have taken into the temperance societies, about five hundred members, and about fifty persons have been truly converted.*** The work seems still to be spreading,

and such a time I have never seen before in my
life. Glorious times truly.
Do try and get all the religions in your heart you
possibly can, for it is the only thing worth having
after all.
Yours, &c.
B. B. Smith.

The way now appeared to be in a measure open; also I thought that
the religious and temperance interest mentioned in the latter portion of Mr. Smith's letter, augured a state of feeling which would
be a protection to me. But fearing still that there might be danger
in visiting Raleigh without the permit from the Governor, or at
least wishing to take every possible precaution, I addressed another
letter to Mr. Smith, and received under date of March 12th, a reply,
from which I copy as follows:

> "The Governor has just returned, and I called upon
> him to get the permit as you requested, but he said
> that he had no authority by law to grant one; and
> he told me to say to you, that you might in perfect
> safety come home in no quiet manner, and remain
> twenty days without being interrupted. I also con-
> sulted Mr. Manly [a lawyer] and he told me the
> same thing.*** *Surely you need not fear anything under
> these circumstances. You had therefore better come on just
> as soon as possible.*"

I need not say, what the reader has already seen, that my life so far
had been one of joy succeeding sorrow, and sorrow following joy;
of hope, of despair; of bright prospects, of gloom; and of as many
hues as ever appear on the varied sky, from the black of midnight,
or the deep brown of a tempest, to the bright warm glow of a clear
noon day. On the 11th of April it was noon with me; I left Boston
on my way for Raleigh with high hopes, intending to pay over the
money for my family and return with them to Boston, which I
intended should be my future home, for there I had found friends
and there I would find a grave. The visit I was making to the South
was to be a farewell one; and I did not dream that my old cradle,
hard as it once had jostled me, would refuse to rock me a pleasant,
or even an affectionate good bye. I thought, too, that the assurances

I had received from the Governor, through Mr. Smith, and the assurances of other friends, were a sufficient guaranty that I might visit the home of my boyhood, of my youth, of my manhood, in peace, especially as I was to stay but for a few days and then to return. With these thoughts, and with the thoughts of my family and freedom, I pursued my way to Raleigh, and arrived there on the 23rd of the month. It was Saturday about four o'clock, p.m. when I found myself once more in the midst of my family. With them I remained over the Sabbath, as it was sweet to spend a little time with them after so long an absence, an absence willed with so much of interest to us, and as I could not do any business until the beginning of the week. On Monday morning between eight and nine o'clock, while I was making ready to leave the house for the first time after my arrival, to go to the store of Mr. Smith, where I was to transact my business with him, two constables, Messrs. Murray and Scott, entered, accompanied by two other men, and summoned me to appear immediately before the police. I accordingly accompanied them to the City Hall, but as it was locked and the officers could not at once find the key, we were told that the court would be held in Mr. Smith's store, a large and commodious room. This was what is termed in common phrase in Raleigh a "call court." The Mayor, Mr. Loring, presided, assisted by William Boylan and Jonathan Bushbye, Esqs. Justices of the peace. There was a large number of people together—more than could obtain admission to the room, and a large company of mobocratic spirits crowded around the door. Mr. Loring read the writ, setting forth that I had been guilty of *delivering abolition lectures in the State of Massachusetts.* He asked me whether I was guilty or not guilty. I told him I did not know whether I had given abolition lectures or not, but if it pleased the court, I would relate the course I had pursued during my absence from Raleigh. He then said that I was at liberty to speak.

The circumstances under which I left Raleigh, said I, are perfectly familiar to you. It is known that I had no disposition to remove from this city, but resorted to every lawful means to remain. After I found that I could not be permitted to stay, I went away leaving behind everything I held dear with the exception of one child, whom I took with me, after paying two hundred and fifty dollars for her. It is also known to you and to many other persons here present, that I had engaged to purchase my wife and children of her master, Mr. Smith, for the sum of twenty-five hundred dollars, and that I had paid of this sum (including my house and lot) eleven hundred and twenty dollars, leaving a balance to be made up of thirteen hundred and eighty dollars. I had previously to that lived in Raleigh, a slave, the property of Mr. Sherwood Haywood, and had purchased my freedom by paying the sum of one thousand dollars. But being driven away, no longer permitted to live in this city, to raise the balance of the money due on my family, my last resort was to call upon the friends of humanity in other places, to assist me.

I went to the city of Boston, and there I related the story of my persecutions here, the same as I have now stated to you. The people gave ear to my statements; and one of them, Rev. Mr. Neale, wrote back, unknown to me, to Mr. Smith, inquiring of him whether the statements made by me were correct. After Mr. Neale received the answer he sent for me, informed me of his having written, and read to me the reply. The letter satisfied Mr. Neale and his friends. He placed it in my hands, remarking that it would, in a great measure, do away with the necessity of using the other documents in my possession. I then with that letter in my hands went out from house to house, from place of business to place of business, and from church to church, relating (where I could gain an ear) the same heart-rending and soul-trying story which I am now repeating to you. In pursuing that course, the people, first one and then another contributed, until I had succeeded in raising the amount alluded to, namely, thirteen hundred and eighty dollars. I may have had contributions from abolitionists; but I did not stop to ask those who assisted me whether they were anti-slavery of pro-slavery, for I considered that the money coming from either, would accomplish the object I had in view. These are the facts; and now, sir, it remains for you to say, whether I have been giving abolition lectures or not.

In the course of my remarks I presented the letter of Mr. Smith to Mr. Neale, showing that I had acted the open part while in Massachusetts; also I referred to my having written to Mr. Smith requesting him to obtain for me the permit of the Governor; and I showed to the court, Mr. Smith's letters in reply, in order to satisfy them that I had reason to believe I should be unmolested in my return.

Mr. Loring then whispered to some of the leading men; after which he remarked that he saw nothing in what I had done, according to my statements, implicating me in a manner worthy of notice. He called upon any present who might be in possession of information tending to disprove what I had said, or to show any wrong on my part, to produce it, otherwise I should be set at liberty. No person appeared against me; so I was discharged.

I started to leave the house; but just before I got to the door I met Mr. James Litchford, who touched me on the shoulder, and I followed him back. He observed to me that if I went out of that room I should in less than five minutes be a dead man; for there was a mob outside waiting to drink my life. Mr. Loring then spoke to me again and said that notwithstanding I had been found guilty of nothing, yet public opinion was law; and he advised me to leave the place the next day, otherwise he was convinced that I should have to suffer death. I replied, "not to-morrow, but to-day." He answered that I could not go out that day, because I had not done my business. I told him that I would leave my business in his hands and in those of other such gentlemen as himself, who might settle it for me and send my family to meet me in Philadelphia. This was concluded upon, and a guard appointed to take me to the depot. I took my seat in the cars, when the mob that had followed us surrounded me, and declared that the cars should not go, if I were permitted to go in them. Mr. Loring inquired what they wanted of me; he told them that there had been an examination, and nothing had been found against me; that they were at the examination invited to speak if they knew of aught to condemn me, but they had remained silent, and that now it was right I should be permitted to leave in peace. They replied that they wanted a more thorough investigation, that they wished to search my trunks (I had but one trunk) and see if I was not in possession of abolitionist papers. It now became evident that I should be unable to get off in the cars; and my friends advised to go the shortest way possible to jail, for my safety. They said that they were persuaded that what the rabble wanted was to get me into their possession, and then to murder me. The mob looked dreadfully enraged, and seemed to lap for blood. The whole city was in an uproar. But the first men and the more wealthy were my friends: and they did everything in their power to protect me. Mr. Boylan, whose name has repeatedly appeared in this publication, and was more than a father to me; and Mr. Smith and Mr. Loring, and many other gentlemen, whose names it would give me pleasure to mention, were exceedingly kind.

The guard then conducted me through the mob to the prison; and I felt joyful that even a prison could protect me. Looking out from the prison window, I saw my trunk in the hands of Messrs.

Johnson, Scott, and others, who were taking it to the City Hall for examination. I understood afterwards that they opened my trunk; and as the lid flew up, Lo! a paper! a paper!! Those about seized it, three or four at once, as hungry dogs would a piece of meat after forty days famine. But the meat quickly turned to a stone; for the paper it happened, was one *printed in Raleigh*, and edited by Weston R. Gales, a nice man to be sure, but no abolitionist. The only other printed or written things in the trunk were some business cards of a firm in Raleigh—not incendiary.

Afterwards I saw from the window Mr. Scott, accompanied by Mr. Johnson, lugging my carpet-bag in the same direction my trunk had gone. It was opened at the City Hall, and found actually to contain a pair of old shoes, and a pair of boots!—but they did not conclude that these were incendiary.

Mr. Smith now came to the prison and told me that the examination had been completed, and nothing found against me; but that it would not be safe for me to leave the prison immediately. It was agreed that I should remain in prison after night-fall, and then steal secretly away, being let out by the keeper, and pass unnoticed to the house of my old and tried friend Mr. Boylan. Accordingly I was discharged between nine and ten o'clock. I went by the back way leading to Mr. Boylan's; but soon and suddenly a large company of men sprang upon me, and instantly I found myself in their possession. They conducted me sometimes high above ground and sometimes dragging me along, but as silently as possible, in the direction of the gallows, which is always kept standing upon the Common, or as it is called "the pines," or "piny old field." I now expected to pass speedily into the world of spirits; I thought of that unseen region to which I seemed to be hastening; and then my mind would return to my wife and children, and the labors I had made to redeem them from bondage. Although I had the money to pay for them according to a bargain already made, it seemed to me some white man would get it, and they would die in slavery, without benefit from my exertions and the contributions of my friends. Then the thought of my own death, to occur in a few brief moments, would rush over me, and I seemed to bid adieu in spirit to all earthly things, and to hold communion already with eternity. But at length I observed those who were carrying me away, changed their course a little from the direct line to the gallows, and hope, a faint beaming, sprung up within me; but then as they were taking me to the woods, I thought they intended to murder me there, in a place where they would be less likely to be interrupted than in so public a spot as where the gallows stood. They conducted me to a rising ground among the trees, and set me down. "Now," said they, "tell us the truth about those abolition lectures you have been giving at the North." I replied that I had related the circumstances before the court in the morning; and could only repeat what I had then said. "But that was not the truth—tell us the truth." I again said that any different story would be false, and as I supposed I was in a few minutes to die, I would not, whatever they might think I would say under other circumstances, pass into the other world with a lie upon my lips. Said one, "you were always, Lunsford, when you were here, a clever fellow, and I did not think you would be engaged in such business as giving abolition lectures." To this and similar remarks, I replied that the people of Raleigh had always said the abolitionists did not believe in buying slaves, but contended that their masters ought to free them without pay. I had been laboring to buy my family; and how then could they suppose me to be in league with the abolitionists?

After other conversations of this kind, and after they seemed to have become tired of questioning me, they held a consultation in a low whisper among themselves. Then a bucket was brought and set down by my side; but what it contained or for what it was intended, I could not divine. But soon, one of the number came forward with a pillow, and then hope sprung up, a flood of light and joy within me. The heavy weight on my heart rolled off; death had passed by and I unharmed. They commenced stripping me until every rag of clothes was removed; and then the bucket was set near, and I discovered it to contain tar. One man, I will do him the honor to record his name, Mr. William Andres, a journeyman printer, when he is any thing, except a tar-and-featherer, put his hands the first into the bucket, and was about passing them to my face. "Don't put any in his face or eyes," said one.* So he desisted; but he, with three other "gentlemen," whose names I should be happy to record if I could recall them, gave me as nice a coat of tar all over, face only excepted, as any one would wish to see. Then they took the pillow and ripped it open at one end, and with the open end commenced the operation of putting a coat of its contents over that of the con-

*I think this was Mr. Burns, a blacksmith in the place, but I am not certain. At any rate, this man was my *friend* (if so he may be called) on this occasion; and it was fortunate for me that the company generally seemed to look up to him for wisdom.

tents of the bucket. A fine escape from the hanging this will be, thought I, provided they do not with a match set fire to the feathers. I had some fear they would. But when the work was completed they gave me my clothes, and one of them handed me my watch which he had carefully kept in his hands; they all expressed great interest in my welfare, advised me how to proceed with my business the next day, told me to stay in the place as long as I wished, and with other such words of consolation they bid me good night.

After I had returned to my family, to their inexpressible joy, as they had become greatly alarmed for my safety, some of the persons who had participated in this outrage, came in (probably influenced by a curiosity to see how the tar and feathers would be got off) and expressed great sympathy for me. They said they regretted that the affair had happened—that they had no objections to my living in Raleigh—I might feel perfectly safe to go out and transact my business preparatory to leaving—I should not be molested.

Meanwhile, my friends understanding that I had been discharged from prison, and perceiving I did not come to them, had commenced a regular search for me, on foot and on horseback, every where; and Mr. Smith called upon the Governor to obtain his official interference; and after my return, a guard came to protect me; but I chose not to risk myself at my own house, and so went to Mr. Smith's, where this guard kept me safely until morning. They seemed friendly indeed, and were regaled with a supper during the night by Mr. Smith. My friend, Mr. Battle, (late private secretary to the Governor,) was with them; and he made a speech to them setting forth the good qualities I had exhibited in my past life, particularly in my connection with the Governor's office.

In the morning Mr. Boylan, true as ever, and unflinching in his friendship, assisted me in arranging my business,* so that I should start with my family *that day* for the north. He furnished us with provisions more than sufficient to sustain the family to Philadelphia, where we intended to make a halt; and sent his own baggage wagon to convey our baggage to the depot, offering also to send his carriage for my family. But my friend, Mr. Malone, had been before

*Of course I was obliged to sacrifice much on my property, leaving in this hurried manner. And while I was in the North, a kind *friend* had removed from the wood-lot, wood that I had cut and corded, for which I had expected to receive over one hundred dollars; thus saving me the trouble of making sale of it, or of being burdened with the money it would bring. I suppose I have no redress. I might add other things as bad.

29

him in this kind offer, which I had agreed to accept.

Brief and sorrowful was the parting from my kind friends; but the worst was the thought of leaving my mother. The cars were to start at ten o'clock in the morning. I called upon my old mistress, Mrs. Haywood, who was affected to weeping by the considerations that naturally came to her mind. She had been kind to me; the day before she and her daughter, Mrs. Hogg, now present, had jointly transmitted a communication to the court representing that in consequence of my good conduct from my youth, I could not be supposed to be guilty of any offence. And now "with tears that ceased not flowing," they gave me their parting blessing. My mother was still Mrs. Haywood's slave, and I her only child. Our old mistress could not witness the sorrow that would attend the parting with my mother. She told her to go with me; and said that if ever I became able to pay two hundred dollars for her, I might; otherwise it should be her loss. She gave her the following paper, which is the ordinary form of a *pass*:

> Raleigh, N.C. April 26, 1842
> Know all persons by these presents, that the bearer of this, Clarissa, a slave, belonging to me, hath my permission to visit the city of New York with her relations, who are in company with her; and it is my desire that she be protected and permitted to pass without molestation or hindrance, on good behavior. Witness my hand this 26th April, 1842.
> Elanor Haywood.
> Witness—J. A. Campbell.

On leaving Mrs. Haywood's, I called upon Mrs. Badger, another daughter, and wife of Judge Badger, previously mentioned. She seemed equally affected; she wept as she gave me her parting counsel. She and Mrs. Hogg and I had been children together, playing in the same yard, while yet none of us had learned that they were of a superior and I of a subject race. And in those infant years there were pencillings made upon the heart, which time and opposite fortunes could not all efface.—May these friends never be slaves as I have been; nor their bosom companions and their little ones be slaves like mine.

When the cars were about to start, the whole city seemed to be gathered at the depot; and among the rest the mobocratic portion, who appeared to be determined still that I should not go peaceably away. Apprehending this, it had been arranged with my friends and the conductor, that my family should be put in the cars and that I should go a distance from the city on foot, and there be taken up as they passed. The mob, therefore, supposing that I was left behind, allowed the cars to start.

Mr. Whiting, known as the agent of the rail road company, was going as far as Petersburg, Va.; and he kindly assisted in purchasing our tickets, and enabling us to pass on unmolested. After he left, Capt. Guyan, of Raleigh, performed the same kind office as far as Alexandria, D.C., and then he placed us in the care of a citizen of Philadelphia, whose name I regret to have forgotten, who protected us quite out of the land of slavery. But for this we should have been quite liable to be detained at several places on our way, much to our embarrassment, at least, if nothing had occurred of a more serious nature.

One accident only had happened: we lost at Washington a trunk containing most of our valuable clothing. This we have not recovered; but our lives have been spared to bless the day that conferred freedom upon us. I felt when my feet struck the pavements in Philadelphia, as though I had passed into another world. I could draw a full long breath, with no one to say to the ribs, "why do ye so?"

On reaching Philadelphia we found that our money had all been expended, but kind friends furnished us with the means of proceeding as far as New-York; and thence we were with equal kindness aided on to Boston.

In Boston and in the vicinity, are persons almost without number, who have done me favors more than I can express. The thought that I was now in my new, though recently acquired home—that my family were with me whence the stern, cruel, hated hand of slavery could never reach us more—the greetings of friends—the interchange of feeling and sympathy—the kindness bestowed upon us, more grateful than rain to the thirsty earth,— the reflections of the past that would rush into my mind,—these and more almost overwhelmed me with emotion, and I had deep and strange communion with my own soul. Next to God from whom every good gift proceeds, I feel under the greatest obligations to my kind friends in Massachusetts. To be rocked in their cradle of Liberty,—Oh, how unlike being stretched on the pillory of slavery! May that cradle rock forever; may many a poor care-worn child of sorrow, many a spirit-bruised (worse than lash-mangled) victim of oppression, there sweetly sleep to the lullaby of Freedom, sung by Massachusetts sons and daughters.

A number of meetings have been held at which friends have contributed to our temporal wants, and individuals have sent us various articles of provision and furniture and apparel, so that our souls have been truly made glad. There are now ten of us in the family, my wife, my mother, and myself, with seven children, and we expect soon to be joined by my father, who several years ago gained his freedom by legacy. The wine fresh from the clustering grapes never filled so sweet a cup as mine. May I and my family be permitted to drink it, remembering whence it came!

I suppose such of my readers as are not accustomed to trade in human beings, may be curious to see the Bills of Sale, by which I have obtained the right to my wife and children. They are both in the hand writing of Mr. Smith. The first—that for Laura is as follows:

> *State of North Carolina, Wake County.*
> Know all men by these presents, that for and in consideration of the sum of two hundred and fifty dollars, to me in hand paid, I have this day bargained and sold; and do hereby bargain, sell and deliver unto Lunsford Lane, a free man of color, a certain negro girl by the name of Laura, aged about seven years, and hereby warrant and defend the right and title of the said Lunsford and his heirs forever, free from their claims of all persons whatsoever.
> In witness whereof, I have hereunto set my hand and seal at Raleigh, this 17th May, 1841.
> B. B. Smith, [seal]
> Witness Robt. W. Haywood

Below is the Bill of Sale for my wife and other six children, to which the papers that follow are attached.

> *State of North Carolina, Wake County.*
> Known all men by these presents, that for and in consideration of the sum of eighteen hundred and

eighty dollars to me in hand paid, the receipt of which is hereby acknowledged, I have this day bargained, sold and delivered unto Lunsford Lane, a free man of color, one dark mulatto woman names Patsy, one boy names Edward, one boy also named William, one boy also named Lunsford, one girl named Maria, one boy also named Ellick, and one girl named Lucy, to have and to hold the said negroes free from the claims of all persons whatsoever.

It witness whereof, I have heretofore affixed my hand and seal the 25th day of April, 1842.

B. B. Smith, [seal.]

Witness—Th. L. West

State of North Carolina, Wake County

Office of the Court of Pleas and Quarter Sessions, April 26, 1842.

The execution of the within bill of sale was this day duly acknowledged before me by B. B. Smith, the executor of the same.

In testimony whereof, I have hereunto affixed the seal of said Court, and subscribed my name at office in Raleigh, the date above.

[L. S.]

Jas. T. Marriott, Clerk.

State of North Carolina, Wake County.

I, Wm. Boylan, presiding magistrate of the Court of Pleas and Quarter Sessions aforesaid, certify that James T. Marriott, who has written and signed the above certificate, is Clerk of the Court aforesaid,—that the same is in due form, and full faith and credit are due to such his official acts.

Given under my hand and private seal (having no seal of office) this 26th day of April, 1842.

Wm. Boylan, P. M. [seal.]

The State of North Carolina.

To all to whom these presents shall come, Greeting:

Be it known, that William Boylan, whose signature appears in his own proper hand writing to the annexed certificate, was at the time of signing the same and now is a Justice of the Peace and Presiding Magistrate for the county of Wake, in the State aforesaid, and as such he is duly qualified and empowered to give said certificate, which is here done in the usual and proper manner; and full faith and credit are due to the same, and ought to be given to all the official acts of the said William Boylan as Presiding Magistrate aforesaid.

In testimony whereof, I, J. M. Morehead, Governor, Captain General and Commander in Chief, have caused the Great Seal of the State to be hereunto affixed, and signed the same at the city of Raleigh, on the 26th day of April, in the year of our Lord one thousand eight hundred and forty-two, and in the sixty-sixth year of Independence of the United States.

J. M. Morehead

By the Governor.

P. Reynolds, Private Secretary.

But thou art born a slave, my child;
Those little hands must toil,
That brow must sweat, that bosom ache
upon another's soil;
And if perchance some tender joy
Should bloom upon thy heart,
Another's hand may enter here,
And tear it soon apart.

Thou art a little joy to me,
But soon thou may'st be sold,
Oh! lovlier to thy mother far
Than any weight of gold;
Or I may see thee scourg'd and driv'n
Hard on the cotton-field,
To fill a cruel master's store,
With what thy blood may yield.

Should some fair maiden win thy heart,
And thou should'st call her thinc;
Should little ones around thee stand,
Or round thy bosom twine,
Thou wilt not know how soon away
These loves may all be riv'n,
Nor what a darkened troop of woe
Through thy lone breast be driv'n.

Thy master may be kind, and give
Thy every wish to thee,
Only deny that greatest wish,
That longing to be free:
Still it will seem a comfort small
That thou hast sweeter bread,
A better hut than other slaves,
Or pillow for thy head.

What joys soe'er may gather round,
What other comforts flow,—
That, like a mountain in the sea,
O'ertops each wave below,
That ever-upward, firm desire

To break the chains, and be
Free as the ocean is, or like
The ocean-winds, be free.

Oh! child! thou art a little slave.
And all of thee that grows,
Will be another's weight of flesh,—
But thine the weight of woes
Thou art a little slave, my child,
And much I grieve and mourn
That to so dark a destiny
A lovely babe I've borne.

And gladly would I lay thee down
To sleep beneath the sod,
And give thy gentle spirit back,
Unmarr'd with grief, to God:
The tears I shed upon that turf
Should whisper peace to me,
And tell me in the spirit land
My lovely babe was free.

I then should know thy peace was sure,
And only long to go
The road which thou had'st gone, and wipe
Away those tears that flow.
Death to the slave has double power;
It breaks the earthly clod,
And breaks the tyrant's sway, that he
May worship only God.
J. P. B.

THE FUGITIVE BLACKSMITH;

OR,

EVENTS IN THE HISTORY

OF

JAMES W. C. PENNINGTON,

PASTOR OF A PRESBYTERIAN CHURCH, NEW YORK,
FORMERLY A SLAVE IN THE STATE OF MARYLAND,
UNITED STATES.

"LET MINE OUTCASTS DWELL WITH THEE, MOAB; BE THOU A COVERT TO THEM
FROM THE FACE OF THE SPOILER.—ISAIAH XVI. 4.

Second Edition.
LONDON:
CHARLES GILPIN, 5, BISHOPSGATE WITHOUT.
1849.

MR. CHARLES GILPIN,
MY DEAR SIR,

The information just communicated to me by you, that another edition of my little book, "The Fugitive Blacksmith," is called for, has agreeably surprised me. The British public has laid me under renewed obligations by this mark of liberality, which I hasten to acknowledge. I would avail myself of this moment, also, to acknowledge the kindness of the gentlemen of the newspaper press for the many favourable reviews which my little book has received. It is to them I am indebted, in no small degree, for the success with which I have been favoured in getting the book before the notice of the public.

Yours truly,
J. W. C. Pennington.
Hoxton, Oct. 15*th,* 1849.

PREFACE

The brief narrative I here introduce to the public, consists of outline notes originally thrown together to guide my memory when lecturing on this part of the subject of slavery. This will account for its style, and will also show that the work is not full.

The question may be asked, Why I have published anything so long after my escape from slavery? I answer I have been induced to do so on account of the increasing disposition to overlook the fact, that THE SIN of slavery lies in the chattel principle, or relation. Especially have I felt anxious to save professing Christians, and my brethren in the ministry, from falling into a great mistake. My feelings are always outraged when I hear them speak of "kind masters,"—"Christian masters,"—"the mildest form of slavery,"—"well fed and clothed slaves," as extenuations of slavery; I am satisfied they either mean to pervert the truth, or they do not know what they say. The being of slavery, its soul and body, lives and moves in the chattel principle, the property principle, the bill of sale principle; the cart-whip, starvation, and nakedness, are its inevitable consequences to a greater or less extent, warring with the dispositions of men.

There lies a skein of silk upon a lady's work-table. How smooth and handsome are the threads. But while that lady goes out to make a call, a party of children enter the apartment, and in amusing themselves, tangle the skein of silk, and now who can untangle it? The relation between master and slave is even as delicate as a skein of silk: it is liable to be entangled at any moment.

The mildest form of slavery, if there be such a form, looking at the chattel principle as the definition of slavery, is comparatively the worst form. For it not only keeps the slave in the most unpleasant apprehension, like a prisoner in chains awaiting his trial; but it actually, in a great majority of cases, where kind masters do exist, trains him under the most favourable circumstances the system admits of, and then plunges him into the worst of which it is capable.

It is under the mildest form of slavery, as it exists in Maryland,

Virginia, and Kentucky, that the finest specimens of coloured females are reared. There are no mothers who rear, and educate in the natural graces, finer daughters than the Ethiopian women, who have the least chance to give scope to their maternal affections. But what is generally the fate of such female slaves? When they are not raised for the express purpose of supplying the market of a class of economical Louisian and Mississippi gentlemen, who do not wish to incur the expense of rearing legitimate families, they are, nevertheless, on account of their attractions, exposed to the most shameful degradation, by the young masters in the families where it is claimed they are so well off. My master once owned a beautiful girl about twenty-four. She had been raised in a family where her mother was a great favourite. She was her mother's darling child. Her master was a lawyer of eminent abilities and great fame, but owing to habits of intemperance, he failed in business, and my master purchased this girl for a nurse. After he had owned her about a year, one of his sons became attached to her, for no honourable purposes; a fact which was not only well-known among all of the slaves, but which became a source of unhappiness to his mother and sisters.

The result was, that poor Rachel had to be sold to "Georgia." Never shall I forget the heart-rending scene, when one day one of the men was ordered to get "the one-horse cart ready to go into town;" Rachel, with her few articles of clothing, was placed in it, and taken into the very town where her parents lived, and there sold to the traders before their weeping eyes. That same son who had degraded her, and who was the cause of her being sold, acted as salesman, and bill of saleman. While this cruel business was being transacted, my master stood aside, and the girl's father, a pious member and exhorter in the Methodist Church, a venerable grey-headed man, with his hat off, besought that he might be allowed to get some one in the place to purchase his child. But no; my master was invincible. His reply was, "She has offended in my family, and I can only restore confidence by sending her out of hearing." After lying in prison a short time, her new owner took her with others to the far South, where her parents heard no more of her.

Here was a girl born and reared under the mildest form of slavery. Her original master was reputed to be even indulgent. He lived in a town, and was a high-bred gentleman, and a lawyer. He had but a few slaves, and had no occasion for an overseer, those negro leeches, to watch and drive them; but when he became embarrassed by his own folly, the chattel principle doomed this girl to be

42

sold at the same sale with his books, house, and horses. With my master she found herself under far more stringent discipline than she had been accustomed to, and finally degraded, and sold where her condition could not be worse, and where she had not the least hope of ever bettering it.

This case presents the legitimate working of the great chattel principle. It is no accidental result—it is the fruit of the tree. You cannot constitute slavery without the chattel principle—and with the chattel principle you cannot save it from these results. Talk not then about kind and christian masters. They are not masters of the system. The system is master of them; and the slaves are their vassals.

These storms rise on the bosom of the calmed waters of the system. You are a slave, a being in whom another owns property. Then you may rise with his pride, but remember the day is at hand when you must also fall with his folly. To-day you may be pampered by his meekness; but to-morrow you will suffer in the storm of his passions.

In the month of September, 1848, there appeared in my study, one morning, in New York City, an aged coloured man of tall and slender form. I saw depicted on his countenance anxiety bordering on despair, still I was confident that he was a man whose mind was accustomed to faith. When I learned that he was a native of my own state, Maryland, having been born in the county of Montgomery, I at once became much interested in him. He had been sent to me by my friend, William Harned, Esq., of the Anti-Slavery Office, 61, John Street. He put into my hand the following bill of distress:—

"Alexander, Virginia, *September 5th,* 1848

"The bearer, Paul Edmondson, is the father of two girls, Mary Jane and Emily Catherine Edmondson. These girls have been purchased by us, and once sent to the South; and upon the positive assurance that the money for them would be raised if they were brought back, they were returned. Nothing, it appears, has as yet been done in this respect by those who promised, and we are on the very eve of sending them south a second time; and we are candid in saying, that if they go again, we will not regard any promises made in relation to them.

"The father wishes to raise money to pay for them, and intends to appeal to the liberality of the humane and the good to aid him, and has requested us to state in writing *the conditions upon which we will sell his daughters.*

"We expect to start our servants to the South in a few days; if the sum of twelve hundred dollars be raised and paid us in fifteen days, or we be assured of that sum, then we will retain them for twenty-five days more, to give an opportunity for raising the other thousand and fifty dollars, otherwise we shall be compelled to send them along with our other servants.

(Signed) "BRUIN AND HILL."

The old man also showed me letters from other individuals, and one from the Rev. Matthew A. Turner, pastor of Asbury Chapel, where himself and his daughters were members. He was himself free, but his wife was a slave. Those two daughters were two out of fifteen children he had raised for the owner of his wife. These two girls had been sold, along with four brothers, to the traders, for an attempt to escape to the North, and gain their freedom.

On the next Sabbath evening, I threw the case before my people, and the first fifty dollars of the sum was raised to restore the old man his daughters. Subsequently the case was taken up under the management of a committee of ministers of the Methodist Episcopal Church, consisting of the Rev. G. Peck, D.D., Rev. E. E. Griswold, and Rev. D. Curry, and the entire sum of 2,250 dollars, (£450.) was raised for two girls, fourteen and sixteen years of age!

But why this enormous sum for two mere children? Ah, reader, they were reared under the mildest form of slavery known to the laws of Maryland! The mother is an invalid, and allowed to live with her free husband; but she is a woman of excellent mind, and has bestowed great pains upon her daughters. If you would know, then, why these girls were held at such a price, even to their own father, read the following extract of a letter from one who was actively engaged in behalf of them, and who had several interviews with the traders to induce them to reduce the price, but without success. Writing from Washington, D. C., September 12th, 1848, this gentleman says to William Harned, "The truth is, *and is confessed to be, that their destination is prostitution;* of this you would be satisfied on seeing them: they are of elegant form, and fine faces."

And such, dear reader, is the sad fate of hundreds of my young countrywomen, natives of my native state. Such is the fate of many who are not only reared under the mildest form of slavery, but of those who have been made acquainted with the milder system of the Prince of Peace.

When Christians, and Christian ministers, then, talk about the "mildest form of slavery,"—"Christian masters," &c., I say my feelings are outraged. It is a great mistake to offer these as an extenuation of the system. It is calculated to mislead the public mind. The opinion seems to prevail that the negro, after having toiled as a slave for centuries to enrich his white brother, to lay the foundation of his proud institutions, after having been sunk as low as slavery can sink him, needs now only a second-rate civilization, a lower standard of civil and religious privileges than the whites claim for themselves.

During the last year or two, we have heard of nothing but revolutions, and the enlargements of the eras of freedom, on both sides of the Atlantic. Our white brethren everywhere are reaching out their hands to grasp more freedom. In the place of absolute monarchies they have limited monarchies, and in the place of limited monarchies they have republics: so tenacious are they of their own liberties.

But when we speak of slavery, and complain of the wrong it is doing us, and ask to have the yoke removed, we are told, "O, you must not be impatient, you must not create undue excitement. You are not so badly off, for many of your masters are kind Christian masters." Yes, sirs, many of our masters are professed Christians; and what advantage is that to us? The grey heads of our fathers are brought down by scores to the grave in sorrow, on account of their young and tender sons, who are sold to the far South, where they have to toil without requite to supply the world's market with *cotton, sugar, rice, tobacco, &c.* Our venerable mothers are borne down with poignant grief at the fate of their children. Our sisters, if not by the law, are by common consent made the prey of vile men, who can bid the highest.

In all the bright achievements we have obtained in the great work of emancipation, if we have not settled the fact that the chattel principle is wrong, and cannot be maintained upon Christian ground, then we have wrought and triumphed to little purpose, and we shall have to do our first work over again.

It is this that has done all the mischief connected with slavery; it is this that threatens still further mischief. Whatever may be the ill or favoured condition of the slave in the matter of mere personal treatment, it is the chattel relation that robs him of his manhood, and transfers his ownership in himself to another. It is this that transfers the proprietorship of his wife and children to another. It is this that throws his family history into utter confusion, and leaves him without a single record to which he may appeal in vindication of his character, or honour. And has a man no sense of honour because he was born a slave? Has he no need of character?

Suppose insult, reproach, or slander, should render it necessary for him to appeal to the history of his family in vindication of his character, where will he find that history? He goes to his native state, to his native county, to his native town; but no where does he find any record of himself *as a man*. On looking at the family record of his old, kind, Christian, master, there he finds his name on a catalogue with the horses, cows, hogs and dogs. However humiliating and degrading it may be to his feelings to find his name written down among the beasts of the field, *that* is just the place, and the *only* place assigned to it by the chattel relation. I beg our Anglo-Saxon brethren to accustom themselves to think that we need something more than mere kindness. We ask for justice, truth and honour as other men do.

My coloured brethren are now widely awake to the degradation which they suffer in having property vested in their persons, and they are also conscious of the deep and corrupting disgrace of having our wives and children owned by other men—men, who have shown to the world that their own virtue is not infallible, and who have given us no flattering encouragement to entrust that of our wives and daughters to them.

I have great pleasure in stating that my dear friend, W. W., spoken of in this narrative, to whom I am so deeply indebted, is still living. I have been twice to see him within four years, and have regular correspondence with him. In one of the last letters I had from him, he authorises me to use his name in connection with this narrative in these words,—"As for using my name, by reference or otherwise, in thy narrative, it is at thy service. I know thee so well James, that I am not afraid of thy making a bad use of it, nor am I afraid or ashamed to have it known that I took thee in and gave thee aid, when I found thee travelling alone and in want.—W. W."

On the second page of the same sheet I have a few lines from his excellent lady, in which she says, "James, I hope thee will not attribute my long silence in writing to indifference. No such feeling can ever exist towards thee in our family. Thy name is mentioned almost every day. Each of the children claims the next letter from thee. It will be for thee to decide which shall have it.—P.W."

In a postscript following this, W. W. says again:—"Understand me, James, that thee is at full liberty to use my name in any way thee wishes in thy narrative. We have a man here from the eastern shore of thy state. He is trying to learn as fast as thee did when here.—W. W."

I hope the reader will pardon me for introducing these extracts. My only apology is, the high gratification I feel in knowing that this family has not only been greatly prospered in health and happiness, but that I am upon the most intimate and pleasant terms with all its members, and that they all still feel a deep and cordial interest in my welfare.

There is another distinguished individual whose sympathy has proved very gratifying to me in my situation—I mean that true friend of the negro, *Gerrit Smith, Esq.* I was well acquainted with the family in which Mr. Smith married in Maryland. My attention has been fixed upon him for the last ten years, for I have felt confident that God had set him apart for some great good to the negro. In a letter dated Petersborough, November 7th, 1848, he says:—

"J. W. C. PENNINGTON,

"Slight as is my *personal* acquaintance with you, I nevertheless am well acquainted with you. I am familiar with many passages in your history—all that part of your history extending from the time when, a sturdy blacksmith, you were running away from Maryland oppression, down to the present, when you are the successor of my lamented friend, Theodore S. Wright. Let me add that my acquaintance with you has inspired me with a high regard for your wisdom and integrity."

Give us a few more such men in America, and slavery will soon be numbered among the things that were. A few men who will not only have the moral courage to aim the severing blow at the chattel relation between master and slave, without parley, palliation or compromise; but who have also the christian fidelity to brave public scorn and contumely, to seize a coloured man by the hand, and elevate him to the position from whence the avarice and oppression of the whites have degraded him. These men have the right view of the subject. They see that in every case where the relation between master and slave is broken, slavery is weakened, and that every coloured man elevated, becomes a step in the ladder upon which his whole people are to ascend. They would not have us accept of some modified form of liberty, while the old mischief working chattel relation remains unbroken, untouched and unabrogated.

J. W. C. PENNINGTON.
13, *Princes Square, London,*
August 15*th*, 1849.

CONTENTS

THE FUGITIVE BLACKSMITH.

CHAPTER I.

MY BIRTH AND PARENTAGE.—
THE TREATMENT OF SLAVES GENERALLY IN MARYLAND.

I WAS born in the state of Maryland, which is one of the smallest and most northern of the slaveholding states; the products of this state are wheat, rye, Indian corn, tobacco, with some hemp, flax, &c. By looking at the map, it will be seen that Maryland, like Virginia her neighbour, is divided by the Chesapeake Bay into eastern and western shores. My birthplace was on the eastern shore, where there are seven or eight small counties; the farms are small, and tobacco is mostly raised.

At an early period in the history of Maryland, her lands began to be exhausted by the bad cultivation peculiar to slave states; and hence she soon commenced the business of breeding slaves for the more southern states. This has given an enormity to slavery, in Maryland, differing from that which attaches to the system in Louisiana, and equalled by none of the kind, except Virginia and Kentucky, and not by either of these in extent.

My parents did not both belong to the same owner: my father belonged to a man named ——; my mother belonged to a man named ——. This not only made me a slave, but made me the slave of him to whom my mother belonged; as the primary law of slavery is, that the child shall follow the condition of the mother.

When I was about four years of age, my mother, an older brother and myself, were given to a son of my master, who had studied for the medical profession, but who had now married wealthy, and was about to settle as a wheat planter in Washington County, on the western shore. This began the first of our family troubles that I knew anything about, as it occasioned a separation between my mother and the only two children she then had, and my father, to a distance of about two hundred miles. But this separation did not continue long; my father being a valuable slave, my master was glad to purchase him.

About this time, I began to feel another evil of slavery—I mean the want of parental care and attention. My parents were not able to give any attention to their children during the day. I often suffered much from *hunger* and other similar causes. To estimate the sad state of a slave child, you must look at it as a helpless human being thrown upon the world without the benefit of its natural guardians. It is thrown into the world without a social circle to flee to for hope, shelter, comfort, or instruction. The social circle, with all its heaven-ordained blessings, is of the utmost importance to the *tender child;* but of this, the slave child, however tender and delicate, is robbed.

There is another source of evil to slave children, which I cannot forbear to mention here, as one which early embittered my life,—I mean the tyranny of the master's children. My master had two sons, about the ages and sizes of my older brother and myself. We were not only required to recognise these young sirs as our young masters, but *they* felt themselves to be such; and, in consequence of this feeling, they sought to treat us with the same air of authority that their father did the older slaves.

Another evil of slavery that I felt severely about this time, was the tyranny and abuse of the overseers. These men seem to look with an evil eye upon children. I was once visiting a menagerie, and being struck with the fact, that the lion was comparatively indifferent to every one around his cage, while he eyed with peculiar keenness a little boy I had; the keeper informed me that such was always the case. Such is true of those human beings in the slave states, called overseers. They seem to take pleasure in torturing the children of slaves, long before they are large enough to be put at the hoe, and consequently under the whip.

We had an overseer, named Blackstone; he was an extremely cruel man to the working hands. He always carried a long hickory whip, a kind of pole. He kept three or four of these in order, that he might not at any time be without one.

I ounce found one of these hickories lying in the yard, and supposing that he had thrown it away, I picked it up, and boy-like, was using it for a horse; he came along from the field, and seeing me with it, fell upon me with the one he then had in his hand, and flogged me most cruelly. From that, I lived in constant dread of that man; and he would show how much he delighted in cruelty by chasing me from my play with threats and imprecations. I have lain for hours in a wood, or behind a fence, to hide from his eye.

At this time my days were extremely dreary. When I was nine years of age, myself and my brother were hired out from home; my brother was placed with a pump-maker, and I was placed with a stonemason. We were both in a town some six miles from home. As the men with whom we lived were not slaveholders, we enjoyed some relief from the peculiar evils of slavery. Each of us lived in a family where there was no other negro.

The slaveholders in that state often hire the children of their slaves out to non-slaveholders, not only because they save themselves the expense of taking care of them, but in this way they get among their slaves useful trades. They put a bright slave-boy with a tradesman, until he gets such a knowledge of the trade as to be able to do his own work, and then he takes him home. I remained with the stonemason until I was eleven years of age: at this time I was taken home. This was another serious period in my childhood; I was separated from my older brother, to whom I was much attached; he continued at his place, and not only learned the trade to great perfection, but finally became the property of the man with whom he lived, so that our separation was permanent, as we never lived nearer after, than six miles. My master owned an excellent blacksmith, who had obtained his trade in the way I have mentioned above. When I returned home at the age of eleven, I was set about assisting to do the mason-work of a new smith's shop. This being done, I was placed at the business, which I soon learned, so as to be called a "first-rate blacksmith." I continued to work at this business for nine years, or until I was twenty-one, with the exception of the last seven months.

In the spring of 1828, my master sold me to a Methodist man, named ——, for the sum of seven hundred dollars. It soon proved that he had not work enough to keep me employed as a smith, and he offered me for sale again. On hearing of this, my old master repurchased me, and proposed to me to undertake the carpentering business. I had been working at this trade six months with a white workman, who was building a large barn when I left. I will now relate the abuses which occasioned me to fly.

Three or four of our farm hands had their wives and families on other plantations. In such cases, it is the custom in Maryland to allow the men to go on Saturday evening to see their families, stay over the Sabbath, and return on Monday morning, not later than "half-an-hour by sun." To overstay their time is a grave fault, for which, especially at busy seasons, they are punished.

One Monday morning, two of these men had not been so fortunate as to get home at the required time: one of them was an uncle of mine. Besides these, two young men who had no families, and for whom no such provision of time was made, having gone somewhere to spend the Sabbath, were absent. My master was greatly irritated, and had resolved to have, as he said, "a general whipping-match among them."

Preparatory to this, he had a rope in his pocket, and a cowhide in his hand, walking about the premises, and speaking to every one he met in a very insolent manner, and finding fault with some without just cause. My father, among other numerous and responsible duties, discharged that of shepherd to a large and valuable flock of Merino sheep. This morning he was engaged in the tenderest of a shepherd's duties;—a little lamb, not able to go alone, lost its mother; he was feeding it by hand. As he stooped over it in the yard, with a vessel of new milk he had obtained, with which to feed it, my master came along, and without the least provocation, began by asking, "Bazil, have you fed the flock?"

"Yes, sir."

"Were you away yesterday?"

"No, sir."

"Do you know why these boys have not got home this morning yet?"

"No, sir, I have not seen any of them since Saturday night."

"By the Eternal, I'll make them know their hour. The fact is, I have too many of you; my people are getting to be the most careless, lazy, and worthless in the country."

"Master," said my father, "I am always at my post; Monday morning never finds me off the plantation."

"Hush, Bazil! I shall have to sell some of you; and then the rest will have enough to do; I have not work enough to keep you all tightly employed; I have too many of you."

All this was said in an angry, threatening, and exceedingly insulting tone. My father was a high-spirited man, and feeling deeply the insult, replied to the last expression,—"If I am one too many, sir, give me a chance to get a purchaser, and I am willing to be sold when it may suit you."

"Bazil, I told you to hush!" and suiting the action to the word, he drew forth the "cowhide" from under his arm, fell upon him with most savage cruelty, and inflicted fifteen or twenty severe stripes with all his strength, over his shoulders and the small of his back. As he raised himself upon his toes, and gave the last stripe, he said, "By the *** I will make you know that I am master of your tongue as well as of your time!"

Being a tradesman, and just at that time getting my breakfast, I was near enough to hear the insolent words that were spoken to my father, and to hear, see, and even count the savage stripes inflicted upon him.

Let me ask any one of Anglo-Saxon blood and spirit, how would you expect a *son* to feel at such a sight?

This act created an open rupture with our family—each member felt the deep insult that had been inflicted upon our head; the spirit of the whole family was roused; we talked of it in our nightly gatherings, and showed it in our daily melancholy aspect. The oppressor saw this, and with the heartlessness that was in perfect keeping with the first insult, commenced a series of tauntings, threatenings, and insinuations, with a view to crush the spirit of the whole family.

Although it was sometime after this event before I took the decisive step, yet in my mind and spirit, I never was a *Slave* after it.

Whenever I thought of the great contrast between my father's employment on that memorable Monday morning, (feeding the little lamb,) and the barbarous conduct of my master, I could not help cordially despising the proud abuser of my sire; and I believe he discovered it, for he seemed to have diligently sought an occasion against me. Many incidents occurred to convince me of this, too tedious to mention; but there is one I will mention, because it will serve to show the state of feeling that existed between us, and how it served to widen the already open breach.

I was one day shoeing a horse in the shop yard. I had been stooping for some time under the weight of the horse, which was large, and was very tired; meanwhile, my master had taken his position on a little hill just in front of me, and stood leaning back on his cane, with his hat drawn over his eyes. I put down the horse's foot, and straightened myself up to rest a moment, and without knowing that he was there, my eye caught his. This threw him into a panic of rage; he would have it that I was watching him. "What are you rolling your white eyes at me for, you lazy rascal?" He came down upon me with his cane, and laid on over my shoulders, arms, and legs, about a dozen severe blows, so that my limbs and flesh were sore for several weeks; and then after several other offensive epithets, left me.

This affair my mother saw from her cottage, which was near; I being one of the oldest sons of my parents, our family was now mortified to the lowest degree. I had always aimed to be trustworthy; and feeling a high degree of mechanical pride, I had aimed to do my work with dispatch and skill, my blacksmith's pride and taste was one thing that had reconciled me so long to remain a slave. I sought to distinguish myself in the finer branches of the business by invention and finish; I frequently tried my hand at making guns and pistols, putting blades in penknives, making fancy hammers, hatchets, sword-canes, &c., &c. Besides I used to assist my father at night in making straw-hats and willow-baskets, by which means we supplied our family with little articles of food, clothing and luxury, which slaves in the mildest form of the system never get from the master; but after this, I found that my mechanic's pleasure and pride were gone. I thought of nothing but the family disgrace under which we were smarting, and how to get out of it.

Perhaps I may as well extend this note a little. The reader will observe that I have not said much about my master's cruel treatment; I have aimed rather to shew the cruelties incident to the system. I have no disposition to attempt to convict him of having been one of the most cruel masters—that would not be true—his prevailing temper was kind, but he was a perpetualist. He was opposed to emancipation; thought free negroes a great nuisance, and was, as respects discipline, a thorough slaveholder. He would not tolerate a look or a word from a slave like insubordination. he would suppress it at once, and at any risk. When he thought it necessary to secure unqualified obedience, he would strike a slave with any weapon, flog him on the bare back, and sell. And this was the kind of discipline he also empowered his overseers and sons to use.

I have seen children go from our plantations to join the chained-gang on its way from Washington to Louisiana; and I have seen men and women flogged—I have seen the overseers strike a man with a hayfork—nay more, men have been maimed by shooting! Some dispute arose one morning between the overseer and one of the farm hands, when the former made at the slave with a hickory club; the slave taking to his heels, started for the woods; as he was crossing the yard, the overseer turned, snatched his gun which was near, and fired at the flying slave, lodging several shots in the calf of one leg. The poor fellow continued his flight, and got into the woods; but he was in so much pain that he was compelled to come out in the evening, and give himself up to his master, thinking he would not allow him to be punished as he had been shot. He was locked up that night; the next morning the overseer was allowed to tie him up and flog him; his master then took his instruments and picked the shot out of his leg, and told him, it served him just right.

My master had a deeply pious and exemplary slave, an elderly man, who one day had a misunderstanding with the overseer, when the latter attempted to flog him. He fled to the woods; it was noon; at evening he came home orderly. The next morning, my master, taking one of his sons with him, a rope and cowhide in his hand, led the poor old man away into the stable; tied him up, and ordered the son to lay on thirty-nine lashes, which he did, making the keen end of the cowhide lap around and strike him in the tenderest part of his side, till the blood sped out, as if a lance had been used.

While my master's son was thus engaged, the sufferer's little daughter, a child six years of age, stood at the door, weeping in agony for the fate of her father. I heard the old man articulating in a low tone of voice; I listened at the intervals between the stripes, and lo! he was praying!

When the last lash was laid on, he was let down; and leaving him to put on his clothes, they passed out of the door, and drove the man's weeping child away! I was mending a hinge to one of the barn doors; I saw and heard what I have stated. Six months after, this same man's eldest daughter, a girl fifteen years old, was sold to slave-traders, where he never saw her more.

This poor slave and his wife were both Methodists, so was the wife of the young master who flogged him. My old master was an Episcopalian.

These are only a few of the instances which came under my notice during my childhood and youth on our plantations; as to those which occurred on other plantations in the neighborhood, I could state any number.

I have stated that my master was watching the movements of our family very closely. Sometime after the difficulties began, we found that he also had a confidential slave assisting him in the business. This wretched fellow, who was nearly white, and of Irish descent, informed our master of the movements of each member of the family by day and by night, and on Sundays. This stirred the spirit of my mother, who spoke to our fellow-slave, and told him that he ought to be ashamed to be engaged in such low business.

Master hearing of this, called my father, mother, and myself before him, and accused us of an attempt to resist and intimidate his "confidential servant." Finding that only my mother had spoken to him, he swore that if she ever spoke another word to him, he would flog her.

I knew my mother's spirit and my master's temper as well. Our social state was now perfectly intolerable. We were on the eve of a general fracas. This last scene occurred on Tuesday; and on Saturday evening following, without counsel or advice from any one, I determined to fly.

CHAPTER II.

THE FLIGHT.

It was the Sabbath: the holy day which God in his infinite wisdom gave for the rest of both man and beast. In the state of Maryland, the slaves generally have the Sabbath, except in those districts where the evil weed, tobacco, is cultivated; and then, when it is the season for setting the plant, they are liable to be robbed of this only rest.

It was in the month of November, somewhat past the middle of the month. It was a bright day, and all was quiet. Most of the slaves were resting about their quarters; others had leave to visit their friends on other plantations, and were absent. The evening previous I had arranged my little bundle of clothing, and had secreted it at some distance from the house. I had spent most of the forenoon in my workshop, engaged in deep and solemn thought.

It is impossible for me now to recollect all the perplexing thoughts that passed through my mind during that forenoon; it was a day of heartaching to me. But I distinctly remember the two great difficulties that stood in the way of my flight: I had a father and mother whom I dearly loved,—I had also six sisters and four brothers on the plantation. The question was, shall I hide my purpose from them? moreover, how will my flight affect them when I am gone? Will they not be suspected? Will not the whole family be sold off as a disaffected family, as is generally the case when one of its members flies? But a still more trying question was, how can I expect to succeed, I have no knowledge of distance or direction. I know that Pennsylvania is a free state, but I know not where its soil begins, or where that of Maryland ends? Indeed, at this time there was no safety in Pennsylvania, New Jersey, or New York, for a fugitive, except in lurking-places, or under the care of judicious friends, who could be entrusted not only with liberty, but also with life itself.

With such difficulties before my mind, the day had rapidly worn away; and it was just past noon. One of my perplexing questions I had settled—I had resolved to let no one into my secret; but the other difficulty was now to be met. It was to be met without the least knowledge of its magnitude, except by imagination. Yet of one thing there could be no mistake, that the consequences of a failure would be most serious. Within my recollection no one had attempted to escape from my master; but I had many cases in my mind's eye, of slaves of other planters who had failed, and who had been made examples of the most cruel treatment, by flogging and selling to the far South, where they were never to see their friends more. I was not without serious apprehension that such would be my fate. The bare possibility was impressively solemn; but the hour was now come, and the man must act and be free, or remain a slave for ever. How the impression came to be upon my mind I cannot tell; but there was a strange and horrifying belief, that if I did not meet the crisis that day, I should be self-doomed—that my ear would be nailed to the door post for ever. The emotions of that moment I cannot fully depict. Hope, fear, dread, terror, love, sorrow, and deep melancholy were mingled in my mind together; my mental state was one of most painful distraction. When I looked at my numerous family—a beloved father and mother, eleven brothers and sisters, &c.; but when I looked at slavery as such; when I looked at it in its mildest form, with all its annoyances; and above all, when I remembered that one of the chief annoyances of slavery, in the most mild form, is the liability of being at any moment sold into the worst form; it seemed that no consideration, not even that of life itself, could tempt me to give up the thought of flight. And then when I considered the difficulties of the way—the reward that would be offered—the human blood-hounds that would be set upon my track—the weariness—the hunger—the gloomy thought, of not only losing all one's friends in one day, but of having to seek and to make new friends in a strange world. But, as I have said, the hour was come, and the man must act, or for ever be a slave.

It was now two o'clock. I stepped into the quarter; there was a strange and melancholy silence mingled with the destitution that was apparent in every part of the house. The only morsel I could see in the shape of food, was a piece of Indian flour bread, it might be half-a-pound in weight. This I placed in my pocket, and giving a last look at the aspect of the house, and at a few small children who were playing at the door, I sallied forth thoughtfully and melancholy, and after crossing the barn-yard, a few moments' walk brought me to a small cave, near the mouth of which lay a pile of stones, and into which I had deposited my clothes. From this, my course lay though thick and heavy woods and back lands to — town, where my brother lived. This town was six miles distance. It was now near three o'clock, but my object was neither to be seen on the road, or to approach the town by daylight, as I was well-known there, and as any intelligence of my having been seen there would at once put the pursuers on my track. This first six miles of my flight, I not only travelled very slowly, therefore, so as to avoid carrying any daylight to this town; but during this walk another very perplexing question was agitating my mind. Shall I call on my brother as I pass through, and shew him what I am about? My brother was older than I, we were much attached; I had been in the habit of looking to him for counsel.

I entered the town about dark, resolved, all things in view, *not* to shew myself to my brother. Having passed through the town without being recognised, I now found myself under cover of night, a solitary wanderer from home and friends; my only guide was the *north star*, by this I knew my general course northward, but at what point I should strike Penn, or when and where I should find a friend, I knew not. Another feeling now occupied my mind,—I felt like a mariner who has gotten his ship outside of the harbour and has spread his sails to the breeze. The cargo is on board—the ship is cleared—and the voyage I must make; besides, this being my first night, almost every thing will depend upon my clearing the coast before the day dawns. In order to do this my flight must be rapid. I therefore set forth in sorrowful earnest, only now and then I was cheered by the *wild* hope, that I should somewhere and at some-time be free.

The night was fine for the season, and passed on with little interruption for want of strength, until, about three o'clock in the morning, I began to feel the chilling effects of the dew.

At this moment, gloom and melancholy again spread through my whole soul. The prospect of utter destitution which threatened me was more than I could bear, and my heart began to melt. What substance is there in a piece of dry Indian bread; what nourishment is there in it to warm the nerves of one already chilled to the heart? Will this afford a sufficient sustenance after the toil of the night? But while these thoughts were agitating my mind, the day dawned upon me, in the midst of an open extent of country, where the only shelter I could find, without risking my travel by daylight, was a corn shock, but a few hundred yards from the road, and here I must pass my first day out. The day was an unhappy one; my hiding-place was extremely precarious. I had to sit in a squatting position the whole day, without the least chance to rest. But, besides this, my scanty pittance did not afford me that nourishment which my hard night's travel needed. Night came again to my relief, and I sallied forth to pursue my journey. By this time, not a crumb of my crust remained, and I was hungry and began to feel the desperation of distress.

As I travelled I felt my strength failing and my spirits wavered; my mind was in a deep and melancholy dream. It was cloudy; I could not see my star, and had serious misgivings about my course.

In this way the night passed away, and just at the dawn of day I found a few sour apples, and took my shelter under the arch of a small bridge that crossed the road. Here I passed the second day in ambush.

This day would have been more pleasant than the previous, but the sour apples, and a draught of cold water, had produced anything but a favourable effect; indeed, I suffered most of the day with severe symptoms of cramp. The day passed away again without any further incident, and as I set out at nightfall, I felt quite satisfied that I could not pass another twenty-four hours without nourishment. I made but little progress during the night, and often sat down, and slept frequently fifteen or twenty minutes. At the dawn of the third day I continued my travel. As I had found my way to a public turnpike road during the night, I came very early in the morning to a toll-gate, where the only person I saw, was a lad about twelve years of age. I inquired of him where the road led to. He informed me it led to Baltimore. I asked him the distance, he said it was eighteen miles.

This intelligence was perfectly astounding to me. My master lived eighty miles from Baltimore. I was now sixty-two miles from home. That distance in the right direction, would have placed me several miles across Mason and Dixon's line, but I was evidently yet in the state of Maryland.

I ventured to ask the lad at the gate another question—Which is the best way to Philadelphia? Said he, you can take a road which turns off about half-a-mile below this, and goes to Getsburgh, or you can go on to Baltimore and take the packet.

I made no reply, but my thought was, that I was as near Baltimore and Baltimore-packets as would answer my purpose.

In a few moments I came to the road to which the lad had referred, and felt some relief when I had gotten out of that great public highway, "The National Turnpike," which I found it to be.

When I had walked a mile on this road, and when it had now gotten to be about nine o'clock, I met a young man with a load of hay. He drew up his horses, and addressed me in a very kind tone, when the following dialogue took place between us.

"Are you travelling any distance, my friend?"

"I am on my way to Philadelphia."

"Are you free?"

"Yes, sir."

"I suppose, then, you are provided with free papers?"

"No, sir. I have no papers."

"Well, my friend, you should not travel on this road: you will be taken up before you have gone three miles. There are men living on this road who are constantly on the look-out for your people; and it is seldom that one escapes them who attempts to pass by day."

He then very kindly gave me advice where to turn off the road at a certain point, and how to find my way to a certain house, where I would meet with an old gentleman who would further advise me whether I had better remain till night, or go on.

I left this interesting young man; and such was my surprise and chagrin at the thought of having so widely missed my way, and my alarm at being in such a dangerous position, that in ten minutes I had so far forgotten his directions as to deem it unwise to attempt to follow them, lest I should miss my way, and get into evil hands.

I, however, left the road, and went into a small piece of wood, but not finding a sufficient hiding-place, and it being a busy part of the day, when persons were at work about the fields, I thought I should excite less suspicion by keeping in the road, so I returned to the road; but the events of the next few moments proved that I committed a serious mistake.

I went about a mile, making in all two miles from the spot where I met my young friend, and about five miles from the toll-gate to which I have referred, and I found myself at the twenty-four miles' stone from Baltimore. It was now about ten o'clock in the forenoon; my strength was greatly exhausted by reason of the want of suitable food; but the excitement that was then going on in my mind, left me little time to think of my *need* of food. Under ordinary circumstances as a traveller, I should have been glad to see the "Tavern," which was near the mile-stone; but as the case stood with me, I deemed it a dangerous place to pass, much less to stop at. I was therefore passing it as quietly and as rapidly as possible, when from the lot just opposite the house, or sign-post, I heard a coarse stern voice cry, "Halloo!"

I turned my face to the left, the direction from which the voice came, and observed that it proceeded from a man who was digging potatoes. I answered him politely; when the following occurred:—

"Who do *you* belong to?"

"I am free, sir."

"Have you got papers?"

"No, sir."

"Well, you must stop here."

By this time he had got astride the fence, making his way into the road. I said,

"My business is onward, sir, and I do not wish to stop."

"I will see then if you don't stop, you black rascal."

He was now in the middle of the road, making after me in a brisk walk.

I saw that a crisis was at hand; I had no weapons of any kind, not even a pocket-knife; but I asked myself, shall I surrender without a struggle. The instinctive answer was "No." What will you do? continue to walk; if he runs after you, run; get him as far from the house as you can, then turn suddenly and smite him on the knee with a stone; that will render him, at least, unable to pursue you.

This was a desperate scheme, but I could think of no other, and my habits as a blacksmith had given my eye and hand such mechanical skill, that I felt quite sure that if I could only get a stone in my hand, and have time to wield it, I should not miss his knee-pan.

He began to breathe short. He was evidently vexed because I did not halt, and I felt more and more provoked at the idea of being thus pursued by a man to whom I had not done the least injury. I had just began to glance my eye about for a stone to grasp, when he made a tiger-like leap at me. This of course brought us to running. At this moment he yelled out "Jake Shouster!" and at the next moment the door of a small house standing to the left was opened, and out jumped a shoemaker girded up in his leather apron, with his knife in hand. He sprang forward and seized me by the collar, while the other seized my arms behind. I was now in the grasp of two men, either of whom were larger bodied than myself, and one of whom was armed with a dangerous weapon.

Standing in the door of the shoemaker's shop, was a third man; and in the potatoe lot I had passed, was still a fourth man. Thus surrounded by superior physical force, the fortune of the day it seemed to me was gone.

My heart melted away, I sunk resistlessly into the hands of my captors, who dragged me immediately into the tavern which was near. I ask my reader to go in with me, and see how the case goes.

GREAT MORAL DILEMMA.

A few moments after I was taken into the bar-room, the news having gone as by electricity, the house and yard were crowded with gossippers, who had left their business to come and see "the runaway nigger." This hastily assembled congregation consisted of men, women, and children, each one had a look to give at, and a word to say about, the "nigger."

But among the whole, there stood one whose name I have never known, but who evidently wore the garb of a man whose profession bound him to speak for the dumb, but he, standing head and shoulders above all that were round about, spoke the first hard sentence against me. Said he, "That fellow is a runaway I know; put him in jail a few days, and you will soon hear where he came from." And then fixing a fiend-like gaze upon me, he continued, "if I lived on this road, *you* fellows would not find such clear running as you do, I'd trap more of you."

But now comes the pinch of the case, the case of conscience to me even at this moment. Emboldened by the cruel speech just recited, my captors enclosed me, and said, "Come now, this matter may easily be settled without you going to jail; who do you belong to, and where did you come from?"

The facts here demanded were in my breast. I knew according to the law of slavery, who I belonged to and where I came from, and I must now do one of three things—I must refuse to speak at all, or I must communicate the fact, or I must tell an untruth. How would an untutored slave, who had never heard of such a writer as Archdeacon Paley, be likely to act in such a dilemma? The first point decided, was, the facts in this case are my private property. These men have no more right to them than a highway robber has to my purse. What will be the consequence if I put them in possession of the facts. In forty-eight hours, I shall have received perhaps one hundred lashes, and be on my way to the Louisiana cotton fields. Of what service will it be to them. They will get a paltry sum of two hundred dollars. Is not my liberty worth more to me than two hundred dollars are to them?

I resolved therefore, to insist that I was free. This not being satisfactory without other evidence, they tied my hands and set out, and went to a magistrate who lived about half a mile distant. It so happened, that when we arrived at his house he was not at home. This was to them a disappointment, but to me it was a relief; but I soon learned by their conversation, that there was still another magistrate in the neighbourhood, and that they would go to him. In about twenty minutes, and after climbing fences and jumping ditches, we, captors and captive, stood before his door, but it was after the same manner as before—he was not at home. By this time the day had worn away to one or two o'clock, and my captors evidently began to feel somewhat impatient of the loss of time. We were about a mile and a quarter from the tavern. As we set out on our return, they began to parley. Finding it was difficult for me to get over fences with my hands tied, they untied me, and said, "Now John," that being the name they had given me, "if you have run away from any one, it would be much better for you to tell us!" but I continued to affirm that I was free. I knew, however, that my situation was very critical, owing to the shortness of the distance I must be from home: my advertisement might overtake me at any moment.

On our way back to the tavern, we passed through a small skirt of wood, where I resolved to make an effort to escape again. One of my captors was walking on either side of me; I made a sudden turn, with my left arm sweeping the legs of one of my captors from under him; I left him nearly standing on his head, and took to my heels. As soon as they could recover they both took after me. We had to mount a fence. This I did most successfully, and making across an open field towards another wood; one of my captors being a long-legged man, was in advance of the other, and consequently nearing me. We had a hill to rise, and during the ascent he gained on me. Once more I thought of self-defence. I am trying to escape peaceably, but this man is determined that I shall not.

My case was now desperate; and I took this desperate thought:

"I will run him a little farther from his coadjutor; I will then suddenly catch a stone, and wound him in the breast." This was my fixed purpose, and I had arrived near the point on the top of the hill, where I expected to do the act, when to my surprise and dismay, I saw the other side of the hill was not only all ploughed up, but we came suddenly upon a man ploughing, who as suddenly left his plough and cut off my flight, by seizing me by the collar, when at the same moment my pursuer seized my arms behind. Here I was again in a sad fix. By this time the other pursuer had come up; I was most savagely thrown down on the ploughed ground with my face downward, the ploughman placed his knee upon my shoulders, one of my captors put his upon my legs, while the other tied my arms behind me. I was then dragged up, and marched off with kicks, punches and imprecations.

We got to the tavern at three o'clock. Here they again cooled down, and made an appeal to me to make a disclosure. I saw that my attempt to escape strengthened their belief that I was a fugitive. I said to them, "If you will not put me in jail, I will now tell you where I am from." They promised. "Well," said I, "a few weeks ago, I was sold from the eastern shore to a slave-trader, who had a large gang, and set out for Georgia, but when he got to a town in Virginia, he was taken sick, and died with the small-pox. Several of his gang also died with it, so that the people in the town became alarmed, and did not wish the gang to remain among them. No one claimed us, or wished to have anything to do with us; I left the rest, and thought I would go somewhere and get work."

When I said this, it was evidently believed by those who were present, and notwithstanding the unkind feeling that had existed, there was a murmur of approbation. At the same time I perceived that a panic began to seize some, at the idea that I was one of a small-pox gang. Several who had clustered near me, moved off to a respectful distance. One or two left the bar-room, and murmured, "better let the small-pox nigger go."

I was then asked what was the name of the slave-trader. Without premeditation, I said, "John Henderson."

"John Henderson!" said one of my captors, "I knew him; I took up a yaller boy for him about two years ago, and got fifty dollars. He passed out with a gang about that time, and the boy ran away from him at Frederickstown. What kind of a man was he?"

At a venture, I gave a description of him. "Yes," said he, "that is the man." By this time, all the gossippers had cleared the coast; our friend, "Jake Shouster," had also gone back to his bench to finish his custom work, after having "lost nearly the whole day, trotting about with a nigger tied," as I heard his wife say as she called him home to his dinner. I was now left alone with the man who first called to me in the morning. In a sober manner, he made this proposal to me: "John, I have a brother living in Risterstown, four miles off, who keeps a tavern; I think you had better go and live with him, till we see what will turn up. He wants an ostler." I at once assented to this. "Well," said he, "take something to eat, and I will go with you."

Although I had so completely frustrated their designs for the moment, I knew that it would by no means answer for me to go into that town, where there were prisons, handbills, newspapers, and travellers. My intention was, to start with him, but not to enter the town alive.

I sat down to eat; it was Wednesday, four o'clock, and this was the first regular meal I had since Sunday morning. This over, we set out, and to my surprise, he proposed to walk. We had gone about a mile and a-half, and were approaching a wood through which the road passed with a bend. I fixed upon that as the spot where I would either free myself from this man, or die in his arms. I had resolved upon a plan of operation—it was this: to stop short, face about, and commence action; and neither ask or give quarters, until I was free or dead!

We had got within six rods of the spot, when a gentleman turned the corner, meeting us on horseback. He came up, and entered into conversation with my captor, both of them speaking in Dutch, so that I knew not what they said. After a few moments, this gentleman addressed himself to me in English, and I then learned that he was one of the magistrates on whom we had called in the morning; I felt that another crisis was at hand. Using his saddle as his bench, he put on an extremely stern and magisterial-like face, holding up his horse not unlike a field-marshal in the act of reviewing troops, and carried me through a most rigid examination in reference to the statement I had made. I repeated carefully all I had said; at the close, he said, "Well, you had better stay among us a few months, until we see what is to be done with you." It was then agreed that we should go back to the tavern, and there settle upon some further plan. When we arrived at the tavern, the magistrate alighted from his horse, and went into the bar-room. He took another close glance at me, and went over some points of the former examination. He seemed quite satisfied at the correctness of my statement, and made the following proposition: that I should go and live with him for a short time, stating that he had a few acres of corn and potatoes to get in, and that he would give me twenty-five cents per day. I most cheerfully assented to this proposal. It was also agreed that I should remain at the tavern with my captor that night, and that he would accompany me in the morning. This part of the arrangement I did not like, but of course I could not say so. Things being thus arranged, the magistrate mounted his horse, and went on his way home.

It had been cloudy and rainy during the afternoon, but the western sky having partially cleared at this moment, I perceived that it was near the setting of the sun.

My captor had left his hired man most of the day to dig potatoes alone; but the waggon being now loaded, it being time to convey the potatoes into the barn, and the horses being all ready for that purpose, he was obliged to go into the potatoe field and give assistance.

I should say here, that his wife had been driven away by the small-pox panic about three o'clock, and had not yet returned; this left no one in the hose, but a boy, about nine years of age.

As he went out, he spoke to the boy in Dutch, which I supposed, from the little fellow's conduct, to be instructions to watch me closely, which he certainly did.

The potatoe lot was across the public road, directly in front of the house; at the back of the house, and about 300 yards distant, there was a thick wood. The circumstances of the case would not allow me to think for one moment of remaining there for the night—the time had come for another effort—but there were two serious difficulties. One was, that I must either deceive or dispatch this boy who is watching me with intense vigilance. I am glad to say, that the latter did not for a moment seriously enter my mind. To deceive him effectually, I left my coat and went to the back door, from which my course would be direct to the wood. When I got to the door, I found that the barn, to which the waggon must soon come, lay just to the right, and overlooking the path I must take to the wood. In front of me lay a garden surrounded by a picket fence, to the left of me was a small gate, and that by passing through that gate would throw me into an open field, and give me clear running to the wood; but on looking through the gate, I saw that my captor, being with the team, would see me if I attempted to start before he moved from the position he then occupied. To add to my difficulty the horses had baulked; while waiting for the decisive moment, the boy came to the door and asked me why I did not come in. I told him I felt unwell, and wished him to be so kind as to hand me a glass of water; expecting while he was gone to get it, the team would clear, so that I could start. While he was gone, another attempt was made to start the team but failed; he came with the water and I quickly used it up by gargling my throat and by drinking a part. I asked him to serve me by giving me another glass: he gave me a look of close scrutiny, but went in for the water. I heard him fill the glass, and start to return with it; when the hind end of the waggon cleared the corner of the house, which stood in a range with the fence along which I was to pass in getting to the wood. As I passed out the gate, I "squared my main yard," and laid my course up the line of fence, I cast a last glance over my right shoulder, and saw the boy just perch his head above the garden picket to look after me; I heard at the same time great confusion with the team, the rain having made the ground slippery, and the horses having to cross the road with a slant and rise to get into the barn, it required great effort after they started to prevent their baulking. I felt some assurance that although the boy might give the alarm, my captor could not leave the team until it was in the barn. I heard the horses' feet on the barn-floor, just as I leaped the fence, and darted into the wood.

The sun was now quite down behind the western horizon, and just at this time a heavy dark curtain of clouds was let down, which seemed to usher in haste the night shade. I have never before or since seen anything which seemed to me to compare in sublimity with the spreading of the night shades at the close of that day. My reflections upon the events of that day, and upon the close of it, since I became acquainted with the Bible, have frequently brought to my mind that beautiful passage in the Book of Job, "He holdeth back the face of His throne, and spreadeth a cloud before it."

Before I proceed to the critical events and final deliverance of the next chapter, I cannot forbear to pause a moment here for reflection. The reader may well imagine how the events of the past day affected my mind. You have seen what was done to me; you have heard what was said to me—you have also seen what I have done, and heard what I have said. If you ask me whether I had expected before I left home, to gain my liberty by shedding men's blood, or breaking their limbs? I answer, no! and as evidence of this, I had provided no weapon whatever; not so much as a penknife—it never once entered my mind. I cannot say that I expected to have the ill fortune of meeting with any human being who would attempt to impede my flight.

If you ask me if I expected when I left home to gain my liberty by fabrications and untruths? I answer, no! my parents, slaves as they were, had always taught me, when they could, that "truth may be blamed but cannot be shamed;" so far as their example was concerned, I had no habits of untruth. I was arrested, and the demand made upon me, "Who do you belong to?" knowing the fatal use these men would make of *my* truth, I at once concluded that they had no more right to it than a highwayman has to a traveller's purse.

If you ask me whether I now really believe that I gained my liberty by those lies? I answer, no! I now believe that I should be free, had I told the truth; but, at that moment, I could not see any other way to baffle my enemies, and escape their clutches.

The history of that day has never ceased to inspire me with a deeper hatred of slavery; I never recur to it but with the most intense horror at a system which can put a man not only in peril of liberty, limb, and life itself, but which may even send him in haste to the bar of God with a lie upon his lips.

Whatever my readers may think, therefore, of the history of events of the day, do not admire in it the fabrications; but *see* in it the impediments that often fall into the pathway of the flying bondman. *See* how human bloodhounds gratuitously chase, catch, and tempt him to shed blood and lie; how, when he would do good, evil is thrust upon him.

CHAPTER III.

A DREARY NIGHT IN THE WOODS— CRITICAL SITUATION THE NEXT DAY.

ALMOST immediately on entering the wood, I not only found myself embosomed in the darkness of the night, but I also found myself entangled in a thick forest of undergrowth, which had been quite thoroughly wetted by the afternoon rain.

I penetrated through the wood, thick and thin, and more or less wet, to the distance I should think of three miles. By this time my clothes were all thoroughly soaked through, and I felt once more a gloom and wretchedness; the recollection of which makes me shudder at this distant day. My young friends in this highly favoured Christian country, surrounded with all the comforts of home and parental care, visited by pastors and Sabbath-school teachers, think of the dreary condition of the blacksmith boy in the dark wood that night; and then consider that thousands of his brethren have had to undergo much greater hardships in their flight from slavery.

I was now out of the hands of those who had so cruelly teased me during the day; but a number of fearful thoughts rushed into my mind to alarm me. It was dark and cloudy, so that I could not see the *north star*. How do I know what ravenous beasts are in this wood? How do I know what precipices may be within its bounds? I cannot rest in this wood to-morrow, for it will be searched by those men from whom I have escaped; but how shall I regain the road? How shall I know when I am on the right road again?

These are some of the thoughts that filled my mind with gloom and alarm.

At a venture I struck an angle northward in search of the road. After several hours of zigzag and laborious travel, dragging through briars, thorns and running vines, I emerged from the wood and found myself wading marshy ground and over ditches.

I can form no correct idea of the distance I travelled, but I came to a road, I should think about three o'clock in the morning. It so happened that I came out near where there was a fork in the road of three prongs.

Now arose a serious query—which is the right prong for me? I was reminded by the circumstance of a superstitious proverb among the slaves, that "the left-hand turning was unlucky," but as I had never been in the habit of placing faith in this or any similar superstition, I am not aware that it had the least weight upon my mind, as I had the same difficulty with reference to the right-hand turning. After a few moments parley with myself, I took the central prong of the road and pushed on with all my speed.

It had not cleared off, but a fresh wind had sprung up; it was chilly and searching. This with my wet clothing made me very uncomfortable; my nerves began to quiver before the searching wind. The barking of mastiffs, the crowing of fowls, and the distant rattling of market waggons, warned me that the day was approaching.

My British reader must remember that in the region where I was, we know nothing of the long hours of twilight you enjoy here.

With us the day is measured more by the immediate presence of the sun, and the night by the prevalence of actual darkness.

The day dawned upon me when I was near a small house and barn, situate close to the road side. The barn was too near the road, and too small to afford secure shelter for the day; but as I cast my eye around by the dim light, I could see no wood, and no larger barn. It seemed to be an open country to a wide extent. The sun was travelling so rapidly from his eastern chamber, that ten or fifteen minutes would spread broad daylight over my track. Whether *my* deed was evil, *you* may judge, but I freely confess that I did *then* prefer darkness rather than light; I therefore took to the mow of the little barn at a great risk, as the events of the day will show. It so happened that the barn was filled with corn fodder, newly cured and lately gotten in. You are aware that however quietly one may crawl into such a bed, he is compelled to make much more noise than if it were a feather-bed; and also considerably more than if it were hay or straw. Besides inflicting upon my own excited imagination the belief that I made noise enough to be heard by the inmates of the house who were likely to be rising at the time, I had the misfortune to attract the notice of a little house-dog, such as we call in that part of the world a "fice," on account of its being not only the smallest species of the canine race, but also, because it is the most saucy, noisy, and teasing of all dogs. This little creature commenced a fierce barking. I had at once great fears that the mischievous little thing would betray me; I fully apprehended that as soon as the man of the house arose, he would come and make search in the barn. It now being entirely daylight, it was too late to retreat from this shelter, even if I could have found another; I, therefore, bedded myself down into the fodder as best I could, and entered upon the annoyances of the day, with the frail hope to sustain my mind.

It was Thursday morning; the clouds that had veiled the sky during the latter part of the previous day and the previous night were gone. It was not until about an hour after the sun rose that I heard any out-door movements about the house. As soon as I heard those movements, I was satisfied there was but one man about the house, and that he was preparing to go some distance to work for the day. This was fortunate for me; the busy movements about the yard, and especially the active preparations in the house for breakfast, silenced my unwelcome little annoyer, the fice, until after the man had gone, when he commenced afresh, and continued with occasional intermissions through the day. He made regular sallies from the house to the barn, and after smelling about, would fly back to the house, barking furiously; thus he strove most skilfully throughout the entire day to raise an alarm. There seemed to be no one about the house but one or two small children and the mother, after the man was gone. About ten o'clock my attention was gravely directed to another trial: how I could pass the day without food. The reader will remember it is Thursday, and the only regular meal I have taken since Sunday, was yesterday, in the midst of great agitation, about four o'clock; that since that I have performed my arduous night's travel. At one moment, I had nearly concluded to go and present myself at the door, and ask the woman of the house to have compassion and give me food; but then I feared the consequences might be fatal, and I resolved to suffer the day out. The wind sprang up fresh and cool; the barn being small and the crevices large, my wet clothes were dried by it, and chilled me through and through.

I cannot now, with pen or tongue, give a correct idea of the feeling of wretchedness I experienced; every nerve in my system quivered, so that not a particle of my flesh was at rest. In this way I passed the day till about the middle of the afternoon, when there seemed to be an unusual stir about the public road, which passed close by the barn. Men seemed to be passing in parties on horseback, and talking anxiously. From a word which I now and then overheard, I had not a shadow of doubt that they were in search of me. One I heard say, "I ought to catch such a fellow, the only liberty he should have for one fortnight, would be ten feet of rope." Another I heard say, "I reckon he is in that wood now." Another said, "Who would have thought that rascal was so 'cute?" All this while the little fice was mingling his voice with those of the horsemen, and the noise of the horses' feet. I listened and trembled.

Just before the setting of the sun, the labouring man of the house returned, and commenced his evening duties about the house and barn; chopping wood, getting up his cow, feeding his pigs, &c., attended by the little brute, who continued barking at short intervals. He came several times into the barn below. While matters were passing thus, I heard the approach of horses again, and as they came up nearer, I was led to believe that all I had heard pass, were returning in one party. They passed the barn and halted at the house, when I recognised the voice of my old captor; addressing the labourer, he asked, "Have you seen a runaway nigger pass here to-day?"

LABOURER.—"No; I have not been at home since early this morning. Where did he come from?"

CAPTOR.—"I caught him down below here yesterday morning. I had him all day, and just at night he fooled me and got away. A party of us have been after him all day; we have been up to the line, but can't hear or see anything of him. I heard this morning where he came from. He is a blacksmith, and a stiff reward is out for him, two hundred dollars."

LAB.—"He is worth looking for."

CAP.—"I reckon so. If I get my clutches on him again, I'll mosey* him down to ——— before I eat or sleep."

Reader, you may if you can, imagine what the state of my mind was at this moment. I shall make no attempt to describe it to you; to my great relief, however, the party rode off, and the labourer after finishing his work went into the house. Hope seemed now to dawn for me once more; darkness was rapidly approaching, but the moments of twilight seemed much longer than they did the evening before. At length the sable covering had spread itself over the earth. About eight o'clock, I ventured to descend from the mow of the barn into the road. The little dog the while began a furious fit of barking, so much so, that I was sure that with what his master had learned about me, he could not fail to believe I was about his premises. I quickly crossed the road, and got into an open field opposite. After stepping lightly about two hundred yards, I halted, and on listening, I picked up two stones, and one in each hand I made off as fast as I could, but I heard nothing more that indicated pursuit, and after going some distance I discharged my encumbrance, as from the reduced state of my bodily strength, I could not afford to carry ballast.

This incident had the effect to start me under great disadvantage to make a good night's journey, as it threw me at once off the road, and compelled me to encounter at once the tedious and laborious task of beating my way across marshy fields, and to drag through woods and thickets where there were no paths.

After several hours I found my way back to the road, but the hope of making anything like clever speed was out of the question. All I could do was to keep my legs in motion, and this I continued to do with the utmost difficulty. The latter part of the night I suffered extremely from cold. There came a heavy frost; I expected at

*An expression which signifies to drive in a hurry.

every moment to fall on the road and perish. I came to a corn-field covered with heavy shocks of Indian corn that had been cut; I went into this and got an ear, and then crept into one of the shocks; eat as much of it as I could, and thought I would rest a little and start again, but weary nature could not sustain the operation of grinding hard corn for its own nourishment, and I sunk to sleep.

When I awoke, the sun was shining around; I started with alarm, but it was too late to think of seeking any other shelter; I therefore nestled myself down, and concealed myself as best I could from the light of day. After recovering a little from my fright, I commenced again eating my whole corn. Grain by grain I worked away at it; when my jaws grew tired, as they often did, I would rest, and then begin afresh. Thus, although I began an early breakfast, I was nearly the whole of the forenoon before I had done.

Nothing of importance occurred during the day, until about the middle of the afternoon, when I was thrown into a panic by the appearance of a party of gunners, who passed near me with their dogs. After shooting one or two birds, however, and passing within a few rods of my frail covering, they went on, and left me once more in hope. Friday night came without any other incident worth naming. As I sallied out, I felt evident benefit from the ear of corn I had nibbled away. My strength was considerably renewed; though I was far from being nourished, I felt that my life was at least safe from death by hunger. Thus encouraged, I set out with better speed than I had made since Sunday and Monday night. I had a presentiment, too, that I must be near free soil. I had not yet the least idea where I should find a home or a friend, still my spirits were so highly elated, that I took the whole of the road to myself; I ran, hopped, skipped, jumped, clapped my hands, and talked to myself. But to the old slaveholder I had left, I said, "Ah! ha! old fellow, I told you I'd fix you."

After an hour or two of such freaks of joy, a gloom would come over me in connexion with these questions, "But where are you going? What are you going to do? What will you do with freedom without father, mother, sisters, and brothers? What will you say when you are asked where you were born? You know nothing of the world; how will you explain the fact of your ignorance?"

These questions made me feel deeply the magnitude of the difficulties yet before me.

Saturday morning dawned upon me; and although my strength seemed yet considerably fresh, I began to feel a hunger somewhat more destructive and pinching, if possible, than I had before. I resolved, at all risk, to continue my travel by day-light, and to ask information of the first person I met.

The events of the next chapter will shew what fortune followed this resolve.

CHAPTER IV.

THE GOOD WOMAN OF THE TOLL-GATE
DIRECTS ME TO W. W.—MY RECEPTION BY HIM.

THE resolution of which I informed the reader at the close of the last chapter, being put into practice, I continued my flight on the public road; and a little after the sun rose, I came in sight of a toll-gate again. For a moment all the events which followed my passing a toll-gate on Wednesday morning, came fresh to my recollection, and produced some hesitation; but at all events, said I, I will try again.

On arriving at the gate, I found it attended by an elderly woman, whom I afterwards learned was a widow, and an excellent Christian woman. I asked her if I was in Pennsylvania. On being informed that I was, I asked her if she knew where I could get employ? She said she did not; but advised me to go to W. W., a Quaker, who lived about three miles from her, whom I would find to take an interest in me. She gave me directions which way to take; I thanked her, and bade her good morning, and was very careful to follow her directions.

In about half an hour I stood trembling at the door of W. W. After knocking, the door opened upon a comfortably spread table; the sight of which seemed at once to increase my hunger sevenfold. Not daring to enter, I said I had been sent to him in search of employ. "Well," said he, "Come in and take thy breakfast, and get warm, and we will talk about it; thee must be cold without any coat." *"Come in and take thy breakfast, and get warm!"* These words spoken by a stranger, but with such an air of simple sincerity and fatherly kindness, made an overwhelming impression upon my mind. They made me feel, spite of all my fear and timidity, that I had, in the providence of God, found a friend and a home. He at once gained my confidence; and I felt that I might confide to him a fact which I had, as yet, confided to no one.

From that day to this, whenever I discover the least disposition in my heart to disregard the wretched condition of any poor or distressed persons with whom I meet, I call to mind these words—*"Come in and take thy breakfast, and get warm."* They invariably remind me of what I was at that time; my condition was as wretched as that of any human being can possibly be, with the exception of the loss of health or reason. I had but four pieces of clothing about my person, having left all the rest in the hands of my captors. I was a starving fugitive, without home or friends—a reward offered for my person in the public papers—pursued by cruel manhunters, and no claim upon him to whose door I went. Had he turned me away, I must have perished. Nay, he took me in, and gave me of his food, and shared with me his own garments. Such treatment I had never before received at the hands of any white man.

A few such men in slaveholding America, have stood, and even now stand, like Abrahams and Lots, to stay its forthcoming and well-earned and just judgment.

The limits of this work compel me to pass over many interesting incidents which occurred during my six months' concealment in that family. I must confine myself only to those which will show the striking providence of God, in directing my steps to the door of W. W., and how great an influence the incidents of that six months has had upon all my subsequent history. My friend kindly gave me employ to saw and split a number of cords of wood, then lying in his yard, for which he agreed with me for liberal pay and board. This inspired me with great encouragement. The idea of beginning to earn something was very pleasant. Next; we confidentially agreed upon the way and means of avoiding surprise, in case any one should come to the house as a spy, or with intention to arrest me. This afforded still further relief, as it convinced me that the whole family would now be on the look out for such persons.

The next theme of conversation was with reference to my education.

"Can thee read or write any, James?" was the question put to me the morning after my arrival, by W. W.

"No, sir, I cannot; my duties as a blacksmith have made me acquainted with the figures on the common mechanics' square. There was a day-book kept in the shop, in which the overseer usually charged the smithwork we did for the neighbours. I have spent entire Sabbaths looking over the pages of that book; knowing the names of persons to whom certain pieces of work were charged, together with their prices, I strove anxiously to learn to write in this way. I got paper, and picked up feathers about the yard, and made ink of —————— berries. My quills being too soft, and my skill in making a pen so poor, that I undertook some years ago to make a steel pen.* In this way I have learnt to make a few of the letters, but I cannot write my own name, nor do I know the letters of the alphabet."

W. W., *(handing a slate and pencil.)*—"Let me see how thee makes letters; try such as thou hast been able to make easily."

A. B. C. L. G.

P. W., *(wife of W. W.)*—"Why, those are better than I can make."

W. W.—"Oh, we can soon get thee in the way, James."

Arithmetic and astronomy became my favourite studies. W. W. was an accomplished scholar; he had been a teacher for some years, and was cultivating a small farm on account of ill-health, which had compelled him to leave teaching. He is one of the most far-sighted and practical men I ever met with. He taught me by familiar conversations, illustrating his themes by diagrams on the slate, so that I caught his ideas with ease and rapidity.

I now began to see, for the first time, the extent of the mischief slavery had done to me. Twenty-one years of my life were gone, never again to return, and I was as profoundly ignorant, comparatively, as a child five years old. This was painful, annoying, and humiliating in the extreme. Up to this time, I recollected to have seen one copy of the New Testament, but the entire Bible I had never seen, and had never heard of the Patriarchs, or of the Lord Jesus Christ. I recollected to have heard two sermons, but had heard no mention in them of Christ, or the way of life by Him. It is quite easy to imagine, then, what was the state of my mind, having been reared in total moral midnight; it was a sad picture of mental and spiritual darkness.

As my friend poured light into my mind, I saw the darkness; it amazed and grieved me beyond description. Sometimes I sank down under the load, and became discouraged, and dared not hope that I could ever succeed in acquiring knowledge enough to make me happy, or useful to my fellow-beings.

My dear friend, W. W., however, had a happy tact to inspire me with confidence; and he, perceiving my state of mind, exerted himself, not without success, to encourage me. He cited to me various instances of coloured persons, of whom I had not heard before, and who had distinguished themselves for learning, such as

---

*This attempt was as early as 1822.

Bannicker, Wheatley, and Francis Williams.

How often have I regretted that the six months I spent in the family of W. W., could not have been six years. The danger of recapture, however, rendered it utterly imprudent that I should remain longer; and early in the month of March, while the ground was covered with the winter's snow, I left the bosom of this excellent family, and went forth once more to try my fortune among strangers.

My dear reader, if I could describe to you the emotions I felt when I left the threshold of W. W.'s door, you could not fail to see how deplorable is the condition of the fugitive slave, often for months and years after he has escaped the immediate grasp of the tyrant. When I left my parents, the trial was great, but I had now to leave a friend who had done more for me than parents could have done as slaves; and hence I felt an endearment to that friend which was heightened by a sense of the important relief he had afforded me in the greatest need, and hours of pleasant and highly profitable intercourse.

About a month previous to leaving the house of W. W., a small circumstance occurred one evening, which I only name to shew the harassing fears and dread in which I lived during most of the time I was there. He had a brother-in-law living some ten miles distant—he was a friend to the slave; he often came unexpectedly and spent a few hours—sometimes a day and a night. I had not, however, ever known him to come at night. One night about nine o'clock, after I had gone to bed, (my lodging being just over the room in which W. W. and his wife were sitting,) I heard the door open and a voice ask, "Where is the boy?" The voice sounded to me like the voice of my master; I was sure it must be his. I sprang and listened for a moment—it seemed to be silent; I heard nothing, and then it seemed to me there was a confusion. There was a window at the head of my bed, which I could reach without getting upon the floor: it was a single sash and opened upon hinges. I quickly opened this window and waited in a perfect tremour of dread for further development. There was a door at the foot of the stairs; as I heard that door open, I sprang for the window, and my head was just, when the gentle voice of my friend W. W. said, "James?"* "Here," said I, "—— has come, and he would like to have thee put up his horse." I drew a breath of relief, but my strength and presence of mind did not return for some hours. I slept none that night; for a

---

*If W. W. had ascended the stairs without calling, I should certainly have jumped out of the window.

moment I could doze away, but the voice would sound in my ears, "Where is that boy?" and it would seem to me it must be the tyrant in quest of his weary prey, and would find myself starting again.

From that time the agitation of my mind became so great that I could not feel myself safe. Every day seemed to increase my fear, till I was unfit for work, study or rest. My friend endeavoured, but in vain, to get me to stay a week longer.

The events of the spring proved that I had not left too soon. As soon as the season for travelling fairly opened, active search was made, and my master was seen in a town, twenty miles in advance of where I had spent my six months.

The following curious fact also came out. That same brother-in-law who frightened me, was putting up one evening at a hotel some miles off, and while sitting quietly by himself in one part of the room, he overheard a conversation between a travelling pedler and several gossippers of the neighborhood, who were lounging away the evening at the hotel.

PEDLER.—"Do you know one W. W. somewhere about here?"

GOSSIPER.—"Yes, he lives ——— miles off."

Ped.—"I understand he had a black boy with him last winter, I wonder if he is there yet?"

Gos.—"I don't know, he most always has a runaway nigger with him."

Ped.—"I should like to find out whether that fellow is there yet."

Brother-in-law, (turning about)—"What does thee know about that boy?"

Ped.—"Well he is a runaway."

Brother-in-law.—"Who did he run away from?"

Ped.—"From Col——— in ———."

Brother-in-law.—"How did thee find out that fact?"

Ped.—"Well, I have been over there peddling."

Brother-in-law.—"Where art thou from?"

Ped.—"I belong in Conn."

Brother-in-law.—"Did thee see the boy's master?"

Ped.—"Yes."

Brother-in-law.—"What did he offer thee to find the boy?"

Ped.—"I agreed to find out where he was, and let him know, and if he got him, I was to receive ———."

Brother-in-law.—"How didst thou hear the boy had been with W. W."

Ped.—"Oh, he is known to be a notorious rascal for enticing away, and concealing slaves; he'll get himself into trouble yet, the slaveholders are on the look out for him."

Brother-in-law.—"W. W. is my brother-in-law; the boy of whom thou speakest is not with him, and to save thee the trouble of abusing him, I can moreover say, he is no rascal."

Ped.—"He may not be there now, but it is because he has sent him off. His master heard of him, and from the description, he is sure it must have been his boy. He could tell me pretty nigh where he was; he said he was a fine healthy boy, twenty-one, a first-rate blacksmith; he would not have taken a thousand dollars for him."

Brother-in-law.—"I know not where the boy is, but I have no doubt he is worth more to himself than he ever was to his master, high as he fixes the price on him; and I have no doubt thee will do better to pursue thy peddling honestly, than to neglect it for the sake of serving negro-hunters at a venture."

All this happened within a month or two after I left my friend. One fact which makes this part of the story deeply interesting to my own mind, is, that some years elapsed before it came to my knowledge.

CHAPTER V.

SEVEN MONTHS' RESIDENCE IN THE FAMILY OF J. K. A MEMBER OF THE SOCIETY OF FRIENDS, IN CHESTER COUNTY, PENNSYLVANIA.—REMOVAL TO NEW YORK—BECOMES A CONVERT TO RELIGION—BECOMES A TEACHER.

On leaving W. W., I wended my way in deep sorrow and melancholy, onward towards Philadelphia, and after travelling two days and a night, I found shelter and employ in the family of J. K., another member of the Society of Friends, a farmer.

The religious atmosphere in this family was excellent. Mrs. K. gave me the first copy of the Holy Scriptures I ever possessed, she also gave me much excellent counsel. She was a preacher in the Society of Friends; this occasioned her with her husband to be much of their time from home. This left the charge of the farm upon me, and besides put it out of their power to render me that aid in my studies which my former friend had. I, however, kept myself closely concealed, by confining myself to the limits of the farm, and using all my leisure time in study. This place was more secluded, and I felt less of dread and fear of discovery than I had before, and although seriously embarrassed for want of an instructor, I realized some pleasure and profit in my studies. I often employed myself in drawing rude maps of the solar system, and diagrams illustrating the theory of solar eclipses. I felt also a fondness for reading the Bible, and committing chapters, and verses of hymns to memory. Often on the Sabbath when alone in the barn, I would break the monotony of the hours by endeavouring to speak, as if I was addressing an audience. My mind was constantly struggling for thoughts, and I was still more grieved and alarmed at its barrenness; I found it gradually freed from the darkness entailed by slavery, but I was deeply and anxiously concerned how I should fill it with useful knowledge. I had a few books, and no tutor.

In this way I spent seven months with J. K., and should have continued longer, agreeably to his urgent solicitation, but I felt that life was fast wearing, and that as I was now free, I must adventure in search of knowledge. On leaving J. K., he kindly gave me the following certificate,—

> "East Nautmeal, Chester County, Pennsylvania,
> *Tenth Month* 5*th*, 1828.
> "I hereby certify, that the bearer, J. W. C. Pennington, has been in my employ seven months, during most of which time I have been from home, leaving my entire business in his trust, and that he has proved a highly trustworthy and industrious young man. He leaves with the sincere regret of myself and family; but as he feels it to be his duty to go where he can obtain education, so as to fit him to be more useful, I cordially commend him to the warm sympathy of the friends of humanity wherever as wise providence may appoint him a home.
> Signed,
> "J. K."

Passing through Philadelphia, I went to New York, and in a short time found employ on Long Island, near the city. At this time, the state of things was extremely critical in New York. It was just two years after the general emancipation in that state. In the city it was a daily occurrence for slaveholders from the southern states to catch their slaves, and by certificate from Recorder Riker take them back. I often felt serious apprehensions of danger, and yet I felt also that I must begin the world somewhere.

I was earning respectable wages, and by means of evening schools and private tuition, was making encouraging progress in my studies.

Up to this time, it had never occurred to me that I was a slave in another and a more serious sense. All my serious impressions of mind had been with reference to the slavery from which I had escaped. Slavery had been my theme of thought day and night.

In the spring of 1829, I found my mind unusually perplexed about the state of the slave. I was enjoying rare privileges in attending a Sabbath school; the great value of Christian knowledge began to be impressed upon my mind to an extent I had not been conscious of before. I began to contrast my condition with that of ten brothers and sisters I had left in slavery, and the condition of children I saw sitting around me on the Sabbath, with their pious teachers, with that of 700,000, now 800,440 slave children, who had no means of Christian instruction.

The theme was more powerful than any my mind had ever encountered before. It entered into the deep chambers of my soul, and stirred the most agitating emotions I had ever felt. The question was, what can I do for that vast body of suffering brotherhood I have left behind. To add to that weight and magnitude of the theme, I learnt for the first time, how many slaves there were. The question completely staggered my mind; and finding myself more and more borne down with it, until I was in an agony; I thought I would make it a subject of prayer to God, although prayer had not been my habit, having never attempted it but once.

I not only prayed, but also fasted. It was while engaged thus, that my attention was seriously drawn to the fact that I was a lost sinner, and a slave to Satan; and soon I saw that I must make another escape from another tyrant. I did not by any means forget my fellow-bondmen, of whom I had been sorrowing so deeply, and travailing in spirit so earnestly; but I now saw that while man had been injuring me, I had been offending God; and that unless I ceased to offend him, I could not expect to have his sympathy in my wrongs; and moreover, that I could not be instrumental in eliciting his powerful aid in behalf of those for whom I mourned so deeply.

This may provoke a smile from some who profess to be the friends of the slave, but who have a lower estimate of experimental Christianity than I believe is due to it; but I am not the less confident that sincere prayer to God, proceeding from a few hearts deeply imbued with experimental Christianity about *that time,* has had much to do with subsequent happy results. At that time the 800,000 bondmen in the British Isles had not seen the beginning of the end of their sufferings—at that time, 20,000 who are now free in Canada, were in bonds—at that time, there was no Vigilance Committee to aid the flying slave—at that time, the two powerful Anti-Slavery Societies of America had no being.

I distinctly remember that I felt the need of enlisting the sympathy of God, in behalf of my enslaved brethren; but when I attempted it day after day, and night after night, I was made to feel, that whatever else I might do, I was not qualified to do that, as I was myself alienated from him by wicked works. In short, I felt that I needed the powerful aid of some in my behalf with God, just as much as I did that of my dear friend in Pennsylvania, when flying from man. "If one man sin against another, the judge shall judge him, but if a man sin against God, who shall entreat for him?"

Day after day, for about two weeks, I found myself more deeply convicted of personal guilt before God. My heart, soul and body were in the greatest distress; I thought of neither food, drink or rest, for days and nights together. Burning with a recollection of the wrongs man had done me—mourning for the injuries my brethren were still enduring, and deeply convicted of the guilt of my own sins against God. One evening, in the third week of the struggle, while alone in my chamber, and after solemn reflection for several hours, I concluded that I could never be happy or useful in that state of mind, and resolved that I would try to become reconciled to God. I was then living in the family of an Elder of the Presbyterian Church. I had not made known my feelings to any one, either in the family or out of it; and I did not suppose that any one had discovered my feelings. To my surprise, however, I found that the family had not only been aware of my state for several days, but were deeply anxious on my behalf. The following Sabbath, Dr. Cox was on a visit in Brooklyn to preach, and was a guest in the family; hearing of my case, he expressed a wish to converse with me, and without knowing the plan, I was invited into a room and left alone with him. He entered skilfully and kindly into my feelings, and after considerable conversation he invited me to attend his service that afternoon. I did so, and was deeply interested.

Without detaining the reader with too many particulars, I will only state that I heard the doctor once or twice after this, at his own place of worship in New York City, and had several personal interviews with him, as the result of which, I hope, I was brought to a saving acquaintance with Him, of whom Moses in the Law and the Prophets did write; and soon connected myself with the church under his pastoral care.

I now returned with all my renewed powers to the great theme—slavery. It seemed now as I looked at it, to be more hideous than ever. I saw it now as an evil under the moral government of God—as a sin not only against man, but also against God. The great and engrossing thought with me was, how shall I now employ my time and my talents so as to tell most effectually upon this system of wrong! As I have stated, there was no Anti-Slavery Society then—there was no Vigilance Committee. I had, therefore, to select a course of action, without counsel or advice from any one who professed to sympathize with the slave. Many, many lonely hours of deep meditation have I passed during the years 1828 and 1829, before the great anti-slavery movement. On the questions, What shall I do for the slave? How shall I act so that he will reap the benefit of my time and talents? At one time I had resolved to go to Africa, and to react from there; but without bias or advice from any mortal, I soon gave up that, as looking too much like feeding a hungry man with a long spoon.

At length, finding that the misery, ignorance, and wretchedness of the free coloured people was by the whites tortured into an argument for slavery; finding myself now among the free people of colour in New York, where slavery was so recently abolished; and finding much to do for their elevation, I resolved to give my strength in that direction. And well do I remember the great movement which commenced among us about this time, for the holding of General Conventions, to devise ways and means for their elevation, which continued with happy influence up to 1834, when we gave way to anti-slavery friends, who had then taken up the labouring oar. And well do I remember that the first time I ever saw those tried friends, Garrison, Jocelyn, and Tappan, was in one of those Conventions, where they came to make our acquaintance, and to secure our confidence in some of their preliminary labours.

My particular mode of labour was still a subject of deep reflection; and from time to time I carried it to the Throne of Grace. Eventually my mind fixed upon the ministry as the desire of my whole heart. I had mastered the preliminary branches of English education, and was engaged in studying logic, rhetoric, and the Greek Testament, without a master. While thus struggling in my laudable work, an opening presented itself which was not less surprising than gratifying. Walking on the street one day, I met a friend, who said to me, "I have just had an application to supply a teacher for a school, and I have recommended you." I said, "My dear friend, I am obliged to you for the kindness; but I fear I cannot sustain an examination for that station." "Oh," said he, "try." I said, "I will," and we separated. Two weeks afterwards, I met the trustees of the school, was examined, accepted, and agreed with them for a salary of two hundred dollars per annum; commenced my school, and succeeded. This was five years, three months, and thirteen days after I came from the South.

As the events of my life since that have been of a public professional nature, I will say no more about it. My object in writing this tract is now completed. It has been to shew the reader the hand of God with a slave; and to elicit your sympathy on behalf of the fugitive slave, by shewing some of the untold dangers and hardships through which he has to pass to gain liberty, and how much he needs friends on free soil; and that men who have felt the yoke of slavery, even in its mildest form, cannot be expected to speak of the system otherwise than in terms of the most unqualified condemnation.

There is one sin that slavery committed against me, which I never can forgive. It robbed me of my education; the injury is irreparable; I feel the embarrassment more seriously now than I ever did before. It cost me two years' hard labour, after I fled, to unshackle my mind; it was three years before I had purged my language of slavery's idioms; it was four years before I had thrown off the crouching aspect of slavery; and now the evil that besets me is a great lack of that general information, the foundation of which is most effectively laid in that part of life which I served as a slave. When I consider how much now, more than ever, depends upon sound and thorough education among coloured men, I am grievously overwhelmed with a sense of my deficiency, and more especially as I can never hope now to make it up. If I know my own heart, I have no ambition but to serve the cause of suffering humanity; all that I have desired or sought, has been to make me more efficient for good. So far I have some consciousness that I have done my utmost; and should my future days be few or many, I am reconciled to meet the last account, hoping to be acquitted of any wilful neglect of duty; but I shall have to go to my last account with this charge against the system of slavery, "*Vile monster! thou hast hindered my usefulness, by robbing me of my early education.*"

Oh! what might I have been now, but for this robbery perpetrated upon me as soon as I saw the light. When the monster heard that a man child was born, he laughed, and said, "It is mine." When I was laid in the cradle, he came and looked on my face, and wrote down my name upon his barbarous list of chattels personal, on the same list where he registered his horses, hogs, cows, sheep, and even his *dogs!* Gracious Heaven, is there no repentance for the misguided men who do these things!

The only harm I wish to slaveholders is, that they may be speedily delivered from the guilt of a sin, which, if not repented of, must bringing down the judgment of Almighty God upon their devoted heads. The least I desire for the slave is, that he may be speedily released from the pain of drinking a cup whose bitterness I have sufficiently tasted, to know that it is insufferable.

CHAPTER VI.

SOME ACCOUNT OF THE FAMILY I LEFT IN SLAVERY—PROPOSAL TO PURCHASE MYSELF AND PARENTS—HOW MET BY MY OLD MASTER.

IT IS but natural that the reader should wish to hear a word about the family I left behind.

There are frequently large slave families with whom God seems to deal in a remarkable manner. I believe my family is an instance.

I have already stated that when I fled, I left a father, mother, and eleven brothers and sisters. These were all, except my oldest brother, owned by the man from whom I fled. It will be seen at once then how the fear of implicating them embarrassed me in the outset. They suffered nothing, however, but a strong suspicion, until about six months after I had left; when the following circumstances took place:—

When I left my friend W. W. in Pennsylvania to go on north, I ventured to write a letter back to one of my brothers, informing him how I was; and this letter was directed to the care of a white man who was hired on the plantation, who worked in the garden with my father, and who professed a warm friendship to our family; but instead of acting in good faith, he handed the letter to my master. I am sorry that truth compels me to say that that man was an Englishman.

From that day the family were handled most strangely. The history begins thus: they were all sold into Virginia, the adjoining state. This was done lest I should have some plan to get them off; but God so ordered that they fell into kinder hands. After a few years, however, their master became much embarrassed, so that he was obliged to pass them into other hands, at least for a term of years. By this change the family was divided, and my parents, with the greater part of their children, were taken to New Orleans. After remaining there several years at hard labour,—my father being in a situation of considerable trust, they were again taken back to Virginia; and by this means became entitled by the laws of that state to their freedom. Before justice, however, could take its course, their old master in Maryland, as if intent to doom them for ever to bondage, repurchased them; and in order to defeat a similar law in Maryland, by which they would have been entitled to liberty, he obtained from the General Assembly of that state the following special act. This will show not only something of his character as a slaveholder, but also his political influence in the state. It is often urged in the behalf of slaveholders, that the law interposes an obstacle in the way of emancipating their slaves when they wish to do so, but here is an instance which lays open the real philosophy of the whole case. They make the law themselves, and when they find the laws operate more in favour of the slaves than themselves, they can easily evade or change it. Maryland being a slave-exporting state, you will see why they need a law to prohibit the importation of slaves; it is a protection to that sort of trade. This law he wished to evade.

"An act for the Relief of ——— of ——— County.
Passed January 17th, 1842.

"Whereas it is represented to this General Assembly that ——— — of ——— county, brought into this state from the state of Virginia, sometime in the month of March last, two negro slaves, to wit, ——— and ——— his wife, who are slaves for life, and who were acquired by the said ——— by purchase, and whereas, the said ——— is desirous of retaining said slaves in this state. THEREFORE, BE IT ENACTED, *by the General Assembly* of Maryland, that the said ——— be, and he is hereby authorized to retain said negroes as slaves for life within this state, provided that the said ——— shall within thirty days after the passage of this act, filed with the clerk of the ——— county court, a list of said slaves so brought into this state, stating their ages, with an affidavit thereto attached, that the same is a true and faithful list of the slaves so removed, and that they were not brought into this state for the purpose of sale, and that they are slaves for life. And *provided also,* that the sum of fifteen dollars for each slave, between the ages of twelve and forty-five years, and the sum of five dollars for each slave above the age of forty-five years and under twelve years of age, so brought into this state, shall be paid to the said clerk of —— county court: to be paid over by him to the treasurer of the western shore, for the use and benefit of the Colonization Society of this state.

> *State of Connecticut.*
> *Office of Secretary of State.*
> "I hereby certify, that the foregoing is a true copy of an act passed by the General Assembly of Maryland, January 17th, 1842, as it appears in the printed acts of the said Maryland, in the Library of the state.
> In testimony whereof, I have hereunto set my hand and seal of said state, at Hartford, this 17th day of August, 1846.
> Charles W. Bradley,
> (SEAL.) Secretary of State.

Thus, the whole family after being twice fairly entitled to their liberty, even by the laws of two slave states, had the mortification of finding themselves again, not only recorded as slaves for life, but also a premium paid upon them, professedly to aid in establishing others of their fellow-beings in a free republic on the coast of Africa; but the hand of God seems to have been heavy upon the man who could plan such a stratagem to wrong his fellows.

The immense fortune he possessed when I left him, (bating one thousand dollars I brought with me in my own body,) and which he seems to have retained till that time, began to fly, and in a few years he was insolvent, so that he was unable to hold the family, and was compelled to think of selling them again. About this time I heard of their state by an underground railroad passenger, who came from that neighbourhood, and resolved to make an effort to obtain the freedom of my parents, and to relieve myself from liability. For this purpose, after arranging for the means to purchase, I employed counsel to make a definite offer for my parents and myself. To his proposal, the following evasive and offensive answer was returned.

> *January* 12*th*, 1846.
> J. H———, Esq.
> "Sir,—Your letter is before me. The ungrateful servant in whose behalf you write, merits no clemency from me. He was guilty of theft when he departed, for which I hope he has made due amends. I have heard he was a respectable man, and calculated to do some good to his fellow-beings. Servants are selling from five hundred and fifty to seven hundred dollars. I will take five hundred and fifty dollars, and liberate him. If my proposition is acceded to, and the money lodged in Baltimore, I will execute the necessary instrument, and deliver it in Baltimore, to be given up on payment being made.
> "Yours, &c.,
> "———."
> "Jim was a first-rate mechanic, (blacksmith) and was worth to me one thousand dollars."

Here he not only refuses to account for my parents, by including them in his return and proposition, but he at the same time attempts to intimidate me by mooting the charge of theft.

I confess I was not only surprised, but mortified, at this result. The hope of being once more united to parents whom I had not seen for sixteen years, and whom I still loved dearly, had so excited my mind, that I disarranged my business relations, disposed of a valuable library of four hundred volumes, and by additional aid obtained among the liberal people of Jamaica, I was prepared to give the extravagant sum of five hundred dollars each for myself, and my father and mother. This I was willing to do, not because I approve of the principle involved as a general rule. But supposing that, as my former master was now an old man not far from his grave, (about which I was not mistaken) and as he knew, by his own shewing, that I was able to do some good, he would be inclined, whatever might have been our former relations and misunderstandings, to meet my reasonable desire to see my parents, and to part this world in reconciliation with each other, as well as with God. I should have rejoiced had his temper permitted him to accede to my offer. But I thought it too bad, a free man of Jesus Christ, living on "free soil," to give a man five hundred dollars for the privilege of being let alone, and to be branded as a thief into the bargain, and that too after I had served him twenty prime years, without the benefit of being taught so much as the alphabet.

I wrote him with my own hand, sometime after this, stating that no proposition would be acceded to by me, which did not include my parents; and likewise fix the sum for myself more reasonable, and also retract the offensive charge; to this he maintained a dignified silence. The means I had acquired by the contributions of kind friends to redeem myself, I laid by, in case the worst should come; and that designed for the purchase of my parents, I used in another kind of operation, as the result of which, my father and two brothers are now in Canada. My mother was sold a second time, south, but she was eventually found. Several of my sisters married free men, who purchased their liberty; and three brothers are owned, by what may be called conscience slaveholders, who hold slaves only for a term of years. My old master has since died; my mother and he are now in the other world together, she is at rest from him. Sometime after his death, I received information from a gentleman, intimate with his heirs, (who are principally females) that the reduced state of the family, afforded not only a good opportunity to obtain a release upon reasonable terms, but also to render the children of my oppressor some pecuniary aid; and much as I had suffered, I must confess this latter was the stronger motive with me, for acceding to their offer made by him.

I have many other deeply interesting particulars touching our family history, but I have detailed as many as prudence will permit, on account of those members who are yet south of Mason and Dixon's line.

I have faith in the hand that has dealt with us so strangely, that all our remaining members will in time be brought together; and then the case may merit a reviewed and enlarged edition of this tract, when other important matter will be inserted.

CHAPTER VII.

THE FEEDING AND CLOTHING OF THE SLAVES IN THE PART OF MARYLAND WHERE I LIVED, &C.

THE slaves are generally fed upon salt pork, herrings and Indian corn.

The manner of dealing it out to them is as follows:—Each working man, on Monday morning, goes to the cellar of the master where the provisions are kept, and where the overseer takes his stand with some one to assist him, when he, with a pair of steel-yards, weighs out to every man the amount of three-and-a-half pounds, to last him till the ensuing Monday—allowing him just half-a-pound per day. Once in a few weeks there is a change made, by which, instead of the three-and-a-half pounds of pork, each man receives twelve herrings, allowing two a-day. The only bread kind the slaves have is that made of Indian meal. In some of the lower counties, the masters usually give their slaves the corn in the ear; and they have to grind it for themselves by night at hand-mills. But my master had a quantity sent to the grist mill at a time, to be ground into coarse meal, and kept it in a large chest in his cellar, where the woman who cooked for the boys could get it daily. This was baked in large loaves, called "steel poun bread." Sometimes as a change it was made into "Johnny Cake," and then at others into mush.

The slaves had no butter, coffee, tea, or sugar; occasionally they were allowed milk, but not statedly; the only exception to this statement was the "harvest provisions." In harvest, when cutting the grain, which lasted from two to three weeks in the heat of summer, they were allowed some fresh meat, rice, sugar, and coffee; and also their allowance of whiskey.

At the beginning of winter, each slave had one pair of coarse shoes and stockings, one pair of pantaloons, and a jacket.

At the beginning of summer, he had two pairs of coarse linen pantaloons and two shirts.

Once in a number of years, each slave, or each man and his wife, had one coarse blanket and enough coarse linen for a "bed-tick." He never had any bedstead or other furniture kind. The men had no hats, waistcoats or handkerchiefs given them, or the women any bonnets. These they had to contrive for themselves. Each labouring man had a small "patch" of ground allowed him; from this he was expected to furnish himself and his boys hats, &c. These patches they had to work by night; from these, also, they had to raise their own provisions, as no potatoes, cabbage, &c., were allowed them from the plantation. Years ago the slaves were in the habit of raising broom-corn, and making brooms to supply the market in the towns; but now of later years great quantities of these and other articles, such as scrubbing-brushes, wooden trays, mats, baskets, and straw hats which the slaves made, are furnished by the shakers and other small manufacturers, from the free states of the north.

Neither my master or any other master, within my acquaintance, made any provisions for the religious instruction of his slaves. They were not worked on the Sabbath. One of the "boys" was required to stay at home and "feed," that is, take care of the stock, every Sabbath; the rest went to see their friends. Those men whose families were on other plantations usually spent the Sabbath with them; some would lie about at home and rest themselves.

When it was pleasant weather my master would ride "into town" to church, but I never knew him to say a word to one of us about going to church, or about our obligations to God, or a future state. But there were a number of pious slaves in our neighbourhood, and several of these my master owned; one of these was an exhorter. He was not connected with a religious body, but used to speak every Sabbath in some part of the neighbourhood. When slaves died, their remains were usually consigned to the grave without any ceremony; but this old gentleman, wherever he heard of a slave having been buried in that way, would send notice from plantation to plantation, calling the slaves together at the grave on the Sabbath, where he'd sing, pray, and exhort. I have known him to go ten or fifteen miles voluntarily to attend these services. He could not read, and I never heard him refer to any Scripture, and state and discourse upon any fundamental doctrine of the gospel; but he knew a number of "spiritual songs by heart," of these he would give two lines at a time very exact, set and lead the tune himself; he would pray with great fervour, and his exhortations were amongst the most impressive I have heard.

The Methodists at one time attempted to evangelize the slaves in our neighbourhood, but the effort was sternly resisted by the masters. They held a Camp Meeting in the neighbourhood, where many of the slaves attended. But one of their preachers for addressing words of comfort to the slaves, was arrested and tried for his life.

My master was very active in this disgraceful affair, but the excellent man, Rev. Mr. G., was acquitted and escaped out of their hands.

Still, it was deemed by his brethren to be imprudent for him to preach any more in the place, as some of the more reckless masters swore violence against him. This good man's name is remembered dearly, till this day, by slaves in that county. I met with a fugitive about a year ago, who remembered distinctly the words spoken by Mr. G., and by which his own mind was awakened to a sense of the value of his soul. He said, in the course of his preaching, addressing himself to the slaves, "You have precious immortal souls, that are worth far more to you than your bodies are to your masters;" or words to that effect. But while these words interested many slaves, they also made many masters exceedingly angry, and they tortured his words into an attempt to excite the slaves to rebellion.

Some of my master's slaves who had families, were regularly married, and others were not; the law makes no provision for such marriages, and the only provision made by the master was, that they should obtain his leave. In some cases, after obtaining leave to take his wife, the slave would ask further leave to go to a minister and be married. I never knew him to deny such a request, and yet, in those cases where the slave did not ask it, he never required him to be married by a minister. Of course, no Bibles, Tracts, or religious books of any kind, were ever given to the slaves; and no ministers or religious instructors were ever known to visit our plantation at any time, either in sickness or in health. When a slave was sick, my master being himself a physician, sometimes attended, and sometimes he called other physicians. Slaves frequently sickened and died, but I never knew any provision made to administer to them the comforts, or to offer to them the hopes of the gospel, or to their friends after their death.

There is no one feature of slavery to which the mind recurs with more gloomy impressions, than to its disastrous influence upon the families of the masters, physically, pecuniarily, and mentally.

It seems to destroy families as by a powerful blight, large and opulent slave-holding families, often vanish like a group of shadows at the third or fourth generation. This fact arrested my attention some years before I escaped from slavery, and of course before I had any enlightened views of the moral character of the system. As far back as I can recollect, indeed, it was a remark among slaves, that every generation of slaveholders are more and more inferior. There were several large and powerful families in our county, including that of my master, which affords to my mind a melan-

choly illustration of this remark. One of the wealthiest slaveholders in the county, was General R., a brother-in-law to my master.
This man owned a large and highly valuable tract of land, called R.'s
Manor. I do not know how many slaves he owned, but the number
was large. He lived in a splendid mansion, and drove his coach and
four. He was for some years a member of Congress. He had a
numerous family of children.

The family showed no particular signs of decay until he had
married a second time, and had considerably increased his number
of children. It then became evident that his older children were
not educated for active business, and were only destined to be a
charge. Of sons, (seven or eight,) not one of them reached the emi-
nence once occupied by the father. The only one that approached
to it, was the eldest, who became an officer in the navy, and obtained
the doubtful glory of being killed in the Mexican war.

General R. himself ran through his vast estate, died intemper-
ate, and left a widow and large number of daughters, some minors,
destitute, and none of his sons fitted for any employment but in the
army and navy.

Slaves have a superstitious dread of passing the dilapidated
dwelling of a man who has been guilty of great cruelties to his
slaves, and who is dead, or moved away. I never felt this dread
deeply but once, and that was one Sabbath about sunset, as I
crossed the yard of General R.'s residence, which was about two
miles from us, after he had been compelled to leave it.

To see the once fine smooth gravel walks, overgrown with grass—
the redundances of the shrubbery neglected—the once finely
painted pricket fences, rusted and falling down—a fine garden in
splendid ruins—the lofty ceiling of the mansion thickly curtained
with cobwebs—the spacious apartments abandoned, while the only
music heard within as a substitute for the voices of family glee that
once filled it, was the crying cricket and cockroaches! Ignorant slave
as I was at that time, I could but pause for a moment, and recur in
silent horror to the fact that, a strange reverse of fortune, had lately
driven from that proud mansion, a large and once opulent family.
What advantage was it now to the members of that family, that the
father and head had for near half a century stood high in the counsels of the state, and had the benefit of the unrequited toil of hundreds of his fellowmen, when they were already grappling with the
annoyances of that poverty, which he had entailed upon others.

My master's family, in wealth and influence, was not inferior to

General R.'s originally. His father was a member of the convention that framed the present constitution of the state; he was, also, for some years chief justice of the state.

My master was never equal to his father, although he stood high at one time. He once lacked but a few votes of being elected Governor of the state: he once sat in the Assembly, and was generally a leading man in his own county. His influence was found to be greatest when exerted in favour of any measure in regard to the control of slaves. He was the first mover in several cruel and rigid municipal regulations in the county, which prohibited slaves from going over a certain number of miles from their master's places on the Sabbath, and from being seen about the town. He once instigated the authorities of the town where he attended service, to break up a Sabbath-school some humane members of the Methodist and Lutheran denominations had set up to teach the free negroes, lest the slaves should get some benefit of it.

But there was a still wider contrast between my master and his own children, eight in number, when I left him. His eldest daughter, the flower of the family, married a miserable and reckless gambler. His eldest son was kind-hearted, and rather a favourite with the slaves on that account; but he had no strength of mind or weight of character. His education was limited, and he had no disposition or tact for business of any kind. He died at thirty-six, intestate; leaving his second wife (a sister to his father's second wife) with several orphan children, a widow with a small estate deeply embarrassed. The second son was once sent to West Point to fit for an officer. After being there a short time, however, he became unsteady, and commenced the study of medicine, but he soon gave that up and preferred to live at home and flog the slaves; and by them was cordially dreaded and disliked, and among themselves he was vulgarly nicknamed on account of his cruel and filthy habits.

These two families will afford a fair illustration of the gloomy history of many others that I could name. This decline of slaveholding families is a subject of observation and daily remark among slaves; they are led to observe every change in the pecuniary, moral, and social state of the families they belong to, from the fact, that as the old master declines, or as his children are married off, they are expecting to fall into their hands, or in cases of insolvency on the part of the old master, they expect to be sold; in either case, it involves a change of master—a subject to which they cannot be indifferent. And it is very rarely the case that a slave's condition is benefited by passing from the old master into the hands of one of his children. Owing to the causes I have mentioned, the decline is so rapid and marked, in almost every point of view, that the children of slaveholders are universally inferior to themselves, mentally, morally, physically, as well as pecuniarily, especially so in the latter point of view; and this is a matter of most vital concern to the slaves. The young master not being able to own as many slaves as his father, usually works what he has more severely, and being liable to embarrassment, the slaves' liability to be sold at an early day is much greater. For the same reason, slaves have a deep interest, generally, in the marriage of a young mistress. Very generally the daughters of slaveholders marry inferior men; men who seek to better their own condition by a wealthy connection. The slaves who pass into the hands of the young master has had some chance to become acquainted with his character, bad as it may be; but the young mistress brings her slaves a new, and sometimes an unknown master. Sometimes these are the sons of already broken down slaveholders. In other cases they are adventurers from the north who remove to the south, and who readily become the most cruel masters.

APPENDIX.

THESE TWO LETTERS ARE SIMPLY INTRODUCED TO SHOW WHAT THE STATE OF MY FEELINGS WAS WITH REFERENCE TO SLAVERY AT THE TIME THEY WERE WRITTEN. I HAD JUST HEARD SEVERAL FACTS WITH REGARD TO MY PARENTS, WHICH HAD AWAKENED MY MIND TO GREAT EXCITEMENT.

To my father, mother, brothers, and sisters.
The following was written in 1844:
DEARLY BELOVED IN BONDS,
About seventeen long years have now rolled away, since in the Providence of Almighty God, I left your embraces, and set out upon a daring adventure in search of freedom. Since that time, I have felt most severely the loss of the sun and moon and eleven stars from my social sky. Many, many a thick cloud of anguish has pressed my brow and sent deep down into my soul the bitter waters of sorrow in consequence. And you have doubtless had your troubles and anxious seasons also about your fugitive star.

I have learned that some of you have been sold, and again

taken back by Colonel ———. How many of you are living and together, I cannot tell. My great grief is, lest you should have suffered this or some additional punishment on account of my *Exodus.*

I indulge the hope that it will afford you some consolation to know that your son and brother is yet alive. That God has dealt wonderfully and kindly with me in all my way. He has made me a Christian, and a Christian Minister, and thus I have drawn my support and comfort from that blessed Saviour, who came *to preach good tidings unto the meek, to bind up the broken hearted, to proclaim liberty to the captives, and the opening of the prison to them that are bound. To proclaim the acceptable year of the Lord and the day of vengeance of our God; to comfort all that mourn. To appoint unto them that mourn in Zion, to give unto them beauty for ashes, the oil of joy for mourning, the garment of praise for the spirit of heaviness, that they might be called trees of righteousness, the planting of the Lord that he might be glorified.*

If the course I took in leaving a condition which had become intolerable to me, has been made the occasion of making that condition worse to you in any way, I do most heartily regret such a change for the worse on your part. As I have no means, however, of knowing if such be the fact, so I have no means of making atonement, but by sincere prayer to Almighty God on your behalf, and also by taking this method of offering to you these consolations of the gospel to which I have just referred, and which I have found to be pre-eminently my own stay and support. My dear father and mother; I have very often wished, while administering the Holy Ordinance of Baptism to some scores of children brought forward by doting parents, that I could see you with yours among the number. And you, my brothers and sisters, while teaching hundreds of children and youths in schools over which I have been placed, what unspeakable delight I should have had in having you among the number; you may all judge of my feeling for these past years, when while preaching from Sabbath to Sabbath to congregations, I have not been so fortunate as even to see father, mother, brother, sister, uncle, aunt, nephew, niece, or cousin in my congregations. While visiting the sick, going to the house of mourning, and burying the dead, I have been a constant mourner for you. My sorrow has been that I know you are not in possession of those hallowed means of grace. I am thankful to you for those mild and gentle traits of character which you took such care to enforce upon me in my youthful days. As an evidence that I prize both you and them, I may say that at the age of thirty-seven, I find them as valuable as any lessons

I have learned, nor am I ashamed to let it be known to the world, that I am the son of a bond man and a bond woman.

Let me urge upon you the fundamental truths of the Gospel of the Son of God. Let repentance towards God and faith in our Lord Jesus Christ have their perfect work in you, I beseech you. Do not be prejudiced against the gospel because it may be seemingly twisted into a support of slavery. The gospel rightly understood, taught, received, felt and practised, is anti-slavery as it is anti-sin. Just so far and so fast as the true spirit of the gospel obtains in the land, and especially in the lives of the oppressed, will the spirit of slavery sicken and become powerless like the serpent with his head pressed beneath the fresh leaves of the prickly ash of the forest.

There is not a solitary decree of the immaculate God that has been concerned in the ordination of slavery, nor does any possible development of his holy will sanctify it.

He has permitted us to be enslaved according to the invention of wicked men, instigated by the devil with intention to bring good out of the evil, but He does not, He cannot approve of it. He has no need to approve of it, even on account of the good which He will bring out of it, for He could have brought about that very good in some other way.

God is never straitened; He is never at a loss for means to work. Could He not have made this a great and wealthy nation without making its riches to consist in our blood, bones, and souls? And could He not also have given the gospel to us without making us slaves?

My friends, let us then, in our afflictions, embrace and hold fast the gospel. The gospel is the fulness of God. We have the glorious and total weight of God's moral character in our side of the scale.

The wonderful purple stream which flowed for the healing of the nations, has a branch for us. Nay, is Christ divided? "The grace of God that bringeth salvation hath appeared to (for) all men, teaching us that denying ungodliness and worldly lust, we should live soberly, righteously, and godly in this present world, looking for that blessed hope and glorious appearing of the great God and our Saviour Jesus Christ, who gave himself for US that he might redeem us from all iniquity, and purify unto himself a peculiar people, zealous of good works."—Titus ii. 11-14.

But you say you have not the privilege of hearing of this gospel of which I speak. I know it; and this is my great grief. But you shall have it; I will send it to you by my humble prayer; I can do it; I will beg our heavenly Father, and he will preach this gospel to you in his holy providence.

You, dear father and mother cannot have much longer to live in this troublesome and oppressive world; you cannot bear the yoke much longer. And as you approach another world, how desirable it is that you should have the prospect of a different destiny from what you have been called to endure in this world during a long life.

But it is the gospel that sets before you the hope of such a blessed rest as is spoken of in the word of God, Job iii. 17, 19. "There the wicked cease from troubling, and there the weary be at rest; there the prisoners rest together; they hear not the voice of the oppressors. The small and great are there; and the servant is free from his master."

Father, I know thy eyes are dim with age and weary with weeping, but look, dear father, yet a little while toward that haven. Look unto Jesus, "the author and finisher of thy faith," for the moment of thy happy deliverance is at hand.

Mother, dear mother, I know, I feel, mother, the pangs of thy bleeding heart, that thou hast endured, during so many years of vexation. Thy agonies are by a genuine son-like sympathy mine; I will, I must, I do share daily in those agonies of thine. But I sincerely hope that with me you bear your agonies to Christ who carries our sorrows.

O come then with me, my beloved family, of weary heart-broken and care-worn ones, to Jesus Christ, "casting all your care upon him, for he careth for you."—2 Peter v. 7.

With these words of earnest exhortation, joined with fervent prayer to God that He may smooth your rugged way, lighten your burden, and given a happy issue out of all your troubles, I must bid you adieu.

Your son and brother,

Jas. P.

Alias J. W. C. Pennington.

To Colonel F——— T———, of H———, Washington County, Md. 1844.

Dear Sir,

It is now, as you are aware, about seventeen years since I left your house and service, at the age of twenty. Up to that time, I was, according to your rule and claim, your slave. Till the age of seven

years, I was, of course, of little or no service to you. At that age, however, you hired me out, and for three years I earned my support;
at the age of ten years, you took me to your place again, and in a
short time after you put me to work at the blacksmith's trade, at
which, together with the carpentering trade, &c., I served you
peaceably until the day I left you, with exception of the short time
you had sold me to S——— H———, Esq., for seven hundred dollars. It is important for me to say to you, that I have no consciousness of having done you any wrong. I called you master when I was
with you from the mere force of circumstances; but I never
regarded you as my master. The nature which God gave me did not
allow me to believe that you had any more right to me than I had
to you, and that was just none at all. And from an early age, I had
intentions to free myself from your claim. I never consulted any one
about it; I had no advisers or instigators; I kept my own counsel
entirely concealed in my own bosom. I never meditated any evil to
your person or property, but I regarded you as my oppressor, and
I deemed it my duty to get out of your hands by peaceable means.

I was always obedient to your commands. I laboured for you
diligently at all times. I acted with fidelity in any matter which you
entrusted me. As you sometimes saw fit to entrust me with considerable money, to buy tools or materials, not a cent was ever coveted
or kept.

During the time I served you in the capacity of blacksmith, your
materials were used economically, your work was done expedi-
tiously, and in the very best style, a style second to no smith in your
neighbourhood. In short, sir, you well know that my habits from
early life were advantageous to you. Drinking, gambling, fighting,
&c., were not my habits. On Sabbaths, holidays, &c., I was frequently at your service, when not even your body-servant was at
home.

Times and times again, I have gone on Sunday afternoon to
H———, six miles, after your letters and papers, when it was as
much my privilege to be "*out of the way*," as it was C———.

But what treatment did you see fit to return me for all this? You,
in the most unfeeling manner, abused my father for no cause but
speaking a word to you, as a man would speak to his fellow-man, for
the sake simply of a better understanding.

You vexed my mother, and because she, as a tender mother
would do, showed solicitude for the virtue of her daughters, you
threatened her in an insulting brutal manner.

You abused my brother and sister without cause, and in like manner you did to myself; you surmised evil against me. You struck me with your walking-cane, called me insulting names, threatened me, swore at me, and became more and more wrathy in your conduct, and at the time I quitted your place, I had good reason to believe you were meditating serious evil against me.

Since I have been out of your hands, I have been signally favoured of God, whence I infer that in leaving you, I acted strictly in accordance with his holy will. I have a conscience void of offence towards God and towards all men, yourself not excepted. And I verily believe that I have performed a sacred duty to God and myself, and a kindness to you, in taking the blood of my soul peaceably off your soul. And now, dear sir, having spoken somewhat pointedly, I would, to convince you of my perfect good will towards you, in the most kind and respectful terms, remind you of your coming destiny. You are now over seventy years of age, pressing on to eternity with the weight of these seventy years upon you. Is not this enough without the blood of some half-score of souls?

You are aware that your right to property in man is now disputed by the civilized world. You are fully aware, also, that the question, whether the Bible sanctions slavery, has distinctly divided this nation in sentiment. On the side of Biblical Anti-slavery, we have many of the most learned, wise and holy men in the land. If the Bible affords no sanction to slavery, (and I claim that it cannot,) then it must be a sin of the deepest dye; and can you, sir, think to go to God in hope with a sin of such magnitude upon your soul?

But admitting that the question is yet doubtful, (which I do only for the sake of argument,) still, sir, you will have the critical hazard of this doubt pressing, in no very doubtful way, upon your declining years, as you descend the long and tedious hill of life.

Would it not seem to be exceedingly undesirable to close an eventful probation of seventy or eighty years, and leave your reputation among posterity suspended upon so doubtful an issue? But what, my dear sir, is a reputation among posterity, who are but worms, compared with a destiny in the world of spirits? And it is in light of that destiny that I would now have you look at this subject. You and I, and all that you claim as your slaves, are in a state of probation; our great business is to serve God under His righteous moral government. Master and slave are the subjects of that government, bound by its immutable requirements, and liable to its sanctions in the next world, though enjoying its forbearance in this. You will pardon me then for pressing this point in earnest good faith. You should, at this stage, review your life without political bias, or adherence to long cherished prejudices, and remember that you are soon to meet those whom you have held, and do hold in slavery, at the awful bar of the impartial Judge of all who doeth right. Then what will become of your own doubtful claims? What will be done with those doubts that agitated your mind years ago; will you answer for threatening, swearing, and using the cowhide among your slaves?

What will become of those long groans and unsatisfied complaints of your slaves, for vexing them with insulting words, placing them in the power of dogish and abusive overseers, or under your stripling, misguided, hot-headed son, to drive and whip at pleasure, and for selling parts or whole families to Georgia? They will all meet you at that bar. Uncle James True, Charles Cooper, Aunt Jenny, and the native Africans; Jeremiah, London, and Donmore, have already gone a-head, and only wait your arrival—Sir, I shall meet you there. The account between us for the first twenty years of my life, will have a definite character upon which one or the other will be able to make out a case.

Upon such a review as this, sir, you will, I am quite sure, see the need of seriousness. I assure you that the thought of meeting you in eternity, and before the dread tribunal of God, with a complaint in my mouth against you, is to me of most weighty and solemn character. And you will see that the circumstances from which this thought arises are of equal moment to yourself. Can the pride of leaving your children possessed of long slave states, of the policy of sustaining in the state the institution of slavery, justify you in overlooking a point of moment to your future happiness?

What excuse could you offer at the bar of God, favoured as you have been with the benefits of a refined education, and through a long life with the gospel of love, should you, when arraigned there, find that you have, all your life long, laboured under a great mistake in regard to slavery, and that in this mistake you had died, and only lifted up your eyes in the light of eternity to be corrected, when it was too late to be corrected in any other way.

I could wish to address you (being bred, born, and raised in your family) *as a father in Israel, or as an elder brother in Christ, but I cannot; mockery is a sin.* I can only say then, dear sir, farewell, till I meet you at the bar of God, where Jesus, who died for us, will judge between us. Now his blood can wash out our stain, break down the middle wall of partition, and reconcile us not only to God but to each other, then the word of his mouth, the sentence will set us at one. As for myself, I am quite ready to meet you face to face at the bar of God. I have done you no wrong; I have nothing to fear when we both fall into the hands of the just God.

I beseech you, dear sir, to look well and consider this matter soundly. In yonder world you can have no slaves—you can be no man's master—you can neither sell, buy, or whip, or drive. Are you then, by sustaining the relation of a slaveholder, forming a character to dwell with God in peace?

With kind regards,

I am, sir, yours respectfully,

J. W. C. Pennington.

LIBERTY'S CHAMPION.

BY A FRIEND OF THE AUTHOR'S.

On the wings of the wind he comes, he comes!
With the rolling billow's speed;
On his breast are the signs of peace and love,
And his soul is served with strength from above:
While his eyes flash fire,
He burns with desire
To achieve the noble deed.

To the shores of the free he goes, he goes!
And smiles as he passes on;
He hears the glad notes of Liberty's song,
And bids the brave sons of freedom be strong.
While his heart bounds high
To his crown in the sky,
He triumphs o'er conquests won.

To the homes of the slave he flies, he flies!
Where manacled mourners cry;
The bursting groan of the mind's o'erflow,
Transfixed on the dark and speaking brow:
With a murmuring sound,
Ascends from the ground,

To the God that reigns on high.

To his loved Father's throne he hastes, he hastes!
And pours forth his soul in grief:
Uprising he finds his strength renewed,
And his heart with fervent love is imbued;
While the heaving sigh,
And the deep-toned cry,
Appeal for instant relief.

To the hard oppressor he cries, he cries,
And points to the bleeding slave;
He tells of the rights of the human soul,
And his eyes with full indignation roll:
While his heart is moved,
And the truth is proved,
He seeks the captive to save.

Again to the foeman he speaks, he speaks,
But utters his cry in vain;
He breathes no curse, no vengeance seeks,—
For the broken hearts or the anguished shrieks,
For the mother's pains,
Or the father's gains,—
Upon the oppressor's name.

To nations of freemen once more he comes,
To raise Liberty's banner high;
He tells of the wrongs of the bonded slave,
And cries aloud, 'mid throngs of the brave,
"O freemen, arise!
Be faithful and wise,
And answer the mourner's cry."

In melting strains of love he calls, he calls,
To the great and good from afar;
Till sympathy wakes to the truthful tale,
And the prayer of the faith, which cannot fail,
Ascends to heaven,
And grace is given,
To nerve for the bloodless war.

The truth with a magic power prevails:
All hearts are moved to the strife;
In a holy phalanx, and with deathless aim,
They seek a peaceful triumph to gain
O'er the tyrant's sway,
In his onward way,
To raise the fallen to life.

At the mighty voice of the glorious free
The chain of the oppressor breaks;
The slave from his bondage springs forth to love,
And, standing erect, his eye fixed above,
He honours his race,
And in the world's face,
The language of liberty speaks.

The oppressor no longer owns a right,
Or property claims in the slave,
But the world, in the glory of freedom's light,
Beams out from the darkness of wide-spread night;
Throughout its length,
In greatness and strength,
The honour of the free and brave.

———

Printed for CHARLES GILPIN, 5, Bishopsgate Street Without.

NARRATIVE

OF

WILLIAM W. BROWN

A
FUGITIVE SLAVE.

WRITTEN BY HIMSELF.

——IS THERE NOT SOME CHOSEN CURSE,
SOME HIDDEN THUNDER IN THE STORES OF HEAVEN,
RED WITH UNCOMMON WRATH, TO BLAST THE MAN
WHO GAINS HIS FORTUNE FROM THE BLOOD OF SOULS?
COWPER.

BOSTON:
PUBLISHED AT THE ANTI-SLAVERY OFFICE,
NO. 25 CORNHILL.
1847.

Andrews & Prentiss, Printers.

TO WELLS BROWN, OF OHIO.

THIRTEEN years ago, I came to your door, a weary fugitive from chains and stripes. I was a stranger, and you took me in. I was hungry, and you fed me. Naked was I, and you clothed me. Even a name by which to be known among men, slavery had denied me. You bestowed upon me your own. Base indeed should I be, if I ever forget what I owe to you, or do anything to disgrace that honored name!

As a slight testimony of my gratitude to my earliest benefactor, I take the liberty to inscribe to you this little Narrative of the sufferings from which I was fleeing when you had compassion upon me. In the multitude that you have succored, it is very possible that you may not remember me; but until I forget God and myself, I can never forget you.

Your grateful friend,
WILLIAM WELLS BROWN.

LETTER
FROM
EDMUND QUINCY, ESQ.

DEDHAM, JULY 1, 1847.
TO WILLIAM W. BROWN.
MY DEAR FRIEND;—I heartily thank you for the privilege of reading the manuscript of your Narrative. I have read it with deep interest and strong emotion. I am much mistaken if it be not greatly successful and eminently useful. It presents a different phase of the infernal slave-system from that portrayed in the admirable story of Mr. Douglass, and gives us a glimpse of its hideous cruelties in other portions of its domain.

Your opportunities of observing the workings of this accursed system have been singularly great. Your experiences in the Field, in the House, and especially on the River in the service of the slave-trader, Walker, have been such as few individuals have had;—no one, certainly, who has been competent to describe them. What I have admired, and marvelled at, in your Narrative, is the simplicity and calmness with which you describe scenes and actions which might well "move the very stones to rise and mutiny" against the National Institution which makes them possible.

You will perceive that I have made very sparing use of your flattering permission to alter what you had written. To correct a few errors, which appeared to be merely clerical ones, committed in the hurry of composition, under unfavorable circumstances, and to suggest a few curtailments, is all that I have ventured to do. I should be a bold man, as well as a vain one, if I should attempt to improve your descriptions of what you have seen and suffered. Some of the scenes are not unworthy of De Foe himself.

I trust and believe that your Narrative will have a wide circulation. I am sure it deserves it. At least, a man must be differently constituted from me, who can rise from the perusal of your Narrative without feeling that he understands slavery better, and hates it worse, than he ever did before.

I am, very faithfully and respectfully,
Your friend,
EDMUND QUINCY.

PREFACE.

THE friends of freedom may well congratulate each other on the appearance of the following Narrative. It adds another volume to the rapidly increasing anti-slavery literature of the age. It has been remarked by a close observer of human nature, "Let me make the songs of a nation, and I care not who makes its laws;" and it may with equal truth be said, that, among a reading people like our own, their books will at least give character to their laws. It is an influence which goes forth noiselessly upon its mission, but fails not to find its way to many a warm heart, to kindle on the altar thereof the fires of freedom, which will one day break forth in a living flame to consume oppression.

This little book is a voice from the prison-house, unfolding the deeds of darkness which are there perpetrated. Our cause has received efficient aid from this source. The names of those who have come from thence, and battled manfully for the right, need not to be recorded here. The works of some of them are an enduring monument of praise, and their perpetual record shall be found in the grateful hearts of the redeemed bondman.

Few persons have had greater facilities for becoming acquainted with slavery, in all its horrible aspects, than WILLIAM W. BROWN. He has been behind the curtain. He has visited its secret chambers. Its iron has entered his own soul. The dearest ties of nature have been riven in his own person. A mother has been cruelly scourged before his own eyes. A father,—alas! slaves have no father. A brother has been made the subject of its tender mercies. A sister has been given up to the irresponsible control of the pale-faced oppressor. This nation looks on approvingly. The American Union sanctions the deed. The Constitution shields the criminals. American religion sanctifies the crime. But the tide is turning. Already, a mighty undercurrent is sweeping onward. The voice of warning, of remonstrance, of rebuke, of entreaty, has gone forth. Hand is linked in hand, and heart mingles with heart, in this great work of the slave's deliverance.

The convulsive throes of the monster, even now, give evidence of deep wounds.

The writer of this Narrative was hired by his master to a "*soul-driver*," and has witnessed all the horrors of the traffic, from the buying up of human cattle in the slave-breeding States, which produced a constant scene of separating the victims from all those whom they loved, to their final sale in the southern market, to be worked up in seven years, or given over to minister to the lust of southern *Christians*.

Many harrowing scenes are graphically portrayed; and yet with that simplicity and ingenuousness which carries with it a conviction of the truthfulness of the picture.

This book will do much to unmask those who have "clothed themselves in the livery of the court of heaven" to cover up the enormity of their deeds.

During the past three years, the author has devoted his entire energies to the anti-slavery cause. Laboring under all the disabilities and disadvantages growing out of his education in slavery—subjected, as he had been from his birth, to all the wrongs and deprivations incident to his condition—he yet went forth, impelled to the work by a love of liberty—stimulated by the remembrance of his own sufferings—urged on by the consideration that a mother, brothers, and sister, were still grinding in the prison-house of bondage, in common with three millions of our Father's children—sustained by an unfaltering faith in the omnipotence of truth and the final triumph of justice—to plead the cause of the slave, and by the eloquence of earnestness carried conviction to many minds, and enlisted the sympathy and secured the co-operation of many to the cause.

His labors have been chiefly confined to Western New York, where he has secured many warm friends, by his untiring zeal, persevering energy, continued fidelity, and universal kindness.

Reader, are you an Abolitionist? What have you done for the slave? What are you doing in his behalf? What do you purpose to do? There is a great work before us. Who will be an idler now? This is the great humanitary movement of the age, swallowing up, for the time being, all other questions, comparatively speaking. The course of human events, in obedience to the unchangeable laws of our being, is fast hastening the final crisis, and

"Have ye chosen, O my people, on whose party ye
shall stand,
Ere the Doom from its worn sandal shakes the dust
against our land?"

Are you a Christian? This is the carrying out of practical
Christianity; and there is no other. Christianity is *practical* in its very
nature and essence. It is a life, springing out of a soul imbued with
its spirit. Are you a friend of the missionary cause? This is the greatest missionary enterprize of the day. Three millions of *Christian*, law-
manufactured heathen are longing for the glad tidings of the
Gospel of freedom. Are you a friend of the Bible? Come, then, and
help us to restore to these millions, whose eyes have been bored out
by slavery, their sight, that they may see to read the Bible. Do you
love God whom you have not seen? Then manifest that love, by
restoring to your brother whom you have seen, his rightful inheri-
tance, of which he has been so long and so cruelly deprived.

It is not for a single generation alone, numbering three millions—sublime as would be that effort—that we are working. It is
for HUMANITY, the wide world over, not only now, but for all
coming time, and all future generations:—

"For he who settles Freedom's principles,
Writes the death-warrant of all tyranny."

It is a vast work—a glorious enterprize—worthy the unswerving
devotion of the entire life-time of the great and the good.

Slaveholding and slaveholders must be rendered disreputable
and odious. They must be stripped of their respectability and
Christian reputation. They must be treated as "MEN-STEALERS—
guilty of the highest kind of theft, and sinners of the first rank."
Their more guilty accomplices in the persons of *northern apologists,*
both in Church and State, must be placed in the same category.
Honest men must be made to look upon their crimes with the same
abhorrence and loathing, with which they regard the less guilty
robber and assassin, until

"The common damned shun their society,
And look upon themselves as fiends less foul."

When a just estimate is placed upon the crime of slaveholding, the work will have been accomplished, and the glorious day ushered in—

> "When man nor woman in all our wide domain,
> Shall buy, or sell, or hold, or be a slave."

J. C. HATHAWAY.
Farmington, N. Y., 1847.

NARRATIVE.

CHAPTER I.

I WAS born in Lexington, Ky. The man who stole me as soon as I was born, recorded the births of all the infants which he claimed to be born his property, in a book which he kept for that purpose. My mother's name was Elizabeth. She had seven children, viz: Solomon, Leander, Benjamin, Joseph, Millford, Elizabeth, and myself. No two of us were children of the same father. My father's name, as I learned from my mother, was George Higgins. He was a white man, a relative of my master, and connected with some of the first families in Kentucky.

My master owned about forty slaves, twenty-five of whom were field hands. He removed from Kentucky to Missouri, when I was quite young, and settled thirty or forty miles above St. Charles, on the Missouri, where, in addition to his practice as a physician, he carried on milling, merchandizing and farming. He had a large farm, the principal productions of which were tobacco and hemp. The slave cabins were situated on the back part of the farm, with the house of the overseer, whose name was Grove Cook, in their midst. He had the entire charge of the farm, and having no family, was allowed a woman to keep house for him, whose business it was to deal out the provisions for the hands.

A woman was also kept at the quarters to do the cooking for the field hands, who were summoned to their unrequited toil every morning at four o'clock, by the ringing of a bell, hung on a post near the house of the overseer. They were allowed half an hour to eat their breakfast, and get to the field. At half past four, a horn was blown by the overseer, which was the signal to commence work; and every one that was not on the spot at the time, had to receive ten lashes from the negro-whip, with which the overseer always went armed. The handle was about three feet long, with the butt-end filled with lead, and the lash six or seven feet in length, made of cowhide, with platted wire on the end of it. This whip was put in requisition very frequently and freely, and a small offence on the part of a slave furnished an occasion for its use. During that time that Mr. Cook was overseer, I was a house servant—a situation preferable to that of a field hand, as I was better fed, better clothed, and not obliged to rise at the ringing of the bell, but about half an hour after. I have often laid and heard the crack of the whip, and the screams of the slave. My mother was a field hand, and one morning was ten or fifteen minutes behind the others in getting into the field. As soon as she reached the spot where they were at work, the overseer commenced whipping her. She cried, "Oh! pray—Oh! pray—Oh! pray"—these are generally the words of slaves, when imploring mercy at the hands of their oppressors. I heard her voice, and knew it, and jumped out of my bunk, and went to the door. Though the field was some distance from the house, I could hear every crack of the whip, and every groan and cry of my poor mother. I remained at the door, not daring to venture any farther. The cold chills ran over me, and I wept aloud. After giving her ten lashes, the sound of the whip ceased, and I returned to my bed, and found no consolation but in my tears. It was not yet daylight.

CHAPTER II.

MY master being a political demagogue, soon found those who were ready to put him into office, for the favors he could render them; and a few years after his arrival in Missouri, he was elected to a seat in the Legislature. In his absence from home, everything was left in charge of Mr. Cook, the overseer, and he soon became more tyrannical and cruel. Among the slaves on the plantation, was one by the name of Randall. He was a man about six feet high, and well-proportioned, and known as a man of great strength and power. He was considered the most valuable and able-bodied slave on the plantation; but no matter how good or useful a slave may be, he seldom escapes the lash. But it was not so with Randall. He had been on the plantation since my earliest recollection, and I had never known of his being flogged. No thanks were due to the master or overseer for this. I have often heard him declare, that no white man should ever whip him—that he would die first.

Cook, from the time that he came upon the plantation, had frequently declared, that he could and would flog any nigger that was put into the field to work under him. My master had repeatedly told him not to attempt to whip Randall, but he was determined to try it. As soon as he was left sole dictator, he thought the time had come to put his threats into execution. He soon began to find fault with Randall, and threatened to whip him, if he did not do better. One day he gave him a very hard task,—more than he could possibly do; and at night, the task not being performed, he told Randall that he should remember him the next morning. On the following morning, after the hands had taken breakfast, Cook called out to Randall, and told him that he intended to whip him, and ordered him to cross his hands and be tied. Randall asked why he wished to whip him. He answered, because he had not finished his task the day before. Randall said that the task was too great, or he should have done it. Cook said it made no difference,—he should whip him. Randall stood silent for a moment, and then said, "Mr. Cook, I have always tried to please you since you have been on the plantation, and I find you are determined not to be satisfied with my work, let me do as well as I may. No man has laid hands on me, to whip me, for the last ten years, and I have long since come to the conclusion not to be whipped by any man living." Cook, finding by Randall's determined look and gestures, that he would resist, called three of the hands from their work, and commanded them to seize Randall, and tie him. The hands stood still;—they knew Randall— and they also knew him to be a powerful man, and were afraid to grapple with him. As soon as Cook had ordered the men to seize him, Randall turned to them, and said—"Boys, you all know me; you know that I can handle any three of you, and the man that lays hands on me shall die. This white man can't whip me himself, and therefore he has called you to help him." The overseer was unable to prevail upon them to seize and secure Randall, and finally ordered them all to go to their work together.

Nothing was said to Randall by the overseer, for more than a week. One morning, however, while the hands were at work in the field, he came into it, accompanied by three friends of his, Thompson, Woodbridge and Jones. They came up to where Randall was at work, and Cook ordered him to leave his work, and go with them to the barn. He refused to go; whereupon he was attacked by the overseer and his companions, when he turned upon them, and laid them, one after another, prostrate on the ground. Woodbridge drew out his pistol, and fired at him, and brought him to the ground by a pistol ball. The others rushed upon him with their clubs, and beat him over the head and face, until they succeeded in tying him. He was then taken to the barn, and tied to a beam. Cook gave him over one hundred lashes with a heavy cowhide, had him washed with salt and water, and left him tied during the day. The next day he was untied, and taken to a blacksmith's shop, and had a ball and chain attached to his leg. He was compelled to labor in the field, and perform the same amount of work that the other hands did. When his master returned home, he was much pleased to find that Randall had been subdued in his absence.

CHAPTER III.

SOON afterwards, my master removed to the city of St. Louis, and purchased a farm four miles from there, which he placed under the charge of an overseer by the name of Friend Haskell. He was a regular Yankee from New England. The Yankees are noted for making the most cruel overseers.

My mother was hired out in the city, and I was also hired out there to Major Freeland, who kept a public house. He was formerly from Virginia, and was a horse-racer, cock-fighter, gambler, and withal an inveterate drunkard. There were ten or twelve servants in the house, and when he was present, it was cut and slash—knock down and drag out. In his fits of anger, he would take up a chair, and throw it at a servant; and in his more rational moments, when he wished to chastise one, he would tie them up in the smoke-house, and whip them; after which, he would cause a fire to be made of tobacco stems, and smoke them. This he called "*Virginia play*."

I complained to my master of the treatment which I received from Major Freeland; but it made no difference. He cared nothing about it, so long as he received the money for my labor. After living with Major Freeland five or six months, I ran away, and went into the woods back of the city; and when night came on, I made my way to my master's farm, but was afraid to be seen, knowing that if Mr. Haskell, the overseer, should discover me, I should be again carried back to Major Freeland; so I kept in the woods. One day, while in the woods, I heard the barking and howling of dogs, and in a short time they came so near, that I knew them to be the blood-hounds of Major Benjamin O'Fallon. He kept five or six, to hunt runaway slaves with.

As soon as I was convinced that it was them, I knew there was no chance of escape. I took refuge in the top of a tree, and the hounds were soon at its base, and there remained until the hunters came up in a half or three quarters of an hour afterwards. There were two men with the dogs, who, as soon as they came up, ordered me to descend. I came down, was tied, and taken to St. Louis jail. Major Freeland soon made his appearance, and took me out, and ordered me to follow him, which I did. After we returned home, I was tied up in the smokehouse, and was very severely whipped. After the Major had flogged me to his satisfaction, he sent out his son Robert, a young man eighteen or twenty years of age, to see that I was well smoked. He made a fire of tobacco stems, which soon set me to coughing and sneezing. This, Robert told me, was the way his father used to do to his slaves in Virginia. After giving me what they conceived to be a decent smoking, I was untied and again set to work.

Robert Freeland was a "chip of the old block." Though quite young, it was not unfrequently that he came home in a state of intoxication. He is now, I believe, a popular commander of a steamboat on the Mississippi river. Major Freeland soon after failed in business, and I was put on board the steamboat Missouri, which plied between St. Louis and Galena. The commander of the boat was William B. Culver. I remained on her during the sailing season, which was the most pleasant time for me that I had ever experienced. At the close of navigation, I was hired to Mr. John Colburn, keeper of the Missouri Hotel. He was from one of the Free States; but a more inveterate hater of the negro, I do not believe ever walked on God's green earth. This hotel was at that time one of the largest in the city, and there were employed in it twenty or thirty servants, mostly slaves.

Mr. Colburn was very abusive, not only to the servants, but to his wife also, who was an excellent woman, and one from whom I never knew a servant to receive a harsh word; but never did I know a kind one to a servant from her husband. Among the slaves employed in the hotel, was one by the name of Aaron, who belonged to Mr. John F. Darby, a lawyer. Aaron was the knife-cleaner. One day, one of the knives was put on the table, not as clean as it might have been. Mr. Colburn, for this offence, tied Aaron up in the wood-house, and gave him over fifty lashes on the bare back with a cowhide, after which, he made me wash him down with rum. This seemed to put him into more agony than the whipping. After being untied, he went home to his master, and complained of the treatment which he had received. Mr. Darby would give no heed to anything he had to say, but sent him directly back. Colburn, learning that he had been to his master with complaints, tied him up again, and gave him a more severe whipping than before. The poor fellow's back was literally cut to pieces; so much so, that he was not able to work for ten or twelve days.

There was also, among the servants, a girl whose master resided in the country. Her name was Patsey. Mr. Colburn tied her up one evening, and whipped her until several of the boarders came out and begged him to desist. The reason for whipping her was this. She was engaged to be married to a man belonging to Major William Christy, who resided four or five miles north of the city. Mr. Colburn had forbid her to see John Christy. The reason of this was said to be the regard which he himself had for Patsey. She went to meeting that evening, and John returned home with her. Mr. Colburn had intended to flog John, if he came within the inclosure; but John knew too well the temper of his rival, and kept at a safe distance;—so he took vengeance on the poor girl. If all the slave-drivers had been called together, I do not think a more cruel man than John Colburn,—and he too a northern man,—could have been found among them.

While living at the Missouri Hotel, a circumstance occurred which caused me great unhappiness. My master sold my mother, and all her children, except myself. They were sold to different persons in the city of St. Louis.

CHAPTER IV.

I WAS soon after taken from Mr. Colburn's, and hired to Elijah P. Lovejoy, who was at that time publisher and editor of the "St. Louis Times." My work, while with him, was mainly in the printing office, waiting on the hands, working the press, &c. Mr. Lovejoy was a very good man, and decidedly the best master that I had ever had. I am chiefly indebted to him, and to my employment in the printing office, for what little learning I obtained while in slavery.

Though slavery is thought, by some, to be mild in Missouri, when compared with the cotton, sugar and rice growing States, yet no part of our slave-holding country, is more noted for the barbarity of its inhabitants, than St. Louis. It was here that Col. Harney, a United States officer, whipped a slave woman to death. It was here that Francis McIntosh, a free colored man from Pittsburgh, was taken from the steamboat Flora, and burned at the stake.

118

During a residence of eight years in this city, numerous cases of extreme cruelty came under my own observation;—to record them all, would occupy more space than could possibly be allowed in this little volume. I shall, therefore, give but a few more, in addition to what I have already related.

Capt. J. B. Brunt, who resided near my master, had a slave named John. He was his body servant, carriage driver, &c. On one occasion, while driving his master through the city,—the streets being very muddy, and the horses going at a rapid rate,—some mud spattered upon a gentleman by the name of Robert More. More was determined to be revenged. Some three or four months after this occurrence, he purchased John, for the express purpose, as he said, "to tame the d——d nigger." After the purchase, he took him to a blacksmith's shop, and had a ball and chain fastened to his leg, and then put him to driving a yoke of oxen, and kept him at hard labor, until the iron around his leg was so worn into the flesh, that it was thought mortification would ensue. In addition to this, John told me that his master whipped him regularly three times a week for the first two months:—and all this to "*tame him.*" A more noble looking man than he, was not to be found in all St. Louis, before he fell into the hands of More; and a more degraded and spirit-crushed looking being was never seen on a southern plantation, after he had been subjected to this "*taming*" process for three months. The last time that I saw him, he had nearly lost the entire use of his limbs.

While living with Mr. Lovejoy, I was often sent on errands to the office of the "Missouri Republican," published by Mr. Edward Charles. Once, while returning to the office with type, I was attacked by several large boys, sons of slave-holders, who pelted me with snow-balls. Having the heavy form of type in my hands, I could not make my escape by running; so I laid down the type and gave them battle. They gathered around me, pelting me with stones and sticks, until they overpowered me, and would have captured me, if I had not resorted to my heels. Upon my retreat, they took possession of the type; and what to do to regain it I could not devise. Knowing Mr. Lovejoy to be a very humane man, I went to the office, and laid the case before him. He told me to remain in the office. He took one of the apprentices with him, and went after the type, and soon returned with it; but on his return informed me that Samuel McKinney had told him that he would whip me, because I had hurt his boy. Soon after, McKinney was seen making his way to the office by one of the printers, who informed me of the fact, and I made my escape through the back door.

McKinney not being able to find me on his arrival, left the office in a great rage, swearing that he would whip me to death. A few days after, as I was walking along Main Street, he seized me by the collar, and struck me over the head five or six times with a large cane, which caused the blood to gush from my nose and ears in such a manner that my clothes were completely saturated with blood. After beating me to his satisfaction, he let me go, and I returned to the office so weak from the loss of blood, that Mr. Lovejoy sent me home to my master. It was five weeks before I was able to walk again. During this time, it was necessary to have some one to supply my place at the office, and I lost the situation.

After my recovery, I was hired to Capt. Otis Reynolds, as a waiter on board the steamboat Enterprize, owned by Messrs. John and Edward Walsh, commission merchants at St. Louis. This boat was then running on the upper Mississippi. My employment on board was to wait on gentlemen, and the captain being a good man, the situation was a pleasant one to me;—but in passing from place to place, and seeing new faces every day, and knowing that they could go where they pleased, I soon became unhappy, and several times thought of leaving the boat at some landing place, and trying to make my escape to Canada, which I had heard much about as a place where the slaves might live, be free, and be protected.

But whenever such thoughts would come into my mind, my resolution would soon be shaken by the remembrance that my dear mother was a slave in St. Louis, and I could not bear the idea of leaving her in that condition. She had often taken me upon her knee, and told me how she had carried me upon her back to the field when I was an infant—how often she had been whipped for leaving her work to nurse me—and how happy I would appear when she would take me into her arms. When these thoughts came over me, I would resolve never to leave the land of slavery without my mother. I thought that to leave her in slavery, after she had undergone and suffered so much for me, would be proving recreant to the duty which I owed to her. Besides this, I had three brothers and a sister there,—two of my brothers having died.

My mother, my brothers Joseph and Millford, and my sister Elizabeth, belonged to Mr. Isaac Mansfield, formerly from one of the Free States, (Massachusetts, I believe.) He was a tinner by trade, and carried on a large manufacturing establishment. Of all my relatives, mother was first, and sister next. One evening, while visiting them, I made some allusion to a proposed journey to Canada, and sister took her seat by my side, and taking my hand in hers, said, with tears in her eyes,—

"Brother, you are not going to leave mother and your dear sister here without a friend, are you?"

I looked into her face, as the tears coursed swiftly down her cheeks, and bursting into tears myself, said—

"No, I will never desert you and mother."

She clasped my hand in hers, and said—

"Brother, you have often declared that you would not end your days in slavery. I see no possible way in which you can escape with us; and now, brother, you are on a steamboat where there is some chance for you to escape to a land of liberty. I beseech you not to let us hinder you. If we cannot get our liberty, we do not wish to be the means of keeping you from a land of freedom."

I could restrain my feelings no longer, and an outburst of my own feelings, caused her to cease speaking upon that subject. In opposition to their wishes, I pledged myself not to leave them in the hand of the oppressor. I took leave of them, and returned to the boat, and laid down in my bunk; but "sleep departed from my eyes, and slumber from my eyelids."

A few weeks after, on our downward passage, the boat took on board, at Hannibal, a drove of slaves, bound for the New Orleans market. They numbered from fifty to sixty, consisting of men and women from eighteen to forty years of age. A drove of slaves on a southern steamboat, bound for the cotton or sugar regions, is an occurrence so common, that no one, not even the passengers, appear to notice it, though they clank their chains at every step. There was, however, one in this gang that attracted the attention of the passengers and crew. It was a beautiful girl, apparently about twenty years of age, perfectly white, with straight light hair and blue eyes. But it was not the whiteness of her skin that created such a sensation among those who gazed upon her—it was her almost unparalleled beauty. She had been on the boat but a short time, before the attention of all the passengers, including the ladies, had been called to her, and the common topic of conversation was about the beautiful slave-girl. She was not in chains. The man who claimed this article of human merchandize was a Mr. Walker,—a well known slave-trader, residing in St. Louis. There was a general anxiety among the passengers and crew to learn the history of the girl. Her master kept close by her side, and it would have been considered impudent for any of the passengers to have spoken to her, and the crew were not allowed to have any conversation with them. When we reached St. Louis, the slaves were removed to a boat bound for New Orleans, and the history of the beautiful slave-girl remained a mystery.

I remained on the boat during the season, and it was not an unfrequent occurrence to have on board gangs of slaves on their way to the cotton, sugar and rice plantations of the South.

Toward the latter part of the summer, Captain Reynolds left the boat, and I was sent home. I was then placed on the farm under Mr. Haskell, the overseer. As I had been some time out of the field, and not accustomed to work in the burning sun, it was very hard; but I was compelled to keep up with the best of the hands.

I found a great difference between the work in a steamboat cabin and that in a corn-field.

My master, who was then living in the city, soon after removed to the farm, when I was taken out of the field to work in the house as a waiter. Though his wife was very peevish, and hard to please, I much preferred to be under her control than the overseer's. They brought with them Mr. Sloane, a Presbyterian minister; Miss Martha Tulley, a niece of theirs from Kentucky; and their nephew William. The latter had been in the family a number of years, but the others were all new-comers.

Mr. Sloane was a young minister, who had been at the South but a short time, and it seemed as if his whole aim was to please the slaveholders, especially my master and mistress. He was intending to make a visit during the winter, and he not only tried to please them, but I think he succeeded admirably. When they wanted singing, he sung; when they wanted praying, he prayed; when they wanted a story told, he told a story. Instead of his teaching my master theology, my master taught theology to him. While I was with Captain Reynolds, my master "got religion," and new laws were made on the plantation. Formerly, we had the privilege of hunting, fishing, making splint brooms, baskets, &c. on Sunday; but this was all stopped. Every Sunday, we were all compelled to attend meeting. Master was so religious, that he induced some others to join him in hiring a preacher to preach to the slaves.

CHAPTER V.

MY master had family worship, night and morning. At night, the slaves were called in to attend; but in the mornings, they had to be at their work, and master did all the praying. My master and mistress were great lovers of mint julep, and every morning, a pitcher-full was made, of which they all partook freely, not excepting little master William. After drinking freely all round, they would have family worship, and then breakfast. I cannot say but I loved the julep as well as any of them, and during prayer was always careful to seat myself close to the table where it stood, so as to help myself when they were all busily engaged in their devotions. By the time prayer was over, I was about as happy as any of them. A sad accident happened one morning. In helping myself, and at the same time keeping an eye on my old mistress, I accidentally let the pitcher fall upon the floor, breaking it in pieces, and spilling the contents. This was a bad affair for me; for as soon as prayer was over, I was taken and severely chastised.

My master's family consisted of himself, his wife, and their nephew, William Moore. He was taken into the family, when only a few weeks of age. His name being that of my own, mine was changed, for the purpose of giving precedence to his, though I was his senior by ten or twelve years. The plantation being four miles from the city, I had to drive the family to church. I always dreaded the approach of the Sabbath; for, during service, I was obliged to stand by the horses in the hot broiling sun, or in the rain, just as it happened.

One Sabbath, as we were driving past the house of D. D. Page, a gentleman who owned a large baking establishment, as I was sitting upon the box of the carriage, which was very much elevated, I saw Mr. Page pursuing a slave around the yard, with a long whip, cutting him at every jump. The man soon escaped from the yard, and was followed by Mr. Page. They came running past us, and the slave perceiving that he would be overtaken, stopped suddenly, and Page stumbled over him, and falling on the stone pavement, fractured one of his legs, which crippled him for life. The same gentleman, but a short time previous, tied up a woman of his, by the name of Delphia, and whipped her nearly to death; yet he was a deacon in the Baptist church, in good and regular standing. Poor Delphia! I was well acquainted with her, and called to see her while upon her sick bed; and I shall never forget her appearance. She was a member of the same church with her master.

Soon after this, I was hired out to Mr. Walker; the same man whom I have mentioned as having carried a gang of slaves down the river, on the steamboat Enterprize. Seeing me in the capacity of steward on the boat, and thinking that I would make a good hand to take care of slaves, he determined to have me for that purpose; and finding that my master would not sell me, he hired me for the term of one year.

When I learned the fact of my having been hired to a negro speculator, or a "soul-driver" as they are generally called among slaves, no one can tell my emotions. Mr. Walker had offered a high price for me, as I afterwards learned, but I suppose my master was restrained from selling me by the fact that I was a near relative of his. On entering the service of Mr. Walker, I found that my opportunity of getting to a land of liberty was gone, at least for the time being. He had a gang of slaves in readiness to start for New Orleans, and in a few days we were on our journey. I am at a loss for language to express my feelings on that occasion. Although my master had told me that he had not sold me, and Mr. Walker had told me that he had not purchased me, I did not believe them; and not until I had been to New Orleans, and was on my return, did I believe that I was not sold.

There was on the boat a large room on the lower deck, in which the slaves were kept, men and women, promiscuously—all chained two and two, and a strict watch kept that they did not get loose; for cases have occurred in which slaves have got off their chains, and made their escape at landing-places, while the boats were taking in wood;—and with all our care, we lost one woman who had been taken from her husband and children, and having no desire to live without them, in the agony of her soul jumped overboard, and drowned herself. She was not chained.

It was almost impossible to keep that part of the boat clean.

On landing at Natchez, the slaves were all carried to the slave-pen, and there kept one week, during which time, several of them were sold. Mr. Walker fed his slaves well. We took on board, at St. Louis, several hundred pounds of bacon (smoked meat) and corn-meal, and his slaves were better fed than slaves generally were in Natchez, so far as my observation extended.

At the end of a week, we left for New Orleans, the place of our final destination, which we reached in two days. Here the slaves were placed in a negro-pen, where those who wished to purchase could call and examine them. The negro-pen is a small yard, surrounded by buildings, from fifteen to twenty feet wide, with the exception of a large gate with iron bars. The slaves are kept in the buildings during the night, and turned out into the yard during the day. After the best of the stock was sold at private sale at the pen, the balance were taken to the Exchange Coffee House Auction Rooms, kept by Isaac L. McCoy, and sold at public auction. After the sale of this lot of slaves, we left New Orleans for St. Louis.

CHAPTER VI.

ON our arrival at St. Louis, I went to Dr. Young, and told him that I did not wish to live with Mr. Walker any longer. I was heart-sick at seeing my fellow-creatures bought and sold. But the Dr. had hired me for the year, and stay I must. Mr. Walker again commenced purchasing another gang of slaves. He bought a man of Colonel John O'Fallon, who resided in the suburbs of the city. This man had a wife and three children. As soon as the purchase was made, he was put in jail for safe keeping, until we should be ready to start for New Orleans. His wife visited him while there, several times, and several times when she went for that purpose was refused admittance.

In the course of eight or nine weeks Mr. Walker had his cargo of human flesh made up. There was in this lot a number of old men and women, some of them with gray locks. We left St. Louis in the steamboat Carlton, Captain Swan, bound for New Orleans. On our way down, and before we reached Rodney, the place where we made our first stop, I had to prepare the old slaves for market. I was ordered to have the old men's whiskers shaved off, and the grey hairs plucked out, where they were not too numerous, in which case he had a preparation of blacking to color it, and with a blacking brush we would put it on. This was new business to me, and was performed in a room where the passengers could not see us. These slaves were also taught how old they were by Mr. Walker, and after going through the blacking process, they looked ten or fifteen years younger; and I am sure that some of those who purchased slaves of Mr. Walker, were dreadfully cheated, especially in the ages of the slaves which they bought.

We landed at Rodney, and the slaves were driven to the pen in the back part of the village. Several were sold at this place, during our stay of four or five days, when we proceeded to Natchez. There we landed at night, and the gang were put in the warehouse until morning, when they were driven to the pen. As soon as the slaves

125

are put in these pens, swarms of planters may be seen in and about them. They knew when Walker was expected, as he always had the time advertised beforehand when he would be in Rodney, Natchez, and New Orleans. These were the principal places where he offered his slaves for sale.

When at Natchez the second time, I saw a slave very cruelly whipped. He belonged to a Mr. Broadwell, a merchant who kept a store on the wharf. The slave's name was Lewis. I had known him several years, as he was formerly from St. Louis. We were expecting a steamboat down the river, in which we were to take passage for New Orleans. Mr. Walker sent me to the landing to watch for the boat, ordering me to inform him on its arrival. While there, I went into the store to see Lewis. I saw a slave in the store, and asked him where Lewis was. Said he, "They have got Lewis hanging between the heavens and the earth." I asked him what he meant by that. He told me to go into the warehouse and see. I went in, and found Lewis there. He was tied up to a beam, with his toes just touching the floor. As there was no one in the warehouse but himself, I inquired the reason of his being in that situation. He said Mr. Broadwell had sold his wife to a planter six miles from the city, and that he had been to visit her,—that he went in the night, expecting to return before daylight, and went without his master's permission. The patrol had taken him up before he reached his wife. He was put in jail, and his master had to pay for his catching and keeping, and that was what he was tied up for.

Just as he finished his story, Mr. Broadwell came in, and inquired what I was doing there. I knew not what to say, and while I was thinking what reply to make, he struck me over the head with the cowhide, the end of which struck me over my right eye, sinking deep into the flesh, leaving a scar which I carry to this day. Before I visited Lewis, he had received fifty lashes. Mr. Broadwell gave him fifty lashes more after I came out, as I was afterwards informed by Lewis himself.

The next day we proceeded to New Orleans, and put the gang in the same negro-pen which we occupied before. In a short time, the planters came flocking to the pen to purchase slaves. Before the slaves were exhibited for sale, they were dressed and driven out into the yard. Some were set to dancing, some to jumping, some to singing, and some to playing cards. This was done to make them appear cheerful and happy. My business was to see that they were placed in those situations before the arrival of the purchasers, and

I have often set them to dancing when their cheeks were wet with tears. As slaves were in good demand at that time, they were all soon disposed of, and we again set out for St. Louis.

On our arrival, Mr. Walker purchased a farm five or six miles from the city. He had no family, but made a housekeeper of one of his female slaves. Poor Cynthia! I knew her well. She was a quadroon, and one of the most beautiful women I ever saw. She was a native of St. Louis, and bore an irreproachable character for virtue and propriety of conduct. Mr. Walker bought her for the New Orleans market, and took her down with him on one of the trips that I made with him. Never shall I forget the circumstances of that voyage! On the first night that we were on board the steamboat, he directed me to put her into a stateroom he had provided for her, apart from the other slaves. I had seen too much of the workings of slavery, not to know what this meant. I accordingly watched him into the stateroom, and listened to hear what passed between them. I heard him make his base offers, and her reject them. He told her that if she would accept his vile proposals, he would take her back with him to St. Louis, and establish her as his housekeeper at his farm. But if she persisted in rejecting them, he would sell her as a field hand on the worst plantation on the river. Neither threats nor bribes prevailed, however, and he retired, disappointed of his prey.

The next morning, poor Cynthia told me what had past, and bewailed her sad fate with floods of tears. I comforted and encouraged her all I could; but I foresaw but too well what the result must be. Without entering into any farther particulars, suffice it to say that Walker performed his part of the contract, at that time. He took her back to St. Louis, established her as his mistress and housekeeper at his farm, and before I left, he had two children by her. But, mark the end! Since I have been at the North, I have been credibly informed that Walker has been married, and, as a previous measure, sold poor Cynthia and her children (she having had two more since I came away) into hopeless bondage!

He soon commenced purchasing to make up the third gang. We took steamboat, and went to Jefferson City, a town on the Missouri river. Here we landed, and took stage for the interior of the State. He bought a number of slaves as he passed the different farms and villages. After getting twenty-two or twenty-three men and women, we arrived at St. Charles, a village on the banks of the Missouri. Here he purchased a woman who had a child in her arms, appearing to be four or five weeks old.

We had been travelling by land for some days, and were in ·hopes to have found a boat at this place for St. Louis, but were disappointed. As no boat was expected for some days, we started for St. Louis by land. Mr. Walker had purchased two horses. He rode one, and I the other. The slaves were chained together, and we took up our line of march, Mr. Walker taking the lead, and I bringing up the rear. Though the distance was not more than twenty miles, we did not reach it the first day. The road was worse than any that I have ever travelled.

Soon after we left St. Charles, the young child grew very cross, and kept up a noise during the greater part of the day. Mr. Walker complained of its crying several times, and told the mother to stop the child's d——d noise, or he would. The woman tried to keep the child from crying, but could not. We put up at night with an acquaintance of Mr. Walker, and in the morning, just as we were about to start, the child again commenced crying. Walker stepped up to her, and told her to give the child to him. The mother tremblingly obeyed. He took the child by one arm, as you would a cat by the leg, walked into the house, and said to the lady,

"Madam, I will make you a present of this little nigger; it keeps such a noise that I can't bear it."

"Thank you, sir," said the lady.

The mother, as soon as she saw that her child was to be left, ran up to Mr. Walker, and falling upon her knees begged him to let her have her child; she clung around his legs, and cried, "Oh, my child! my child! master, do let me have my child! oh, do, do, do. I will stop its crying, if you will only let me have it again." When I saw this woman crying for her child so piteously, a shudder,—a feeling akin to horror, shot through my frame. I have often since in imagination heard her crying for her child:—

"O, master let me stay to catch
My baby's sobbing breath,
His little glassy eye to watch,
And smooth his limbs in death,

And cover him with grass and leaf,
Beneath the large oak tree:
It is not sullenness, but grief,—
O, master, pity me!

The morn was chill—I spoke no word,
But feared my babe might die,
And heard all day, or thought I heard,
My little baby cry.

At noon, oh, how I ran and took
My baby to my breast!
I lingered—and the long lash broke
My sleeping infant's rest.

I worked till night—till darkest night,
In torture and disgrace;
Went home and watched till morning light,
To see my baby's face.

Then give me but one little hour—
O! do not lash me so!
One little hour—one little hour—
And gratefully I'll go."

Mr. Walker commanded her to return into the ranks with the other slaves. Women who had children were not chained, but those that had none were. As soon as her child was disposed of, she was chained in the gang.

The following song I have often heard the slaves sing, when about to be carried to the far south. It is said to have been composed by a slave.

"See these poor souls from Africa
Transported to America;
We are stolen, and sold to Georgia,
Will you go along with me?
We are stolen, and sold to Georgia,
Come sound the jubilee!

See wives and husbands sold apart,
Their children's screams will break my heart;—
There's a better day a coming,
Will you go along with me?
There 's a better day a coming,
Go sound the jubilee!

O, gracious Lord! when shall it be,
That we poor souls shall all be free;
Lord, break them slavery powers—
Will you go along with me?
Lord break them slavery powers,
Go sound the jubilee!

Dear Lord, dear Lord, when slavery'll cease,
Then we poor souls will have our peace;—
There 's a better day a coming,
Will you go along with me?
There 's a better day a coming,
Go sound the jubilee!"

We finally arrived at Mr. Walker's farm. He had a house built during our absence to put slaves in. It was a kind of domestic jail. The slaves were put in the jail at night, and worked on the farm during the day. They were kept here until the gang was completed, when we again started for New Orleans, on board the steamboat North America, Capt. Alexander Scott. We had a large number of slaves in this gang. One, by the name of Joe, Mr. Walker was training up to take my place, as my time was nearly out, and glad was I. We made our first stop at Vicksburg, where we remained one week and sold several slaves.

Mr. Walker, though not a good master, had not flogged a slave since I had been with him, though he had threatened me. The slaves were kept in the pen, and he always put up at the best hotel, and kept his wines in his room, for the accommodation of those who called to negotiate with him for the purchase of slaves. One day while we were at Vicksburg, several gentlemen came to see him for this purpose, and as usual the wine was called for. I took the tray and started around with it, and having accidentally filled some of the glasses too full, the gentlemen spilled the wine on their clothes as they went to drink. Mr. Walker apologized to them for my carelessness, but looked at me as though he would see me again on this subject.

After the gentlemen had left the room, he asked me what I meant by my carelessness and said that he would attend to me. The next morning, he gave me a note to carry to the jailer, and a dollar in money to give to him. I suspected that all was not right, so I went down near the landing where I met with a sailor, and walking up to him, asked him if he would be so kind as to read the note for me. He read it over, and then looked at me. I asked him to tell me what was in it. Said he,

"They are going to give you hell."

"Why?" said I.

He said, "This is a note to have you whipped, and says that you have a dollar to pay for it."

He handed me back the note, and off I started. I knew not what to do, but was determined not to be whipped. I went up to the jail—took a look at it, and walked off again. As Mr. Walker was acquainted with the jailer, I feared that I should be found out if I did not go, and be treated in consequence of it still worse.

While I was meditating on the subject, I saw a colored man about my size walk up, and the thought struck me in a moment to send him with my note. I walked up to him, and asked him who he belonged to. He said he was a free man, and had been in the city but a short time. I told him I had a note to go into the jail, and get a trunk to carry to one of the steamboats; but was so busily engaged that I could not do it, although I had a dollar to pay for it. He asked me if I would not give him the job. I handed him the note and the dollar, and off he started for the jail.

I watched to see that he went in, and as soon as I saw the door close behind him, I walked around the corner, and took my station, intending to see how my friend looked when he came out. I had been there but a short time, when a colored man came around the corner, and said to another colored man with whom he was acquainted—

"They are giving a nigger scissors in the jail."

"What for?" said the other. The man continued,

"A nigger came into the jail, and asked for the jailer. The jailer came out, and he handed him a note, and said he wanted to get a trunk. The jailer told him to go with him, and he would give him the trunk. So he took him into the room, and told the nigger to give up the dollar. He said a man had given him the dollar to pay for getting the trunk. But that lie would not answer. So they made him strip himself, and then they tied him down, and are now whipping him."

I stood by all the while listening to their talk, and soon found out that the person alluded to was my customer. I went into the street opposite the jail, and concealed myself in such a manner that I could not be seen by any one coming out. I had been there but a short time, when the young man made his appearance, and looked around for me. I, unobserved, came forth from my hiding-place, behind a pile of brick, and he pretty soon saw me and came up to me complaining bitterly, saying that I had played a trick upon him. I denied any knowledge of what the note contained, and asked him what they had done to him. He told me in substance what I heard the man tell who had come out of the jail.

"Yes," said he, "they whipped me and took my dollar, and gave me this note."

He showed me the note which the jailer had given him, telling him to give it to his master. I told him I would give him fifty cents for it,—that being all the money I had. He gave it to me, and took his money. He had received twenty lashes on his bare back, with the negro-whip.

I took the note and started for the hotel where I had left Mr. Walker. Upon reaching the hotel, I handed it to a stranger whom I had not seen before, and requested him to read it to me. As near as I can recollect, it was as follows:—

> "DEAR SIR:—By your direction, I have given your
> boy twenty lashes. He is a very saucy boy, and tried
> to make me believe that he did not belong to you,
> and I put it on to him well for lying to me.
> I remain,
> Your obedient servant."

It is true that in most of the slave-holding cities, when a gentleman wishes his servants whipped, he can send him to the jail and have it done. Before I went in where Mr. Walker was, I wet my cheeks a little, as though I had been crying. He looked at me, and inquired what was the matter. I told him that I had never had such a whipping in my life, and handed him the note. He looked at it and laughed;—"and so you told him that you did not belong to me." "Yes, sir," said I. "I did not know that there was any harm in that." He told me I must behave myself, if I did not want to be whipped again.

This incident shows how it is that slavery makes its victims lying and mean; for which vices it afterwards reproaches them, and uses them as arguments to prove that they deserve no better fate. I have often, since my escape, deeply regretted the deception I practised upon this poor fellow; and I heartily desire that it may be, at some time or other, in my power to make him amends for his vicarious sufferings in my behalf.

CHAPTER VII.

IN a few days we reached New Orleans, and arriving there in the night, remained on board until morning. While at New Orleans this time, I saw a slave killed; an account of which has been published by Theodore D. Weld, in his book entitled, "Slavery as it is." The circumstances were as follows. In the evening, between seven and eight o'clock, a slave came running down the levee, followed by several men and boys. The whites were crying out, "Stop that nigger; stop that nigger;" while the poor panting slave, in almost breathless accents, was repeating, "I did not steal the meat—I did not steal the meat." The poor man at last took refuge in the river. The whites who were in pursuit of him, run on board of one of the boats to see if they could discover him. They finally espied him under the bow of the steamboat Trenton. They got a pike-pole, and tried to drive him from his hiding place. When they would strike at him, he would dive under the water. The water was so cold, that it soon became evident that he must come out or be drowned.

While they were trying to drive him from under the bow of the boat or drown him, he would in broken and imploring accents say, "I did not steal the meat; I did not steal the meat. My master lives up the river. I want to see my master. I did not steal the meat. Do let me go home to master." After punching him, and striking him over the head for some time, he at last sunk in the water, to rise no more alive.

On the end of the pike-pole with which they were striking him was a hook which caught in his clothing, and they hauled him up on the bow of the boat. Some said he was dead, others said he was "*playing possum*," while others kicked him to make him get up, but it was of no use—he was dead.

As soon as they became satisfied of this, they commenced leaving, one after another. One of the hands on the boat informed the captain that they had killed the man, and that the dead body was lying on the deck. The captain came on deck, and said to those who were remaining, "You have killed this nigger; now take him off of my boat." The captain's name was Hart. The dead body was dragged on shore and left there. I went on board of the boat where our gang of slaves were, and during the whole night my mind was occupied with what I had seen. Early in the morning, I went on shore to see if the dead body remained there. I found it in the same position that it was left the night before. I watched to see what they would do with it. It was left there until between eight and nine o'clock, when a cart, which takes up the trash out of the streets, came along, and the body was thrown in, and in a few minutes more was covered over with dirt which they were removing from the streets. During the whole time, I did not see more than six or seven persons around it, who, from their manner, evidently regarded it as no uncommon occurrence.

During our stay in the city, I met with a young white man with whom I was well acquainted in St. Louis. He had been sold into slavery, under the following circumstances. His father was a drunkard, and very poor, with a family of five or six children. The father died, and left the mother to take care of and provide for the children as best she might. The eldest was a boy, named Burrill, about thirteen years of age, who did chores in a store kept by Mr. Riley, to assist his mother in procuring a living for the family. After working with him two years, Mr. Riley took him to New Orleans to wait on him while in that city on a visit, and when he returned to St. Louis, he told the mother of the boy that he had died with the yellow fever. Nothing more was heard from him, no one supposing him to be alive. I was much astonished when Burrill told me his story. Though I sympathized with him, I could not assist him. We were both slaves. He was poor, uneducated, and without friends; and if living, is, I presume, still held as a slave.

After selling out this cargo of human flesh, we returned to St. Louis, and my time was up with Mr. Walker. I had served him one year, and it was the longest year I ever lived.

CHAPTER VIII.

I WAS sent home, and was glad enough to leave the service of one who was tearing the husband from the wife, the child from the mother, and the sister from the brother,—but a trial more severe and heart-rending than any which I had yet met with awaited me. My dear sister had been sold to a man who was going to Natchez, and was lying in jail awaiting the hour of his departure. She had expressed her determination to die, rather than go to the far south, and she was put in jail for safe keeping. I went to the jail the same day that I arrived, but as the jailor was not in, I could not see her.

I went home to my master, in the country, and the first day after my return, he came where I was at work, and spoke to me very politely. I knew from his appearance that something was the matter. After talking about my several journeys to New Orleans with Mr.

Walker, he told me that he was hard pressed for money, and as he had sold my mother and all her children except me, he thought it would be better to sell me than any other one, and that as I had been used to living in the city, he thought it probable that I would prefer it to a country life. I raised up my head, and looked him full in the face. When my eyes caught his, he immediately looked to the ground. After a short pause, I said,

"Master, mother has often told me that you are a near relative of mine, and I have often heard you admit the fact; and after you have hired me out, and received, as I once heard you say, nine hundred dollars for my services,—after receiving this large sum, will you sell me to be carried to New Orleans or some other place?"

"No," said he, "I do not intend to sell you to a negro trader. If I had wished to have done that, I might have sold you to Mr. Walker for a large sum, but I would not sell you to a negro trader. You may go to the city, and find you a good master."

"But," said I, "I cannot find a good master in the whole city of St. Louis."

"Why?" said he.

"Because there are not good masters in the State."

"Do you not call me a good master?"

"If you were, you would not sell me."

"Now I will give you one week to find a master in, and surely you can do it in that time."

The price set by my evangelical master upon my soul and body was the trifling sum of five hundred dollars. I tried to enter into some arrangement by which I might purchase my freedom; but he would enter into no such arrangement.

I set out for the city with the understanding that I was to return in a week with some one to become my new master. Soon after reaching the city, I went to the jail, to learn if I could once more see my sister; but could not gain admission. I then went to mother, and learned from her that the owner of my sister intended to start for Natchez in a few days.

I went to the jail again the next day, and Mr. Simonds, the keeper, allowed me to see my sister for the last time. I cannot give a just description of the scene at that parting interview. Never, never can be erased from my heart the occurrences of that day! When I entered the room where she was, she was seated in one corner, alone. There were four other women in the same room, belonging to the same man. He had purchased them, he said, for his own use. She was seated with her face towards the door where I entered, yet she did not look up until I walked up to her. As soon as she observed me, she sprung up, threw her arms around my neck, leaned her head upon by breast, and, without uttering a word, burst into tears. As soon as she recovered herself sufficiently to speak, she advised me to take mother, and try to get out of slavery. She said there was no hope for herself,—that she must live and die a slave. After giving her some advice, and taking from my finger a ring and placing it upon hers, I bade her farewell forever, and returned to my mother, and then and there made up my mind to leave for Canada as soon as possible.

I had been in the city nearly two days, and as I was to be absent only a week, I thought best to get on my journey as soon as possible. In conversing with mother, I found her unwilling to make the attempt to reach a land of liberty, but she counselled me to get my liberty if I could. She said, as all her children were in slavery, she did not wish to leave them. I could not bear the idea of leaving her among those pirates, when there was a prospect of being able to get away from them. After much persuasion, I succeeded in inducing her to make the attempt to get away.

The time fixed for our departure was the next night. I had with me a little money that I had received, from time to time, from gentlemen for whom I had done errands. I took my scanty means and purchased some dried beef, crackers and cheese, which I carried to mother, who had provided herself with a bag to carry it in. I occasionally thought of my old master, and of my mission to the city to find a new one. I waited with the most intense anxiety for the appointed time to leave the land of slavery, in search of a land of liberty.

The time at length arrived, and we left the city just as the clock struck nine. We proceeded to the upper part of the city, where I had been two or three times during the day, and selected a skiff to carry us across the river. The boat was not mine, nor did I know to whom it did belong; neither did I care. The boat was fastened with a small pole, which, with the aid of a rail, I soon loosened from its moorings. After hunting round and finding a board to use as an oar, I turned to the city, and bidding it a long farewell, pushed off my boat. The current running very swift, we had not reached the middle of the stream before we were directly opposite the city.

We were soon upon the Illinois shore, and, leaping from the boat, turned it adrift, and the last I saw of it, it was going down the river at good speed. We took the main road to Alton, and passed through just at daylight, when we made for the woods, where we remained during the day. Our reason for going into the woods was, that we expected that Mr. Mansfield (the man who owned my mother) would start in pursuit of her as soon as he discovered that she was missing. He also knew that I had been in the city looking for a new master, and we thought probably he would go out to my master's to see if he could find my mother, and in so doing, Dr. Young might be led to suspect that I had gone to Canada to find a purchaser.

We remained in the woods during the day, and as soon as darkness overshadowed the earth, we started again on our gloomy way, having no guide but the NORTH STAR. We continued to travel by night, and secrete ourselves in woods by day; and every night, before emerging from our hiding-place, we would anxiously look for our friend and leader,—the NORTH STAR.

CHAPTER IX.

AS we travelled towards a land of liberty, my heart would at times leap for joy. At other times, being, as I was, almost constantly on my feet, I felt as though I could travel no further. But when I thought of slavery with its Democratic whips—its Republican chains—its evangelical blood-hounds, and its religious slave-holders—when I thought of all this paraphernalia of American Democracy and Religion behind me, and the prospect of liberty before me, I was encouraged to press forward, my heart was strengthened, and I forgot that I was tired or hungry.

On the eighth day of our journey, we had a very heavy rain, and in a few hours after it commenced, we had not a dry thread upon our bodies. This made our journey still more unpleasant. On the tenth day, we found ourselves entirely destitute of provisions, and how to obtain any we could not tell. We finally resolved to stop at some farmhouse, and try to get something to eat. We had no sooner determined to do this, than we went to a house, and asked them for some food. We were treated with great kindness, and they not only gave us something to eat, but gave us provisions to carry with us. They advised us to travel by day, and lye by at night. Finding ourselves about one hundred and fifty miles from St. Louis, we concluded that it would be safe to travel by daylight, and did not leave the house until the next morning. We travelled on that day through a thickly settled country, and through one small village. Though we were fleeing from a land of oppression, our hearts were still there. My dear sister and two beloved brothers were behind us, and the idea of giving them up, and leaving them forever, made us feel sad. But with all this depression of heart, the thought that I should one day be free, and call my body my own, buoyed me up, and made my heart leap for joy. I had just been telling mother how I should try to get employment as soon as we reached Canada, and how I intended to purchase us a little farm, and how I would earn money enough to buy sister and brothers, and how happy we would be in our own FREE HOME,—when three men came up on horseback, and ordered us to stop.

I turned to the one who appeared to be the principal man, and asked him what he wanted. He said he had a warrant to take us up. The three immediately dismounted, and one took from his pocket a handbill, advertising us as runaways, and offering a reward of two hundred dollars for our apprehension, and delivery in the city of St. Louis. The advertisement had been put out by Isaac Mansfield and John Young.

While they were reading the advertisement, mother looked me in the face, and burst into tears. A cold chill ran over me, and such a sensation I never experienced before, and I hope never to again. They took out a rope and tied me, and we were taken back about six miles, to the house of the individual who appeared to be the leader. We reached there about seven o'clock in the evening, had supper, and were separated for the night. Two men remained in the room during the night. Before the family retired to rest, they were all called together to attend prayers. The man who but a few hours before had bound my hands together with a strong cord, read a chapter from the Bible, and then offered up prayer, just as though God sanctioned the act he had just committed upon a poor panting, fugitive slave.

The next morning, a blacksmith came in, and put a pair of handcuffs on me, and we started on our journey back to the land of whips, chains and Bibles. Mother was not tied, but was closely watched at night. We were carried back in a wagon, and after four days travel, we came in sight of St. Louis. I cannot describe my feelings upon approaching the city.

As we were crossing the ferry, Mr. Wiggins, the owner of the ferry, came up to me, and inquired what I had been doing that I was in chains. He had not heard that I had run away. In a few minutes, we were on the Missouri side, and were taken directly to the jail. On the way thither, I saw several of my friends, who gave me a nod of recognition as I passed them. After reaching the jail, we were locked up in different apartments.

CHAPTER X.

I HAD been in jail but a short time when I heard that my master was sick, and nothing brought more joy to my heart than that intelligence. I prayed fervently for him—not for his recovery, but for his death. I knew he would be exasperated at having to pay for my apprehension, and knowing his cruelty, I feared him. While in jail, I learned that my sister Elizabeth, who was in prison when we left the city, had been carried off four days before our arrival.

I had been in jail but a few hours when three negro-traders, learning that I was secured thus for running away, came to my prison-house and looked at me, expecting that I would be offered for sale. Mr. Mansfield, the man who owned mother, came into the jail as soon as Mr. Jones, the man who arrested us, informed him that he had brought her back. He told her that he would not whip her, but would sell her to a negro-trader, or take her to New Orleans himself. After being in jail about one week, master sent a man to take me out of jail, and send me home. I was taken out and carried home, and the old man was well enough to sit up. He had me brought into the room where he was, and as I entered, he asked me where I had been? I told I had acted according to his orders. He had told me to look for a master, and I had been to look for one. He answered that he did not tell me to go to Canada to look for a master. I told him that as I had served him faithfully, and had been the means of putting a number of hundreds of dollars into his pocket, I thought I had a right to my liberty. He said he had promised my father that I should not be sold to supply the New Orleans market, or he would sell me to a negro-trader.

I was ordered to go into the field to work, and was closely watched by the overseer during the day, and locked up at night. The overseer gave me a severe whipping on the second day that I was in the field. I had been at home but a short time, when master was able to ride to the city; and on his return, he informed me that he had sold me to Samuel Willi, a merchant tailor. I knew Mr. Willi. I had lived with him three or four months some years before, when he hired me of my master.

Mr. Willi was not considered by his servants as a very bad man, nor was he the best of masters. I went to my new home, and found my new mistress very glad to see me. Mr. Willi owned two servants before he purchased me,—Robert and Charlotte. Robert was an excellent white-washer, and hired his time from his master, paying him one dollar per day, besides taking care of himself. He was known in the city by the name of Bob Music. Charlotte was an old woman, who attended to the cooking, washing, &c. Mr. Willi was not a wealthy man, and did not feel able to keep many servants around his house; so he soon decided to hire me out, and as I had been accustomed to service in steamboats, he gave me the privilege of finding such employment.

I soon secured a situation on board the steamer Otto, Capt. J. B. Hill, which sailed from St. Louis to Independence, Missouri. My former master, Dr. Young, did not let Mr. Willi know that I had run away, or he would not have permitted me to go on board a steamboat. The boat was not quite ready to commence running, and therefore I had to remain with Mr. Willi. But during this time, I had to undergo a trial, for which I was entirely unprepared. My mother, who had been in jail since her return until the present time, was now about being carried to New Orleans, to die on a cotton, sugar, or rice plantation!

I had been several times to the jail, but could obtain no interview with her. I ascertained, however, the time the boat in which she was to embark would sail, and as I had not seen mother since her being thrown into prison, I felt anxious for the hour of sailing to come. At last, the day arrived when I was to see her for the first time after our painful separation, and, for aught that I knew, for the last time in this world!

At about ten o'clock in the morning I went on board of the boat, and found her there in company with fifty or sixty other slaves. She was chained to another woman. On seeing me, she immediately dropped her head upon her heaving bosom. She moved not, neither did she weep. Her emotions were too deep for tears. I approached, threw my arms around her neck, kissed her, and fell upon my knees, begging her forgiveness, for I thought myself to blame for her sad condition; for if I had not persuaded her to accompany me, she would not then have been in chains.

She finally raised her head, looked me in the face, (and such a look none but an angel can give!) and said, "*My dear son, you are not to blame for my being here. You have done nothing more than less than your duty. Do not, I pray you, weep for me. I cannot last long upon a cotton plantation. I feel that my heavenly master will soon call me home, and then I shall be out of the hands of the slave-holders!"*

I could bear no more—my heart struggled to free itself from the human form. In a moment she saw Mr. Mansfield coming toward that part of the boat, and she whispered into my ear, "*My child, we must soon part to meet no more this side of the grave. You have ever said that you would not die a slave; that you would be a freeman. Now try to get your liberty! You will soon have no one to look after but yourself!"* and just as she whispered the last sentence into my ear, Mansfield came up to me, and with an oath, said, "Leave here this instant; you have been the means of my losing one hundred dollars to get this wench back,"—at the same time kicking me with a heavy pair of boots. As I left her, she gave one shriek, saying, "God be with you!" It was the last time that I saw her, and the last word I heard her utter.

I walked on shore. The bell was tolling. The boat was about to start. I stood with a heavy heart, waiting to see her leave the wharf. As I thought of my mother, I could but feel that I had lost

"———the glory of my life,
My blessing and my pride!
I half forgot the name of slave,
When she was by my side."

CHAPTER XI.

THE love of liberty that had been burning in my bosom, had well nigh gone out. I felt as though I was ready to die. The boat moved gently from the wharf, and while she glided down the river, I realized that my mother was indeed

"Gone,—gone,—sold and gone,
To the rice swamp dank and lone!"

After the boat was out of sight, I returned home; but my thoughts were so absorbed in what I had witnessed, that I knew not what I was about half of the time. Night came, but it brought no sleep to my eyes.

In a few days, the boat upon which I was to work being ready, I went on board to commence. This employment suited me better than living in the city, and I remained until the close of navigation; though it proved anything but pleasant. The captain was a drunken, profligate, hard-hearted creature, not knowing how to treat himself, or any other person.

The boat, on its second trip, brought down Mr. Walker, the man of whom I have spoken in a previous chapter, as hiring my time. He had between one and two hundred slaves, chained and manacled. Among them was a man that formerly belonged to my old master's brother, Aaron Young. His name was Solomon. He was a preacher, and belonged to the same church with his master. I was glad to see the old man. He wept like a child when he told me how he had been sold from his wife and children.

The boat carried down, while I remained on board, four or five gangs of slaves. Missouri, though a comparatively new State, is very much engaged in raising slaves to supply the southern market. In a former chapter, I have mentioned that I was once in the employ of a slave-trader, or driver, as he is called at the south. For fear that some may think that I have misrepresented a slave-driver, I will here give an extract from a paper published in a slaveholding State, Tennessee, called the "Millennial Trumpeter."

"Droves of negroes, chained together in dozens and scores, and hand-cuffed, have been driven through our country in numbers far surpassing any previous year, and these vile slave-drivers and dealers are swarming like buzzards around a carrion. Through this county, you cannot pass a few miles in the great roads without having every feeling of humanity insulted and lacerated by this spectacle, nor can you go into any county or any neighborhood, scarcely, without seeing or hearing of some of these despicable creatures, called negro-drivers.

"Who is a negro-driver? One whose eyes dwell with delight on lacerated bodies of helpless men, women and children; whose soul feels diabolical raptures at the chains, and hand-cuffs, and cart-whips, for inflicting tortures on weeping mothers torn from helpless babes, and on husbands and wives torn asunder forever!"

Dark and revolting as is the picture here drawn, it is from the pen of one living in the midst of slavery. But though these men may cant about negro-drivers, and tell what despicable creatures they are, who is it, I ask, that supplies them with the human beings that they are tearing asunder? I answer, as far as I have any knowledge of the State where I came from, that those who raise slaves for the market are to be found among all classes, from Thomas H. Benton down to the lowest political demagogue, who may be able to purchase a woman for the purpose of raising stock, and from the Doctor of Divinity down to the most humble lay member in the church.

It was not uncommon in St. Louis to pass by an auction-stand, and behold a woman upon the auction-block, and hear the seller crying out, "*How much is offered for this woman? She is a good cook, good washer, a good obedient servant. She has got religion!*" Why should this man tell the purchasers that she has religion? I answer, because in Missouri, and as far as I have any knowledge of slavery in the other States, the religious teaching consists in teaching the slave that he must never strike a white man; that God made him for a slave; and that, when whipped, he must not find fault,—for the Bible says, "He that knoweth his master's will, and doeth it not, shall be beaten with many stripes!" And slaveholders find such religion very profitable to them.

After leaving the steamer Otto, I resided at home, in Mr. Willi's family, and again began to lay my plans for making my escape from slavery. The anxiety to be a freeman would not let me rest day or night. I would think of the northern cities that I had heard so much about;—of Canada, where so many of my acquaintances had found refuge. I would dream at night that I was in Canada, a freeman, and on waking in the morning, weep to find myself so sadly mistaken.

"I would think of Victoria's domain,
And in a moment I seemed to be there!
But the fear of being taken again,
Soon hurried me back to despair."

Mr. Willi treated me better than Dr. Young ever had; but instead of making me contented and happy, it only rendered me the more miserable, for it enabled me better to appreciate liberty. Mr. Willi was a man who loved money as most men do, and without looking for an opportunity to sell me, he found one in the offer of Captain Enoch Price, a steamboat owner and commission merchant, living in the city of St. Louis. Captain Price tendered seven hundred dollars, which was two hundred more than Mr. Willi had paid. He therefore thought best to accept the offer. I was wanted for a carriage driver, and Mrs. Price was very much pleased with the captain's bargain. His family consisted besides of one child. He had three servants besides myself—one man and two women.

Mrs. Price was very proud of her servants, always keeping them well dressed, and as soon as I had been purchased, she resolved to have a new carriage. And soon one was procured, and all preparations were made for a turn-out in grand style, I being the driver.

One of the female servants was a girl some eighteen or twenty years of age, named Maria. Mrs. Price was very soon determined to have us united, if she could so arrange matters. She would often urge upon me the necessity of having a wife, saying that it would be so pleasant for me to take one in the same family! But getting married, while in slavery, was the last of my thoughts; and had I been ever so inclined, I should not have married Maria, as my love had already gone in another quarter. Mrs. Price soon found out that her efforts at this match-making between Maria and myself would not prove successful. She also discovered (or thought she had) that I was rather partial to a girl named Eliza, who was owned by Dr. Mills. This induced her at once to endeavor the purchase of Eliza, so great was her desire to get me a wife!

Before making the attempt, however, she deemed it best to talk to me a little upon the subject of love, courtship, and marriage. Accordingly one afternoon she called me into her room— telling me to take a chair and sit down. I did so, thinking it rather strange, for servants are not very often asked thus to sit down in the same room with the master or mistress. She said that she had found out that I did not care enough about Maria to marry her. I told her that was true. She then asked me if there was not a girl in the city that I loved. Well, now, this was coming into too close quarters with me! People, generally, don't like to tell their love stories to everybody that may think fit to ask about them, and it was so with me. But, after blushing awhile and recovering myself, I told her that I did not want a wife. She then asked me, if I did not think something of Eliza. I told her that I did. She then said that if I wished to marry Eliza, she would purchase her if she could.

I gave but little encouragement to this proposition, as I was determined to make another trial to get my liberty, and I knew that if I should have a wife, I should not be willing to leave her behind; and if I should attempt to bring her with me, the chances would be difficult for success. However, Eliza was purchased, and brought into the family.

CHAPTER XII.

BUT the more I thought of the trap laid by Mrs. Price to make me satisfied with my new home, by getting me a wife, the more I determined never to marry any woman on earth until I should get my liberty. But this secret I was compelled to keep to myself, which placed me in a very critical position. I must keep upon good terms with Mrs. Price and Eliza. I therefore promised Mrs. Price that I would marry Eliza; but said that I was not then ready. And I had to keep upon good terms with Eliza, for fear that Mrs. Price would find out that I did not intend to get married.

I have here spoken of marriage, and it is very common among slaves themselves to talk of it. And it is common for slaves to be married; or at least have the marriage ceremony performed. But there is no such thing as slaves being lawfully married. There has never yet a case occurred where a slave has been tried for bigamy. The man may have as many women as he wishes, and the women as many men; and the law takes no cognizance of such acts among slaves. And in fact some masters, when they have sold the husband from the wife, compel her to take another.

There lived opposite Captain Price's, Doctor Farrar, well known in St. Louis. He sold a man named Ben, to one of the traders. He also owned Ben's wife, and in a few days he compelled Sally (that was her name) to marry Peter, another man belonging to him. I asked Sally "why she married Peter so soon after Ben was sold." She said, "because master made her do it."

Mr. John Calvert, who resided near our place, had a woman named Lavinia. She was quite young, and a man to whom she was about to be married was sold, and carried into the country near St. Charles, about twenty miles from St. Louis. Mr. Calvert wanted her to get a husband; but she had resolved not to marry any other man, and she refused. Mr. Calvert whipped her in such a manner that it was thought she would die. Some of the citizens had him arrested, but it was soon hushed up. And that was the last of it. The woman did not die, but it would have been the same if she had.

Captain Price purchased me in the month of October, and I remained with him until December, when the family made a voyage to New Orleans, in a boat owned by himself, and named the "Chester." I served on board, as one of the stewards. On arriving at New Orleans, about the middle of the month, the boat took in freight for Cincinnati; and it was decided that the family should go up the river in her, and what was of more interest to me, I was to accompany them.

The long looked for opportunity to make my escape from slavery was near at hand.

Captain Price had some fears as to the propriety of taking me near a free State, or a place where it was likely I could run away, with a prospect of liberty. He asked me if I had ever been in a free State. "Oh yes," said I, "I have been in Ohio; my master carried me into that State once, but I never liked a free State."

It was soon decided that it would be safe to take me with them, and what made it more safe, Eliza was on the boat with us, and Mrs. Price, to try me, asked if I thought as much as ever of Eliza. I told her that Eliza was very dear to me indeed, and that nothing but death should part us. It was the same as if we were married. This had the desired effect. The boat left New Orleans, and proceeded up the river.

I had at different times obtained little sums of money, which I had reserved for a "rainy day." I procured some cotton cloth, and made me a bag to carry provisions in. The trials of the past were all lost in hopes for the future. The love of liberty, that had been burning in my bosom for years, and had been well nigh extinguished, was now resuscitated. At night, when all around was peaceful, I would walk the decks, meditating upon my happy prospects.

I should have stated, that before leaving St. Louis, I went to an old man named Frank, a slave, owned by a Mr. Sarpee. This old man was very distinguished (not only among the slave population, but also the whites) as a fortune-teller. He was about seventy years of age, something over six feet high, and very slender. Indeed, he was so small around his body that it looked as though it was not strong enough to hold up his head.

Uncle Frank was a very great favorite with the young ladies, who would go to him in great numbers to get their fortunes told. And it was generally believed that he could really penetrate into the mysteries of futurity. Whether true or not, he had the *name*, and that is about half of what one needs in this gullible age. I found Uncle Frank seated in the chimney corner, about ten o'clock at night. As soon as I entered, the old man left his seat. I watched his movement as well as I could by the dim light of the fire. He soon lit a lamp, and coming up, looked me full in the face, saying, "Well, my son, you have come to get uncle to tell your fortune, have you?" "Yes," said I. But how the old man should know what I had come for, I could not tell. However, I paid the fee of twenty-five cents, and he commenced by looking into a gourd, filled with water. Whether the old man was a prophet, or the son of a prophet, I cannot say; but there is one thing certain, many of his predictions were verified.

I am no believer in soothsaying; yet I am sometimes at a loss to know how Uncle Frank could tell so accurately what would occur in the future. Among the many things he told was one which was enough to pay me for all the trouble of hunting him up. It was that *I should be free!* He further said, that in trying to get my liberty, I would meet with many severe trials. I thought to myself, any fool could tell me that!

The first place in which we landed in a free State was Cairo, a small village at the mouth of the Ohio river. We remained here but a few hours, when we proceeded to Louisville. After unloading some of the cargo, the boat started on her upward trip. The next day was the first of January. I had looked forward to New Year's day as the commencement of a new era in the history of my life. I had decided upon leaving the peculiar institution that day.

During the last night that I served in slavery, I did not close my eyes a single moment. When not thinking of the future, my mind dwelt on the past. The love of a dear mother, a dear sister, and three dear brothers, yet living, caused me to shed many tears. If I could only have been assured of their being dead, I should have felt satisfied; but I imagined I saw my dear mother in the cotton-field, followed by a merciless task-master, and no one to speak a consoling word to her! I beheld my dear sister in the hands of a slave-driver, and compelled to submit to his cruelty! None but one placed in such a situation can for a moment imagine the intense agony to which these reflections subjected me.

CHAPTER XIII.

AT last the time for action arrived. The boat landed at a point which appeared to me the place of all others to start from. I found that it would be impossible to carry anything with me, but what was upon my person. I had some provisions, and a single suit of clothes, about half worn. When the boat was discharging her cargo, and the passengers engaged carrying their baggage on and off shore, I improved the opportunity to convey myself with my little effects on land. Taking up a trunk, I went up the wharf, and was soon out of the crowd. I made directly for the woods, where I remained until night, knowing well that I could not travel, even in the State of

Ohio, during the day, without danger of being arrested.

I had long since made up my mind that I would not trust myself in the hands of any man, white or colored. The slave is brought up to look upon every white man as an enemy to him and his race; and twenty-one years in slavery had taught me that there were traitors, even among colored people. After dark, I emerged from the woods into a narrow path, which led me into the main travelled road. But I knew not which way to go. I did not know North from South, East from West. I looked in vain for the North Star; a heavy cloud hid it from my view. I walked up and down the road until near midnight, when the clouds disappeared, and I welcomed the sight of my friend,—truly the slave's friend,—the North Star!

As soon as I saw it, I knew my course, and before daylight I travelled twenty or twenty-five miles. It being in the winter, I suffered intensely from the cold; being without an overcoat, and my other clothes rather thin for the season. I was provided with a tinderbox, so that I could make up a fire when necessary. And but for this, I should certainly have frozen to death; for I was determined not to go to any house for shelter. I knew of a man belonging to Gen. Ashly, of St. Louis, who had run away near Cincinnati, on the way to Washington, but had been caught and carried back into slavery; and I felt that a similar fate awaited me, should I be seen by any one. I travelled by night, and lay by during the day.

On the fourth day, my provisions gave out, and then what to do I could not tell. Have something to eat, I must; but how to get it was the question! On the first night after my food was gone, I went to a barn on the road-side, and there found some ears of corn. I took ten or twelve of them, and kept on my journey. During the next day, while in the woods, I roasted my corn and feasted upon it, thanking God that I was so well provided for.

My escape to a land of freedom now appeared certain, and the prospects of the future occupied a great part of my thoughts. What should be my occupation, was a subject of much anxiety to me; and the next thing what should be my name? I have before stated that my old master, Dr. Young, had no children of his own, but had with him a nephew, the son of his brother, Benjamin Young. When this boy was brought to Doctor Young, his name being William, the same as mine, my mother was ordered to change mine to something else. This, at the time, I thought to be one of the most cruel acts that could be committed upon my rights; and I received several very severe whippings for telling people that my name was

William, after orders were given to change it. Though young, I was old enough to place a high appreciation upon my name. It was decided, however, to call me "Sandford," and this name I was known by, not only upon my master's plantation, but up to the time that I made my escape. I was sold under the name of Sandford.

But as soon as the subject came to my mind, I resolved on adopting my old name of William, and let Sandford go by the board, for I always hated it. Not because there was anything peculiar in the name; but because it had been forced upon me. It is sometimes common at the south, for slaves to take the name of their masters. Some have a legitimate right to do so. But I always detested the idea of being called by the name of either of my masters. And as for my father, I would rather have adopted the name of "Friday," and been known as the servant of some Robinson Crusoe, than to have taken his name. So I was not only hunting for my liberty, but also hunting for a name; though I regarded the latter as of little consequence, if I could but gain the former. Travelling along the road, I would sometimes speak to myself, sounding my name over, by way of getting used to it, before I should arrive among civilized human beings. On the fifth or sixth day, it rained very fast, and it froze about as fast as it fell, so that my clothes were one glare of ice. I travelled on at night until I became so chilled and benumbed—the wind blowing into my face—that I found it impossible to go any further, and accordingly took shelter in a barn, where I was obliged to walk about to keep from freezing.

I have ever looked upon that night as the most eventful part of my escape from slavery. Nothing but the providence of God, and that old barn, saved me from freezing to death. I received a very severe cold, which settled upon my lungs, and from time to time my feet had been frost-bitten, so that it was with difficulty I could walk. In this situation I travelled two days, when I found that I must seek shelter somewhere, or die.

The thought of death was nothing frightful to me, compared with that of being caught, and again carried back into slavery. Nothing but the prospect of enjoying liberty could have induced me to undergo such trials, for

> "Behind I left the whips and chains,
> Before me were sweet Freedom's plains!"

This, and this alone, cheered me onward. But I at last resolved to seek protection from the inclemency of the weather, and therefore I secured myself behind some logs and brush, intending to wait there until some one should pass by; for I thought it probable that I might see some colored person, or, if not, some one who was not a slaveholder; for I had an idea that I should know a slaveholder as far as I could see him.

CHAPTER XIV.

THE first person that passed was a man in a buggy-wagon. He looked too genteel for me to hail him. Very soon, another passed by on horse-back. I attempted speaking to him, but fear made my voice fail me. As he passed, I left my hiding-place, and was approaching the road, when I observed an old man walking towards me, leading a white horse. He had on a broad-brimmed hat and a very long coat, and was evidently walking for exercise. As soon as I saw him, and observed his dress, I thought to myself, "You are the man that I have been looking for!" Nor was I mistaken. He was the very man!

On approaching me, he asked me, "if I was not a slave." I looked at him some time, and then asked him "if he knew of any one who would help me, as I was sick." He answered that he would; but again asked, if I was not a slave. I told him I was. He then said that I was in a very pro-slavery neighborhood, and if I would wait until he went home, he would get a covered wagon for me. I promised to remain. He mounted his horse, and was soon out of sight.

After he was gone, I meditated whether to wait or not; being apprehensive that he had gone for some one to arrest me. But I finally concluded to remain until he should return; removing some few rods to watch his movements. After a suspense of an hour and a half or more, he returned with a two horse covered-wagon, such as are usually seen under the shed of a Quaker meeting-house on Sundays and Thursdays; for the old man proved to be a Quaker of the George Fox stamp.

He took me to his house, but it was some time before I could be induced to enter it; not until the old lady came out, did I venture into the house. I thought I saw something in the old lady's cap that told me I was not only safe, but welcome, in her house. I was not, however, prepared to receive their hospitalities. The only fault I found with them was their being too kind. I had never had a white man to treat me as an equal, and the idea of a white lady waiting on me at the table was still worse! Though the table was loaded with the good things of this life, I could not eat. I thought if I could only be allowed the privilege of eating in the kitchen, I should be more than satisfied!

Finding that I could not eat, the old lady, who was a "Thompsonian," made me a cup of "composition," or "number six;" but it was so strong and hot, that I called it *"number seven!"* However, I soon found myself at home in this family. On different occasions, when telling these facts, I have been asked how I felt upon finding myself regarded as a man by a white family; especially just having run away from one. I cannot say that I have ever answered the question yet.

The fact that I was in all probability a freeman, sounded in my ears like a charm. I am satisfied that none but a slave could place such an appreciation upon liberty as I did at that time. I wanted to see mother and sister, that I might tell them "I was free!" I wanted to see my fellow slaves in St. Louis, and let them know that the chains were no longer on my limbs. I wanted to see Captain Price, and let him learn from my own lips that I was no more a chattel, but a man! I was anxious, too, thus to inform Mrs. Price that she must get another coachman. And I wanted to see Eliza more than I did either Mr. or Mrs. Price!

The fact that I was a freeman—could walk, talk, eat and sleep as a man, and no one to stand over me with the blood-clotted cowhide—all this made me feel that I was not myself.

The kind friend that had taken me in was named Wells Brown. He was a devoted friend of the slave; but was very old, and not in the enjoyment of good health. After being by the fire awhile, I found that my feet had been very much frozen. I was seized with a fever which threatened to confine me to my bed. But my Thompsonian friends soon raised me, treating me as kindly as if I had been one of their own children. I remained with them twelve or fifteen days, during which time they made me some clothing, and the old gentleman purchased me a pair of boots.

I found that I was about fifty or sixty miles from Dayton, in the State of Ohio, and between one and two hundred miles from Cleaveland, on lake Erie, a place I was desirous of reaching on my way to Canada. This I know will sound strangely to the ears of people in foreign lands, but it is nevertheless true. An American citizen was fleeing from a Democratic, Republican, Christian government, to receive protection under the monarchy of Great

Britain. While the people of the United States boast of their freedom, they at the same time keep three millions of their own citizens in chains; and while I am seated here in sight of Bunker Hill Monument, writing this narrative, I am a slave, and no law, not even in Massachusetts, can protect me from the hands of the slaveholder!

Before leaving this good Quaker friend, he inquired what my name was besides William. I told him that I had no other name. "Well," said he, "thee must have another name. Since thee has got out of slavery, thee has become a man, and men always have two names."

I told him that he was the first man to extend the hand of friendship to me, and I would give him the privilege of naming me.

"If I name thee," said he, "I shall call thee Wells Brown, after myself."

"But," said I, "I am not willing to lose my name of William. As it was taken from me once against my will, I am not willing to part with it again upon any terms."

"Then," said he, "I will call thee William Wells Brown."

"So be it," said I; and I have been known by that name ever since I left the house of my first white friend, Wells Brown.

After giving me some little change, I again started for Canada. In four days I reached a public house, and went in to warm myself. I there learned that some fugitive slaves had just passed through the place. The men in the bar-room were talking about it, and I thought that it must have been myself they referred to, and I was therefore afraid to start, fearing they would seize me; but I finally mustered courage enough, and took my leave. As soon as I was out of sight, I went into the woods, and remained there until night, when I again regained the road, and travelled on until the next day.

Not having had any food for nearly two days, I was faint with hunger, and was in a dilemma what to do, as the little cash supplied me by my adopted father, and which had contributed to my comfort, was now all gone. I however concluded to go to a farm-house, and ask for something to eat. On approaching the door of the first one presenting itself, I knocked, and was soon met by a man who asked me what I wanted. I told him that I would like something to eat. He asked me where I was from, and where I was going. I replied that I had come some way, and was going to Cleaveland.

After hesitating a moment or two, he told me that he could give me nothing to eat, adding, "that if I would work, I could get something to eat."

I felt bad, being thus refused something to sustain nature, but did not dare tell him that I was a slave.

Just as I was leaving the door, with a heavy heart, a woman, who proved to be the wife of this gentleman, came to the door, and asked her husband what I wanted? He did not seem inclined to inform her. She therefore asked me herself. I told her that I had asked for something to eat. After a few other questions, she told me to come in, and that she would give me something to eat.

I walked up to the door, but the husband remained in the passage, as if unwilling to let me enter.

She asked him two or three times to get out of the way, and let me in. But as he did not move, she pushed him on one side, bidding me walk in! I was never so glad to see a woman push a man aside! Ever since that act, I have been in favor of "woman's rights!"

After giving me as much food as I could eat, she presented me with ten cents, all the money then at her disposal, accompanied with a note to a friend, a few miles further on the road. Thanking this angel of mercy from an overflowing heart, I pushed on my way, and in three days arrived at Cleaveland, Ohio.

Being an entire stranger in this place, it was difficult for me to find where to stop. I had no money, and the lake being frozen, I saw that I must remain until the opening of navigation, or go to Canada by way of Buffalo. But believing myself to be somewhat out of danger, I secured an engagement at the Mansion House, as a table waiter, in payment for my board. The proprietor, however, whose name was E. M. Segur, in a short time, hired me for twelve dollars per month; on which terms I remained until spring, when I found good employment on board a lake steamboat.

I purchased some books, and at leisure moments perused them with considerable advantage to myself. While at Cleaveland, I saw, for the first time, an anti-slavery newspaper. It was the "*Genius of Universal Emancipation,*" published by Benjamin Lundy, and though I had no home, I subscribed for the paper. It was my great desire, being out of slavery myself, to do what I could for the emancipation of my brethren yet in chains, and while on Lake Erie, I found many opportunities of "helping their cause along."

It is well known, that a great number of fugitives make their escape to Canada, by way of Cleaveland; and while on the lake, I always made arrangement to carry them on the boat to Buffalo or Detroit, and thus effect their escape to the "promised land." The friends of the slave, knowing that I would transport them without charge, never failed to have a delegation when the boat arrived at Cleaveland. I have sometimes had four or five on board, at one time.

In the year 1842, I conveyed, from the first of May to the first of December, sixty-nine fugitives over Lake Erie to Canada. In 1843, I visited Malden, in Upper Canada, and counted seventeen, in that small village, who owed their escape to my humble efforts.

Soon after coming North, I subscribed for the Liberator, edited by that champion of freedom, William Lloyd Garrison. I labored a season to promote the temperance cause among the colored people, but for the last three years, have been pleading for the victims of American slavery.

WILLIAM WELLS BROWN.

Boston, Mass., June, 1847.

MY LIFE IN THE SOUTH

By
JACOB STROYER.

NEW AND ENLARGED EDITION.

SALEM, MASS.:
Newcomb & Gauss, Printers.
1898.

Rev. Jacob Stroyer's book is intensely interesting, because it is a story of personal experience. It is also a book of great educational worth, because it deals plainly and justly with slavery, as that institution existed both in time of peace and in time of war, from the standpoint of one who was himself a slave.

C. H. Puffer,

Pastor First Universalist Church.

Salem, Mass., Nov. 9, 1898.

The author of this book—Mr. Stroyer—has been for years a worthy resident of this city, doing an excellent work among the colored people. His story, graphically told, is one of many which must interest every lover of the Nation's history, in both its dark and bright pages.

De Witt S. Clark, Salem.

Oct. 25, 1989.

Mr. Stroyer's account of his experiences in the War of the Rebellion is history at first hand. And his point of view is one from which little has been written. There have been any number of accounts by observers in both the Federal and the Confederate ranks. But not many have come from the slaves who were forced to work against a cause which they knew was their own. This fact gives Mr. Stroyer's narrative an uncommon interest. I take pleasure in commending Mr. Stroyer as an earnest and worthy Christian man, who has deeply at heart the welfare of his people.

Jas. F. Brodie

Salem, Mass., September 19, 1898.

Mr. Stroyer's account of his experience in slavery and during the war is of great interest and value as a trustworthy description of the condition and life of slaves *by one of themselves.* His memory is remarkably keen and his narrative vivid and at times both touching and thrilling. The book is a great credit to its author and deserves a generous reception and a wide circulation.

John Wright Buckham.

August 13, 1879.

In this book Mr. Stroyer has given us, with a most simple and effective realism, the inside view of the institution of slavery. It is worth reading, to know how men, intelligent enough to report their experience, felt under the yoke. The time has come when American slavery can be studied historically, without passion, save such as mixes itself with the wonder that so great an evil could exist so long as a social form or a political idol. The time has not come when such study is unnecessary; for to deal justly by white or black in the United States, their previous relations must be understood, and nothing which casts light on the most universal and practical of those relations is without value today. I take pleasure, therefore, in saying that I consider Mr. Stroyer a competent and trustworthy witness to these details of plantation life.

E. C. Bolles.

City of Salem, Mayor's Office, Nov. 5, 1884. }

This is to certify that since the year 1876 I have known Rev. Jacob Stroyer as a preacher and minister to the colored people of this city. He is earnest, devoted and faithful.

He is endeavoring by the sale of this book to realize the means to enable him, by a course of study, to better fit himself as a minister to preach in the South.

I most cheerfully commend him in his praiseworthy efforts.

Wm. M. Hill, *Mayor.*

Mr. Stroyer's book is a setting forth in a fresh and unique manner of the old and bitter wrongs of American slavery. It is an inside view of a phase of our national life which has happily passed away forever. Although it concerns itself largely with incidents and details, it is not without the historical value which attaches to reliable personal reminiscences. The author has made commendable progress in intellectual culture, and is worthy of generous assistance in his effort to fit himself still more perfectly for labor among his needy brethren in the South.

E. S. Atwood.

PREFACE.

Fourth Edition.

When the author first presented his book to the public he did not anticipate the very great favor with which it would be received. The first edition was soon disposed of, a second and a third were called for, and those were as generously received as had been their predecessors. The present edition, the fourth, besides all that was in those former publications, contains some new material relating to the author's personal experiences in the Civil War.

Thanking the people for the support given, and hoping that this latest effort will meet approval, the author presents the story of himself and his once oppressed brethren.

CHAPTER I.

My father was born in Sierra Leone, Africa. Of his parents and his brothers and sisters I know nothing. I only remember that it was said that his father's name was Moncoso, and his mother's Mongomo, which names are known only among the native Africans. He was brought from Africa when but a boy, and sold to old Colonel Dick Singleton, who owned a great many plantations in South Carolina, and when the old colonel divided his property among his children, father fell to the second son, Col. M. R. Singleton.

Mother never was sold, but her parents were; they were owned by one Mr. Crough, who sold them and the rest of the slaves, with the plantation, to Col. Dick Singleton, upon whose place mother was born. I was born on this extensive plantation, twenty-eight miles southeast of Columbia, South Carolina, in the year 1849. I belonged to Col. M. R. Singleton, and was held in slavery up to the time of the emancipation proclamation issued by President Lincoln.

THE CHILDREN.

My father had fifteen children: four boys and three girls by his first wife and eight by his second. Their names were as follow: of the boys—Toney, Aszerine, Duke and Dezine; of the girls—Violet, Priscilla, and Lydia. Those of his second wife were as follows: Footy, Embrus, Caleb, Mitchell, Cuffey and Jacob, and of the girls, Catherine and Retta.

SAND HILL DAYS.

Col. M. R. Singleton was like many other rich slave owners in the South, who had summer seats four, six or eight miles from the plantations, where they carried the little negro boys and girls too small to work.

Our summer seat, or the sand hill, as the slaves used to call it, was four miles from the plantation. Among the four hundred and sixty-five slaves owned by the colonel there were a great many children. If my readers had visited Col. Singleton's plantation the last of May or the first of June in the days of slavery, they would have seen three or four large plantation wagons loaded with little negroes of both sexes, of various complexions and conditions, who were being carried to this summer residence, and among them they would have found the author of this little work in his sand-hill days.

My readers would naturally ask how many seasons these children were taken to the summer seats? I answer, until, in the judgment of the overseer, they were large enough to work; then they were kept at the plantation. How were they fed? There were three or four women who were too old to work on the plantation who were sent as nurses to the summer seats with the children; they did the cooking. The way in which these old women cooked for 80, and sometimes 150 children, in my sand-hill days, was this:—they had two or three large pots, which held about a bushel each, in which they used to cook corn flour, stirred with large wooden paddles. The food was dealt out with the paddles into each child's little wooden tray or tin pail, which was furnished by the parents according to their ability.

With this corn flour, which the slaves called mush, each child used to get a gill of sour milk brought daily from the plantation in a large wooden pail on the head of a boy or man. We children used to like the sour milk, or hard clabber as it was called by the slaves; but that seldom changed diet, namely the mush, was hated worse than medicine. Our hatred was increased against the mush from the fact that they used to give us molasses to eat with it, instead of clabber. The hateful mixture made us anxious for Sundays to come, when our mothers, fathers, sisters and brothers would bring something from the plantation, which, however poor, we considered very nice, compared with what we had during the week days. Among the many desirable things our parents brought us the most delightful was cow pease, rice, and a piece of bacon, cooked together; the mixture was called by the slaves "hopping John."

THE STORY OF GILBERT.

A few large boys were sent yearly to the sand-hill among the smaller ones, as guides. At the time to which I am referring there was one by the name of Gilbert, who used to go around with the smaller boys in the woods to gather bushes and sticks for the old women to cook our food with.

Gilbert was a cruel boy. He used to strip his little fellow negroes while in the woods, and whip them two or three times a week, so that their backs were all scarred, and threatened them with severer punishment if they told; this state of things had been going on for quite a while. As I was a favorite with Gilbert, I always had managed to escape a whipping, with the promise of keeping the secret of the punishment of the rest, which I did, not so much that I was afraid of Gilbert, as because I always was inclined to mind my own business. But finally, one day, Gilbert said to me, "Jake," as he used to call me, "you am a good boy, but I'm gwine to wip you some to-day, as I wip dem toder boys." Of course I was required to strip off my only garment, which was an Osnaburg linen shirt, worn by both sexes of the negro children in the summer. As I stood trembling before my merciless superior, who had a switch in his hand, thousands of thoughts went through my little mind as to how to get rid of the whipping. I finally fell upon a plan which I hoped would save me from a punishment that was near at hand. There were some carpenters in the woods, some distance from us, hewing timber; they were far away, but it was a clear morning, so we could hear their voices and the sound of the axes. Having resolved in my mind what I would do, I commenced reluctantly to take off my shirt, at the same time pleading with Gilbert, who paid no attention to my prayer, but said, "Jake, I is gwine to wip you today as I did dem toder boys." Having satisfied myself that no mercy was to be found with Gilbert, I drew my shirt off and threw it over his head, and bounded forward on a run in the direction of the sound of the carpenters. By the time he got from the entanglement of my garment, I had quite a little start of him. Between my starting point and the place where the carpenters were at work I jumped over some bushes five or six feet high. Gilbert soon gained upon me, and sometimes touched me with his hands, but as I had on nothing for him to hold to, he could not take hold of me. As I began to come in sight of the carpenters, Gilbert begged me not to go to them, for he knew that it would be bad for him, but as that was not a time for me to listen to his entreaties, I moved on faster. As I got near to the carpenters, one of them ran and met me, into whose arms I jumped. The man into whose arms I ran was Uncle Benjamin, my mother's uncle. As he clasped me in his arms, he said, "Bres de Lo, my son, wat is de matter?" But I was so exhausted that it was quite a while before I could tell him my trouble; when recovered from my breathless condition, I told him that Gilbert had been in the habit of stripping the boys and whipping them two or three times a week, when we went into the woods, and threatened them with greater punishment if they told. I said he had never whipped me before, but I was cautioned to keep the secret, which I had done up to this time; but he said he was going to whip me this morning, so I threw my shirt over his head and ran here for protection. Gilbert did not follow me after I got in sight of the carpenters, but sneaked away. Of course my body was all bruised and scratched by the bushes. Acting as a guide for Uncle Benjamin, I took him to where I had left my garment.

At this time the children were scattered around in the woods, waiting for what the trouble would bring; they all were gathered up and taken to the sand-hill house, examined, and it was found, as I have stated, that their backs were all scarred. Gilbert was brought to trial, severely whipped, and they made him beg all the children to pardon him for his treatment to them. But he never was allowed to go into the woods with the rest of the children during that season. My sand-hill associates always thanked me for the course I took, which saved them and myself from further punishment by him.

MASTER AND MISTRESS VISITING.

When master and mistress were to visit their little negroes at the sand-hill, the news was either brought by the overseer who resided at the above named place, and went back and forth to the plantation, or by one of master's house servants, a day ahead. The preparation required to receive our white guests was that each little negro was to be washed, and clad in the best dress he or she had. But before this was done, the unsuccessful attempt was made to straighten out our unruly wools with some small cards, or Jim-Crows as we called them.

On one occasion an old lady, by the name of Janney Cuteron, attempted to straighten out my wool with one of those Jim-crows; as she hitched the teeth of the instrument in my unyielding wool with her great masculine hand, of course I was jerked flat on my back. This was the common fate of most of my associates, whose wools were of the same nature, but with a little water and the strong application of the Jim-crow, the old lady soon combed out my wool into some sort of shape.

As our preparations were generally completed three-quarters of an hour before our guests came, we were placed in line, the boys together and the girls by themselves. We were then drilled in the art of addressing our expected visitors. The boys were required to bend the body forward with head down, and rest the body on the left foot, and scrape the right foot backward on the ground, while uttering the words, "how dy Massie and Missie." The girls were required to use the same words, accompanied with a courtesy. But when Master and Mistress had left, the little African wools were neglected until the news of their next visit.

Our sand-hill days were very pleasant, outside of the seldom changed diet, namely the mush, which we had sometimes to eat with molasses, the treatment of Gilbert, and the attempt to straighten out our unruly wools.

I said that my father was brought from Africa when but a boy, and was sold to old Col. Dick Singleton; and when the children were of age, the Colonel divided his plantations among them, and father fell to Col. M. R. Singleton, who was the second son.

On this large plantation there were 465 slaves; there were not so many when it was given to Col. M. R., but increased to the above stated number, up to the time of emancipation.

My father was not a field hand; my first recollection of him was that he used to take care of hogs and cows in the swamp, and when too old for that work he was sent to the plantation to take care of horses and mules, as master had a great many for the use of his farm.

I have stated that father said that his father's name in Africa was Moncoso, and his mother's Mongomo, but I never learned what name he went by before he was brought to this country. I only know that he stated that Col. Dick Singleton gave him the name of

William, by which he was known up to the day of his death. Father had a surname, Stroyer, which he could not use in public, as the surname Stroyer would be against the law; he was known only by the name of William Singleton, because that was his master's name. So the title Stroyer was forbidden him, and could be used only by his children after the emancipation of the slaves.

There were two reasons given by the slave holders why they did not allow a slave to use his own name, but rather that of the master. The first was that, if he ran away, he would not be so easily detected by using his own name as by that of his master. The second was that to allow him to use his own name would be sharing an honor which was due only to his master, and that would be too much for a negro, said they, who was nothing more than a servant. So it was held as a crime for a slave to be caught using his own name, a crime which would expose him to severe punishment. But thanks be to God that those days have passed, and we now live under the sun of liberty.

MOTHER.

Mother's name was Chloe. She belonged to Col. M. R. Singleton too; she was a field hand, and never was sold, but her parents were once.

Mr. Crough who, as I have said had owned this plantation on which mother lived, had sold the plantation to Col. Dick Singleton, with mother's parents on it, before she was born.

Most of the family from which mother came, had trades of some kind; some were carpenters, some were blacksmiths, some house servants, and others were made drivers over the other negroes. Of course the negro drivers would be under a white man, who was called the overseer. Sometimes the negro drivers were a great deal worse to their fellow negroes than were the white men.

Mother had an uncle by the name of Esau, whom master thought more of than he did of the overseer. Uncle Esau was more cruel than was any white man master ever had on his plantation. Many of the slaves used to run away from him into the woods. I have known some of the negroes to run away from the cruel treatment of Uncle Esau, and to stay off eight or ten months. They were so afraid of him that they used to say that they would rather see the devil than to see him; they were glad when he died. But while so much was said of Uncle Esau, which was also true of many other negro drivers, the overseers themselves were not guiltless of cruelty to the defenceless slaves.

I have said that most of the family from which mother came had trades of some kind; but she had to take her chance in the field with those who had to weather the storm. But my readers are not to think that those whom I have spoken of as having trades were free from punishment, for they were not; some of them had more trouble than had the field hands. At times the overseer, who was a white man, would go to the shop of the blacksmith, or carpenter, and would pick a quarrel with him, so as to get an opportunity to punish him. He would say to the negro, "Oh, ye think yourself as good as ye master, ye ——." Of course he knew what the overseer was after, so he was afraid to speak; the overseer, hearing no answer, would turn to him and cry out, "ye so big ye can't speak to me, ye ——," and then the conflict would begin, and he would give that man such a punishment as would disable him for two or three months. The merciless overseer would say to him, "Ye think because ye have a trade ye are as good as ye master, ye ——; but I will show ye that ye are nothing but a nigger."

I said that my father had two wives and fifteen children: four boys and three girls by the first, and six boys and two girls by the second wife. Of course he did not marry his wives as they do now, as it was not allowed among the slaves, but he took them as his wives by mutual agreement. He had my mother after the death of his first wife. I am the third son of his second wife.

My readers would very naturally like to know whether some of the slaves did not have more than one woman. I answer, they had; for as they had no law to bind them to one woman, they could have as many as they pleased by mutual agreement. But notwithstanding, they had a sense of the moral law, for many of them felt that it was right to have but one woman; they had different opinions about plurality of wives, as have the most educated and refined among the whites.

I met one of my fellow negroes one day, who lived next neighbor to us, and I said to him, "Well, Uncle William, how are you, to-day?" His answer was "Thank God, my son, I have two wives now, and must try and make out with them until I get some more." But while you will find many like him, others would rebuke the idea of having more than one wife. But, thanks be to God, the day has come when no one need to plead ignorance, for master and servant are both bound by the same law.

I did not go to the sand-hill, or summer seat, my alloted time, but stopped on the plantation with father, as I said that he used to take care of horses and mules. I was around with him in the barn yard when but a very small boy; of course that gave me an early relish for the occupation of hostler, and I soon made known my preference to Col. Singleton, who was a sportsman, and an owner of fine horses. And, although I was too small to work, the Colonel granted my request; hence I was allowed to be numbered among those who took care of the fine horses, and learned to ride. But I soon found that my new occupation demanded a little more than I cared for.

It was not long after I had entered my new work before they put me upon the back of a horse which threw me to the ground almost as soon as I had reached his back. It hurt me a little, but that was not the worst of it, for when I got up there was a man standing near with a switch in hand, and he immediately began to beat me. Although I was a very bad boy, this was the first time I had been whipped by any one except father and mother, so I cried out in a tone of voice as if I would say, this is the first and last whipping you will give me when father gets hold of you.

When I had got away from him I ran to father with all my might, but soon found my expectation blasted, as father very coolly said to me, "Go back to your work and be a good boy, for I cannot do anything for you." But that did not satisfy me, so on I went to mother with my complaint and she came out to the man who had whipped me; he was a groom, a white man master had hired to train the horses. Mother and he began to talk, then he took a whip and started for her, and she ran from him, talking all the time. I ran back and forth between mother and him until he stopped beating her. After the fight between the groom and mother, he took me back to the stable yard and gave me a severe flogging. And, although mother failed to help me at first, still I had faith that when he had taken me back to the stable yard, and commenced whipping me, she would come and stop him, but I looked in vain, for she did not come.

Then the idea first came to me that I, with my dear father and mother and the rest of my fellow negroes, was doomed to cruel treatment through life, and was defenceless. But when I found that father and mother could not save me from punishment, as they themselves had to submit to the same treatment, I concluded to appeal to the sympathy of the groom, who seemed to have full control over me; but my pitiful cries never touched his sympathy, for things seemed to grow worse rather than better; so I made up my mind to stem the storm the best I could.

I have said that Col. Singleton had fine horses, which he kept for racing, and he owned two very noted ones, named Capt. Miner and Inspector. Perhaps some of my readers have already heard of Capt. Miner, for he was widely known, having won many races in Charlestown and Columbia, S. C., also in Augusta, Ga., and New York. He was a dark bay, with short tail. Inspector was a chestnut sorrel, and had the reputation of being a very great horse. These two horses have won many thousand dollars for the colonel. I rode these two horses a great many times in their practice gallops, but never had the opportunity to ride them in a race before Col. Singleton died, for he did not live long after I had learned so that I could ride for money. The custom was, that when a boy had learned the trade of a rider, he would have to ride what was known as a trial, in the presence of a judge, who would approve or disapprove his qualifications to be admitted as a race rider, according to the jockey laws of South Carolina at that time.

I have said that I loved the business and acquired the skill very early, and this enabled me to pass my examination creditably, and to be accepted as a capable rider, but I passed through some very severe treatment before reaching that point.

This white man who trained horses for Col. Singleton was named Boney Young; he had a brother named Charles, who trained for the colonel's brother, John Singleton. Charles was a good man, but Boney our trainer, was as mean as Charles was good; he could smile in the face of one who was suffering the most painful death at his hands.

One day, about two weeks after Boney Young and mother had the conflict, he called me to him, as though he were in the pleasantest mood; he was singing. I ran to him as if to say by action, I will do anything you bid me, willingly. When I got to him he said, "Go and bring me a switch, sir." I answered, "yes, sir," and off I went and brought him one; then he said, "come in here, sir;" I answered, "yes, sir;" and I went into a horse's stall, but while I was going in a thousand thoughts passed through my mind as to what he wanted me to go into the stall for, but when I had got in I soon learned, for he gave me a first-class flogging.

A day or two after that he called me in the same way, and I went again, and he sent me for a switch. I brought him a short stubble that was worn out, which he took and beat me on the head with. Then he said to me, "Go and bring me a switch, sir;" I answered

"Yes, sir;" and off I went the second time, and brought him one very little better than the first; he broke that over my head also, saying, "Go and bring me a switch, sir;" I answered, "Yes, sir," and off I went the third time, and brought one which I supposed would suit him. Then he said to me, "Come in here, sir." I answered, "Yes, sir." When I went into the stall, he told me to lie down, and I stooped down; he kicked me around for a while, then, making me lie on my face, he whipped me to his satisfaction.

That evening when I went home to father and mother, I said to them, "Mr. Young is whipping me too much now, I shall not stand it, I shall fight him." Father said to me, "You must not do that, because if you do he will say that your mother and I advised you to do it, and it will make it hard for your mother and me, as well as for yourself. You must do as I told you, my son: do your work the best you can, and do not say anything." I said to father, "But I don't know what I have done that he should whip me; he does not tell me what wrong I have done, he simply calls me to him and whips me when he gets ready." Father said, "I can do nothing more than to pray to the Lord to hasten the time when these things shall be done away; that is all I can do." When mother had stripped me and looked at the wounds that were upon me she burst into tears, and said, "If he were not so small I would not mind it so much; this will break his constitution; I am going to master about it, because I know he will not allow Mr. Young to treat this child so."

And I thought to myself that had mother gone to master about it, it would have helped me some, for he and she had grown up together and he thought a great deal of her. But father said to mother, "You better not go to master, for while he might stop the child from being treated badly, Mr. Young may revenge himself through the overseer, for you know that they are very friendly to each other." So said father to mother, "You would gain nothing in the end; the best thing for us to do is to pray much over it, for I believe that the time will come when this boy with the rest of the children will be free, though we may not live to see it."

When father spoke of liberty his words were of great comfort to me, and my heart swelled with the hope of a future, which made every moment seem an hour to me.

Father had a rule, which was strictly carried out as far as possible under the slave law, which was to put his children to bed early; but that night the whole family sat up late, while father and mother talked over the matter. It was a custom among the slaves not to allow their children under certain ages to enter into conversation with them; hence we could take no part with father and mother. As I was the object of their sympathy, I was allowed the privilege of answering the questions about the whipping the groom gave me.

When the time came for us to go to bed we all knelt down in family prayer, as was our custom; father's prayer seemed more real to me that night than ever before, especially in the words, "Lord, hasten the time when these children shall be their own free men and women."

My faith in father's prayer made me think that the Lord would answer him at the farthest in two or three weeks, but it was fully six years before it came, and father had been dead two years before the war.

After prayer we all went to bed; next morning father went to his work in the barn-yard, mother to hers in the field, and I to mine among the horses; before I started, however, father charged me carefully to keep his advice, as he said that would be the easiest way for me to get along.

But in spite of father's advice, I had made up my mind not to submit to the treatment of Mr. Young as before, seeing that it did not help me any. Things went smoothly for a while, until he called me to him, and ordered me to bring him a switch. I told him that I would bring him no more switches for him to whip me with, but that he must get them himself. After repeating the command very impatiently, and I refusing, he called to another boy named Hardy, who brought the switch, and then taking me into the stall he whipped me unmercifully.

After that he made me run back and forth every morning from a half to three quarters of an hour every two hundred and fifty yards, and every now and then he would run after me, and whip me to make me run faster. Besides that, when I was put upon a horse, if it threw me he would whip me, if it were five times a day. So I did not gain anything by refusing to bring switches for him to whip me with.

One very cold morning in the month of March, I came from home without washing my face, and Mr. Young made two of the slave boys take me down to a pond where the horses and mules used to drink; they threw me into the water and rubbed my face with sand until it bled, then I was made to run all the way to the stable, which was about a quarter of a mile. This cruel treatment soon hardened me so that I did not care for him at all.

A short time afterwards I was sent with the other boys about four or five miles from home, up the public road, to practice the horse, and they gave me a very wild animal to ride, which threw me very often. Mr. Young did not go with us, but sent a colored groom every morning, who was very faithful to every task alloted him; he was instructed to whip me every time the horse threw me while away from home. I got many little floggings by the colored groom, as the horse threw me a great many times, but the floggings I got from him were very feeble compared with those of the white man; hence I was better content to go away with the colored groom than to be at home where I should have worse punishment.

But the time was coming when they ceased to whip me for being thrown by horses. One day, as I was riding along the road, the horse that I was upon darted at the sight of a bird, which flew across the way, throwing me upon a pile of brush. The horse stepped on my cheek, and the head of a nail in his shoe went through my left cheek and broke a tooth, but it was done so quickly that I hardly felt it. It happened that he did not step on me with his whole weight, if he had my jaw would have been broken. When I got up the colored groom was standing by me, but he could not whip me when he saw the blood flowing from my mouth, so he took me down to the creek, which was but a short distance from the place, and washed me, and then taking me home, sent for a doctor, who dressed the wound.

When Mr. Young saw my condition, he asked how it was done, and upon being told he said it ought to have killed me. After the doctor had dressed my face, of course I went home, thinking they would allow me to stay until I got well, but I had no sooner arrived than the groom sent for me; I did not answer, as my jaw pained me very much. When he found that I did not come, he came after me himself, and said if I did not come to the stable right away, he would whip me, so I went with him. He did not whip me while I was in that condition, but he would not let me lie down, so I suffered very much from exposure.

When mother came that night from the farm and saw my condition, she was overcome with grief; she said to father, "this wound is enough to kill the child, and that merciless man will not let him lie down until he gets well; this is too hard." Father said to her, "I know it is very hard, but what can we do? for if we try to keep this boy in the house it will cause us trouble." Mother said, "I wish they would take him out of the world, then he would be out of pain, and we should not have to fret about him, for he would be in heaven."

Then she took hold of me and said, "Does it hurt you, son?" meaning my face, and I said, "Yes, mamma," and she shed tears; but she had no little toys to give me to comfort me; she could only promise me such as she had, which were eggs and chickens.

Father did not show his grief for me as mother did, but he tried to comfort mother all he could, and at times would say to me, "Never mind, my son, you will be a man bye and bye," but he did not know what was passing through my mind at that time. Though I was very small I thought that if, while a boy, my treatment was so severe, it would be much worse when I became a man, and having had a chance to see how men were being punished, it was a very poor consolation to me.

Finally the time came for us to go to bed, and we all knelt in family prayer. Father thanked God for having saved me from a worse injury, and then he prayed for mother's comfort, and also for the time which he predicted would come, that is, the time of freedom, when I and the rest of the children would be our own masters and mistresses; then he commended us to God, and we all went to bed. The next morning I went to my work with a great deal of pain. They did not send me up the road with the horses in that condition, but I had to ride the old horses to water, and work around the stable until I was well enough to go with the other boys. But I am happy to say that from the time I got hurt by that horse I was never thrown except through carelessness, neither was I afraid of a horse after that.

Notwithstanding father and mother fretted very much about me, they were proud of my success as a rider, but my hardships did not end here.

A short time after, I was taken to Columbia and Charleston, S.C., where they used to have the races. That year Col. Singleton won a large sum of money by the well-known horse, Capt. Miner, and that was the same season that I rode my trial race. The next year, before the time of racing, Col. Singleton died at his summer seat. After master's death, mistress sold all the race horses, and that put an end to sporting horses in that family.

I said that Boney Young, Col. Singleton's groom, had a brother by the name of Charles, who trained horses for the colonel's brother, John Singleton. Boney was a better trainer, but Charles was a better man to the negroes. It was against the law for a slave to buy spirituous liquors without a ticket, but Charles used to give the boys tickets to buy rum and whiskey with. He also allowed them to steal the neighbor's cows and hogs.

I remember that on one occasion his boys killed a cow belonging to a man by the name of Le Brun; soon after the meat was brought to the stable, Le Brun rode up on horseback with a loaded shot gun and threatened to shoot the party with whom the beef was found. Of course the negroes' apartments were searched; but as that had been anticipated, Mr. Young had made them put the meat in his apartment, and, as it was against the law of South Carolina for a white man to search another's house, or any apartment, without very strong evidence, the meat was not found. Before searching among the negroes, Mr. Young said to Le Brun, "You may search, but you won't find your beef here, for my boys don't steal." Le Brun answered, "Mr. Young, your word might be true, sir, but I would trust a nigger with money a great deal sooner than I would with cows and hogs." Mr. Young answered, "That might be true, but you won't find your beef here."

After their rooms and clothes had been searched, blood was found under some of their finger nails, which increased Le Brun's suspicion that they were of the party who stole his cow; but Mr. Young answered, "that blood is from rabbits my boys caught today." Mr. Le Brun tried to scare one of the boys, to make him say it was the blood of his cow. Mr. Young said, "Mr. Le Brun, you have searched and did not find your beef, as I told you that you would not; also I told you that the blood under their finger nails is from rabbits caught today. You will have to take my word, sir, without going to further trouble; furthermore, these boys belong to Mr. Singleton, and if you want to take further steps you will have to see him." Finding that he was not allowed to do as he wanted to, Mr. Le Brun made great oaths and threats as he mounted his horse to leave, that he would shoot the very first one of those boys he should catch near his cattle. He and Mr. Young never did agree after that.

But poor Mr. Young, as good as he was to the negroes, was an enemy to himself, for he was a very hard drinker. People who knew him before I did said they never had seen him drink tea, coffee, or water, but rather rum and whiskey; he drank so hard that he used to go into a crazy fit; he finally put an end to his life by cutting his throat with a razor, at a place called O'Handly's race course, about three miles from Columbia, S. C. This was done just a few days before one of the great races.

Boney Young drank, too, but not so hard as Charles. He lived until just after the late war, and, while walking one day through one of the streets of the above named city, dropped dead, with what was supposed to have been heart disease.

Boney had a mulatto woman, named Moriah, who had been originally brought from Virginia by negro traders, but had been sold to several different masters later. The trouble was that she was very beautiful, and wherever she was sold her mistresses became jealous of her, so that she changed owners very often. She was finally sold to Boney Young, who had no wife; and she lived with him until freed by the emancipation proclamation. She had two daughters; the elder's name was Annie, but we used to call her sissie; the younger's name was Josephine. Annie looked just like her father, Boney Young, while Josephine looked enough like Charles to have been his daughter. It was easy enough to tell that the mother had sprung from the negro race, but the girls could pass for white. Their mother, Moriah, died in Columbia some time after the war. Annie went off and was married to a white man, but I don't know what became of Josephine.

A short time before master's death he stood security for a northern man, who was cashier of one of the largest banks in the city of Charleston. This man ran away with a large sum of money, leaving the colonel embarrassed, which fact made him very fretful and peevish. He had been none too good before to his slaves, and that made him worse, as you knew that the slave holders would revenge themselves on the slaves whenever they became angry. I had seen master whip his slaves a great many times, but never so severely as he did that spring before he died.

One day, before he went to his summer seat, he called a man to him, stripped and whipped him so that the blood ran from his body like water thrown upon him in cupfuls, and when the man stepped from the place where he had been tied, the blood ran out of his shoes. He said to the man, "You will remember me now, sir, as long as you live." The man answered, "Yes, master, I will."

Master went away that spring for the last time; he never returned alive; he died at his summer seat. When they brought his remains home all of the slaves were allowed to stop at home that day to see the last of him, and to lament with mistress. After all the slaves who cared to do so had seen his face, they gathered in groups around mistress to comfort her; they shed false tears, saying, "Never mind, missis, massa gone home to heaven." While some were saying this, others said, "Thank God, massa gone home to hell." Of course the most of them were glad that he was dead; but they were

173

gathered there for the express purpose of comforting mistress. But after master's death mistress was a great deal worse than he had been.

When the master died there was a great change of things on the plantation; the creditors came in for settlement, so all of the fine horses, and some others, such as carriage horses, and a few mules also, were sold. The slaves whom master had bought himself had to be sold, but those who had been born on the plantation, given to him by his father, old Col. Dick Singleton, could not be sold until the grandchildren were of age.

As I have stated, my hardships and trials did not end with the race horses; you will now see them in another form.

After all the fine horses had been sold, mistress ordered the men and boys who were taking care of the horses to be put into the field, and I was among them, though small; but I had become so attached to the horses that they could get no work out of me, so they began to whip me, but every time they whipped me I would leave the field and run home to the barnyard.

Finally mistress engaged a very bad man as overseer, in place of old Ben Usome, whose name was William Turner. Two or three days after his arrival he took me into the field and whipped me until I was sick, so I went home.

I went to mistress and told her that the overseer had whipped me; she asked if I had done the work that he had given me. I told her that master had promised me that, when I got too heavy to ride race horses, he would send me to learn the carpenter's trade; she asked me if, in case she put me to a trade, I would work, and I told her I would. So she consented.

But the overseer did not like the idea of having me work at the trade which was my choice. He said to mistress, "That is the worst thing you can do, madam, to allow a negro to have his choice about what he shall do. I have had some experience as an overseer for many years, and I think I am able to give a correct statement about the nature of negroes in general. I know a gentleman who allowed his negroes to have their own way about things on his plantation, and the result was that they got as high as their master. Besides that, madam, their influence rapidly spreads among the neighbors, and if such should be allowed, South Carolina would have all masters and mistresses, and no servants; and, as I have said, I know somewhat about the nature of negroes; I notice, madam, that this boy will put you to a great deal of trouble unless you begin to subdue him now while he is young. A very few years' delay will enable him to have a great influence among his fellow negroes, for that boy can read very well now, and you know, madam, it is against the law for a negro to get an education, and if you allow him to work at the carpenter's trade it will thus afford him the opportunity of acquiring a better education, because he will not be directly under the eye of one who will see that he makes no further advancement."

Then mistress asked me, "Can you read, Jacob?" I did not want her to know that I had taken notice of what they were saying, so I answered, "I don't know, ma'am." The overseer said, "He does not know what is meant, madam, but I can make him understand me." Then he took a newspaper from his pocket and said to me, "Can you say these words?" I took the paper and began to read, then he took it from me.

Mistress asked when I had learned to read and who had taught me. The overseer did not know, but said he would find out from me. Turning to me he took the paper from his pocket again, and said, "Jacob, who told you to say words in the book?" I answered, "Nobody, sir; I said them myself." He repeated the question three or four times, and I gave the same answer every time. Then mistress said, "I think it would be better to put him to trade than to have him in the field, because he will be away from his fellow negroes, and will be less liable to influence them if we can manage to keep him away." The overseer said, "That might be true, madam, but if we can manage to keep him from gaining any more education he will eventually lose what little he has; and now, madam, if you will allow me to take him in hand, I will bring him out all right without injuring him." Just at this juncture a carriage drove up to the gate, and I ran as usual to open it, the overseer went about his business, and mistress went to speak to the persons in the carriage. I never had a chance to hear their conclusion.

A few days after the conversation between the overseer and mistress, I was informed by one of the slaves, who was a carpenter, that she had ordered that I should go to work at the trade with him. This gave me great joy, as I was very anxious to know what they had decided to do with me. I went to my new trade with great delight, and soon began to imagine what a famous carpenter I should make, and what I should say and do when I had learned the trade. Everything seemed to run smoothly with me for about two months, when suddenly I was told one morning that I must go into the field to drop cotton seed, but I did not heed the call, as mistress was not at home, and I knew she had just put me to the trade, also that the overseer was trying to get mistress' consent to have me work out in the field.

The next morning the overseer came into the carpenter's shop and said, "Did I not order ye into the field, sir?" I answered, "Yes, sir." "Well, why did ye not go?" I answered, "Mistress has put me here to learn the trade." He said, "I will give ye trade." So he stripped me and gave me a severe whipping, and told me that that was the kind of trade I needed, and said he would give me many of them. The next day I went into the field, and he put me to drop cotton seed, as I was too small to do anything else. I would have made further resistance, but mistress was very far away from home, and I had already learned the lesson that father and mother could render me no help, so I thought submission to him the easiest for me.

When I had got through with the cotton seed, in about three weeks, I went back to the carpenter's shop to work; so he came there and gave me another severe whipping, and said to me, "Ye want to learn the carpenter's trade, but I will have ye to the trade of the field." But that was the last whipping he gave me, and the last of his whip.

A few days after my last whipping the slaves were ordered down into the swamp across the river to clear up new grounds, while the already cleared lands were too wet from rain that had fallen that night. Of course I was among them to do my part; that is, while the men quartered up dry trees, which had been already felled in the winter, and rolled the logs together, the women, boys and girls piled the brushes on the logs and burned them.

We had to cross the river in a flat boat, which was too small to carry over all the slaves at once, so they had to make several trips.

Mr. Turner, the overseer, went across in the first flat; he did not ride down to the work place, but went on foot, while his horse, which was trained to stand alone without being hitched, was left at the landing place. My cousin and I crossed in the last boat. When we had got across we lingered behind the crowd at the landing; when they all were gone we went near the horse and saw the whip with which I was whipped a few days before fastened to the saddle. I said to him, "Here is the whip old Turner whipped me with the other day." He said, "It ought to be put where he will never get it to whip anybody with again." I answered my cousin, "If you will keep the secret I will put it where old Bill, as we used to call Mr. Turner, will never use it any more." He agreed to keep the secret, and then asked me how I would put the whip away. I told him if he would find me a string and a piece of iron I would show him how. He ran down to the swamp barn, which was a short distance from the margin of the river, and soon returned with the string and iron exactly suited for the work. I tied the iron to the whip, went into the flat boat, and threw it as far as I could into the river. My cousin and I watched it until it went out of sight under water; then, as guilty boys generally do after mischievous deeds, we dashed off in a run, hard as we could, among the other negroes, and acted as harmless as possible. Mr. Turner made several inquiries, but never learned what had become of his whip.

A short time after this, in the time of the war, in the year 1863, when a man was going round to the different plantations gathering slaves from their masters to carry off to work on fortifications and to wait on officers, there were ten slaves sent from Mrs. Singleton's plantation, and I was among them. They carried us to Sullivan's Island at Charleston, S. C., and I was there all of that year. I thanked God that it afforded me a better chance for an education than I had had at home, and so I was glad to be on the island. Though I had no one to teach me, as I was thrown among those of my fellow negroes who were fully as lame as I was in letters, yet I felt greatly relieved from being under the eye of the overseer, whose intention was to keep me from further advancement. The year after I had gone home I was sent back to Fort Sumpter—in the year 1864. I carried my spelling book with me, and, although the northerners were firing upon us, I tried to keep up my study.

In July of the same year I was wounded by the Union soldiers, on a Wednesday evening. I was taken to the city of Charleston, to Dr. Regg's hospital, and there I stayed until I got well enough to travel, when I was sent to Columbia, where I was when the hour of liberty was proclaimed to me, in 1865. This was the year of jubilee, the year which my father had spoken of in the dark days of slavery, when he and mother sat up late talking of it. He said to mother, "The time will come when this boy and the rest of the children will be their own masters and mistresses." He died six years before that day came, but mother is still enjoying liberty with her children.

And no doubt my readers would like to know how I was wounded in the war. We were obliged to do our work in the night, as they were firing on us in the day, and on a Wednesday night, just as we went out, we heard the cry of the watchman. "Look out." There was a little lime house near the southwest corner of the fort, and some twelve or thirteen of us ran into it, and all were killed but two; a shell came down on the lime house and burst, and a piece cut my face open. But as it was not my time to die, I lived to enjoy freedom.

I said that when I got so I could travel I was sent from Dr. Ragg's hospital in Charleston to Col. Singleton's plantation near Columbia, in the last part of the year 1864. I did not do any work during the remainder of that year, because I was unwell from my wound received in the fort.

About that time Gen. Sherman came through Georgia with his hundred thousand men, and camped at Columbia, S. C. The slave holders were very uneasy as to how they should save other valuables, as they saw that slavery was a hopeless case. Mistress had some of her horses, mules, cows and hogs carried down into the swamp, while the others which were left on the plantation were divided out to the negroes for safe keeping, as she had heard that the Yankees would not take anything belonging to the slaves. A little pig of about fifty or sixty pounds was given to me for safe keeping. A few of the old horses and mules were taken from the plantation by the Union soldiers, but they did not trouble anything else.

After Columbia had been burned, and things had somewhat quieted, along in the year 1865, the negroes were asked to give up the cows and hogs given them for safe keeping; all the rest gave up theirs, but mine was not found. No doubt my readers want to know what had become of it. Well, I will tell you. You all know that Christmas was a great day with both masters and slaves in the South, but the Christmas of 1864 was the greatest which had ever come to the slaves, for, although the proclamation did not reach us until 1865, we felt that the chains which had bound us so long were well nigh broken.

So I killed the pig that Christmas, gathered all of my associates, and had a great feast, after which we danced the whole week. Mother would not let me have my feast in her cabin, because she was afraid that the white people would charge her with advising me to kill the pig, so I had it in one of the other slave's cabins.

When the overseer asked me for the pig given me, I told him that I killed it for my Christmas feast. Mistress said to me, "Jacob, why did you not ask me for the pig if you wanted it, rather than take it without permission?" I answered, "I would have asked, but thought, as I had it in hand, it wasn't any use asking for it." The overseer wanted to whip me for it, but as Uncle Sam had already broken the right arm of slavery, through the voice of the proclamation of 1863, he was powerless.

When the yoke had been taken from my neck I went to school in Columbia, S. C., awhile, then to Charleston. Afterward I came to Worcester, Mass., in February, 1869. I studied quite a while in the evening schools at Worcester, and also a while in the academy of the same place. During that time I was licensed a local preacher of the African Methodist Episcopal church, and sometime later was ordained deacon at Newport, R. I.

A short time after my ordination I was sent to Salem, Mass., where I have remained, carrying on religious work among my people, trying in my feeble way to preach that gospel which our blessed Saviour intended for the redemption of all mankind, when he proclaimed, "Go ye into all the world and preach the gospel." In the meantime I have been striking steady blows for the improvement of my education, in preparing myself for a field of work among my more unfortunate brethren in the South.

I must say that I have been surrounded by many good friends, including the clergy, since I have been in Salem, whose aid has enabled me to serve a short term in the Wesleyan school at Wilbraham, Mass., also to begin a course of theological studies at Talladega college in Alabama, which I am endeavoring to complete by the sale of this publication.

CHAPTER II.—SKETCHES.

THE SALE OF MY TWO SISTERS.

I have stated that my father had fifteen children—four boys and three girls by his first wife, and six boys and two girls by his second. Their names are as follows: Toney, Azerine, Duke and Dezine, of the girls, Violet, Priscilla and Lydia; those of the second wife as follows: Footy, Embrus, Caleb, Mitchell, Cuffee, and Jacob, who is the author, and the girls, Catherine and Retta.

As I have said, old Col. Dick Singleton had two sons and two daughters, and each had a plantation. Their names were John, Matt, Marianna and Angelico. They were very agreeable together, so that if one wanted negro help from another's plantation, he or she could have it, especially in cotton picking time.

John Singleton had a place about twenty miles from master's, and master used to send him slaves to pick cotton. At one time my master, Col. M. R. Singleton, sent my two sisters, Violet and Priscilla, to his brother John, and while they were there they married two of the men on his place. By mutual consent master allowed them to remain on his brother's place. But some time after this John Singleton had some of his property destroyed by water, as is often the case in the South at the time of May freshets, what is known in the North as high tides.

One of these freshets swept away John Singleton's slave houses, his barns, with horses, mules and cows. These caused his death by a broken heart, and since he owed a great deal of money his slaves had to be sold. A Mr. Manning bought a portion of them, and Charles Login the rest. These two men were known as the greatest slave traders in the South. My sisters were among the number that Mr. Manning bought.

He was to take them into the state of Louisiana for sale, but some of the men did not want to go with him, and he put those in prison until he was ready to start. My sisters' husbands were among the prisoners in the Sumterville jail, which was about twenty-five or thirty miles across the river from master's place. Those who did not show any unwillingness to go were allowed to visit their relatives and friends for the last time. So my sisters, with the rest of their unfortunate companions, came to master's place to visit us. When the day came for them to leave, some, who seemed to have been willing to go at first, refused, and were handcuffed together and guarded on their way to the cars by white men. The women and children were driven to the depot in crowds, like so many cattle, and the sight of them caused great excitement among master's negroes. Imagine a mass of uneducated people shedding tears and yelling at the top of their voices in anguish.

The victims were to take the cars at a station called Clarkson turnout, which was about four miles from master's place. The excitement was so great that the overseer and driver could not control the relatives and friends of those that were going away, as a large crowd of both old and young went down to the depot to see them off. Louisiana was considered by the slaves a place of slaughter, so those who were going did not expect to see their friends again. While passing along many of the negroes left their masters' fields and joined us as we marched to the cars; some were yelling and wringing their hands, while others were singing little hymns that they had been accustomed to for the consolation of those that were going away, such as

"When we all meet in heaven,
There is no parting there;
When we all meet in heaven,
There is parting no more."

We arrived at the depot and had to wait for the cars to bring the others from the Sumterville jail, but they soon came in sight, and when the noise of the cars had died away, we heard wailing and shrieks from those in the cars. While some were weeping, others were fiddling, picking banjo, and dancing as they used to do in their cabins on the plantations. Those who were so merry had very bad masters, and even though they stood a chance of being sold to one as bad or even worse, yet they were glad to be rid of the one they knew.

While the cars were at the depot a large crowd of white people gathered, laughing and talking about the prospect of negro traffic; but when the cars began to start, and the conductor cried out, "All who are going on this train must get on board without delay," the colored people cried out with one voice as though the heavens and earth were coming together, and it was so pitiful that those hard-hearted white men, who had been accustomed to driving slaves all their lives, shed tears like children. As the cars moved away we heard the weeping and wailing from the slaves as far as human voice could be heard; and from that time to the present I have neither seen nor heard from my sisters, nor any of those who left Clarkson depot on that memorable day.

THE WAY THE SLAVES LIVED.

Most of the cabins in the time of slavery were built so as to contain two families; some had partitions, while others had none. When there were no partitions each family would fit up its own part as it could; sometimes they got old boards and nailed them up, stuffing the cracks with rags; when they could not get boards they hung up old clothes. When the family increased the children all slept together, both boys and girls, until one got married; then a part of another cabin was assigned to that one, but the rest would have to remain with their mother and father, as in childhood, unless they could get with some of their relatives or friends who had small families, or unless they were sold; but of course the rules of modesty were held in some degrees by the slaves, while it could not be expected that they could entertain the highest degree of it, on account of their condition. A portion of the time the young men slept in the apartment known as the kitchen, and the young women slept in the room with their mother and father. The two families had to use one fireplace. One who was accustomed to the way in which the slaves lived in their cabins could tell as soon as they entered whether they were friendly or not, for when they did not agree the fires of the two families did not meet on the hearth, but there was a vacancy between them, that was a sign of disagreement. In a case of this kind, when either of the families stole a hog, cow or sheep from the master, he had to carry it to some of his friends, for fear of being betrayed by the other family. On one occasion a man, who lived with one unfriendly, stole a hog, killed it, and carried some of the meat home. He was seen by some one of the other family, who reported him to the overseer, and he gave the man a severe whipping. Sometime afterward this man who had been betrayed thought he would get even with his enemy; so about two months later he killed another hog, and, after eating a part of it, stole into the apartment of the other family and hid a portion of the meat among the old clothes. Then he told the overseer that he had seen the man go out late that night and that he had not come home until the late morning; when he did come he had called his wife to the window and she had taken something in. He did not know what it was, but if the overseer would go there right away he would find it. The overseer went and searched and found the meat, so the man was whipped. He told the overseer that the other man put it in his apartment while the family were away, but the overseer told him that every man must be responsible for his own apartment.

No doubt you would like to know how the slaves could sleep in their cabins in summer, when it was so very warm. When it was too warm for them to sleep comfortably, they all slept under trees until it grew too cool, that is along in the month of October. Then they took up their beds and walked.

JOE AND THE TURKEY.

Joe was a boy who was waiter to his master, one Mr. King, and he and his wife were very fond of company. Mrs. King always had chickens and turkey for dinner, but at one time the company was so large that they did not leave anything for the servants; so that day, finding that all had been eaten, while mistress and master were busy with the company, Joe killed a turkey, dressed it and put it into the pot, but, as he did not cut it up, the turkey's knees stuck out of the pot, and, as he could not cover them up, he put one of his shirts over them. When Mrs. King called Joe, he answered, but did not go right away as he generally did, and when he did go his mistress said, "Joe, what was the matter with you?" he answered, "Noffing, missis." Then he went and opened the gate for the company. Soon after, Joe was back in the kitchen again, and Mrs. King went down to see what he was doing; seeing the pot on she said, "Joe, what is in that pot?" he said, "noffing, missis, but my shirt; am gwine to wash it." She did not believe him, so she took a fork and stuck it in the pot, taking out the shirt, and she found the turkey. She asked him how the turkey had got into the pot; he said he did not know but reckoned the turkey got in himself, as the fowls were very fond of going into the kitchen. So Joe was whipped because he allowed the turkey to get into the pot.

THE CUSTOM OF CHRISTMAS.

Both masters and slaves regarded Christmas as a great day. When the slaveholders had made a large crop they were pleased, and gave the slaves from five to six days, which were much enjoyed by the negroes, especially by those who could dance. Christmas morning was held sacred both by master and slaves, but in the afternoon, or in a part of the next day, the slaves were required to devote themselves to the pleasure of their masters. Some of the masters would buy presents for the slaves, such as hats and tobacco for the men, handkerchiefs and little things for the women; these things were given after they had been pleased with them; after either dancing or something for their amusement.

When the slaves came up to their masters and mistresses, the latter would welcome them, the men would take off their hats and bow and the women would make a low courtesy. There would be two or three large pails filled with sweetened water, with a gallon or two of whiskey in each; this was dealt out to them until they were partly drunk; while this was going on, those who could talk very well would give tokens of well wishing to their master and mistress, and some who were born in Africa, would sing some of their songs, or tell different stories of the customs in Africa. After this they would spend half a day in dancing in some large cotton house or on a scaffold, the master providing fiddlers who came from other plantations if there were none on the place, and who received from fifteen to twenty dollars on these occasions.

A great many of the strict members of the church who did not dance would be forced to do it to please their masters; the favorite tunes were "The Fisher's Hornpipe," "The Devil's Dream," and "Black-eyed Susan." No one can describe the intense emotion in the negro's soul on those occasions when they were trying to please their masters and mistresses.

After the dancing was over we had our presents, master giving to the men, and mistress to the women; then the slaves would go to their quarters and continue to dance the rest of the five or six days, and would sometimes dance until eight o'clock Sunday morning. The cabins were mostly made of logs, and there were large cracks in them so that a person could see the light in them for miles in the night, and of course the sun's rays would shine through them in the daytime, so on Sunday morning when they were dancing and did not want to stop you would see them filling up the cracks with old rags. The idea was that it would not be Sunday inside if they kept the sun out, and thus they would not desecrate the Sabbath; and these things continued until the freedom of the slaves.

Perhaps my readers would like to know if most of the negroes were inclined to violate the Sabbath. They were; as the masters would make them do unnecessary work, they got into the habit of disregarding the day as one for rest, and did many things Sunday that would not be allowed in the North. At that time, if you should go through the South on those large cotton and rice plantations, while you would find some dancing on Sunday, others would be in the woods and fields hunting rabbits and other game, and some would be killing pigs belonging to their masters or neighbors. I remember when a small boy I went into the woods one Sunday morning with one of my fellow negroes whose name was Munson, but we called him Pash, and we killed one of master's pigs, hid it under the leaves until night, then took it home and dressed it. That was the only time I killed a pig, but I knew of thousands of cases like this in the time of slavery. But thank God, the year of Jubilee has come, and the negroes can return from dancing, from hunting, and from the master's pig pens on Sundays and become observers of the Sabbath, of good moral habits and men of equal rights before the law.

PUNISHMENTS INFLICTED ON DIFFERENT ONES.

One of my fellow negroes, who belonged to Col. M. R. Singleton, visited the plantation of the Col.'s sister; the overseer of that plantation had forbidden strangers to go there, but this man, whose name was Harry, would go. The overseer heard of him but could not catch him, but the overseer of master's place sent him to Mr. Jackson (the overseer of master's sister's place). Mr. Jackson tied him and hit him three hundred lashes and then said to him, "Harry, if you were not such a good nigger I should have given you a first class whipping, but as you are a good fellow, and I like you so well, I thought I would give you a light flogging now; you must be a good nigger and behave yourself, for if I ever have to take hold of you again, I shall give you a good whipping." When Mr. Jackson had loosed him from where he had tied him, Harry was so exhausted that he fell down, so Mr. Jackson sent him home in a cart, and he had to stay at home from work a month or two, and was never the same man again.

THE PUNISHMENT AND SALE OF MONDAY.

There was a man who belonged to master by the name of Monday, who was a good field hand; in summer the tasks generally performed by the slaves were more than they could do, and in consequence they were severely whipped, but Monday would not wait to be whipped, but would run away before the overseer or driver could get to him. Sometimes master would hire a white man who did nothing else but hunt runaway slaves for a living; this man would take from fifteen to twenty hounds with him to hunt Monday, but often he would be out three or four months; when he was caught and brought home, he was put in prison and was whipped every day for a week or two, but just as soon as he could he would run away again.

At one time when he had been brought home, one of his arms was tied and he was put in care of a keeper who made him work with the other slaves, days, and put him in confinement nights, but for all this he got away from his keeper and went into the woods again. The last time he ran away two white men were hired to hunt him; they had about twenty-five blood hounds, but this time Monday fell in with another slave who had run away from his master and had been in the woods seven years, and they together were able to kill a greater portion of the hounds. Finally the white men caught his companion, but did not catch Monday, though they chased him two or three days longer, but he came home himself; they did not whip him and he went to work in the field. Things went on very nicely with him for two or three weeks, until one day a white man was seen riding through the fields with the overseer; of course the slaves did not mistrust his object, as white men often visited master's plantation, but that night, when all the slaves were sleeping, the man that was seen in the daytime went to the door of Monday's cabin and called him out of his bed, and when he had come to his door, the stranger, whom he had never seen before that day, handcuffed him and said, "You now belong to me." Most of the slaves found it out, as Monday was put in a cart and carried through the streets of the negro quarters, and there was quite an excitement, but Monday was never heard from again.

THE STORY OF JAMES HAY.

There was a slave named James Hay, who belonged to a neighbor of master's; he was punished a great many times because he could not get his task done. The other slaves pitied him because he seemed unable to perform his task. One evening he got a severe whipping; the next morning as the slaves were having their tasks assigned them, an old lady by the name of Aunt Patience went by, and said, "Never mind, Jim, my son, the Lord will help you with your task today;" he answered, "Yes, ma'am." He began his work very faithfully and continued until it was half done, then he lay down under a tree; the others, not understanding his motive, thought he was tired and was taking a rest, but he did not return to his task until the overseer called him and asked him why he did not have his work nearer done. He said, "Aunt Patience told me this morning that the Lord would help me today, and I thought as I did half of the task, the Lord might have finished the other half if he intended to help me at all." The overseer said, "You see that the Lord did not come to help you and we shall not wait for him, but we will help you;" so Jim got a severe punishment. Sometime after this, Jim Hay was called upon by some professors of religion; they asked him if he was not tired of serving the devil, and told him that the Lord was good and had helped many of his people, and would help all who asked him and then take them home to heaven. Jim said that if the Lord would not do half an acre of his task for him when he depended on him, he did not think he could trust him, and Jim never became a Christian to my knowledge.

THE STORY OF MR. USOM AND JACK.

One Sunday when the boys were at the overseer's, Mr. Usom's house, as we generally were, he said to one, "Jack, don't you think that hell is a very hot place, if it is as they describe it?" Jack said, "Yes, massa." Mr. Usom said, "Well, how do you think it will be with poor fellows that have to go there?" "Well, Massa Bob, I will tell you what I tinks about it, I tinks us niggers need not trouble usselves about hell, as the white folks." "How is that, Jack?" Jack answered, "Because us niggers have to work out in the hot sun, and if we go to hell it would not be so bad for us because us used to heat, but it will be bad for white folks because they is not used to hot weather."

THE STORY OF JAMES SWINE AND HIS DEATH.

There was a negro who belonged to one Mr. Clarkson; he was called Jim Swine; his right name was James, but he was called Jim Swine because he loved hog meat and would often steal hogs from his master or from the neighbors; he was a very able-bodied man, weighing about two hundred and twenty-five pounds, and a very good field hand. Of course it is generally known that a great many of the slaves were poorly fed, so it was natural that they should take anything they could to sustain life. As his master had only a few hogs, he stole many from the neighbors and was punished a great many times for it.

Sometimes he was punished when a hog was missing, even though they did not find the meat with him. Jim was not in the habit of running away much, but if they whipped him when he had not stolen the hog they accused him of taking, he would go away into the woods and stay until he got ready to come home. He was so strong that they were afraid of him; three or four men would not attack him when in the woods. The last time Jim stole hogs he was caught in the act of taking one from my master, Col. Singleton. They tied him, and Mr. Clarkson's overseer was sent for, who was his own son, Thomas Clarkson. Jim was taken home, whipped, and a cured middling of a hog was tied around his neck; he was then made to work along with the other slaves in the day and was put in prison in the night for two weeks. One morning when the overseer went to his place of confinement to take him into the field, he found him dead, with a large piece of meat hanging to his neck. The news of his death soon went abroad, also the cause of it, and when old Mr. Clarkson found it out he was very angry at his son Thomas, and his punishment was, that he was driven from his plantation with orders never to return, and that he should not have any of his property. This seemed to grieve Thomas very much, and he made several attempts to regain his father's affections, but failed. Finally, one night, Thomas made an outcry that he had found a pearl of great price, that the Lord had pardoned his sins, and that he was at peace with all mankind. When his father heard of this, he sent for him to come home, and he gave him quite a sum of money and willed him the portion of property that he had said he should keep from him. But poor Jim was not there to forgive him.

A MAN MISTAKEN FOR A HOG.

Two negroes went to steal hogs from their masters. The swine were under a barn, as in the South barns were made high enough for hogs to stand under. The man who went under the barn said to the other, you must strike the hog that goes the slowest; then he went under the barn on his knees to drive them out while the other stood with his club ready to strike, but they ran out so fast he could not hit them, except the last as he thought, which came just slow enough, and he struck. While the supposed hog was kicking, he jumped upon it to stab it with his knife but found it was his companion.

CUSTOM OF WITCHES AMONG SLAVES.

The witches among slaves were supposed to have been persons who worked with them every day, and were called old hags or jack lanterns. Those, both men and women, who, when they had grown old looked old, were supposed to be witches. Sometimes, after eating supper, the negroes would gather in each other's cabins which looked over the large openings on the plantation, and when they would see a light at a great distance and see it open and shut, they would say, "There is an old hag," and if it came from a direction in which those lived whom they called witches, one would say, "Dat looks like old Aunt Susan;" another would say, "No, dat look like man hag;" still another, "I tink dat look like old Uncle Renty."

When the light had disappeared they said that the witch had got into the plantation and changed itself into a person and had gone about on the place talking with the people like others until those whom it wanted to bewitch went to bed, then it would change itself to a witch again. They claimed that the witches rode human beings like horses, and that the spittle that ran on the side of the cheek when one slept, was the bridle that the witch rode with. Sometimes a baby would be smothered by its mother, and they would charge it to a witch. If they went out hunting at night and were lost, it was believed that a witch had led them off, especially if they fell into a pond or creek. I was very much troubled with witches when a little boy and am now sometimes, but it is only when I eat a hearty supper and immediately go to bed. It was said by some of the slaves that the witches would sometimes go into the rooms of the cabins and hide themselves until the family went to bed, and therefore when any one claimed that he had gone into the apartment before bed time and thought he had seen a witch, if he had an old Bible in the cabin, that would be taken into the room, and the person who carried the Bible would say as he went in, "In de name of de Fader and of de Son and de Holy Gos wat you want?" Then the Bible would be put in the corner where the person thought he had seen the witch, as it was generally believed that if this were done the witch could not stay. When they could not get the Bible they used red pepper and salt pounded together and scattered in the room, but in this case they generally felt the effects of it more than the witch, for when they went to bed it made them cough all night. When I was a little boy my mother sent me into the cabin room for something, and as I got in I saw something black and white, but did not stop to see what it was, and running out said there was a witch in the room. But father, having been born in Africa, did not believe in such things, so he called me a fool and whipped me and the witch got scared and ran out the door. It turned out to be our own black and white cat that we children played with every day. Although it proved to be the cat, and father did not believe in witches, still I held the idea that there were such things, for I thought the majority of the people believed it, and that they ought to know more than could one man. Sometime after I was free, in travelling from Columbia to Camden, a distance of about thirty-two miles, night overtook me when about half way there; it was very dark and rainy, and as I approached a creek I saw a great number of lights of those witches opening and shutting. I did not know what to do and thought of turning back, but when I looked behind I saw some witches in the distance, so I said, "If I turn back those will meet me and I shall be in as much danger as if I go on, and I thought of what some of my fellow negroes had said about their leading men into ponds and creeks. There was a creek just ahead, so I concluded that I should be drowned that night; however, I went on, as I saw no chance of turning back. When I came near the creek one of the witches flew into my face. I jumped back and grasped it, but it proved to be one of those lightning bugs, and I thought that if all the witches were like that one, I should not be in any great danger from them.

THE DEATH OF CYRUS AND STEPNEY.

Old Col. Dick Singleton had several state places as I have mentioned. In the South, the rich men who had a great deal of money bought all the plantations they could get and obtained them very cheap. The Colonel had some ten or twenty places and had slaves settled on each of them.

He had four children, and after each had received a plantation, the rest were called state places, and these could not be sold until all the grandchildren should become of age; after they all had received places, the rest could be sold.

One of the places was called Biglake. The slaves on these places were treated more cruelly than on those where the owner lived, for the overseers had full sway.

One day the overseer at Biglake punished the slaves so that some of them fell exhausted. When he came to the two men, Cyrus and Stepney, they resisted, but were taken by force and severely punished. A few days afterwards the overseer died, and those two men were taken up and hanged on the plantation without judge or jury.

After that another overseer was hired, with orders to arm himself, and every slave who did not submit to his punishment was to be shot immediately. At times, when the overseer was angry with a man he would strike him on the head with a club and kill him instantly, and they would bury him in the field. Some would run away and come to M. R. Singleton, my master, but he would only tell them to go home and behave. Then they were handcuffed or chained and carried back to Biglake, and when we would hear from them again the greater part would have been murdered. When they were taken from master's place, they would bid us good bye and say they knew they should be killed when they got home.

Oh! who can paint the sad feeling in our minds when we saw these, our own race, chained and carried home to drink the bitter cup of death from the merciless oppressors, with no one near to say, "Spare him, God made him," or to say, "Have mercy on him, for Jesus died for him." His companions dared not groan above a whisper for fear of sharing the same fate; but thanks that the voice of the Lord was heard in the North, which said, "Go quickly to the South and let my prison-bound people go free, for I have heard their cries from cotton, corn and rice plantations, saying, how long before thou wilt come to deliver us from this chain?" and the Lord said to them, "Wait, I will send you John Brown who shall be the key to the door of your liberty, and I will harden the heart of Jefferson Davis your *devil*, that I may show him and his followers my power; then shall I send you Abraham Lincoln, mine *angel*, who shall lead you from the land of bondage to the land of liberty." Our fathers all died in "the wilderness," but thank God, the children reached "the promised land."

THE WAY THE SLAVES DETECTED THIEVES AMONG THEMSELVES.
The slaves had three ways of detecting thieves, one with a Bible, one with a sieve, and another with graveyard dust. The first way was this:—four men were selected, one of whom had a Bible with a string attached, and each man had his own part to perform. Of course this was done in the night as it was the only time they could attend to such matters as concerned themselves. These four would commence at the first cabin with every man of the family, and one who held the string attached to the Bible would say, "John or Tom," whatever the person's name was, "you are accused of stealing a chicken or a dress from Sam at such a time," then one of the other two would say, "John stole the chicken," and another would say, "John did not steal the chicken." They would continue their assertions for at least five minutes, then the man would put a stick in the loop of the string that was attached to the Bible, and holding it as still as he could, one would say, "Bible, in the name of the Father and of the Son and of the Holy Ghost, if John stole that chicken, turn," that is, if the man had stolen what he was accused of, the Bible was to turn around on the string, and that would be a proof that he did steal it. This was repeated three times before they left that cabin, and it would take those men a month sometimes when the plantation was very large, that is if they did not find the right person before they got through the whole place.

The second way they had of detecting thieves was very much like the first, only they used a sieve instead of a Bible; they stuck a pair of scissors in the sieve with a string hitched to it and a stick put through the loop of the string and the same words were used as for the Bible. Sometimes the Bible and the sieve would turn upon the names of persons whose characters were beyond suspicion. When this was the case they would either charge the mistake to the men who fixed the Bible and the sieve, or else the man who was accused by the turning of the Bible and the sieve, would say that he passed near the coop from which the fowl was stolen, then they would say, "Bro. John we see dis how dat ting work, you pass by de chicken coop de same night de hen went away."

But when the Bible or the sieve turned on the name of one whom they knew often stole, and he did not acknowledge that he had stolen the chicken of which he was accused, he would have to acknowledge his previously stolen goods or that he had thought of stealing at the time when the chicken or the dress was stolen. Then this examining committee would justify the turning of the Bible or sieve on the above statement of the accused person.

The third way of detecting thieves was taught by the fathers and mothers of the slaves. They said no matter how untrue a man might have been during his life, when he came to die he had to tell the truth and had to own everything he had ever done, and whatever dealing those alive had with anything pertaining to the dead, must be true, or they would immediately die and go to hell to burn in fire and brimstone. So in consequence of this, the graveyard dust was the truest of the three ways in detecting thieves. The dust would be taken from the grave of a person who had died last and put into a bottle with water. Then two of the men of the examining committee would use the same words as in the case of the Bible and the sieve, "John stole that chicken," "John did not steal that chicken," and after this had gone on for about five minutes, then one of the other two who attended to the Bible and the sieve would say, "John, you are accused of stealing that chicken that was taken from Sam's chicken coop at such a time." "In the name of the Father and the Son and the Holy Ghost, if you have taken Sam's chicken don't drink this water, for if you do you will die and go to hell and be burned in fire and brimstone, but if you have not you may take it and it will not hurt you." So if John had taken the chicken he would own it rather than take the water.

Sometimes those whose characters were beyond suspicion would be proven thieves when they tried the graveyard dust and water. When the right person was detected, if he had any chickens he had to give four for one, and if he had none he made it good by promising that he would do so no more. If all the men on the plantation passed through the examination and no one was found guilty, the stolen goods would be charged to strangers. Of course these customs were among the negroes for their own benefit, for they did not consider it stealing when they took anything from their master.

JOSH AND THE CORN.

A man engaged in stripping fodder put some green ears of corn in the fire to roast as the slaves generally do in fodder stripping time, although they were whipped when caught. Before the ears were roasted enough, the overseer approached, and Josh took the ears out with some live coals stuck to them and put them in his shirt bosom. In running away his clothes took fire and Josh jumped into a creek to put it out. The overseer said to him, "Josh, what are you doing there?" He answered, "It is so warm today I taught I would go in de creek to git cool off, sir." "Well, have you got cooled off, Josh?" "Oh! yes, sir, very much cooler, sir."

Josh was a very hearty eater, so that the peck of corn flour allowed the slaves for a week's ration lasted him only a half. He used to lug large sticks of wood on his shoulders from the woods, which was from a mile to a mile and a half away, to first one and then another of his fellow negroes, who gave him something to eat; and in that way he made out his week's rations.

His habit was to bring the wood at night, throw it down at the cabin door, and, as he walked in, some one of the family would say, "Well, Josh, you fetched us a piece of wood." He would burst into one of his jolly laughs and answer, "Yes." Soon after they had given him something to eat, Josh would bid them good night, but when he went, the wood disappeared too. He would throw it down at another cabin door as before, go in and get something to eat; but every time when he went away the wood would be missing until he had found enough to eat, when he would leave it at the last cabin. Those to whom Josh carried the wood accused others of stealing it, and when they asked him about it, he only laughed and said that the wood was at the door when he came out.

Josh continued the trick for quite a while. Finally one night he brought a stick of wood and threw it down at a cabin door, walked in and got something to eat as usual. But as he came in, the man of the family, to whom he carried the wood, bade him good night, and said that he had business out which would keep him so late, that Josh would be gone before he got back. While Josh was busy laughing and talking with the rest of the family the man went out, and secreted himself in the chimney corner of another cabin, and it was not long after he took his stand before Josh bade the family good night, came out whistling, and shouldered the wood, but as he started off the watchman cried out, "Is that you, Josh?" Josh threw the wood down and answered, "O no, tisn't me." Of course

Josh was so funny one couldn't get angry with him if he wanted to; but the rest of the slaves found out after that how the wood Josh brought them, was missing.

But poor Josh died at last, away from home, he was sent with some of the other negroes from Mrs. M. R. Singleton's plantation at Columbia, in the year 1864, to build fortifications as a defence, under Gen. Wade Hampton against Gen. Sherman, and while there he was taken sick and died, under the yoke of slavery, having heard of freedom but not living to enjoy it.

RUNAWAY SLAVES.

My readers, have, no doubt, already heard that there were men in the South who made it their business in the days of slavery to raise and train hounds especially to hunt slaves with. Most of the owners hired such men on condition that they were to capture and return their runaway slaves, without being bruised and torn by the dogs. The average sums paid hunters were ten, fifteen and twenty-five dollars for capturing a slave; very many times, these sums were taken from the overseer's salary, as they were more or less the cause of slaves running away.

My readers want to know whether the runaway slaves ever returned to the overseers and their masters without being caught by the hunters. Sometimes they did and sometimes they never returned. Some stayed their lifetime; others, who would have returned, fell sick and died in the woods.

My readers ask, how did the slaves at home know when their fellow negroes, the runaways, sickened or died in the woods. In general, some one on the plantation from which they ran away, or confidential friends on some other plantation, had communication with them, so that if anything happened to them the slaves at home would find out through such parties. And sometimes the masters and overseers would find out about their death, but indirectly, however, because if it was known that any one on the plantation had dealings with the runaway, he would be punished, even though the information should be gladly received by the master and overseer.

Sometimes groups of runaway slaves, of eight, ten and even twenty, belonging to different owners, got together in the woods, which made it very difficult and dangerous for slave hunters to capture those whom they were hired to hunt. In such cases sometimes these runaways killed both hunters and dogs. The thick forests in which they lived could not be searched on horseback, neither could man or dog run in them. The only chances the hunters had of catching runaway slaves were either to rout them from those thick forests or attack them when they came out in the opening to seek food.

Of course the runaways were mostly armed, and when attacked in the forests they would fight. My readers ask, how had they obtained arms and what were those arms, since slaves were not allowed to have deadly weapons? Some had large knives made by their fellow negroes who were blacksmiths, others stole guns from white men who were accustomed to lay them carelessly around when they were out hunting game. The runaways who stole the guns were kept in powder and shot by some of the other slaves at home, who bought such from poor white men who kept little country stores in the different parts of the South.

The runaway slaves generally had fathers, brothers, cousins, or confidential friends who met them at certain appointed places, and brought them such things as were needed. The most they wanted from their fellow negroes at home were salt and little corn flour; for they lived principally on beef and swine meat, taken either from their own masters or some other's stock.

My readers ask, did not some of the slaves at home betray their fellow negroes, the runaways, to the white man? I answer, they did; but often such were well spotted, and if the runaway slaves got a chance at them while in the woods would mob or kill them. On the other hand when they met those whom they could trust, instead of injuring them, they exchanged beef and swine meat with them for bread, corn flour, and salt, such as they needed in the woods.

THE RUNAWAY SLAVES IN THE HOUSE.

Instead of going into the woods, sometimes runaway slaves lived right around the overseer's and master's houses for months. A slaves named Isom, ran away from Thomas Clarkson, his master's son, who was the overseer. Mr. Clarkson was satisfied, as he said, that the unaccustomed runaway, whom he thought was in the woods could not stay from home long, but finding that he stayed longer than expected, Mr. Clarkson hired a slave hunter with his dogs to hunt him.

The hunter came early to the plantation and took breakfast with Mr. Clarkson on the day they began to hunt for the runaway slave. While sitting at breakfast, Mr. Clarkson said to the hunter, "My father brought up that boy as a house servant, and petted him so that it takes all the salt in the country to cure him. Father had too much religion to keep his negroes straight; but I don't believe in that. I think a negro ought to be overhauled every little while to keep him in his place, and that is just the reason why I took the overseership on this plantation."

The Hunter. "Well, what caused your boy to run away, Mr. Clarkson?"

Mr. Clarkson. "Well he ran away because I gave him an overhauling, to keep him in the place of a negro."

Mr. Clarkson's wife. "Well, Thomas, I told you the other day, before you did it, that I didn't see any need of your whipping Isom, because I thought he was a good boy."

Mr. Clarkson. "Yes, my dear, if South Carolina had many more such Presbyterians as you and Father Boston (he meant old Mr. Clarkson), in a short time there would be no slaves in the state; then who would you have to work for you?"

I wish to state a fact to my readers. While there were exceptions, as a general thing the Presbyterians made better masters than did any other denomination among the slave holders in the South.

Mrs. Clarkson. "Yes, Thomas, if you were such a Presbyterian as you charged Father Boston and me with being, you could have saved yourself the trouble and money which it will cost to hunt him."

Mr. Clarkson. "Well, we will not discuss the matter of religion any further." (To the hunter.) "That boy has been away now for several days since I whipped him. I thought that he would have returned home long before this time, as this is the first time he has ever run away; but I rather conclude that he got with some experienced runaways. Now do you think that you can capture him without his being hurt, or torn by your dogs?"

Mrs. Clarkson. "That is just what I am afraid will be done to that boy."

The Hunter. "O, no fear of that, madam, I shall use care in hunting him. I have but one dog which is dangerous for tearing runaway negroes; I will chain him here until I capture your boy."

The hunter blew his horn which gathered his dogs, chained the one he spoke of, then he and Mr. Clarkson started on a chase for the runaway slave, who, secreted in the house, had heard every word they had said about him.

After the hunter and Mr. Clarkson had gone, Mrs. Clarkson went to her room (as a general thing the southern mistresses hardly ever knew what went on in their dining rooms and kitchens after meal hours), and Isom, the runaway slave, sat at the same table and ate his breakfast.

After two or three days of vain search in the woods for the runaway slave, Mr. Clarkson asked some of the other negroes on the plantation, if they saw him, to tell him if he came home he would not whip him. Of course, as a general thing, when they stayed in the woods until they were captured, they were whipped but they were not when they came home themselves. One morning after several days of fruitless search in the woods for the runaway slave by the overseer and the hunter, while at breakfast, Isom came up to the door. As soon as Mr. Clarkson learned that the runaway slave was at the door he got up from his breakfast and went out.

"Well, Isom," said Mr. Clarkson. "Well, Massa Thomas," said Isom. "Where have you been?" said Mr. Clarkson. "I been in the woods, sir," answered Isom. Of course it would not have been well for him to tell Mr. Clarkson that he was hidden and fed right in the house, for it would have made it bad for the other negroes who were house servants, among whom he had a brother and sister.

Mr. Clarkson. "Isom, did you get with some other runaways?" "Yes, sir," said Isom. Of course Isom's answer was in keeping with the belief of Mr. Clarkson that he had got in with some experienced runaway in the woods. "How many were with you?" asked Mr. Clarkson. "Two," answered Isom. "What are their names, and to whom do they belong?" asked Mr. Clarkson. "I don't know, sir," said Isom. "Didn't you ask their names?" said Mr. Clarkson. "No, sir," said Isom. "Can you describe them?" asked Mr. Clarkson. "One is big, like you, and the other was little like the man who was hunting me," said Isom. "Where did you see the hunter?" asked Mr. Clarkson. "In the woods, sir," said Isom. "Isom, do you want something to eat?" asked Mr. Clarkson. "Yes, sir," said Isom. He sent him around to the kitchen and told the cook to give him something to eat.

Mrs. Clarkson thought a great deal of Isom, so while he was in the kitchen eating, she went in and had a long talk with him about how he got along since he had been away, as they supposed.

As I have said, in general, when runaway slaves came home themselves, they were not whipped, but were either handcuffed or put in stocks, and locked up for two or three days.

While Isom was eating and talking with Mrs. Clarkson, Mr. Clarkson appeared at the kitchen door with a pistol in one hand and handcuffs in the other. Mrs. Clarkson said, "What are you going to do, Thomas?" "I want Isom as soon as he is through eating," said Mr. Clarkson. "You are not going to lock him up, are you Thomas?" said Mrs. Clarkson. Mrs. Clarkson's name was Henrietta, but her pet name was Henie. Mr. Clarkson said, "Henie, I shan't hurt Isom."

Isom, who had a smooth, black, round face, full eyes, white teeth, was a very beautiful negro. When he saw the pistol and hand-cuffs in Mr. Clarkson's hands, those large eyes of his were stretched so wide, one could see the white, like great sheets in them.

Mrs. Clarkson said, "Thomas, please don't lock up Isom; he won't run away again. You won't, will you, Isom?" "No, mamma massie Henie, I won't," said Isom. "Yes, Henie," said Mr. Clarkson, "he says so, but will he not?" "Thomas," said Mrs. Clarkson, "I will take the responsibility if you do as I ask you to; I will keep Isom around the house and will assure you that he will not run away."

Mr. Clarkson wanted to lock Isom up very much, but he knew what a strong will his wife had, and how hard it would be to get her right when she had got wrong, hence he complied with her request. So Isom worked around the house for a long time. The hunter was to rest a few days, and then resume his work, but Mr. Clarkson wrote to him that his services would be no longer needed, as the runaway slave whom he was employed to hunt had returned himself. I never learned whether the hunter got paid for what he had done.

MR. BLACK, THE SLAVE HUNTER.

There was a white man in Richland County, South Carolina, named Mr. Black, who made his living by hunting runaway slaves. I knew him as well as I did one of my fellow negroes on Col. Singleton's plantation. He was of dark complexion, short stature, spare built, with long, jet black, coarse hair. He bore the description of what some would call a good man, but he was quite the reverse; he was one of the most heartless men I have ever seen.

Mr. Black was a very successful hunter, although sometimes all of his bloodhounds were killed by runaway slaves, and he barely escaped with his life. He used to ride a small bay mare in hunting, which was the only horse he owned. She was a thin, rawboned crea-ture and looked as though she could hardly walk, but knew the busi-ness about as well as her master; and in such troubles as above stated she used to carry him pretty fast out of danger. Mr. Black caught several runaway slaves belonging to Col. Singleton.

I have known him to chase runaway slaves out of the forest right through the colonel's plantation, through a crowd of other negroes, and his dogs would never mistake any among the crowd for the ones they were after. When these hound dogs chased the runaways through farms in that way, many of them were killed and buried in the cotton or corn field by some among the crowd of negroes through which they passed. In general the slaves hated bloodhounds, and would kill them any time they got a chance, but especially on such occasions as above stated, to keep them from capturing runaways.

Once eight slaves ran away from Col. Singleton's plantation, and Mr. Black, with twenty-five hound dogs, was hired to hunt them up. The dogs struck trail of the runaways late one afternoon, and chased them all that night, during which time they got scattered. Next morning three of the runaways were chased through a crowd of their fellow negroes, who were working in the cotton field. While chasing the runaways some among the crowd killed six of the dogs, including the two leading ones, and buried them in the cotton beds or rows, as we used to call them.

Mr. Black, the hunter, though a mile or more off, knew that something had happened from the irregular barking of the other dogs, and also because he did not hear the yelling of the two leading dogs. So he blew his horn, called the rest of his dogs, and gave up the chase until he had replaced his leading dogs by others, which he always had on hand at home.

Slave hunters generally had one or two among the pack of hound dogs, called trailers or leaders, which the others, fifty or more, were trained to follow. So if anything happened to the leaders while on chase, the rest would become confused, and could not follow the runaway. But if the leaders were hurt or killed after the runaways were captured, the rest would surround and guard them until the hunter reached them, as he was always a mile or more behind.

After the leading dogs had been replaced, Mr. Black resumed the chase, and caught some of the runaways, but the rest came home themselves.

The last runaway slave Mr. Black was hired to hunt belonged to Col. M. R. Singleton, and was named Dick, but instead of Dick he caught a slave belonging to a man in Sumterville county, who had been in the woods seven years. This runaway slave had another name at home, but while in the woods had assumed the name of Champion, for his success in keeping slave hunters from capturing him up to that time.

Mr. Black, the hunter, chased Dick and Champion two days and nights; on the morning before the capture of the latter they swam across the Water-ree river. After they got across they were separated; the dogs followed Champion, and ran him down that morning about eleven o'clock. Champion had a gun and pistol; as the first dog ran up and opened his mouth to take hold of him he discharged the contents of the pistol in his mouth and killed him instantly. The rest of the dogs did not take hold of him, but surrounded him and held him at bay until the hunter reached the spot.

When Mr. Black rode up within gunshot, Champion aimed at him with a loaded double barrel gun, but the caps of both barrels snapped from being wet by running through the bushes. Mr. Black had a gun and pistol, too; he attempted to shoot the negro, but William Turner, Col. Singleton's overseer, who hired Mr. Black to hunt Dick, the runaway from the colonel's plantation, would not let him do it. Mr. Black then attempted to strike Champion with the breech of his gun, but Champion kicked him down, and as he drew his knife to stab Mr. Black, Mr. Turner, the overseer, struck him on the back of his head with the butt of a loaded whip. This stunned him for a few moments, and by the time he had regained his senses they had handcuffed him.

After the negro had been handcuffed, Mr. Black wanted to abuse him, because he had killed the dog, and attempted to shoot him, but Mr. Turner, the overseer, would not let him. Champion was taken to Col. Singleton's plantation, locked up in the dungeon under the overseer's house, and his master was notified of his capture; he was a mulatto negro, and his master, who was his father, sent for him at Col. Singleton's plantation; but I never learned whether Mr. Black, the hunter, was ever paid for capturing him. Dick, the runaway negro from Col. Singleton's place, came home himself sometime after Champion, his companion, had been captured.

Mr. Black, the slave hunter, was very poor, and had a large family; he had a wife, with eight or ten helpless children, whom I knew as well as I did my fellow negroes on the colonel's plantation. But as cruel as Mr. Black was to runaway slaves, his family was almost wholly supported by negroes; I have known in some cases that they stole from their master to help this family. The negroes were so kind to Mr. Black's family that his wife turned against him for his cruelty to runaway slaves.

I have stated that some of the masters and overseers hired the hunters, on condition that they would capture and return the run-away slaves, unbruised and untorn by their dogs; while others, in a mad fit of passion, would say to them, "I want you to bring my run-away nigger home, dead or alive."

All of the slave hunters used to practice cruelty upon the run-away slaves; more especially upon those whose masters would say to hunters "bring them dead or alive." But among all the slave hunters in the part of South Carolina where the author of this work lived, Mr. Black was the most cruel.

It was rumored that many of the runaway slaves that were never heard of afterward, were captured and killed in the woods by Mr. Black, but no special clue to this could be found. Finally Mr. Black was hired to capture a runaway slave in Barnwell County, S. C. This slave was with another, who was thought well of by his master, but hated by the overseer. In the chase, the two runaways separated, and the dogs followed the second instead of the one whom Mr. Black had been hired to hunt. Mr. Black had another hunter with him by the name of Motley. The negro killed several of the dogs, and gave Messrs. Black and Motley a hard fight. After the negro had been captured, they killed him, cut him up and gave his remains to the living dogs.

The companion of the murdered slave was not caught. A few days after the chase, while wandering around in the wood in a somewhat excited state, he came to a spot where the bushes and leaves seemed to have been in a stirred-up condition, as though there had been tussling by two parties. On looking around in this disordered spot, he found pieces of clothing here and there in rags, looking just like the suit worn by his companion, who was then a victim of a most cruel death from the hands of the hunters. On closer examination, he saw spots of blood here and there upon the leaves, which awakened his suspicion; on looking a little way from this spot, he saw some leaves which looked as though they had been moved by hands and put there, and on removing the leaves, he found that the earth had been freshly dug and filled in again. Digging down in the spot, he soon discovered pieces of the person of a dead man, whom he could not identify, but was satisfied that it was the remains of his companion, from whom he had been compelled to separate a few days before. This sight frightened the runaway negro so, that he left the woods, went home to his master and told the story; but as a negro's word was not to be taken against a white man's in the days of slavery, no special notice was taken of what he had said. Still some of the white people were secretly watching Mr. Black, the slave hunter, as he had been before suspected of killing runaway slaves in the woods.

The master of the murdered negro was still ignorant of his death; he was in hopes that his slave would return. But finding that his slave did not return as expected, the master became uneasy, and offered a reward to any one who could give a clue of his negro. In the meantime, he discharged the overseer who had been the cause of his slave running away; and he also kept the overseer's salary of four hundred dollars, which was the annual pay for overseeing his plantation.

Mr. Black's house was in Richland county, and as he was the last who had hunted runaway slaves in Barnwell county before the murder, suspicion rested on him. Still no one said anything to him, but he was very closely watched by men of his own county, whose interest was not in the hatefulness of the crime committed, but rather in the reward offered by the master to any who could give information of his runaway slave.

Sometime after the case had occurred, another white man of Richland county became quite a friend to Mr. Black, the slave hunter; this apparent friendship soon led Mr. Black to tell the secret, which speedily brought him to trial. While he and his pretended friend were on a drinking spree, in the midst of the merriment,—of course the conversation was how to control negroes, as that was the principal topic or the poor white men South, in the days of slavery.

In the conversation, this friend spoke of several plans which he said, if properly carried out, "would keep a nigger in his place." After the friend had said so much to Mr. Black, the slave hunter, the latter felt that he could tell his secret without endangering himself, so he answered: "The way to show a nigger that would resist a white man, his place, is to put him among the missing. Not long since, I went to Barnwell county to hunt a runaway nigger, and my dogs struck trail of another instead of the one I wanted to capture. After quite a long chase my dogs ran him down, and before I reached him he killed several of them, and gave me a hard fight when I got to him. Motley and I were together; I shot him down, and Motley and I cut him up and gave the pieces to the remainder of my dogs; that is the way I put a nigger in his place."

After the secret had been revealed, Mr. Black's friend excused himself, and the former saw him no more until he appeared as a witness against him. The companion of the murdered negro was summoned to carry the investigating party, including the murderer, to the spot where his companion had been buried.

Mr. Black was tried and found to be guilty. After sentence had been passed, he confessed the commission of that crime, and also told that he had killed several runaway negroes previously in his own county. So Mr. Black and Motley, his companion, were both hanged in Barnwell county, S. C. The system of slavery outlived Mr. Black, the slave hunter, just six years.

MANNING BROWN AND AUNT BETTY.

A man by the name of Manning Brown was nursed by an old colored woman he called mamma Betty. She was naturally good natured and a devout Christian, and Mr. Brown gained many of her good qualities when he was under her entire control, at which time he was said to be a boy of very fine sense of feeling and quite promising. But when approaching manhood Mr. Brown fell among a class of other white men who, in the days of slavery, were unbridled in their habits. With this class of men he began to drink, and step by step in this rapid stride he soon became a confirmed drunkard. This habit so overcoated the good influence he had gained from the colored woman, that it rendered him dangerous not only to his enemies, but also to his friends.

Manning Brown was feared by most of the other white men in Richland county, S. C., and, strange to say, although he was dangerous to white men, yet he never lost the respect he had for colored people in his boyhood days. He ate, drank and slept among colored people after he was a grown man, and in many cases when other white men, who were called patrols, caught colored people away from home without tickets, and were about to whip them, Mr. Brown would ride up and say, "The first man who raises a whip at one of those negroes I will blow his brains out." Knowing that he would shoot a man as quick as he would a bird, even if ten patrols were together, when Mr. Brown made such threats, they never would attempt to whip the negroes.

Mr. Brown owned a plantation with forty slaves on it; his good treatment of them enabled him to get more work out of them than most owners got out of their slaves. His slaves thought so much of their "Massa Manning," as they used to call him, that they did everything in their power to please him. But while he was so good to colored people, he was dangerous to many of the white people and feared by them.

A man by the name of Peter Gafney fought a duel with his brother-in-law, whose name was Dr. Ray; the former, who was quite a marksman, was killed by the latter, who was considered a very poor one. This led many who were in favor of Mr. Gafney to feel that there had been foul play by Dr. Ray, the contestant. Mr. Brown, who acted as a second for Mr. Gafney in the fight, felt the loss of his old friend very deeply. A short time after this he sent a challenge to Dr. Ray, stating, "You may either meet me at a certain time, on the spot where you killed P. T. Gafney, for a duel, or I will shoot you on first sight wherever I meet you. Yours, M. Brown."

But Dr. Ray refused in the face of the threat to accept the challenge. Knowing the disposition of Mr. Brown, the people in that county were inflamed with excitement, because the doctor was liable at any moment while riding in the road to be killed. In fear of meeting Mr. Brown, the doctor gave up visiting the most of his sick patients, and almost wholly confined himself to his large plantation. At the same time Mr. Brown was closely watched by his friends to keep him from waylaying the doctor.

A short time after this threat Mr. Brown commenced to drink harder than ever, so that at times he did not know his own family. But the providence of God was slowly leading Mr. Brown through the unknown paths to a sudden change of life, as we shall soon see.

Mr. Brown's family consisted of a wife, one child, and Aunt Betty, the old colored woman who had brought him up. She was the only mother he knew, for his own mother had died when he was an infant, and her dying request had been that mamma Betty, the old woman, should bring up this boy, who was an only child; and when Mr. Brown got married he took Aunt Betty into his family and told her she need not do any work only what she chose to do, and that he would take care of her the balance of her days. And Mrs. Brown regarded Aunt Betty more as a mother-in-law than as a negress servant. Sometimes when Mr. Brown would not listen to his wife, he would to his mamma Betty, when he was sober enough to know her. One afternoon, while Mr. Brown was in one of those drunken fits, he went into his bedroom and lay down across the bed, talking to himself. His wife went in to speak to him, but as she entered he jumped up and got his loaded double barrelled gun and threatened to shoot her. Frightened at this, she ran out of the room and screamed saying, "O, my God, mamma Betty, please go in and speak to your Massa Manning, for he threatened to shoot me."

With that old familiar confidence in one who had often listened to her advice, Aunt Betty went into the house and to the room where she found Mr. Brown lying across the bed, with the gun by his side. On entering the room, as she was advancing toward the bed, she said, "Massa Manning, what is the matter with you? You naughty boy, what is the matter?" On saying these words, before she had reached the bed, Mr. Brown rose, with the gun in hand, and discharged the contents of both barrels at the old woman; she dropped instantly to the floor. Mr. Brown lay across the bed as before, with the gun by his side, talking to himself, and soon dropped to sleep. Mrs. Brown fainted away several times under the excitement.

Aunt Betty lived about an hour. Soon after she had been shot she wanted to see Mr. Brown, but when told that she could not, she said, "O, my Lord, I wanted to see my child before I die, and I know that he would want to see his mamma Betty, too, before she leaves him." During the time she lived she prayed for Mr. Brown, and requested that he would change his course of life, become a Christian, and meet her in heaven. After singing one of her familiar hymns, Aunt Betty said to some one who stood by her bedside, "I want you to tell Massa Manning that he must not feel bad for what he did to me, because I know that if he was in his right mind he would not hurt me any more than he would himself. Tell him that I have prayed to the Lord for him that he may be a good boy, and I want him to promise that he will be a Christian and meet me in heaven." With these words Aunt Betty became speechless, dying a few moments afterwards. The doctor was sent for, but had to come from such a distance that she died before he reached there.

When Mr. Brown awoke from his drunken state in the night, and learned the sad news of Aunt Betty's death, of which he had been the cause, he clasped his hands and cried out, "What! is it possible that my mamma Betty, the only mother I ever knew, was killed by my hands?" He ran into the room where the corpse was and clasped the remains of the old negress in his arms and cried, "Mamma Betty, mamma Betty, please speak to me as you used to." But that voice was hushed in death.

The doctor, overseer and others tried to quiet him, but they could not. That night Mr. Brown took the train to Columbia, the capital of South Carolina, and gave himself up to the law next day. He was told that it was all right; that the old negress was his slave. But Mr. Brown was dissatisfied; he came back home and invited all the white neighbors and slaves to Aunt Betty's funeral, in which he and his family took part. After the excitement was over the message of Aunt Betty was delivered to Mr. Brown; he was told that her last request had been that he would meet her in heaven. He answered, "I will." Mr. Brown then and there took an oath that he would drink no more strong drinks. He then disposed of his slaves, but how I did not learn. Soon after this he was converted and became one of the ablest preachers in Richland county, S. C. Mr. Brown's conversion freed Dr. Ray from his threat. The doctor was so glad of this that he paid quite a large sum towards Mr. Brown's salary for preaching.

CHAPTER III—
MY EXPERIENCE IN THE
CIVIL WAR.

My knowledge of the Civil War, extends from the time when the first gun was fired on Fort Sumter in April, 1861, to the close of the War.

While the slaves were not pressed into the Confederate service as soldiers, yet they were used in all the slave-holding states at war points, not only to build fortifications, but also to work on vessels used in the war.

The slaves were gathered in each state, anywhere from 6000 to 8000 or more, from different plantations, carried to some centre and sent to various war points in the state.

It would be impossible to describe the intense excitement which prevailed among the Confederates in their united efforts to raise troops to meet the Union forces. They were loud in their expressions of the certainty of victory.

Many of the poor white men were encouraged by the promise of from three to five negroes to each man who would serve in the Confederate service, when the Confederate government should have gained the victory.

On the other hand, the negroes were threatened with an increase of the galling yoke of slavery. These threats were made with significant expressions, and the strongest assumption that the negro was the direct cause of the war.

HOW SLAVES WERE GATHERED AND CARRIED TO WAR POINTS.

No sooner had the war commenced in the spring of 1861, than the slaves were gathered from the various plantations, and shipped by freight cars, or boats, to some centre, and apportioned out and sent to work at different war points. I do not know just how many slaves the Confederate Government required each master to furnish for its service, but I know that 15 of the 465 slaves on my master's, Col. M. R. Singleton's, plantation, were sent to work on fortifications each year during the war.

The war had been going on two years before my turn came. In the summer of 1863 with thousands of other negroes, gathered from the various parts of the state, I was freighted to the city of Charleston, South Carolina, and the group in which my lot fell was sent to Sullivan's Island. We were taken on a boat from the city of Charleston, and landed in a little village, situated nearly opposite Fort Sumter, on this island. Leaving behind us Fort Moultrie, Fort Beauregard, and several small batteries, we marched down the white sandy beach of the island, below Fort Marshall, to the very extreme point, where a little inlet of water divides Sullivan's from Long Island, and here we were quartered under Capt. Charles Haskell.

From this point on the island, turning our faces northward, with Morris Island northwest of us, and looking directly north out into the channel, we saw a number of Union gun boats, like a flock of black sheep feeding on a plain of grass; while the men pacing their decks looked like faithful shepherds watching the flock. While we negroes remained upon Sullivan's Island, we watched every movement of the Union fleet, with hearts of joy to think that they were a part of the means by which the liberty of four and one-half millions of slaves was to be effected in accordance with the emancipation proclamation made the January preceding. We kept such close watch upon them that some one among us, whether it was night or day, would be sure to see the discharge of a shot from the gun boat before the sound of the report was heard. During that summer there was no engagement between the Union fleet and the Confederates at that point in South Carolina. The Union gun boats, however, fired occasional shots over us, six miles, into the city of Charleston. They also fired a few shells into a marsh between Sullivan's Island and Mount Pleasant, but with no damage to us.

WHAT WORK THE NEGROES DID ON THE ISLAND.

After we had reached the island, our company was divided. One

207

part was quartered at one end of the Island, around Fort Moultrie, and we were quartered at the other end, at Fort Marshall. Our work was to repair forts, build batteries, mount guns, and arrange them. While the men were engaged at such work, the boys of my age, namely, thirteen, and some older, waited on officers and carried water for the men at work, and in general acted as messengers between different points on the island.

ENGAGEMENT ON LONG ISLAND.

Though there was no fighting on Sullivan's Island during my stay there, Confederate soldiers at times crossed the inlet from Sullivan's to Long Island, in the night and engaged in skirmishes with Union soldiers, who had entered the upper end of that island and camped there. Whether these Confederate scouts were ever successful in routing the Union forces on the island or not I have never learned, but I know that they were several times repulsed with considerable loss.

NEGROES ESCAPE.

The way the Confederates came to the knowledge that Union soldiers were on Long Island was that the group of negroes who preceded us on Sullivan's Island had found out that Union soldiers were camping on the upper end of Long Island. So one night quite a number of them escaped by swimming across the inlet that divides Sullivan's Island and Long Island, and succeeded in reaching the Union line.

The next day it was discovered that they had swum across the inlet, and the following night they were pursued by a number of Confederate scouts who crossed in a flat boat. Instead of the capture of the negroes, who would have been victims of the most cruel death, the Confederate scouts were met by soldiers from the Union line, and after a hot engagement they were repulsed, as they usually were.

BUILDING A BATTERY ON LONG ISLAND.

Finally the Confederates took a large number of the group of which I was a member from Sullivan's to the south shore of Long Island and there built a battery, and mounted several small field guns upon it. As they were afraid of being discovered in the daytime we were obliged to work on the battery nights and were taken back to Sullivan's in the morning, until the work was complete.

We were guarded by Confederate soldiers while building the battery, as, without a guard it would have been easy for any of us to have reached the Union line on the north end of Long Island. Sullivan's Island was about five miles long.

A NEGRO SERVANT MURDERED.

One of the most heartless deeds committed while I was on Sullivan's Island, was that of the murder of a negro boy by his master, a Confederate officer to whom the boy had been a body servant. What the rank of this officer was I am not sure, but I think he was a Major, and that he was from the state of Georgia. It was a common thing for southern men to carry dirks, especially during the war. This officer had one, and for something the boy displeased him in, he drew the knife and made a fatal stab between the boy's collar bone and left shoulder. As the victim fell at the brutal master's feet, we negroes who had witnessed the fiendish and cowardly act upon a helpless member of our race, expected an immediate interference from the hand of justice in some form or other. But we looked and waited in vain, for the horrible deed did not seem to have changed the manner of those in authority in the least, but they rather treated it as coolly as though nothing had happened. Finding that the Confederates failed to lay the hand of justice upon the officer, we, with our vague ideas of moral justice, and with our extreme confidence that God would somehow do more for the oppressed negroes than he would ordinarily for any other people, anxiously waited a short time for some token of Divine vengeance, but as we found that no such token as we desired, in the heat of our passion, came, we finally concluded to wait God's way and time, as to how, and when this, as every other wrong act, should be visited with his unfailing justice.

But aside from this case we fared better on these fortifications than we had at home on the plantations. This was the case at least with those of us who were on Sullivan's Island. Our work in general on the fortifications was not hard, we had a great deal of spare time, and although we knew that our work in the Confederate service was against our liberty, yet we were delighted to be in military service.

We felt an exalted pride that, having spent a little time at these war points, we had gained some knowledge which would put us beyond our fellow negroes at home on the plantations, while they would increase our pride by crediting us with far more knowledge than it was possible for us to have gained.

Our daily rations from the Commissary was a quart of rice or hard-tack, and a half pound of salt pork or corn-beef.

The change from the cabins and from the labor on the old plantations so filled our cup of joy that we were sorry when the two months of our stay on the island was ended.

At the end of about two months, I, with the rest of my fellow negroes of that groups, was sent back to the plantation again, while others took our places.

MY EXPERIENCE IN FORT SUMTER.

In the summer of 1864, when I was in my fourteenth year, another call was made for negro laborers for the Confederate government, and fifteen from our plantation, including myself, with thousands from other plantations, were sent down to Charleston again.

There the negroes were apportioned in groups to be sent to the different fortifications. My lot fell among the group of three hundred and sixty, who were assigned to Fort Sumter. I shall never forget with what care they had to move in carrying us in a steamer from the government wharf in Charleston to John's island wharf, on account of the network of torpedo mines in Charleston Harbor.

From John's island wharf they carried us in rowboats to Fort Sumter, and, as those boats could not carry many, it took all night to convey us with other freightage to Fort Sumter.

The steamer which carried us from Charleston to John's island wharf had to run at night. Indeed every move the Confederates made about there near the close of the war had to be made at night because the Yankees on gunboats outside the channel and those on Morris island kept so close a watch it was very dangerous to convey us from John's island wharf to Fort Sumter because the oars dipping into the salt water at night made sparks like fire, and thus the Yankees on Morris island were able to see us. Indeed their shots oftentimes took effect.

Many of the negroes were killed. Of the fifteen from our plantation, one boy of about my age was struck by a parrot shell while climbing from the boat into the fort. We were told of the perils we were to meet, both before and after we reached our destination. For one of the most disheartening things was the sad report of the survivors of those whose places we were to fill. As the rowboats left them on John's island wharf and as we were about to embark they told us of the great danger to which we would be exposed,—of the liability of some of us being killed before we reached the fort, which proved true, and of how fast their comrades were killed in Fort Sumter. A number, it was said, died from fright before reaching Sumter.

THE OFFICERS AND QUARTERS.

The officers who were then in command of the fort were Capt. J. C. Mitchell and Major John Johnson. The name of the overseer in charge of the negroes in the fort was Deburgh,—whether that was his right name I can not say.

Deburgh was a foreigner by birth. He was one of the most cruel men I ever knew. As he and his atrocious deeds will come up later in this history, I will say no more of him here.

CONDITION OF THE FORT.

Fort Sumter, which previous to this, had not only been silenced by the Union forces, but also partly demolished, had but one gun mounted on it, on the west side. That cannon we used to call the "Sundown Gun," because it was fired every evening as the sun went down,—as well as at sunrise. On this west side the Confederate officers and soldiers were sheltered in the bomb-proof safe during bombardment. On the east side of the fort, facing Morris island, opposite Fort Wagner, there was another apartment called the "Rat-hole" in which we negroes were quartered.

WHAT THE NEGROES DID IN FORT SUMTER.

Fort Sumter had been so badly damaged by the Union forces in 1863, that unless something had been done upon the top, the continued bombardment which it suffered up to the close of the war, would have rendered it uninhabitable.

The fort was being fired upon every five minutes with mortar and parrot shells by the Yankees from Morris Island.

The principal work of the negroes was to secure the top and other parts against the damage from the Union guns.

Large timbers were put on the rampart of the fort, and boards laid on them, then baskets, without bottoms, about two feet wide, and four feet high, were put close together on the rampart, and filled with sand by the negroes.

The work could only be done at night, because, besides the bombardment from Fort Wagner which was about a mile or little less from us, there were also sharp-shooters there who picked men off whenever they showed their heads on the rampart.

The mortar and parrot shells rained alternately upon Fort Sumter every five minutes, day and night, but the sharp-shooters could only fire by day-light.

The negroes were principally exposed to the bombardment. The only time the few Confederate soldiers were exposed to danger was while they were putting the Chevaldefrise on the parapet at night.

The "Chevaldefrise" is a piece of timber with wooden spikes pointed with iron, and used for defence on fortifications.

In the late war between the Spaniards and the Americans, the former used barbed wire for the same purpose.

If my readers could have been in Fort Sumter in the summer of 1964 they would have heard the sentinel cry, every five minutes, "Look out! Mortar!" Then they would have seen the negroes running about in the fort yard in a confused state, seeking places of safety from the missiles sure to bring death to one or more of them. Another five minutes, and again the cry of the sentinel, "Look out," means a parrot shell, which is far more deadly than is the mortar because it comes so quickly that one has no chance to seek a place of safety.

The next moment the survivors of us, expecting that it would be our turn next, would be picking up, here and there, parts of the severed bodies of our fellow negroes; many of those bodies so mutilated as not to be recognizable.

DEBURGH, THE OVERSEER.

Deburgh, the overseer, of whom I have spoken, was a small man, of light complexion, and very light hair.

If my readers could have been in Fort Sumter in July, 1864, they would have seen Deburgh with a small bar of iron or a piece of shell in his hand, forcing the surviving portion of the negroes back into line and adding to these, other negroes kept in the Rat-hole as reserves to fill the places of those who were killed and wounded.

They would also have heard him swearing at the top of his voice, while forcing the negroes to rearrange themselves in line from the base of the fort to the top.

This arrangement of the negroes, enabled them to sling to each other the bags of sand which was put in the baskets on the top of the fort. My readers ask, what was the sand put on the fort for? It was to smother the fuses of such shells as reached the ramparts before bursting.

After the bombardment of Fort Sumter in 1863, by the Union forces, its top of fourteen or sixteen feet in thickness, built of New Hampshire granite, was left bare. From that time all through 1864, the shells were so aimed as to burst right over the fort; and it was pieces of these shells which flew in every direction that were so destructive.

The fuses of many of these shells fired on Fort Sumter did not burn in time to cause the shells to burst before falling. Now as the shells fell on the rampart of the fort instead of falling and bursting on the stone, they buried themselves harmlessly in the sand, which put out the fuse and also kept them from bursting.

But while the destruction of life was lessened by the sand, it was fully made up by the hand of that brute, the overseer. God only knows how many negroes he killed in Fort Sumter under the shadow of night. Every one he reached, while forcing the slaves back into working position after they had been scattered by the shells, he would strike on the head with the piece of iron he carried in his hand, and, as his victim fell, would cry out to some other negro, "Put that fellow in his box," meaning his coffin.

Whether the superior officers in Fort Sumter knew that Deburgh was killing the negroes off almost as fast as the shells from Fort Wagner, or whether they did not know, and did not care, I never have learned. But I have every reason to believe that one of them at least, namely, Major John Johnson, would not have allowed such a wholesale slaughter, had he known. On the other hand I believe that Capt. J. C. Mitchell was not only mean enough to have allowed it, but that he was fully as heartless himself.

Whatever became of Deburgh, whether he was killed in Fort Sumter or not, I never knew.

OUR SUPERIOR OFFICERS.

The two officers in command of Fort Sumter in July of 1864 were Capt. J. C. Mitchell, and Major John Johnson.

Major Johnson was as kind, gentle, and humane to the negroes as could have been expected.

On the other hand, the actions of Capt. Mitchell were harsh and very cruel. He had a bitter hatred toward the Yankees, and during the rain of shells on Fort Sumter, he sought every opportunity to expose the negroes to as much danger as he dared.

I remember that one night Capt. Mitchell ordered us outside

of Fort Sumter to a projection of the stonebed upon which the Fort was built, right in front of Fort Wagner. At that place we were in far greater danger from the deadly missiles of the Union forces than we were exposed to on the inside of Sumter, and I could see no other reasons for his ordering us outside of the fort that night than that we might be killed off faster.

It seems that during the incessant firing on Fort Sumter the officers held a consultation as to whether it was not best to evacuate the fort. It was at this time that it was rumored,—a rumor that we had every reason to believe,—that Capt. Mitchell plotted to lock us negroes up in our quarters in Sumter, known as the Rat-hole; and put powder to it and arrange it so that both the negroes and the Yankees should be blown up, when the latter should have taken possession after the evacuation of the fort by the Confederates.

But we learned that Major John Johnson, who has since become an Episcopal minister, in Charleston, S. C., wholly refused to agree with Capt. Mitchell in such a barbarous and cowardly act, and, as though Providence were watching over the innocent and oppressed negroes, and over the Yankees as well, because they were fighting in a righteous cause, Capt. Mitchell's career and further chances of carrying out his cruel intentions were cut short. He was mortally wounded by the sharp-shooters of Fort Wagner, on the 14th of July, 1864, and died four hours afterwards.

OUR RATIONS IN SUMTER.

The working forces of negroes in Sumter with the exception of the boys who carried messages to the different parts of the fort day and night, were locked up days, and turned out nights, to work. We drew our rations of hard-tack and salt pork twice a day; mornings when we ceased work and turned in for the day, and again, between three and four o'clock in the afternoon, so as to have supper eaten in time to go to work at dark.

We often ate our salt pork raw with the hard-tack, as there were no special means of cooking in the negroes' apartment. We were not only in danger, while at work, from the continued rain of shells, but oftentimes when we were put in line to draw our rations some of us were killed or wounded.

I cannot say how they got fresh water in Fort Sumter, as I do not remember seeing any brought there in boats, neither did I notice any conveniences there for the catching of rain water.

The water we negroes used was kept in large hogsheads with

coal tar in them; I do not know what the tar was put in the water for unless it was for our health. The "rat-hole" into which we were locked, was like a sweat box; it was so hot and close, that, although we were exposed to death by shells when we were turned out to work, we were glad to get into the fresh air.

We had little cups in which they used to give us whiskey mornings when we went in, and again when we were going out to work at night.

I don't know how many of the forty survivors of the three hundred and sixty of us who were carried into the Fort in the summer of 1864 besides myself are still alive. But if there are any with the keen tenderness of a negro, they cannot help joining me in an undying sense of gratitude to Major John Johnson, not only for his kind and gentle dealings with us which meant so much to a negro in the days of slavery, but also for his humane protection, which saved us from some of the danger from shells to which we were exposed in Sumter.

A short time after Capt. J. C. Mitchell had been killed, Major Johnson was dangerously wounded in the head by a piece of shell.

MY LAST NIGHT IN FORT SUMTER AND
THE GLORIOUS END OF THE WAR.

During the time we spent in Fort Sumter we had not seen a clear day or night. In harmony with the continual danger by which we were surrounded, the very atmosphere wore the pall of death; for it was always rainy and cloudy. The mutilated bodies of the negroes, mingled with the black mud and water in the fort yard, added to the awfulness of the scene. Pieces of bombshells and other pieces of iron, and also large southern pine timbers were scattered all over the yard of the fort. There was also a little lime house in the middle of the yard, into which we were warned not to go when seeking places of safety from the deadly missiles at the cry of the sentinel.

The orders were that we should get as near the centre of the fort yard as possible and lie down. The reason for this was that the shells which were fired upon Sumter were so measured that they would burst in the air, and the pieces would generally fly toward the sides of the fort. But the orders were not strictly carried out, because, at the warning cries of the sentinel, we became confused. That night, at the cry of the sentinel, I ran and lay down on one of the large southern pine timbers, and several of my fellow negroes followed and piled in upon me. Their weight was so heavy that I cried out as for life. The sense of that crush I feel at certain times even now.

At the next report of a shell I ran toward the lime house, but some one tripped me up, and, by the time I had got to my feet again, twelve or thirteen others were crowded into it. Another negro and I reached the doorway, but we were not more than there before a mortar shell came crashing down upon the little lime house, and all within were so mangled that their bodies were not recognizable.

Only we two were saved. My companion had one of his legs broken, and a piece of shell had wounded me over my right eye and cut open my under lip. At the moment I was wounded I was not unconscious, but I did not know what had hurt me. I became almost blind from the effect of my wounds, but not directly after I was wounded, and I felt no pain for a day or so. With other wounded I was taken to the bombproof in the fort. I shall never forget this first and last visit to the hospital department. To witness the rough handling of the wounded patients, to see them thrown on a table as one would a piece of beef, and to see the doctor use his knife and saw, cutting off a leg, or arm, and sometimes both, with as much indifference as if he were simply cutting up beef, and to hear the doctor say, of almost every other one of these victims, after a leg or an arm was amputated, "Put that fellow in his box," meaning his coffin, was an awful experience. After the surgeon had asked to whom I belonged, he dressed my wounds.

My readers will remember that I stated that no big boat could run to Fort Sumter at that time, on account of the bombardment. We had to be conveyed back to John's Island wharf in rowboats, which was the nearest distance a steamer could go to Fort Sumter.

As one of those rowboats was pushed out to take the dead and wounded from the fort, and as the former were put into the boat, which was generally done before they put in the latter, fortunately, just before the wounded were put in, a Parrott shell was fired into it from Fort Wagner by the Union forces, which sank both the boat and the coffins, with their remains.

My readers would ask how the Confederates disposed of the negroes who were killed in Fort Sumter. Those who were not too badly mutilated were sent over to the city of Charleston and were buried in a place which was set apart to bury the negroes. But others, who were so badly cut up by shells, were put into boxes, with pieces of iron in them, and carried out a little away from Sumter and thrown overboard.

I was then taken to John's Island wharf, and from there to the city of Charleston in a steamer, and carried to Doctor Rag's hospital, where I stopped until September. Then I was sent back home to my master's plantation. Quoting the exact words of Major John Johnson, a Confederate officer under whom I was a part of the time at the above-named place, I would say: "July 7th, Fort Sumter's third great bombardment, lasting sixty days and nights, with a total of 14,666 rounds fired at the fort, with eighty-one casualties."

WHAT TOOK PLACE AFTER.

I said that after I got well enough to travel I was sent back home to my master's plantation, about a hundred miles from the city of Charleston, in central South Carolina. This was in September of 1864, and I, with the rest of my fellow-negroes on this extensive plantation, and with other slaves all over the South, were held in suspense waiting the final outcome of the emancipation proclamation, issued January, 1963, but as the war continued, it had not taken effect until the spring of 1865.

Here I had less work than before the war, for the nearer the war approached its close the less the slaves had to do, as the masters were at the end of their wits what to do. In the latter part of 1864 Gen. Sherman, with his army of a hundred thousand men and almost as many stragglers, covered the space of about sixty miles in width while marching from Georgia through South Carolina. The army camped around Columbia, the capital of South Carolina, for a short time. Early in the spring of 1865 the commissary building first took fire, which soon spread to such extent that the whole city of Columbia was consumed; just a few houses on the suburbs were left.

The commissary building was set on fire by one of the two parties, but it was never fully settled whether it was done by Gen. Sherman's men or by the Confederates, who might have, as surmised by some, as they had to evacuate the city, set it on fire to keep Gen. Sherman's men from getting the food. After this Columbia was occupied by a portion of Sherman's men, while the others marched on toward North Carolina.

THE GLORIOUS END.

In closing this brief sketch of my experiences in the war, I would ask my readers to go back of the war a little with me. I want to show them a few of the dark pictures of the slave system. Hark! I hear the clanking of the ploughman's chains in the fields; I hear the tramping of the feet of the hoe-hands. I hear the coarse and harsh voice of the negro driver and the shrill voice of the white overseer swearing at the slaves. I hear the swash of the lash upon the backs of the unfortunates; I hear them crying for mercy from the merciless. Amidst these cruelties I hear the fathers and mothers pour out their souls in prayer,—"O, Lord, how long!" and their cries not only awaken the sympathy of their white brothers and sisters of the North, but also mightily trouble the slave masters of the South.

The firing on Fort Sumter, in April of 1861, brought hope to the slaves that the long looked for year of jubilee was near at hand. And though the South won victory after victory, and the Union reeled to and fro like a drunken man, the negroes never lost hope, but faithfully supported the Union cause with their prayers.

Thank God, where Christianity exists slavery cannot exist.

At last came freedom. And what joy it brought! I am now standing, in imagination, on a high place just outside the city of Columbia, in the spring of 1865. The stars and stripes float in the air. The sun is just making its appearance from behind the hills, and throwing its beautiful light upon green bush and tree. The mocking birds and jay birds sing this morning more sweetly than ever before. Beneath the flag of liberty there is congregated a perfect network of the emancipated slaves from the different plantations, their swarthy faces, from a distance, looking like the smooth water of a black sea. Their voices, like distant thunder, rend the air,—

"Old master gone away, and the darkies all at home,
There must be now the kingdom come and the year of jubilee."
The old men and women, bent over by reason of age and servitude, bound from their staves, praising God for deliverance.

NARRATIVE

OF THE

LIFE OF
MOSES
GRANDY,

LATE A SLAVE
IN THE
UNITED STATES OF AMERICA.

"SLAVERY IS A MASS, A SYSTEM OF ENORMITIES, WHICH INCON-TROVERTIBLY BIDS DEFIANCE TO EVERY REGULATION WHICH INGE-NUITY CAN DEVISE, OR POWER EFFECT, BUT A TOTAL EXTINCTION. WHY OUGHT SLAVERY TO BE ABOLISHED? BECAUSE *IT IS INCURABLE INJUSTICE*. WHY IS INJUSTICE TO REMAIN FOR A SINGLE HOUR?"   WILLIAM PITT.

SECOND AMERICAN FROM THE LAST LONDON EDITION.

SOLD FOR THE BENEFIT OF HIS RELATIONS STILL IN SLAVERY.

BOSTON:
OLIVER JOHNSON, 25 CORNHILL.
1844.

$*_*^*$ It is not improbable that some of the proper names in the following pages are incorrectly spelled. M.G., through the laws of the slave states, is perfectly illiterate; his pronunciation being the only guide.

INTRODUCTION.

About a fortnight ago, the subject of the following brief Memoir came to me, bearing with him a letter from a dear friend and distinguished abolitionist in the United States, from which the following is an extract:—'I seize my pen in haste to gratify a most worthy colored friend of mine, by giving him a letter of introduction to you, as he intends sailing this week (August 8th, 1842) for Liverpool and London, *via* New Orleans. His name is Moses Grandy. He knows what it is to have been a slave, and what are the tender mercies of the southern slave-drivers. His history is not only authentic, but most extraordinary, and full of thrilling interest. Could it be published, it would make a deep sensation in every quarter. He was compelled to buy his freedom *three times over!* He paid for it $1,850. He has since bought his wife, and one or two of his children; and before going to England will first go to New Orleans, to purchase some of his other children, if he can find them, who are still held in captivity. His benevolence, affection, kindness of heart, and elasticity of spirit, are truly remarkable. He has a good head, a fine countenance, and a great spirit, notwithstanding his education has been obtained in the horrible school of slavery. Just get him to tell you his narrative, and if you happen to have an anti-slavery meeting, let him tell his tale to a British audience.' In the letter of another highly esteemed friend, he is spoken of as 'unsurpassed for faithfulness and perseverance;' in the letter of a third, as a 'worthy and respectable man.' On examining a book containing a list of the donations made him by American friends, in aid of his noble design to rescue from the miseries of slavery his relations, I found the names and certificates of persons of the highest respectability. It will be amply sufficient with those who are acquainted with the Abolitionists of the United States, for me to name General Fessenden, and Nathan Winslow, Esq., of Portland, Maine; the Rev. A. A. Phelps, Ellis Gray Loring, and Samuel E. Sewall, Esqs., of Boston, Massachusetts. Being satisfied, by these indubitable vouchers, of Moses Grandy's title to credit, I listened to his artless tale with entire confidence, and with a feeling of interest which all will participate who peruse the following pages. Considering his Narrative calculated to promote a more extensive knowledge of the workings of American slavery, and that its sale might contribute to the object which engages so entirely the mind of Moses, namely, the redemption of those who are in bonds, belonging to his family, I resolved to commit it to the press, as nearly as possible in the language of Moses himself. I have carefully abstained from casting a single reflection or animadversion of my own. I leave the touching story of the self-liberated captive to speak for itself, and the wish of my heart will be gratified, and my humble effort on his behalf be richly rewarded, if this little book is the means of obtaining for my colored brother the assistance which he seeks, or of increasing the zeal of those who are associated for the purpose of 'breaking every yoke and setting the oppressed free.'

GEORGE THOMPSON.

9, *Blandford Place, Regent's Park,*
October 18*th*, 1842.

NARRATIVE.

My name is Moses Grandy. I was born in Camden county, North Carolina. I believe I am fifty-six years old. Slaves seldom know exactly how old they are; neither they nor their masters set down the time of a birth; the slaves, because they are not allowed to write or read, and the masters, because they only care to know what slaves belong to them.

The master, Billy Grandy, whose slave I was born, was a hard-drinking man; he sold away many slaves. I remember four sisters and four brothers; my mother had more children, but they were dead or sold away before I can remember. I was the youngest. I remember well my mother often hid us all in the woods, to prevent master selling us. When we wanted water, she sought for it in any hole or puddle formed by falling trees or otherwise. It was often full of tadpoles and insects. She strained it, and gave it round to each of us in the hollow of her hand. For food, she gathered berries in the woods, got potatoes, raw corn, &c. After a time, the master would send word to her to come in, promising he would not sell us. But, at length, persons came who agreed to give the prices he set on us. His wife, with much to be done, prevailed on him not to sell me; but he sold my brother, who was a little boy. My mother, frantic with grief, resisted their taking her child away. She was beaten, and held down; she fainted; and, when she came to herself, her boy was gone. She made much outcry, for which the master tied her up to a peach-tree in the yard, and flogged her.

Another of my brothers was sold to Mr. Tyler, Dewan's Neck, Pasquotank county. This man very much ill treated many colored boys. One very cold day, he sent my brother out, naked and hungry, to find a yoke of steers; the boy returned without finding them, when his master flogged him, and sent him out again. A white lady, who lived near, gave him food, and advised him to try again; he did so, but, it seems, again without success. He piled up a heap of leaves, and laid himself down in them, and died there. He was found through a flock of turkey buzzards hovering over him; these birds had pulled his eyes out.

My young master and I used to play together; there was but two days' difference in our ages. My old master always said he would give me to him. When he died, all the colored people were divided amongst his children, and I fell to young master; his name was James Grandy. I was then about eight years old. When I became old enough to be taken away from my mother and put to field work, I was hired out for the year, by auction, at the court house, every January: this is the common practice with respect to slaves belonging to persons who are under age. This continued till my master and myself were twenty-one years old.

The first who hired me was Mr. Kemp, who used me pretty well; he gave me plenty to eat, and sufficient clothing.

The next was old Jemmy Coates, a severe man. Because I could not learn his way of hilling corn, he flogged me naked with a severe whip, made of a very tough sapling; this lapped round me at each stroke; the point of it at last entered my belly and broke off, leaving an inch and a half outside. I was not aware of it until, on going to work again, it hurt my inside very much, when, on looking down, I saw it sticking out of my body. I pulled it out, and the blood spouted after it. The wound festered, and discharged very much at the time, and hurt me for years after.

In being hired out, sometimes the slaves gets a good home, and sometimes a bad one: when he gets a good one, he dreads to see January come; when he has a bad one, the year seems five times as long as it is.

I was next with Mr. Enoch Sawyer, of Camden county. My business was to keep ferry, and do other odd work. It was cruel living. We had not near enough of either victuals or clothes. I was half starved for half my time. I have often ground the husks of Indian corn over again in a hand-mill, for the chance of getting something to eat out of it which the former grinding had left. In severe frosts, I was compelled to go into the fields and woods to work, with my naked feet cracked and bleeding from extreme cold: to warm them, I used to rouse an ox or hog, and stand on the place where it had lain. I was at that place three years, and very long years they seemed to me. The trick by which he kept me so long was this: the court house was but a mile off. At hiring day, he prevented me from going till he went himself and bid for me. On the last occasion, he was detained for a little while by other business; so I ran as quickly as I could, and got hired before he came up.

Mr. George Furley was my next master; he employed me as a car-boy in the Dismal Swamp; I had to drive lumber, &c. I had plenty to eat and plenty of clothes. I was so overjoyed at the change, that I then thought I would not have left the place to go to heaven.

Next year I was hired by Mr. John Micheau, of the same county, who married my young mistress, one of the daughters of Mr. Grandy, and sister of my present owner. This master gave us very few clothes, and but little to eat. I was almost naked. One day he came into the field, and asked why no more work was done. The older people were afraid of him; so I said that the reason, we were so hungry we could not work. He went home and told the mistress to give us plenty to eat, and at dinner-time we had plenty. We came out shouting for joy, and went to work with delight. From that time we had food enough, and he soon found that he had a great deal more work done. The field was quite alive with people striving who should do most.

He hired me for another year. He was a great gambler. He kept me up five nights together, without sleep night or day, to wait on the gambling table. I was standing in the corner of the room, nodding for want of sleep, when he took up the shovel and beat me with it; he dislocated my shoulder, and sprained my wrist, and broke the shovel over me. I ran away, and got another person to hire me.

This person was Mr. Richard Furley, who, after that, hired me at the court house every year till my master came of age. He gave me a pass to work for myself; so I obtained work by the piece where I could, and paid him out of my earnings what we had agreed on; I maintained myself on the rest, and saved what I could. In this way

I was not liable to be flogged and ill used. He paid seventy, eighty, or ninety dollars a year for me, and I paid him twenty or thirty dollars a year more than that.

When my master came of age, he took all his colored people to himself. Seeing that I was industrious and persevering, and had obtained plenty of work, he made me pay him almost twice as much as I had paid Mr. Furley. At that time the English blockaded the Chesapeake, which made it necessary to send merchandise from Norfolk to Elizabeth City by the Grand Canal, so that it might get to sea by Pamlico Sound and Ocracock Inlet. I took some canal boats on shares; Mr. Grice, who married my other young mistress, was the owner of them. I gave him one half of all I received for freight; out of the other half I had to victual and man the boats, and all over that expense was my own profit.

Some time before this, my brother Benjamin returned from the West Indies, where he had been two years with his master's vessel. I was very glad to hear of it, and got leave to go see him. While I was sitting with his wife and him, his wife's master came and asked him to fetch a can of water; he did so, and carried it into the store. While I was waiting for him, and wondering at his being so long away, I heard the heavy blows of a hammer; after a little while I was alarmed, and went to see what was going on. I looked into the store, and saw my brother lying on his back on the floor, and Mr. Williams, who had bought him, driving staples over his wrists and ankles; an iron bar was afterwards put across his breast, which was also held down by staples. I asked what he had been doing, and was told that he had done nothing amiss, but that his master had failed, and he was sold towards paying the debts. He lay in that state all that night; next day he was taken to jail, and I never saw him again. This is the usual treatment under such circumstances. I had to go by my mother's next morning, but I feared to tell her what had happened to my brother. I got a boy to go and tell her. She was blind and very old, and was living in a little hut, in the woods, after the usual manner of old, worn-out slaves; she was unable to go to my brother before he was taken away, and grieved after him greatly.

It was some time after this that I married a slave belonging to Mr. Enoch Sawyer, who had been so hard a master to me. I left her at home (that is, at his house,) one Thursday morning, when we had been married about eight months. She was well, and seemed likely to be so. We were nicely getting together our little necessaries. On the Friday, as I was at work, as usual, with the boats, I heard a noise behind me, on the road which ran by the side of the canal. I turned to look, and saw a gang of slaves coming. When they came up to me, one of them cried out, "Moses, my dear!" I wondered who among them should know me, and found it was my wife. She cried out to me, 'I am gone!' I was struck with consternation. Mr. Rogerson was with them, on his horse, armed with pistols. I said to him, 'For God's sake, have you bought my wife?' He said he had; when I asked him what she had done, he said she had done nothing, but that her master wanted money. He drew out a pistol, and said that, if I went near the wagon on which she was, he would shoot me. I asked for leave to shake hands with her, which he refused, but said I might stand at a distance and talk with her. My heart was so full that I could say very little. I asked leave to give her a dram. He told Mr. Burgess, the man who was with him, to get down and carry it to her. I gave her the little money I had in my pocket, and bade her farewell. I have never seen or heard of her from the day to this. I loved her as I loved my life.

Mr. Grice found that I served him faithfully. He and my young mistress, his wife, advised me, as I was getting money fast, to try to buy myself. By their advice, I asked my master what he would take for me. He wanted $800; and, when I said that was too much, he replied, he could get $1000 for me any minute. Mr. Grice afterwards went with me to him; he said to him that I had already been more profitable to him than any five others of his negroes, and reminded him that we had been playfellows. In this way he got him to consent to take $600 for me. I then went heartily to work, and, whenever I paid him for my time, I paid him something, also, towards my freedom, for which he gave me receipts. When I made him the last payment of the $600 for my freedom, he tore up all the receipts. I told him he ought not to have done so; he replied it did not signify, for, as soon as court day came, he should give me my free papers. On Monday, in court week, I went to him; he was playing at billiards, and would not go with me, but told me to come again the next day; the next day he did the same, and so on daily. I went to his sister, Mrs. Grice, and told her I feared that he did not mean to give them to me; she said she feared so too, and sent for him. He was a very wicked young man; he came, and cursed her, and went out of the house. Mr. Grice was from home; on his return, he went to my master, and told him he ought to give me my free papers; that I had paid for myself, and it was court week, so that there was no excuse. He promised he would; instead of which, he rode away, and kept away till court was over. Before the next court came, he sold me to Mr. Trewitt for $600.

The way in which Mr. Trewitt came to buy me was this: I had left the boats, and had gone with a schooner collecting lumber in Albemarle Sound for the merchants. Coming to Elizabeth City, I found a new store had been opened by Mr. Grice, which Mr. Sutton was keeping: the latter gentleman was glad to see me, and was desirous that I should return to my old employment with the canal boats, as lumber was in great demand at Norfolk. I did so, and sold some cargoes to Mr. Moses Myers, of Norfolk. As I was waiting at the door of his store for settlement, he came up with Mr. Trewitt, whom I did not then know. Mr. Myers said to Mr. Trewitt, 'Here is a captain doing business for you.' Mr. Trewitt then asked me who had chartered the boats, and to whom I belonged. I told him Mr. Sutton had chartered me, and that I had belonged to Mr. James Grandy, but had bought myself. He said he would buy me; on which Mr. Myers told him he could not, as I had already bought myself, and further said I was one of their old war captains, and had never lost a single thing of the property intrusted to me. Mr. Trewitt said he would buy me, and would see about it as soon as he got to Elizabeth City. I thought no more about it. On my return voyage, I delivered a cargo at Elizabeth City, for Mr. Trewitt. I had been at Mr. Grice's, the owner of the boats; and, on my going away from him to meet Mr. Trewitt for settlement, he said he would go with me, as he wanted money. Opposite the custom house we met Mr. Trewitt, who said, "Well, captain, I have bought you.' Mr. Grice said, 'Let us have no nonsense; go and settle with him.' Angry words passed between them, one saying he had bought me, and the other denying that he had or could, as I had bought myself already. We all went to Mr. Grice's dwelling house; there Mr. Trewitt settled with me about the freight, and then, jumping up, said, 'Now I will show you, Mr. Grice, whether I am a liar or not.' He fetched the bill of sale; on reading it, Mr. Grice's color changed, and he sent for Mrs. Grice. When she read it, she began to cry; seeing that, I began to cry too. She sent me to her brother, who was at Mr. Wood's boarding house. He was playing at billiards. I said to him, 'Master James, have you sold me?' He said, 'No.' I said he had; when he turned round and went into another room, crying; I followed him. All the gentlemen followed us, saying, 'Captain Grandy, what is the matter?' I told them Master James had sold me again. They asked him why he had done it; he said it was because people had jeered him by saying I had more sense than he had. They would not suffer him to remain in the boarding house, but turned him out, there and then, with all his trunks and boxes. Mrs. Grice, his sister, sued him in my name for my liberty, but he gained the cause. The court maintained that I, and all I could do, belonged to him, and that he had a right to do as he pleased with me and all my earnings, as his own property, until he had taken me to the court house, and given me my free papers, and until, besides that, I had been a year and a day in the Northern States to gain my residence.

So I was forced to go to Mr. Trewitt. He agreed that, if I would pay him the same wages as I paid my late master, and the $600 he gave for me, he would give me my free papers. He bought two canal boats, and, taking me out of Mr. Grice's employment, set me to work them on the same terms as I did for my former master. I was two years and a half in earning $600 to pay for myself the second time. Just when I had completed the payment, he failed. On Christmas eve he gave me a letter to take to Mr. Mews, at Newbegun Creek. I was rather unwilling to take it, wishing to go to my wife; I told him, too, I was going to his office to settle with him. He offered to give me two dollars to take the letter, and said he would settle when I came back: then Mr. Shaw came from another room, and said his vessel was ready loaded, but he had nobody he could trust with his goods; he offered me five dollars to take the vessel down, and deliver the goods to Mr. Knox, who also was at Newbegun Creek. The wind was fair, and the hands on board, so I agreed; it being Christmas eve, I was glad of something to carry to my wife. I ran the vessel down to the mouth of the creek, and anchored; when the moon rose, I went up the river. I reached the wharf, and commenced taking out the goods that night, and delivered them all safely to Mr. Knox next morning. I then took the letter to Mr. Mews, who read it, and, looking up at me, said, 'Well, you belong to me.' I thought he was joking, and said, 'How? What way?' He said, 'Don't you recollect when Trewitt chartered Wilson Sawyer's brig to the West Indies?' I said, I did. He told me Trewitt then came to him to borrow $600, which he would not lend, except he had a mortgage on me: Trewitt was to take it up at a certain time, but never did. I asked him whether he really took the mortgage on me. He replied that he certainly thought Trewitt would have taken up the mortgage, but he had failed, and was not worth a cent, and he, Mews, must have his money. I asked him whether he had not helped me and my young mistress in the court house, when master James fooled me before. He said he did help me all he could, and that he should not have taken a mortgage on me, but that he thought Trewitt would take it up. Trewitt must have received some of the last payments from me, after he had given the mortgage, and knew he should fail; for the mortgage was given two months before this time.

My head seemed to turn round and round; I was quite out of my senses; I went away towards the woods; Mr. Mews sent his waiter after me to persuade me to go back. At first I refused, but afterwards went. He told me he would give me another chance to buy myself, and I certainly should have my freedom that time. He said Mr. Enoch Sawyer wanted to buy me, to be his overseer in the Swamp. I replied that I would never try again to buy myself, and that they had already got $1,200 from me. My wife* (this was my second wife) belonged to Mr. Sawyer; he told me that her master would not allow me to go to see her, if I would not consent to what he now proposed; for any colored person going on the grounds of a white man, after being warned off, is liable to be flogged, or even shot. I thus found myself forced to go, although no colored man wishes to live at the house where his wife lives, for he has to endure the continual misery of seeing her flogged and abused, without daring to say a word in her defence.

In the service of Mr. Sawyer, I got into a fair way of buying myself again; for I undertook the lightering of shingles or boards out of the Dismal Swamp, and hired hands to assist me. But my master had become security for his two sons-in-law at Norfolk, who failed; in consequence of which he sold eighteen colored people, his share of the Swamp, and two plantations. I was one of the slaves he kept, and after that had to work in the corn-field the same as the rest. The overseer was a bad one; his name was Brooks. The horn

---

*It will be observed that the narrator married a second wife, without having heard of the decease of the first. To explain this fact, it is necessary to state, that the frequent occurrence of cases where husbands and wives, members of Christian societies, were finally separated by sale, led the ministers, some years ago, to deliberate on the subject: they decided that such separation might be considered as the death of the parties to each other, and they therefore agreed to consider subsequent marriages not immoral. The practice is general. It is scarcely necessary to remark, that a more unequivocal and impressive proof of the heinous nature of the system could hardly exist. It breaks up the fondest connections, it tears up the holiest attachments, and induces the ministers of religion, as much as in them lies, to carve the divine law to a fitting with its own infernal exigencies.

was blown at sunrise; the colored people had then to march before the overseer to the field, he on horseback. We had to work, even in long summer days, till twelve o'clock, before we tasted a morsel, men, women, and children all being served alike. At noon the cart appeared with our breakfast. It was in large trays, and was set on the ground. There was bread, of which a piece was cut off for each person; then there was small hominy boiled, that is, Indian-corn, ground in the hand-mill, and besides this two herrings for each of the men and women, and one for each of the children. Our drink was the water in the ditches, whatever might be its state; if the ditches were dry, water was brought to us by the boys. The salt fish made us always thirsty, but no other drink than water was ever allowed. However thirsty a slave may be, he is not allowed to leave his employment for a moment to get water; he can only have it when the hands in working have reached the ditch, at the end of the roads. The overseer stood with his watch in his hand, to give us just an hour; when he said, 'Rise,' we had to rise and go to work again. The women who had children laid them down by the hedge-row, and gave them straws and other trifles to play with; here they were in danger from snakes; I have seen a large snake found coiled round the neck and face of a child, when its mother went to suckle it at dinner-time. The hands work in a line by the side of each other; the overseer puts the swiftest hands in the fore row, and all must keep up with them. One black man is kept on purpose to whip the others in the field; if he does not flog with sufficient severity, he is flogged himself; he whips severely, to keep the whip from his own back. If a man have a wife in the same field with himself, he chooses a row by the side of hers, that, with extreme labor, he may, if possible, help her. But he will not be in the same field if he can help it; for, with his hardest labor, he often cannot save her from being flogged, and he is obliged to stand by and see it; he is always liable to see her taken home at night, stripped naked, and whipped before all the men. On the estate I am speaking of, those women who had sucking children suffering much from their breasts becoming full of milk, the infants being left at home; they therefore could not keep up with the other hands. I have seen the overseer beat them with raw hide, so that blood and milk flew mingled from their breasts. A woman who gives offence in the field, and is large in the family way, is compelled to lie down over a hole made to receive her corpulency, and is flogged with the whip, or beat with a paddle, which has holes in it; at every hole comes a blister. One of my sisters was so severely punished in this way, that labor was brought on, and the child was born in the field. This very overseer, Mr. Brooks, killed in this manner a girl named Mary; her father and mother were in the field at the time. He killed, also, a boy about twelve years old. He had no punishment, or even trial, for either.

There was no dinner till dark, when he gave the order to knock off and go home. The meal then was the same as in the morning, except that we had meat twice a week.

On very few estates are the colored people provided with any bedding: the best masters give only a blanket; this master gave none; a board, which the slave might pick up any where on the estate, was all he had to lie on. If he wished to procure bedding, he could only do so by working at nights. For warmth, therefore, the negroes generally sleep near a large fire, whether in the kitchen, or in their log huts; their legs are often in this way blistered and greatly swelled, and sometimes badly burnt: they suffer severely from this cause.

When the water-mill did not supply meal enough, we had to grind with the hand-mill. The night was employed in this work, without any thing being taken from the labor of the day. We had to take turn at it, women as well as men; enough was to be ground to serve for the following day.

I was eight months in the field. My master, Mr. Sawyer, agreed to allow me eight dollars a month, while so employed, towards buying myself; it will be seen he did not give me even that. When I first went to work in the corn-field, I had paid him $230 towards this third buying of my freedom. I told him, one night, I could not stand his field work any longer; he asked, why; I said I was almost starved to death, and had long been unaccustomed to this severe labor. He wanted to know why I could not stand it as well as the rest. I told him he knew well I had not been used to it for a long time; that his overseer was the worst that had ever been on the plantation, and that I could not stand it. He said he would direct Mr. Brooks to give each of us a pint of meal or corn every evening, which we might bake, and which would serve us next morning, till our breakfast came at noon. The black people were much rejoiced that I got this additional allowance for them. But I was not satisfied; I wanted liberty.

On Sunday morning, as master was sitting in his porch, I went to him, and offered to give him the $230 I had already paid him, if, beside them, he would take for my freedom the $600 he had

231

given for me. He drove me away, saying I had no way to get the money. I sat down for a time, and went to him again. I repeated my offer to procure the $600, and he again said I could not. He called his wife out of the room to the porch, and said to her, 'Don't you think Moses has taken to getting drunk?' She asked me if it was so; I denied it, when she inquired what was the matter. Master replied, 'Don't you think he wants me to sell him?' She said, 'Moses, we would not take any money for you. Captain Cormack put a thousand dollars for you on the supper table last Friday night, and Mr. Sawyer would not touch it; he wants you to be overseer in the Dismal Swamp.' I replied, 'Captain Cormack never said any thing to me about buying me; I would cut my throat from ear to ear rather than go to him. I know what made him say so; he is courting Miss Patsey, and he did it to make himself look big.' Mistress laughed and turned away, and slammed to the door; master shook himself with laughing, and put the paper he was reading before his face, knowing that I spoke the truth. Captain Cormack was an old man who went on crutches. Miss Patsey was the finest of master's daughters. Master drove me away from him again.

On Monday morning, Mr. Brooks, the overseer, blew the horn as usual for all to go to the field. I refused to go. I went to master, and told him that if he would give me a paper, I would go and fetch the $600; he then gave me a paper, stating that he was willing to take that sum for my freedom: so I hired an old horse and started for Norfolk, fifty miles off.

When I reached Deep Creek, I went to the house of Captain Edward Minner. He was very glad to see me, for in former days I had done much business for him; he said how sorry he had been to hear that I was at field work. He inquired where I was going. I said, to Norfolk, to get some of the merchants to let me have money to buy myself. He replied, 'What did I always say to you? Was it not, that I would let you have the money at any time, if you would only tell me when you could be sold?' He called Mrs. Minner into the room, and told her I could be sold for my freedom; she was rejoiced to hear it. He said, 'Put up your horse at Mr. Western's tavern, for you need go no farther; I have plenty of old rusty dollars, and no man shall put his hand on your collar again to say you are a slave. Come and stay with me to-night, and in the morning I will get Mr. Garret's horse, and go with you.'

Next morning we set off, and found master at Major Farrence's, at the cross canal, where I knew he was to be that day, to sell his share of the canal. When I saw him, he told me to go forward home, for he would not sell me. I felt sick and sadly disappointed. Captain Minner stepped up to him, and showed him the paper he had given me, saying, 'Mr. Sawyer, is not this your hand-writing?' He replied, "Mistress said, the last word when I came away, I was not to sell him, but send him home again.' Captain Minner said, 'Mind, gentlemen, I do not want him for a slave; I want to buy him for freedom. He will repay me the money, and I shall not charge him a cent of interest for it. I would not have a colored person, to drag me down to hell, for all the money in the world.' A gentleman who was by said it was a shame I should be so treated; I had bought myself so often that Mr. Sawyer ought to let me go. The very worst man as an overseer over the persons employed in digging the canal, Mr. Wiley M'Pherson, was there; he was never known to speak in favor of a colored person; even he said that Mr. Sawyer ought to let me go, as I had been sold so often. At length, Mr. Sawyer consented I should go for $650, and would take no less. I wished Captain Minner to give the extra $50, and not stand about it. I believe it was what M'Pherson said that induced my master to let me go; for he was well known for his great severity to colored people; so that after even he had said so, master could not stand out. The Lord must have opened M'Pherson's heart to say it.

I have said this M'Pherson was an overseer where slaves were employed in cutting canals. The labor there is very severe. The ground is often very boggy; the negroes are up to the middle, or much deeper, in mud and water, cutting away roots and baling out mud; if they can keep their heads above water, they work on. They lodge in huts, or, as they are called, camps, made of shingles or boards. They lie down in the mud which has adhered to them, making a great fire to dry themselves, and keep off the cold. No bedding whatever is allowed them; it is only by work done over his task that any of them can get a blanket. They are paid nothing, except for the overwork. Their masters come once a month to receive the money for their labor; then, perhaps, some few very good masters will give them $2 each, some others $1, some a pound of tobacco, and some nothing at all. The food is more abundant than that of field slaves: indeed, it is the best allowance in America—it consists of a peck of meal and six pounds of pork per week; the pork is commonly not good; it is damaged, and is bought, as cheap as possible, at auctions.

M'Pherson gave the same task to each slave; of course, the weak ones often failed to do it. I have often seen him tie up persons and flog them in the morning, only because they were unable to get the previous day's task done; after they were flogged, pork or beef brine was put on their bleeding backs to increase the pain; he sitting by, resting himself, and seeing it done. After being thus flogged and pickled, the sufferers often remained tied up all day, the feet just touching the ground, the legs tied, and pieces of wood put between the legs. All the motion allowed was a slight turn of the neck. Thus exposed and helpless, the yellow flies and musquitoes in great numbers would settle on the bleeding and smarting back, and put the sufferer to extreme torture. This continued all day, for they were not taken down till night. In flogging, he would sometimes tie the slave's shirt over his head, that he might not flinch when the blow was coming; sometimes he would increase his misery, by blustering, and calling out that he was coming to flog again, which he did or did not, as happened. I have seen him flog them with his own hands till their entrails were visible; and I have seen the sufferers dead when they were taken down. He never was called to account in any way for it.

It is not uncommon for flies to blow the sores made by flogging; in that case, we get a strong weed growing in those parts, called the Oak of Jerusalem; we boil it at night, and wash the sores with the liquor, which is extremely bitter. On this the creepers or maggots come out. To relieve them in some degree, after severe flogging, their fellow-slaves rub their backs with part of their little allowance of fat meat.

For fear the slaves should run away, while unable to work from flogging, he kept them chained till they could work again. This man had from 500 to 700 men under his control. When out of other employment, I sometimes worked under him, and saw his doings. I believe it was the word of this man which gained my freedom. He is dead, but there are yet others like him on public works.

When the great kindness of Captain Minner had set me clear of Mr. Sawyer, I went to my old occupation of working the canal boats. These I took on shares, as before. After a time, I was disabled for a year from following this employment by a severe attack of rheumatism, caught by frequent exposure to severe weather. I was anxious, however, to be earning something towards the repayment of Captain Minner, lest any accident, unforeseen by him or me, should even yet deprive me of the liberty for which I so longed, and for which I had suffered so much. I therefore had myself carried in a lighter up a cross canal in the Dismal Swamp, and to the other side of Drummond's Lake. I was left on the shore, and there I built myself a little hut, and had provisions brought to me as opportunity served. Here, among snakes, bears, and panthers, whenever my strength was sufficient, I cut down a juniper-tree, and converted it into cooper's timber. The camp, like those commonly set up for negroes, was entirely open on one side; on that side a fire is lighted at night, and a person sleeping puts his feet towards it. One night I was awoke by some animal smelling my face, and snuffing strongly; I felt its cold muzzle. I suddenly thrust out my arms, and shouted with all my might; it was frightened, and made off. I do not know whether it was a bear or a panther; but it seemed as tall as a large calf. I slept, of course, no more that night. I put my trust in the Lord, and continued on the spot; I was never attacked again.

I recovered, and went to the canal boats again; by the end of three years from the time he laid down the money, I entirely repaid my very kind and excellent friend. During this time he made no claim whatever on my services; I was altogether on the footing of a free man, as far as a colored man can there be free.

When, at length, I had repaid Captain Minner, and had got my free papers, so that my freedom was quite secure, my feelings were greatly excited. I felt to myself so light, that I could almost think I could fly; in my sleep I was always dreaming of flying over woods and rivers. My gait was so altered by my gladness, that people often stopped me, saying, 'Grandy, what is the matter?' I excused myself as well as I could; but many perceived the reason, and said, 'O! he is so pleased with having got his freedom.' Slavery will teach any man to be glad when he gets freedom.

My good master, Captain Minner, sent me to Providence, in Rhode Island, to stay a year and a day, in order to gain my residence. But I staid only two months. Mr. Howard's vessel came there laden with corn. I longed much to see my master and mistress, for the kindness they had done me, and so went home in the schooner. On my arrival, I did not stop at my own house, except to ask my wife at the door how she and the children were in health, but went up the town to see Captain and Mrs. Minner. They were very glad to see me, and consulted with me about my way of getting a living. I wished to go on board the New York and Philadelphia packets, but feared I should be troubled for my freedom. Captain Minner thought I might venture, and I therefore engaged myself. I continued in that employment till his death, which happened about a year after my return from Providence. Then I returned to Boston; for, while he lived, I knew I could rely on his protection; but when I lost my friend, I thought it best to go wholly to the Northern States.

At Boston I went to work at sawing wood, sawing with the whip-saw, laboring in the coal-yards, loading and unloading vessels, &c. After laboring in this way for a few months, I went a voyage to St. John's, in Porto Rico, with Captain Cobb, in the schooner *New Packet*. On the return voyage, the vessel got ashore on Cape Cod; we left her, after doing in vain what we could to right her: she was afterwards recovered. I went several other voyages, and particularly two to the Mediterranean: the last was to the East Indies, in the ship *James Murray*, Captain Woodbury, owner Mr. Gray. My entire savings, up to the period of my return from this voyage, amounted to $300; I sent it to Virginia, and bought my wife. She came to me at Boston. I dared not go myself to fetch her, lest I should be again deprived of my liberty, as often happens to free colored people.

At the time, called the time of the Insurrection, about eight years ago, when the whites said the colored people were going to rise, and shot, hanged, and otherwise destroyed many of them, Mrs. Minner thought she saw me in the street, and fainted there. The soldiers were seizing all the blacks they could find, and she knew, if I were there, I should be sure to suffer with the rest. She was mistaken; I was not there.

My son's master, at Norfolk, sent a letter to me at Boston, to say, that if I could raise $450, I might have his freedom; he was then fifteen years old. I had again saved $300. I knew the master was a drinking man, and was therefore very anxious to get my son out of his hands. I went to Norfolk, running the risk of my liberty, and took my $300 with me, to make the best bargain I could. Many gentlemen in Boston, my friends, advised me not to go myself; but I was anxious to get my boy's freedom, and I knew that nobody in Virginia had any cause of complaint against me. So, notwithstanding their advice, I determined to go.

When the vessel arrived there, they said it was against the law for me to go ashore. The mayor of the city said I had been among the cursed Yankees too long; he asked me whether I did not know that it was unlawful for me to land, to which I replied, that I did not know it, for I could neither read nor write. The merchants for whom I had formerly done business came on board, and said they cared for neither the mare (mayor) nor the horse, and insisted that I should go ashore. I told the mayor the business on which I came, and he gave me leave to stay nine days, telling me that if I were not gone in that time, he would sell me for the good of the state.

I offered my boy's master the $300; he counted the money, but put it back to me, refusing to take less than $450. I went on board to return to Boston. We met with head winds, and put back three times to Norfolk, anchoring each time just opposite the jail. The nine days had expired, and I feared the mayor would find me on board and sell me. I could see the jail, full of colored people, and even the whipping-post, at which they were constantly enduring the lash. While we were lying there by the jail, two vessels came from Eastern Shore, Virginia, laden with cattle and colored people. The cattle were lowing for their calves, and the men and women were crying for their husbands, wives, or children. The cries and groans were terrible, notwithstanding there was a whipper on board each vessel, trying to compel the poor creatures to keep silence. These vessels lay close to ours. I had been a long time away from such scenes; the sight affected me very much, and added greatly to my fears.

One day I saw a boat coming from the shore with white men in it. I thought they were officers coming to take me; and such was my horror of slavery, that I twice ran to the ship's waist to jump overboard into the strong ebb tide then running, to drown myself; but a strong impression on my mind restrained me each time.

Once more we got under way for New York; but, meeting again with head winds, we ran into Maurice's River, in Delaware Bay. New Jersey, in which that place lies, is not a slave state. So I said to the captain, 'Let me have a boat, and set me on the free land once more; then I will travel home over land; for I will not run the risk of going back to Virginia any more.' The captain said there was no danger, but I exclaimed, 'No, no! captain, I will not try it; put my feet on free land once again, and I shall be safe.' When I once more touched the free land, the burden of my mind was removed; if two ton weight had been taken off me, the relief would not have seemed so great.

From Maurice's Creek I travelled to Philadelphia, and at that place had a letter written to my wife, at Boston, thanking God that I was on free land again. On arriving at Boston, I borrowed $150 of a friend, and, going to New York, I obtained the help of Mr. John Williams to send the $450 to Norfolk; thus, at length, I bought my son's freedom. I met him at New York, and brought him on to Boston.

Six other of my children, three boys and three girls, were sold to New Orleans. Two of these daughters have bought their own freedom. The eldest of them, Catherine, was sold three times after she was taken away from Virginia; the first time was by auction. Her last master but one was a Frenchman; she worked in his sugar-cane and cotton fields. Another Frenchman inquired for a girl, on whom he could depend, to wait on his wife, who was in a consumption. Her master offered him my daughter; they went into the field to see her, and the bargain was struck. Her new master gave her up to his sick wife, on whom she waited till her death. As she had waited exceedingly well on his wife, her master offered her a chance of buying her freedom. She objected to his terms as too high; for he required her to pay him $4 a week out of her earnings, and $1,200 for her freedom. He said he could get more for her, and told her she might get plenty of washing, at a dollar a dozen: at last she agreed. She lived near the river side, and obtained plenty of work. So anxious was she to obtain her freedom, that she worked nearly all her time, days and nights, and Sundays. She found, however, she gained nothing by working on Sundays, and therefore left it off. She paid her master punctually her weekly hire, and also something towards her freedom, for which he gave her receipts. A good stewardess was wanted for a steamboat on the Mississippi; she was hired for the place at $30 a month, which is the usual salary; she also had liberty to sell apples and oranges on board; and, commonly, the passengers give from twenty-five cents to a dollar to a stewardess who attends them well. Her entire incoming, wages and all, amounted to about sixty dollars a month. She remained at this employment till she had paid the entire sum of $1,200 for her freedom.

As soon as she obtained her free papers, she left the steamboat, thinking she could find her sister Charlotte. Her first two trials were unsuccessful; but on the third attempt she found her at work in the cane-field. She showed her sister's master her own free papers, and told him how she had bought herself; he said that, if her sister would pay him as much as she paid her master, she might go too. They agreed, and he gave her a pass. The two sisters went on board a steamboat, and worked together for the wages of one, till they had saved the entire $1,200 for the freedom of the second sister. The husband of Charlotte was dead; her children were left behind in the cotton and cane-fields; their master refuses to take less than $2,400 for them; their names and ages are as follows: Zeno, about fifteen; Antoinette, about thirteen; Joseph, about eleven; and Josephine, about ten years old. Of my other children,

I only know that one, a girl, named Betsey, is a little way from Norfolk, in Virginia. Her master, Mr. William Dixon, is willing to sell her for $500.

I do not know where any of my other four children are, nor whether they be dead or alive. It will be very difficult to find them out: for the names of slaves are commonly changed with every change of master: they usually bear the name of the master to whom they belong at the time: they have no family name of their own by which they can be traced. Through this circumstance, and their ignorance of reading and writing, to which they are compelled by law, all trace between parents and children, who are separated from them in childhood, is lost in a few years. When, therefore, a child is sold away from its mother, she feels that she is parting from it forever; there is little likelihood of her ever knowing what of good or evil befalls it. The way of finding out a friend or relative who has been sold away for any length of time, or to any great distance, is to trace them, if possible, to one master after another, or if that cannot be done, to inquire about the neighborhood where they are supposed to be, until some one is found who can tell that such or such a person belonged to such or such a master; and the person supposed to be the one sought for, may, perhaps, remember the names of the persons to whom his father and mother belonged: there is little to be learned from his appearance, for so many years may have passed away that he may have grown out of the memory of his parents, or his nearest relations. There are thus no lasting family ties to bind relations together, not even the nearest, and this aggravates their distress when they are sold from each other. I have little hope of finding my four children again.

I have lived in Boston ever since I bought my freedom, except during the last year, which I have spent at Portland, in the state of Maine.

I have yet said nothing of my father. He was often sold through the failure of his successive owners. When I was a little boy, he was sold away from us to a distance: he was then so far off that he could not come to see us oftener than once a year. After that, he was sold to go still farther away, and then he could not come at all. I do not know what has become of him.

When my mother became old, she was sent to live in a little lonely log-hut in the woods. Aged and worn-out slaves, whether men or women, are commonly so treated. No care is taken of them, except, perhaps, that a little ground is cleared about the hut, on which the old slave, if able, may raise a little corn. As far as the owner is concerned, they live or die, as it happens: it is just the same thing as turning out an old horse. Their children, or other near relations, if living in the neighborhood, take it by turns to go at night with a supply saved out of their own scanty allowance of food, as well as to cut wood and fetch water for them: this is done entirely through the good feelings of the slaves, and not through the masters' taking care that it is done. On these night-visits, the aged inmate of the hut is often found crying on account of sufferings from disease or extreme weakness, or from want of food or water in the course of the day: many a time, when I have drawn near to my mother's hut, I have heard her grieving and crying on these accounts: she was old and blind too, and so unable to help herself. She was not treated worse than others: it is the general practice. Some few good masters do not treat their old slaves so: they employ them in doing light jobs about the house and garden.

My eldest sister is in Elizabeth City. She has five children, who, of course, are slaves. Her master is willing to sell her for $100: she is growing old. One of her children, a young man, cannot be bought under $900.

My sister Tamar, who belonged to the same master with myself, had children very fast. Her husband had hard owners, and lived at a distance. When a woman who has many children belongs to an owner who is under age, as ours was, it is customary to put her and the children out yearly to the person who will maintain them for the least money, the person taking them having the benefit of whatever work the woman can do. But my sister was put to herself in the woods. She had a bit of ground cleared, and was left to hire herself out to labor. On the ground she raised corn and flax; and obtained a peck of corn, some herrings, or a piece of meat, for a day's work among the neighboring owners. In this way she brought up her children. Her husband could help her but little. As soon as each of the children became big enough, it was sold away from her.

After parting thus with five, she was sold along with the sixth, (about a year and a half old,) to the speculators; these are persons who buy slaves in Carolina and Virginia, to sell them in Georgia and New Orleans. After travelling with them more than one hundred miles, she made her escape, but could not obtain her child to take it with her. On her journey homeward she travelled by night, and hid herself in thick woods by day. She was in great danger on the road, but in three weeks reached the woods near us: there she had to keep herself concealed: I, my mother, and her husband, knew where she was: she lived in a den she made for herself. She sometimes ventured down to my mother's hut, where she was hid in a hollow under the floor. Her husband lived ten miles off; he would sometimes set off after his day's work was done, spend part of the night with her, and get back before next sunrise: sometimes he would spend Sunday with her. We all supplied her with such provisions as we could save. It was necessary to be very careful in visiting her; we tied pieces of wood or bundles of rags to our feet, that no track might be made.

In the wood she had three children born; one of them died. She had not recovered from the birth of the youngest when she was discovered and taken to the house of her old master.

She was afterwards sold to Culpepper, who used her very cruelly. He was beating her dreadfully, and the blood was streaming from her head and back one day when I happened to go to his house. I was greatly grieved, and asked his leave to find a person to buy her: instead of answering me, he struck at me with an axe, and I was obliged to get away as fast as I could. Soon after this he failed, and she was offered for sale in Norfolk; there Mr. Johnson bought her and her two children, out of friendship for me: he treated her exceedingly well, and she served him faithfully; but it was not long before she was claimed by a person to whom Culpepper had mortgaged her before he sold her to Johnson. This person sold her to Long, of Elizabeth City, where again she was very badly treated. After a time, this person sold her to Georgia: she was very ill at the time, and was taken away in a cart. I hear from her sometimes, and am very anxious to purchase her freedom, if ever I should be able. Two of her children are now in North Carolina, and are longing to obtain their freedom. I know nothing of the others, nor am I likely ever to hear of them again.

The treatment of slaves is mildest near the borders, where the free and slave states join: it becomes more severe, the farther we go from the free states. It is more severe in the west and south than where I lived. The sale of slaves most frequently takes place from the milder to the severer parts: there is great traffic in slaves in that direction, which is carried on by the speculators. On the frontier between the slave and free States there is a guard; no colored person can go over a ferry without a pass. By these regulations, and the great numbers of patrols, escape is made next to impossible.

Formerly slaves were allowed to have religious meetings of their own; but after the insurrection which I spoke of before, they were forbidden to meet even for worship. Often they are flogged if they are found singing or praying at home. They may go to the places of worship used by the whites; but they like their own meetings better. My wife's brother Isaac was a colored preacher. A number of slaves went privately into a wood to hold meetings; when they were found out, they were flogged, and each was forced to tell who else was there. Three were shot, two of whom were killed, and the other was badly wounded. For preaching to them, Isaac was flogged, and his back pickled; when it was nearly well, he was flogged and pickled again, and so on for some months; then his back was suffered to get well, and he was sold. A little while before this, his wife was sold away with an infant at her breast; and out of six children, four had been sold away by one at a time. On the way with his buyers he dropped down dead; his heart was broken.

Having thus narrated what has happened to myself, my relatives and near friends, I will add a few matters about slaves and colored people in general.

Slaves are under fear in every word they speak. If, in their master's kitchen, they let slip an expression of discontent, or a wish for freedom, it is often reported to the master or mistress by the children of the family who may be playing about: severe flogging is often the consequence.

I have already said that it is forbidden by law to teach colored persons to read or write. A few well-disposed white young persons, of the families to which the slaves belonged, have ventured to teach them, but they dare not let it be known they have done so.

The proprietors get new land cleared in this way. They first 'dead' a piece of ground in the woods adjoining the plantation: by 'deading' is meant killing the trees, by cutting a nick all round each, quite through the bark. Out of this ground each colored person has a piece as large as he can tend after his other work is done; the women have pieces in like manner. The slave works at night, cutting down the timber and clearing the ground; after it is cleared, he has it for his own use for two or three years, as may be agreed on. As these new clearings lie between the woods and the old cultivated land, the squirrels and raccoons first come at the crops on them, and thus those on the planter's land are saved from much waste. When the negro has had the land for the specified time, and it has become fit for the plough, the master takes it, and he is removed to another new piece. It is no uncommon thing for the land to be taken from him before the time is out, if it has sooner become fit for the plough. When the crop is gathered, the master comes to see how much there is of it; he then gives the negro an order to sell that quantity; without that order, no storekeeper dare buy it. The slave lays out the money in something tidy to go to meeting in, and something to take to his wife.

The evidence of a black man, or of even so many black men, stands for nothing against that of one white; in consequence of it the free negroes are liable to great cruelties. They have had their dwellings entered, their bedding and furniture destroyed, and themselves, their wives and children, beaten; some have even been taken, with their wives, into the woods, and tied up, flogged, and left there. There is nothing which a white man may not do against a black one, if he only takes care that no other white man can give evidence against him.

A law has lately been passed in New Orleans prohibiting any free colored person from going there.

The coasting packets of the ports on the Atlantic commonly have colored cooks. When a vessel goes from New York or Boston to a port in the slaveholding states, the black cook is usually put in jail till the vessel sails again.

No colored person can travel without a pass. If he cannot show it, he may be flogged by any body; in such a case he often is seized and flogged by the patrols. All through the slave states there are patrols; they are so numerous that they cannot be easily escaped.

The only time when a man can visit his wife, when they are on different estates, is Saturday evening and Sunday. If they be very near to each other, he may sometimes see her on Wednesday evening. He must always return to his work by sunrise; if he fail to do so, he is flogged. When he has got together all the little things he can for his wife and children, and has walked many miles to see them, he may find that they have all been sold away, some in one direction, and some in another. He gives up all hope of seeing them again, but he dare not utter a word of complaint.

It often happens that, when a slave wishes to visit his wife on another plantation, his own master is busy or from home, and therefore he cannot get a pass. He ventures without it. If there be any little spite against his wife or himself, he may be asked for it when he arrives, and, not having it, he may be beaten with thirty-nine stripes, and sent away. On his return, he may be seized by the patrol, and flogged again for the same reason; and he will not wonder if he is again seized and beaten for the third time.

If a negro has given offence to the patrol, even by so innocent a matter as dressing tidily to go to a place of worship, he will be seized by one of them, and another will tear up his pass; while one is flogging him, the others will look another way; so when he or his master makes complaint of his having been beaten without cause, and he points out the person who did it, the others will swear they saw no one beat him. His oath, being that of a black man, would stand for nothing; but he may not even be sworn; and, in such a case, his tormentors are safe, for they were the only whites present.

In all the slave states there are men who make a trade of whipping negroes; they ride about inquiring for jobs of persons who keep no overseer; if there is a negro to be whipped, whether man of woman, this man is employed when he calls, and does it immediately; his fee is half a dollar. Widows and other females, having negroes, get them whipped in this way. Many mistresses will insist on the slave who has been flogged begging pardon for her fault on her knees, and thanking her for the correction.

A white man, who lived near me in Camden county, Thomas Evidge, followed this business. He was also sworn whipper at the court house. A law was passed that any white man detected in stealing should be whipped. Mr. Dozier frequently missed hogs, and flogged many of his negroes on suspicion of stealing them; when he could not, in his suspicions, fix on any one in particular, he flogged them all round, saying that he was sure of having punished the right one. Being one day shooting in his woods, he heard the report of another gun, and shortly after met David Evidge, the nephew of the whipper, with one of his hogs on his back, which had just been shot. David was sent to prison, convicted of the theft, and sentenced to be flogged. His uncle, who vapored about greatly in flogging slaves, and taunted them with unfeeling speeches while he did it, could not bear the thought of flogging his nephew, and hired a man to do it. The person pitched on chanced to be a sailor; he laid it well on the thief; pleased enough were the colored people to see a white back for the first time subjected to the lash.

Another man of the same business, George Wilkins, did no greater credit to the trade. Mr. Carnie, on Western Branch, Virginia, often missed corn from his barn. Wilkins, the whipper, was very officious in pointing out this slave and that, as very likely to be the thief; with nothing against them but his insinuations, some were very severely punished, being flogged by this very Wilkins, and others, at his instigation, were sold away. One night, Mr. Carnie, unknown to his colored people, set a steel trap in the barn; some of the negroes, passing the barn before morning, saw Wilkins standing there, but were not aware he was caught. They called the master, that he might seize the thief before he could escape; he came and teased Wilkins during the night; in the morning, he exposed him to the view of the neighbors, and then set him at liberty without further punishment.

The very severe punishments to which slaves are subjected, for trifling offences, or none at all, their continued liability to all kinds of ill usage, without a chance of redress, and the agonizing feelings they endure at being separated from the dearest connections, drive many of them to desperation, and they abscond. They hide themselves in the woods, where they remain for months, and, in some cases, for years. When caught, they are flogged with extreme severity, their backs are pickled, and the flogging repeated as before described: after months of this torture, the back is allowed to heal, and the slave is sold away. Especially is this done when the slave has attempted to reach a free state.

In violent thunder-storms, when the whites have got between feather-beds to be safe from the lightning, I have often seen negroes, the aged as well as others, go out, and, lifting up their hands, thank God that judgment was coming at last. So cruelly are many of them used, that judgment, they think, would be a happy release from their horrible slavery.

The proprietors, though they live in luxury, generally die in debt: their negroes are so hardly treated that no profit is made by their labor. Many of them are great gamblers. At the death of a proprietor, it commonly happens that his colored people are sold towards paying his debts. So it must and will be with the masters while slavery continues: when freedom is established, I believe they will begin to prosper greatly.

Before I close this Narrative, I ought to express my grateful thanks to the many friends in the Northern States, who have encouraged and assisted me: I shall never forget to speak of their kindness, and to pray for their prosperity. I am delighted in saying, that not only to myself, but to very many other colored persons, they have lent a benevolent and helping hand. Last year, gentlemen whom I know bought no less than ten families from slavery: and this year they are pursuing the same good work. But for these numerous and heavy claims on their means and their kindness, I should have had no need to appeal to the generosity of the British public; they would gladly have helped me to redeem all my children and relations.

When I first went to the Northern States,—which is about ten years ago,—although I was free as to the law, I was made to feel severely the difference between person of different colors. No black man was admitted to the same seats in churches with the whites, nor to the inside of public conveyances, nor into street coaches or cabs: we had to be content with the decks of steamboats in all weathers, night and day, not even our wives or children being allowed to go below, however it might rain, or snow, or freeze; in various other ways, we were treated as though we were of a race of men below the whites. But the abolitionists boldly stood up for us, and, through them, things are much changed for the better. Now, we may sit in any part of the pews of many places of worship, and are even asked into the pews of respectable white families; many public conveyances now make no distinction between white and black. We begin to feel that we are really on the same footing as our fellow-citizens. They see we can and do conduct ourselves with propriety, and they are now admitting us, in many cases, to the same standing with themselves.

During the struggles which have procured for us this justice from our fellow-citizens, we have been in the habit of looking in public places for some well-known abolitionists, and, if none that we knew were there, we addressed any person dressed as a Quaker; these classes always took our part against ill usage, and we have to thank them for many a contest in our behalf.

We were greatly delighted by the zealous efforts and powerful eloquence in our cause of Mr. George Thompson, who came from our English friends to aid our suffering brethren. He was hated and mobbed by bad men amongst the whites; they put his life in great danger, and threatened destruction to all who sheltered him. We prayed for him, and did all we could to defend him. The Lord preserved him, and thankful were we when he escaped from our country with his life. At that time, and ever since, we have had a host of American friends, who have labored for the cause night and day; they have nobly stood up for the rights and honor of the colored man; but they did so at first in the midst of scorn and danger. Now, thank God, the case is very different. William Lloyd Garrison, who was hunted for his life by a mob in the streets of New York, has lately been chairman of a large meeting in favor of abolition, held in Faneuil Hall, the celebrated public hall of Boston, called the

'Cradle of Liberty.'

I am glad to say also that numbers of my colored brethren now escape from slavery; some by purchasing their freedom, others by quitting, through many dangers and hardships, the land of bondage. The latter suffer many privations in their attempts to reach the free states. They hide themselves, during the day, in the woods and swamps; at night, they travel, crossing rivers by swimming or by boats they may chance to meet with, and passing over hills and meadows which they do not know: in these dangerous journeys they are guided by the north-star, for they only know that the land of freedom is in the north. They subsist only on such wild fruit as they can gather, and as they are often very long on their way, they reach the free states almost like skeletons. On their arrival they have no friends but such as pity those who have been in bondage, the number of whom, I am happy to say, is increasing; but if they can meet with a man in a broad-brimmed hat and Quaker coat, they speak to him without fear—relying on him as a friend. At each place the escaped slave inquires for an abolitionist or a Quaker, and these friends of the colored man help them on their journey northwards, until they are out of the reach of danger.

Our untiring friends, the abolitionists, once obtained a law that no colored person should be seized as a slave within the free states; this law would have been of great service to us, by ridding us of all anxiety about our freedom while we remained there; but I am sorry to say, that it has lately been repealed, and that now, as before, any colored person who is said to be a slave, may be seized in the free states and carried away, no matter how long he may have resided there, as also may his children born there. I hope this law will soon be altered again. At present many escaped slaves are forwarded by their friends to Canada, where, under British rule, they are quite safe. There is a body of ten thousand of them in Upper Canada; they are known for their good order, and loyalty to the British government; during the late troubles, they could always be relied on for the defence of the British possessions against the lawless Americans who attempted to invade them.

As to the settlement of Liberia, on the coast of Africa, the free colored people of America do not willingly go to it. America is their home: if their forefathers lived in Africa, they themselves know nothing of that country. None but free colored people are taken there: if they would take slaves, they might have plenty of colonists. Slaves will go any where for freedom.

We look very much to England for help to the cause of the slaves. Whenever we hear of the people of England doing good to black men, we are delighted, and run to tell each other the news. Our kind friends, the abolitionists, are very much encouraged when they hear of meetings and speeches in England in our cause. The first of August, the day when the slaves in the West Indies were made free, is always kept as a day of rejoicing by the American colored free people.

I do hope and believe that the cause of freedom to the blacks is becoming stronger and stronger every day. I pray for the time to come when freedom shall be established all over the world. Then will men love as brethren; they will delight to do good to one another; and they will thankfully worship the Father of All.

And now I have only to repeat my hearty thanks to all who have done any thing towards obtaining liberty for my colored brethren, and especially to express my gratitude to those who have helped me to procure for myself, my wife, and so far of my children, the blessing of freedom—a blessing of which none can know the value, but he who has been a slave. Whatever profit may be obtained by the sale of this book, and all donations with which I may be favored, will be faithfully employed in redeeming my remaining children and relatives from the dreadful condition of slavery.

NOTE.

I have paid the following sums to redeem myself and relatives from slavery, viz:

For my own freedom,	$1,850
For my wife's freedom,	300
For my son's freedom,	450
Grandchild's freedom,	400
To redeem my kidnapped son,	60
	$3,060

I now wish to raise $100 to buy the freedom of my sister Mary, who is a slave at Elizabeth City, N. C. Her master says he will take that sum for her.

M. G.
Boston, Jan. 19, 1844.

INCIDENTS

IN THE

LIFE OF A
SLAVE GIRL

LINDA BRENT

EDITED BY
L. MARIA CHILD

CONTENTS

INTRODUCTION
BY L. MARIA CHILD

The author of the following autobiography is personally known to me, and her conversation and manners inspire me with confidence. During the last seventeen years, she has lived the greater part of the time with a distinguished family in New York, and has so deported herself as to be highly esteemed by them. This fact is sufficient, without further credentials of her character. I believe those who know her will not be disposed to doubt her veracity, though some incidents in her story are more romantic than fiction.

At her request, I have revised her manuscript; but such changes as I have made have been mainly for purposes of condensation and orderly arrangement. I have not added any thing to the incidents, or changed the import of her very pertinent remarks. With trifling exceptions, both the ideas and the language are her own. I pruned excrescences a little, but otherwise I had no reason for changing her lively and dramatic way of telling her own story. The names of both persons and places are known to me; but for good reasons I suppress them.

It will naturally excite surprise that a woman reared in Slavery should be able to write so well. But circumstances will explain this. In the first place, nature endowed her with quick perceptions. Secondly, the mistress, with whom she lived till she was twelve years old, was a kind, considerate friend, who taught her to read and spell. Thirdly, she was placed in favorable circumstances after she came to the North; having frequent intercourse with intelligent persons, who felt a friendly interest in her welfare, and were disposed to give her opportunities for self-improvement.

I am well aware that many will accuse me of indecorum for presenting these pages to the public; for the experiences of this intelligent and much-injured woman belong to a class which some call delicate subjects, and others indelicate. This peculiar phase of Slavery has generally been kept veiled; but the public ought to be made acquainted with its monstrous features, and I willingly take the responsibility of presenting them with the veil withdrawn. I do this for the sake of my sisters in bondage, who are suffering wrongs so foul, that our ears are too delicate to listen to them. I do it with the hope of arousing conscientious and reflecting women at the North to a sense of their duty in the exertion of moral influence on the question of Slavery, on all possible occasions. I do it with the hope that every man who reads this narrative will swear solemnly before God that, so far as he has power to prevent it, no fugitive from Slavery shall ever be sent back to suffer in that loathsome den of corruption and cruelty.

PREFACE
BY LINDA BRENT

Reader, be assured this narrative is no fiction. I am aware that some of my adventures may seem incredible; but they are, nevertheless, strictly true. I have not exaggerated the wrongs inflicted by Slavery; on the contrary, my descriptions fall far short of the facts. I have concealed the names of places, and given persons fictitious names. I had no motive for secrecy on my own account, but I deemed it kind and considerate towards others to pursue this course.

I wish I were more competent to the task I have undertaken. But I trust my readers will excuse deficiencies in consideration of circumstances. I was born and reared in Slavery; and I remained in a Slave State twenty-seven years. Since I have been at the North, it has been necessary for me to work diligently for my own support, and the education of my children. This has not left me much leisure to make up for the loss of early opportunities to improve myself; and it has compelled me to write these pages at irregular intervals, whenever I could snatch an hour from household duties.

When I first arrived in Philadelphia, Bishop Paine advised me to publish a sketch of my life, but I told him I was altogether incompetent to such an undertaking. Though I have improved my mind somewhat since that time, I still remain of the same opinion; but I trust my motives will excuse what might otherwise seem presumptuous. I have not written my experiences in order to attract attention to myself; on the contrary, it would have been more pleasant to me to have been silent about my own history. Neither do I care to excite sympathy for my own sufferings. But I do earnestly desire to arouse the women of the North to a realizing sense of the condition of two millions of women at the South, still in bondage, suffering what I suffered, and most of them **far** worse. I want to add my testimony to that of abler pens to convince the people of the Free States what Slavery really is. Only by experience can any one realize how deep, and dark, and foul is that pit of abominations. May the blessing of God rest on this imperfect effort in behalf of my persecuted people!

1

CHILDHOOD

I was born a slave; but I never knew it till six years of happy childhood had passed away. My father was a carpenter, and considered so intelligent and skillful in his trade, that, when buildings out of the common line were to be erected, he was sent for from long distances, to be head workman. On condition of paying his mistress two hundred dollars a year, and supporting himself, he was allowed to work at his trade, and manage his own affairs. His strongest wish was to purchase his children; but, though he several times offered his hard earnings for that purpose, he never succeeded. In complexion my parents were a light shade of brownish yellow, and were termed mulattoes. They lived together in a comfortable home; and, though we were all slaves, I was so fondly shielded that I never dreamed I was a piece of merchandise, trusted to them for safe keeping, and liable to be demanded of them at any moment. I had one brother, William, who was two years younger than myself—a bright, affectionate child. I had also a great treasure in my maternal grandmother, who was a remarkable woman in many respects. She was the daughter of a planter in South Carolina, who, at his death, left her mother and his three children free, with money to go to St. Augustine, where they had relatives. It was during the Revolutionary War; and they were captured on their passage, carried back, and sold to different purchasers. Such was the story my grandmother used to tell me; but I do not remember all the particulars. She was a little girl when she was captured and sold to the keeper of a large hotel. I have often heard her tell how hard she fared during childhood. But as she grew older she evinced so much intelligence, and was so faithful, that her master and mistress could not help seeing it was for their interest to take care of such a valuable piece of property. She became an indispensable personage in the household, officiating in all capacities, from cook and wet nurse to seamstress. She was much praised for her cooking; and her nice crackers became so famous in the neighborhood that many people were desirous of obtaining them. In consequence of numerous requests of this kind, she asked permission of her mistress to bake crackers at night, after all the household work was done; and she obtained leave to do it, provided she would clothe herself and her children from the profits. Upon these terms, after working hard all day for her mistress, she began her midnight bakings, assisted by her two oldest children. The business proved profitable; and each year she laid by a little, which was saved for a fund to purchase her children. Her master died, and the property was divided among his heirs. The widow had her dower in the hotel, which she continued to keep open. My grandmother remained in her service as a slave; but her children were divided among her master's children. As she had five, Benjamin, the youngest one, was sold, in order that each heir might have an equal portion of dollars and cents. There was so little difference in our ages that he seemed more like my brother than my uncle. He was a bright, handsome lad, nearly white; for he inherited the complexion my grandmother had derived from Anglo-Saxon ancestors. Though only ten years old, seven hundred and twenty dollars were paid for him. His sale was a terrible blow to my grandmother; but she was naturally hopeful, and she went to work with renewed energy, trusting in time to be able to purchase some of her children. She had laid up three hundred dollars, which her mistress one day begged as a loan, promising to pay her soon. The reader probably knows that no promise or writing given to a slave is legally binding; for, according to Southern laws a slave, *being* property, can *hold* no property. When my grandmother lent her hard earnings to her mistress, she trusted solely to her honor. The honor of a slaveholder to a slave!

To this good grandmother I was indebted for many comforts. My brother Willie and I often received portions of the crackers, cakes, and preserves, she made to sell; and after we ceased to be children we were indebted to her for many more important services.

Such were the unusually fortunate circumstances of my early childhood. When I was six years old, my mother died; and then, for the first time, I learned, by the talk around me, that I was a slave. My mother's mistress was the daughter of my grandmother's mistress. She was the foster sister of my mother; they were both nourished at my grandmother's breast. In fact, my mother had been weaned at three months old, that the babe of the mistress might obtain sufficient food. They played together as children; and, when they became women, my mother was a most faithful servant to her whiter foster sister. On her death-bed her mistress promised that her children should never suffer for any thing; and during her lifetime she kept her word. They all spoke kindly of my dead mother, who had been a slave merely in name, but in nature was noble and womanly. I grieved for her, and my young mind was troubled with the thought who would now take care of me and my little brother. I was told that my home was now to be with her mistress; and I found it a happy one. No toilsome or disagreeable duties were imposed upon me. My mistress was so kind to me that I was always glad to do her bidding, and proud to labor for her as much as my young years would permit. I would sit by her side for hours, sewing diligently, with a heart as free from care as that of any freeborn white child. When she thought I was tired, she would send me out to run and jump; and away I bounded, to gather berries or flowers to decorate her room. Those were happy days—too happy to last. The slave child had no thought for the morrow; but there came that blight, which too surely waits on every human being born to be a chattel.

When I was nearly twelve years old, my kind mistress sickened and died. As I saw the cheek grow paler, and the eye more glassy, how earnestly I prayed in my heart that she might live! I loved her; for she had been almost like a mother to me. My prayers were not answered. She died, and they buried her in the little churchyard, where, day after day, my tears fell upon her grave.

I was sent to spend a week with my grandmother. I was now old enough to begin to think of the future; and again and again I asked myself what they would do with me. I felt sure I should never find another mistress so kind as the one who was gone. She had promised my dying mother that her children should never suffer for any thing; and when I remembered that, and recalled her many proofs of attachment to me, I could not help having some hopes that she had left me free. My friends were almost certain it would be so. They thought she would be sure to do it, on account of my mother's love and faithful service. But, alas! we all know that the memory of a faithful slave does not avail much to save her children from the auction block.

After a brief period of suspense, the will of my mistress was read, and we learned that she had bequeathed me to her sister's daughter, a child of five years old. So vanished our hopes. My mistress had taught me the precepts of God's Word: "Thou shalt love thy neighbor as thyself." "Whatsoever ye would that men should do unto you, do ye even so unto them." But I was her slave, and I suppose she did not recognize me as her neighbor. I would give much to blot out from my memory that one great wrong. As a child, I loved my mistress; and, looking back on the happy days I spent with her, I try to think with less bitterness of this act of injustice. While I was with her, she taught me to read and spell; and for this privilege, which so rarely falls to the lot of a slave, I bless her memory.

She possessed but few slaves; and at her death those were all distributed among her relatives. five of them were my grandmother's children, and had shared the same milk that nourished her mother's children. Notwithstanding my grandmother's long and faithful service to her owners, not one of her children escaped the auction block. These God-breathing machines are no more, in the sight of their masters, than the cotton they plant, or the horses they tend.

II
THE NEW MASTER AND MISTRESS

Dr. Flint, a physician in the neighborhood, had married the sister of my mistress, and I was now the property of their little daughter. It was not without murmuring that I prepared for my new home; and what added to my unhappiness, was the fact that my brother William was purchased by the same family. My father, by his nature, as well as by the habit of transacting business as a skillful mechanic, had more of the feelings of a freeman than is common among slaves. My brother was a spirited boy; and being brought up under such influences, he early detested the name of master and mistress. One day, when his father and his mistress both happened to call him at the same time, he hesitated between the two; being perplexed to know which had the strongest claim upon his obedience. He finally concluded to go to his mistress. When my father reproved him for it, he said, "You both called me, and I didn't know which I ought to go to first."

"You are my child," replied our father, "and when I call you, you should come immediately, if you have to pass through fire and water."

Poor Willie! He was now to learn his first lesson of obedience to a master. Grandmother tried to cheer us with hopeful words, and they found an echo in the credulous hearts of youth.

When we entered our new home we encountered cold looks, cold words, and cold treatment. We were glad when the night came. On my narrow bed I moaned and wept, I felt so desolate and alone.

I had been there nearly a year, when a dear little friend of mine was buried. I heard her mother sob, as the clods fell on the coffin of her only child, and I turned away from the grave, feeling thankful that I still had something left to love. I met my grandmother, who said, "Come with me, Linda;" and from her tone I knew that something sad had happened. She led me apart from the people, and then said, "My child, your father is dead." Dead! How could I believe it? He had died so suddenly I had not even heard that he was sick. I went home with my grandmother. My heart rebelled against God, who had taken from me mother, father, mistress, and friend. The good grandmother tried to comfort me. "Who knows the ways of God?" said she. "Perhaps they have been kindly taken from the evil days to come." Years afterwards I often thought of this. She promised to be a mother to her grandchildren, so far as she might be permitted to do so; and strengthened by her love, I returned to my master's. I thought I should be allowed to go to my father's house the next morning; but I was ordered to go for flowers, that my mistress's house might be decorated for an evening party. I spent the day gathering flowers and weaving them into festoons, while the dead body of my father was lying within a mile of me. What cared my owners for that? He was merely a piece of property. Moreover, they thought he had spoiled his children, by teaching them to feel that they were human beings. This was blasphemous doctrine for a slave to teach; presumptuous in him, and dangerous to the masters.

The next day I followed his remains to a humble grave beside that of my dear mother. There were those who knew my father's worth, and respected his memory.

My home now seemed more dreary than ever. The laugh of the little slave-children sounded harsh and cruel. It was selfish to feel so about the joy of others. My brother moved about with a very grave face. I tried to comfort him, by saying, "Take courage, Willie; brighter days will come by and by."

"You don't know any thing about it, Linda," he replied. "We shall have to stay here all our days; we shall never be free."

I argued that we were growing older and stronger, and that perhaps we might, before long, be allowed to hire our own time, and then we could earn money to buy our freedom. William declared this was much easier to say than to do; moreover, he did not intend to buy his freedom. We held daily controversies upon this subject.

Little attention was paid to the slaves' meals in Dr. Flint's house. If they could catch a bit of food while it was going, well and good. I gave myself no trouble on that score, for on my various errands I passed my grandmother's house, where there was always something to spare for me. I was frequently threatened with punishment if I stopped there; and my grandmother, to avoid detaining me, often stood at the gate with something for my breakfast or dinner. I was indebted to *her* for all my comforts, spiritual or temporal. It was *her* labor that supplied my scanty wardrobe. I have a vivid recollection of the linsey-woolsey dress given me every winter by Mrs. Flint. How I hated it! It was one of the badges of slavery.

While my grandmother was thus helping to support me from her hard earnings, the three hundred dollars she had lent her mistress were never repaid. When her mistress died, her son-in-law, Dr. Flint, was appointed executor. When grandmother applied to him for payment, he said the estate was insolvent, and the law prohibited payment. It did not, however, prohibit him from retaining the silver candelabra, which had been purchased with that money. I presume they will be handed down in the family, from generation to generation.

My grandmother's mistress had always promised her that, at her death, she should be free; and it was said that in her will she made good the promise. But when the estate was settled, Dr. Flint told the faithful old servant that, under existing circumstances, it was necessary she should be sold.

On the appointed day, the customary advertisement was posted up, proclaiming that there would be a "public sale of negroes, horses, &c." Dr. Flint called to tell my grandmother that he was unwilling to wound her feelings by putting her up at auction, and that he would prefer to dispose of her at private sale. My grandmother saw through his hypocrisy; she understood very well that he was ashamed of the job. She was a very spirited woman, and if he was base enough to sell her, when her mistress intended she should be free, she was determined the public should know it. She had for a long time supplied many families with crackers and preserves; consequently, "Aunt Marthy," as she was called, was generally known, and every body who knew her respected her intelligence and good character. Her long and faithful service in the family was also well known, and the intention of her mistress to leave her free. When the day of sale came, she took her place among the chattels, and at the first call she sprang upon the auction-block. Many voices called out, "Shame! Shame! Who is going to sell *you*, aunt Marthy? Don't stand there! That is no place for *you*." Without saying a word, she quietly awaited her fate. No one bid for her. At last, a feeble voice said, "Fifty dollars." It came from a maiden lady, seventy years old, the sister of my grandmother's deceased mistress. She had lived forty years under the same roof with my grandmother; she knew how faithfully she had served her owners, and how cruelly she had been defrauded of her rights; and she resolved to protect her. The auctioneer waited for a higher bid; but her wishes were respected; no one bid above her. She could neither read nor write; and when the bill of sale was made out, she signed it with a cross. But what consequence was that, when she had a big heart overflowing with human kindness? She gave the old servant her freedom.

At that time, my grandmother was just fifty years old. Laborious years had passed since then; and now my brother and I were slaves to the man who had defrauded her of her money, and tried to defraud her of her freedom. One of my mother's sisters, called Aunt Nancy, was also a slave in his family. She was a kind, good aunt to me; and supplied the place of both housekeeper and waiting maid to her mistress. She was, in fact, at the beginning and end of every thing.

Mrs. Flint, like many southern women, was totally deficient in energy. She had not strength to superintend her household affairs; but her nerves were so strong, that she could sit in her easy chair and see a woman whipped, till the blood trickled from every stroke of the lash. She was a member of the church; but partaking of the Lord's supper did not seem to put her in a Christian frame of mind. If dinner was not served at the exact time on that particular Sunday, she would station herself in the kitchen, and wait till it was dished, and then spit in all the kettles and pans that had been used for cooking. She did this to prevent the cook and her children from eking out their meager fare with the remains of the gravy and other scrapings. The slaves could get nothing to eat except what she chose to give them. Provisions were weighed out by the pound and ounce, three times a day. I can assure you she gave them no chance to eat wheat bread from her flour barrel. She knew how many biscuits a quart of flour would make, and exactly what size they ought to be.

Dr. Flint was an epicure. The cook never sent a dinner to his table without fear and trembling; for if there happened to be a dish not to his liking, he would either order her to be whipped, or compel her to eat every mouthful of it in his presence. The poor, hungry creature might not have objected to eating it; but she did object to having her master cram it down her throat till she choked.

They had a pet dog, that was a nuisance in the house. The cook was ordered to make some Indian mush for him. He refused to eat, and when his head was held over it, the froth flowed from his mouth into the basin. He died a few minutes after. When Dr. Flint came in, he said the mush had not been well cooked, and that was the reason the animal would not eat it. He sent for the cook, and compelled her to eat it. He thought that the woman's stomach was stronger than the dog's; but her sufferings afterwards proved that he was mistaken. This poor woman endured many cruelties from her master and mistress; sometimes she was locked up, away from her nursing baby, for a whole day and night.

When I had been in the family a few weeks, one of the plantation slaves was brought to town, by order of his master. It was near night when he arrived, and Dr. Flint ordered him to be taken to the work house, and tied up to the joist, so that his feet would just escape the ground. In that situation he was to wait till the doctor had taken his tea. I shall never forget that night. Never before, in my life, had I heard hundreds of blows fall, in succession, on a human being. His piteous groans, and his "O, pray don't massa," rang in my ear for months afterwards. There were many conjectures as to the cause of this terrible punishment. Some said master accused him of stealing corn; others said the slave had quarreled with his wife, in presence of the overseer, and had accused his master of being the father of her child. They were both black, and the child was very fair.

I went into the work house next morning, and saw the cowhide still wet with blood, and the boards all covered with gore. The poor man lived, and continued to quarrel with his wife. A few months afterwards Dr. Flint handed them both over to a slave-trader. The guilty man put their value into his pocket, and had the satisfaction of knowing that they were out of sight and hearing. When the mother was delivered into the trader's hands, she said, "You *promised* to treat me well." To which he replied, "You have let your tongue run too far; damn you!" She had forgotten that it was a crime for a slave to tell who was the father of her child.

From others than the master persecution also comes in such cases. I once saw a young slave girl dying soon after the birth of a child nearly white. In her agony she cried out, "O Lord, come and take me!" Her mistress stood by, and mocked at her like an incarnate fiend. "You suffer, do you?" she exclaimed. "I am glad of it. You deserve it all, and more too."

The girl's mother said, "The baby is dead, thank God; and I hope my poor child will soon be in heaven, too."

"Heaven!" retorted the mistress. "There is no such place for the like of her and her bastard."

The poor mother turned away, sobbing. Her dying daughter called her, feebly, and as she bent over her, I heard her say, "Don't grieve so, mother; God knows all about it; and He will have mercy upon me."

Her sufferings, afterwards, became so intense, that her mistress felt unable to stay; but when she left the room, the scornful smile was still on her lips. Seven children called her mother. The poor black woman had but the one child, whose eyes she saw closing in death, while she thanked God for taking her away from the greater bitterness of life.

III

THE SLAVES' NEW YEAR'S DAY

Dr. Flint owned a fine residence in town, several farms, and about fifty slaves, besides hiring a number by the year. Hiring-day at the south takes place on the 1st of January.

On the 2d, the slaves are expected to go to their new masters. On a farm, they work until the corn and cotton are laid. They then have two holidays. Some masters give them a good dinner under the trees. This over, they work until Christmas eve. If no heavy charges are meantime brought against them, they are given four or five holidays, whichever the master or over-seer may think proper. Then comes New Year's eve; and they gather together their little alls, or more properly speaking, their little nothings, and wait anxiously for the dawning of day. At the appointed hour the grounds are thronged with men, women, and children, waiting, like criminals, to hear their doom pronounced. The slave is sure to know who is the most humane, or cruel master, within forty miles of him.

It is easy to find out, on that day, who clothes and feeds his slaves well; for he is surrounded by a crowd, begging, "Please, massa, hire me this year. I will work very hard, massa."

If a slave is unwilling to go with his new master, he is whipped, or locked up in jail, until he consents to go, and promises not to run away during the year. Should he chance to change his mind, thinking it justifiable to violate an extorted promise, woe unto him if he is caught! The whip is used till the blood flows at his feet; and his stiffened limbs are put in chains, to be dragged in the field for days and days!

If he lives until the next year, perhaps the same man will hire him again, without even giving him an opportunity of going to the hiring-ground. After those for hire are disposed of, those for sale are called up.

O, you happy free women, contrast your New Year's day with that of the poor bond-woman! With you it is a pleasant season, and the light of the day is blessed. Friendly wishes meet you every where, and gifts are showered upon you. Even hearts that have been estranged from you soften at this season, and lips that have been silent echo back, "I wish you a happy New Year." Children bring their little offerings, and raise their rosy lips for a caress. They are your own, and no hand but that of death can take them from you.

But to the slave mother New Year's day comes laden with peculiar sorrows. She sits on her cold cabin floor, watching the children who may all be torn from her the next morning; and often does she wish that she and they might die before the day dawns. She may be an ignorant creature, degraded by the system that has brutalized her from childhood; but she has a mother's instincts, and is capable of feeling a mother's agonies.

On one of these sale days, I saw a mother lead seven children to the auction-block. She knew that *some* of them would be taken from her; but they took all. The children were sold to a slave-trader, and their mother was bought by a man in her own town. Before night her children were all far away. She begged the trader to tell her where he intended to take them; this he refused to do. How *could* he, when he knew he would sell them, one by one, wherever he could command the highest price? I met that mother in the street, and her wild, haggard face lies to-day in my mind. She wrung her hands in anguish, and exclaimed, "Gone! All gone! Why *don't* God kill me?" I had no words wherewith to comfort her. Instances of this kind are of daily, yea, of hourly occurrence.

Slaveholders have a method, peculiar to their institution, of getting rid of *old* slaves, whose lives have been worn out in their service. I knew an old woman, who for seventy years faithfully served her master. She had become almost helpless, from hard labor and disease. Her owners moved to Alabama, and the old black woman was left to be sold to any body who would give twenty dollars for her.

IV

THE SLAVE WHO DARED TO FEEL LIKE A MAN

Two years had passed since I entered Dr. Flint's family, and those years had brought much of the knowledge that comes from experience, though they had afforded little opportunity for any other kinds of knowledge.

My grandmother had, as much as possible, been a mother to her orphan grandchildren. By perseverance and unwearied industry, she was now mistress of a snug little home, surrounded with the necessaries of life. She would have been happy could her children have shared them with her. There remained but three children and two grandchildren, all slaves. Most earnestly did she strive to make us feel that it was the will of God: that He had seen fit to place us under such circumstances; and though it seemed hard, we ought to pray for contentment.

It was a beautiful faith, coming from a mother who could not call her children her own. But I, and Benjamin, her youngest boy, condemned it. We reasoned that it was much more the will of God that we should be situated as she was. We longed for a home like hers. There we always found sweet balsam for our troubles. She was so loving, so sympathizing! She always met us with a smile, and listened with patience to all our sorrows. She spoke so hopefully, that unconsciously the clouds gave place to sunshine. There was a grand big oven there, too, that baked bread and nice things for the town, and we knew there was always a choice bit in store for us.

But, alas! even the charms of the old oven failed to reconcile us to our hard lot. Benjamin was now a tall, handsome lad, strongly and gracefully made, and with a spirit too bold and daring for a slave. My brother William, now twelve years old, had the same aversion to the word master that he had when he was an urchin of seven years. I was his confidant. He came to me with all his troubles. I remember one instance in particular. It was on a lovely spring morning, and when I marked the sunlight dancing here and there, its beauty seemed to mock my sadness. For my master, whose restless, craving, vicious nature roved about day and night, seeking whom to devour, had just left me, with stinging, scorching words; words that scathed ear and brain like fire. O, how I despised him! I thought how glad I should be, if some day when he walked the earth, it would open and swallow him up, and disencumber the world of a plague.

When he told me that I was made for his use, made to obey his command in *every* thing; that I was nothing but a slave, whose will must and should surrender to his, never before had my puny arm felt half so strong.

So deeply was I absorbed in painful reflections afterwards, that I neither saw nor heard the entrance of any one, till the voice of William sounded close beside me. "Linda," said he, "what makes you look so sad? I love you. O, Linda, isn't this a bad world? Every body seems so cross and unhappy. I wish I had died when poor father did."

I told him that every body was *not* cross, or unhappy; that those who had pleasant homes, and kind friends, and who were not afraid to love them, were happy. But we, who were slave-children, without father or mother, could not expect to be happy. We must be good; perhaps that would bring us contentment.

"Yes," he said, "I try to be good; but what's the use? They are all the time troubling me." Then he proceeded to relate his afternoon's difficulty with young master Nicholas. It seemed that the brother of master Nicholas had pleased himself with making up stories about William. Master Nicholas said he should be flogged, and he would do it. Whereupon he went to work; but William fought bravely, and the young master, finding he was getting the better of him, undertook to tie his hands behind him. He failed in that likewise. By dint of kicking and fisting, William came out of the skirmish none the worse for a few scratches.

He continued to discourse on his young master's *meanness;* how he whipped the *little* boys, but was a perfect coward when a tussle ensued between him and white boys of his own size. On such occasions he always took to his legs. William had other charges to make against him. One was his rubbing up pennies with quicksilver, and passing them off for quarters of a dollar on an old man who kept a fruit stall. William was often sent to buy fruit, and he earnestly inquired of me what he ought to do under such circumstances. I told him it was certainly wrong to deceive the old man, and that it was his duty to tell him of the impositions practiced by his young master. I assured him the old man would not be slow to comprehend the whole, and there the matter would end. William thought it might with the old man, but not with *him*. He said he did not mind the smart of the whip, but he did not like the *idea* of being whipped.

While I advised him to be good and forgiving I was not unconscious of the beam in my own eye. It was the very knowledge of my own shortcomings that urged me to retain, if possible, some sparks of my brother's God-given nature. I had not lived fourteen years in slavery for nothing. I had felt, seen, and heard enough, to read the characters, and question the motives, of those around me. The war of my life had begun; and though one of God's most powerless creatures, I resolved never to be conquered. Alas, for me!

If there was one pure, sunny spot for me, I believed it to be in Benjamin's heart, and in another's, whom I loved with all the ardor of a girl's first love. My owner knew of it, and sought in every way to render me miserable. He did not resort to corporal punishment, but to all the petty, tyrannical ways that human ingenuity could devise.

I remember the first time I was punished. It was in the month of February. My grandmother had taken my old shoes, and replaced them with a new pair. I needed them; for several inches of snow had fallen, and it still continued to fall. When I walked through Mrs. Flint's room, their creaking grated harshly on her refined nerves. She called me to her, and asked what I had about me that made such a horrid noise. I told her it was my new shoes. "Take them off," said she; "and if you put them on again, I'll throw them into the fire."

I took them off, and my stockings also. She then sent me a long distance, on an errand. As I went through the snow, my bare feet tingled. That night I was very hoarse; and I went to bed thinking the next day would find me sick, perhaps dead. What was my grief on waking to find myself quite well!

I had imagined if I died, or was laid up for some time, that my mistress would feel a twinge of remorse that she had so hated "the little imp," as she styled me. It was my ignorance of that mistress that gave rise to such extravagant imaginings.

Dr. Flint occasionally had high prices offered for me; but he always said, "She don't belong to me. She is my daughter's property, and I have no right to sell her." Good, honest man! My young mistress was still a child, and I could look for no protection from her. I loved her, and she returned my affection. I once heard her father allude to her attachment to me; and his wife promptly replied that it proceeded from fear. This put unpleasant doubts into my mind. Did the child feign what she did not feel, or was her mother jealous of the mite of love she bestowed on me? I concluded it must be the latter. I said to myself, "Surely, little children are true."

One afternoon I sat at my sewing, feeling unusual depression of spirits. My mistress had been accusing me of an offense, of which I assured her I was perfectly innocent; but I saw, by the contemptuous curl of her lip, that she believed I was telling a lie.

I wondered for what wise purpose God was leading me through such thorny paths, and whether still darker days were in store for me. As I sat musing thus, the door opened softly, and William came in. "Well, brother," said I, "what is the matter this time?"

"O Linda, Ben and his master have had a dreadful time!" said he.

My first thought was that Benjamin was killed. "Don't be frightened, Linda," said William; "I will tell you all about it."

It appeared that Benjamin's master had sent for him, and he did not immediately obey the summons. When he did, his master was angry, and began to whip him. He resisted. Master and slave fought, and finally the master was thrown. Benjamin had cause to tremble; for he had thrown to the ground his master—one of the richest men in town. I anxiously awaited the result.

That night I stole to my grandmother's house, and Benjamin also stole thither from his master's. My grandmother had gone to spend a day or two with an old friend living in the country.

"I have come," said Benjamin, "to tell you good by. I am going away."

I inquired where.

"To the north," he replied.

I looked at him to see whether he was in earnest. I saw it all in his firm, set mouth. I implored him not to go, but he paid no heed to my words. He said he was no longer a boy, and every day made his yoke more galling. He had raised his hand against his master, and was to be publicly whipped for the offense. I reminded him of the poverty and hardships he must encounter among strangers. I told him he might be caught and brought back; and that was terrible to think of.

He grew vexed, and asked if poverty and hardships with freedom, were not preferable to our treatment in slavery. "Linda," he continued, "we are dogs here; foot-ball, cattle, every thing that's mean. No, I will not stay. Let them bring me back. We don't die but once."

He was right; but it was hard to give him up. "Go," said I, "and break your mother's heart."

I repented of my words ere they were out.

"Linda," said he, speaking as I had not heard him speak that evening, "how *could* you say that? Poor mother! Be kind to her, Linda; and you, too, cousin Fanny."

Cousin Fanny was a friend who had lived some years with us.

Farewells were exchanged, and the bright, kind boy, endeared to us by so many acts of love, vanished from our sight.

It is not necessary to state how he made his escape. Suffice it to say, he was on his way to New York when a violent storm overtook the vessel. The captain said he must put into the nearest port. This alarmed Benjamin, who was aware that he would be advertised in every port near his own town. His embarrassment was noticed by the captain. To port they went. There the advertisement met the captain's eye. Benjamin so exactly answered its description, that the captain laid hold on him, and bound him in chains. The storm passed, and they proceeded to New York. Before reaching that port Benjamin managed to get off his chains and throw them overboard. He escaped from the vessel, but was pursued, captured, and carried back to his master.

When my grandmother returned home and found her youngest child had fled, great was her sorrow; but, with characteristic piety, she said, "God's will be done." Each morning, she inquired if any news had been heard from her boy. Yes, news *was* heard. The master was rejoicing over a letter, announcing the capture of his human chattel.

That day seems but as yesterday, so well do I remember it. I saw him led through the streets in chains, to jail. His face was ghastly pale, yet full of determination. He had begged one of the sailors to go to his mother's house and ask her not to meet him. He said the sight of her distress would take from him all self-control. She yearned to see him, and she went; but she screened herself in the crowd, that it might be as her child had said.

We were not allowed to visit him; but we had known the jailer for years, and he was a kind-hearted man. At midnight he opened the jail door for my grandmother and myself to enter, in disguise. When we entered the cell not a sound broke the stillness. "Benjamin, Benjamin!" whispered my grandmother. No answer. "Benjamin!" she again faltered. There was a jingle of chains. The moon had just risen, and cast an uncertain light through the bars of the window. We knelt down and took Benjamin's cold hands in ours. We did not speak. Sobs were heard, and Benjamin's lips were unsealed; for his mother was weeping on his neck. How vividly does memory bring back that sad night! Mother and son talked together. He asked her pardon for the suffering he had caused her. She said she had nothing to forgive; she could not blame his desire for freedom. He told her that when he was captured, he broke away, and was about casting himself into the river, when thoughts of her came over him, and he desisted. She asked if he did not also think of God. I fancied I saw his face g grow fierce in the moonlight. He answered, "No, I did not think of him. When a man is hunted like a wild beast he forgets there is a God, a heaven. He forgets every thing in his struggle to get beyond the reach of the bloodhounds."

"Don't talk so, Benjamin," said she. "Put your trust in God. Be humble, my child, and your master will forgive you."

"Forgive me for *what*, mother? For not letting him treat me like a dog? No! I will never humble myself to him. I have worked for him for nothing all my life, and I am repaid with stripes and imprisonment. Here I will stay till I die, or till he sells me."

The poor mother shuddered at his words. I think he felt it; for when he next spoke, his voice was calmer. "Don't fret about me, mother. I ain't worth it," said he. "I wish I had some of your goodness. You bear every thing patiently, just as though you thought it was all right. I wish I could."

She told him she had not always been so; once, she was like him; but when sore troubles came upon her, and she had no arm to lean upon, she learned to call on God, and he lightened her burdens. She besought him to do likewise.

We overstayed our time, and were obliged to hurry from the jail.

Benjamin had been imprisoned three weeks, when my grandmother went to intercede for him with his master. He was immovable. He said Benjamin should serve as an example to the rest of his slaves; he should be kept in jail till he was subdued, or be sold if he got but one dollar for him. However, he afterwards relented in some degree. The chains were taken off, and we were allowed to visit him.

As his food was of the coarsest kind, we carried him as often as possible a warm supper, accompanied with some little luxury for the jailer.

Three months elapsed, and there was no prospect of release or of a purchaser. One day he was heard to sing and laugh. This piece of indecorum was told to his master, and the overseer was ordered to re-chain him. He was now confined in an apartment with other prisoners, who were covered with filthy rags. Benjamin was chained near them, and was soon covered with vermin. He worked at his chains till he succeeded in getting out of them. He passed them through the bars of the window, with a request that they should be taken to his master, and he should be informed that he was covered with vermin.

This audacity was punished with heavier chains, and prohibition of our visits.

My grandmother continued to send him fresh changes of clothes. The old ones were burned up. The last night we saw him in jail his mother still begged him to send for his master, and beg his pardon. Neither persuasion nor argument could turn him from his purpose. He calmly answered, "I am waiting his time."

Those chains were mournful to hear.

Another three months passed, and Benjamin left his prison walls. We that loved him waited to bid him a long and last farewell. A slave-trader had bought him. You remember, I told you what price he brought when ten years of age. Now he was more than twenty years old, and sold for three hundred dollars. The master had been blind to his own interest. Long confinement had made his face too pale, his form too thin; moreover, the trader had heard something of his character, and it did not strike him as suitable for a slave. He said he would give any price if the handsome lad was a girl. We thanked God that he was not.

Could you have seen that mother clinging to her child, when they fastened the irons upon his wrists; could you have heard her heart-rending groans, and seen her bloodshot eyes wander wildly from face to face, vainly pleading for mercy; could you have witnessed that scene as I saw it, you would exclaim, *Slavery is damnable!*

Benjamin, her youngest, her pet, was forever gone! She could not realize it. She had had an interview with the trader for the purpose of ascertaining if Benjamin could be purchased. She was told it was impossible, as he had given bonds not to sell him till he was out of the state. He promised that he would not sell him till he reached New Orleans.

With a strong arm and unvaried trust, my grandmother began her work of love. Benjamin must be free. If she succeeded, she knew they would still be separated; but the sacrifice was not too great. Day and night she labored. The trader's price would treble that he gave; but she was not discouraged.

She employed a lawyer to write to a gentleman, whom she knew, in New Orleans. She begged him to interest himself for Benjamin, and he willingly favored her request. When he saw Benjamin, and stated his business, he thanked him; but said he preferred to wait a while before making the trader an offer. He knew he had tried to obtain a high price for him, and had invariably failed. This encouraged him to make another effort for freedom. So one morning, long before day, Benjamin was missing. He was riding over the blue billows, bound for Baltimore.

For once his white face did him a kindly service. They had no suspicion that it belonged to a slave; otherwise, the law would have been followed out to the letter, and the *thing* rendered back to slavery. The brightest skies are often overshadowed by the darkest clouds. Benjamin was taken sick, and compelled to remain in Baltimore three weeks. His strength was slow in returning; and his desire to continue his journey seemed to retard his recovery. How could he get strength without air and exercise? He resolved to venture on a short walk. A by-street was selected, where he thought himself secure of not being met by any one that knew him; but a voice called out, "Halloo, Ben, my boy! what are you doing *here?*"

His first impulse was to run; but his legs trembled so that he could not stir. He turned to confront his antagonist, and behold, there stood his old master's next door neighbor! He thought it was all over with him now; but it proved otherwise. That man was a miracle. He possessed a goodly number of slaves, and yet was not quite deaf to that mystic clock, whose ticking is rarely heard in the slaveholder's breast.

"Ben, you are sick," said he. "Why, you look like a ghost. I guess I gave you something of a start. Never mind, Ben, I am not going to touch you. You had a pretty tough time of it, and you may go on your way rejoicing for all me. But I would advise you to get out of this place plaguy quick, for there are several gentlemen here from our town." He described the nearest and safest route to New York, and added, "I shall be glad to tell your mother I have seen you. Good by, Ben."

Benjamin turned away, filled with gratitude, and surprised that the town he hated contained such a gem—a gem worthy of a purer setting.

This gentleman was a Northerner by birth, and had married a southern lady. On his return, he told my grandmother that he had seen her son, and of the service he had rendered him.

Benjamin reached New York safely, and concluded to stop there until he had gained strength enough to proceed further. It happened that my grandmother's only remaining son had sailed for the same city on business for his mistress. Through God's providence, the brothers met. You may be sure it was a happy meeting. "O Phil," exclaimed Benjamin, "I am here at last." Then he told him how near he came to dying, almost in sight of free land, and how he prayed that he might live to get one breath of free air. He said life was worth something now, and it would be hard to die. In the old jail he had not valued it; once, he was tempted to destroy it; but something, he did not know what, had prevented him; perhaps it was fear. He had heard those who profess to be religious declare there was no heaven for self-murderers; and as his life had been pretty hot here, he did not desire a continuation of the same in another world. "If I die now," he exclaimed, "thank God, I shall die a freeman!"

He begged my uncle Phillip not to return south; but stay and work with him, till they earned enough to buy those at home. His brother told him it would kill their mother if he deserted her in her trouble. She had pledged her house, and with difficulty had raised money to buy him. Would he be bought?

"No, never!" he replied. "Do you suppose, Phil, when I have got so far out of their clutches, I will give them one red cent? No! And do you suppose I would turn mother out of her home in her old age? That I would let her pay all those hard-earned dollars for me, and never to see me? For you know she will stay south as long as her other children are slaves. What a good mother! Tell her to buy *you*, Phil. You have been a comfort to her, and I have been a trouble. And Linda, poor Linda; what'll become of her? Phil, you don't know what a life they lead her. She has told me something about it, and I wish old Flint was dead, or a better man. When I was in jail, he asked her if she didn't want him to ask my master to forgive me, and take me home again. She told him, No; that I didn't want to go back. He got mad, and said we were all alike. I never despised my own master half as much as I do that man. There is many a worse slaveholder than my master; but for all that I would not be his slave."

While Benjamin was sick, he had parted with nearly all his clothes to pay necessary expenses. But he did not part with a little pin I fastened in his bosom when we parted. It was the most valuable thing I owned, and I thought none more worthy to wear it. He had it still.

His brother furnished him with clothes, and gave him what money he had.

They parted with moistened eyes; and as Benjamin turned away, he said, "Phil, I part with all my kindred." And so it proved. We never heard from him again.

Uncle Phillip came home; and the first words he uttered when he entered the house were, "Mother, Ben is free! I have seen him in New York." She stood looking at him with a bewildered air. "Mother, don't you believe it!" he said, laying his hand softly upon her shoulder. She raised her hands, and exclaimed, "God be praised! Let us thank him." She dropped on her knees, and poured forth her heart in prayer. Then Phillip must sit down and repeat to her every word Benjamin had said. He told her all; only he forbore to mention how sick and pale her darling looked. Why should he distress her when she could do him no good?

The brave old woman still toiled on, hoping to rescue some of her other children. After a while she succeeded in buying Phillip. She paid eight hundred dollars, and came home with the precious document that secured his freedom. The happy mother and son sat together by the old hearthstone that night, telling how proud they were of each other, and how they would prove to the world that they could take care of themselves, as they had long taken care of others. We all concluded by saying, "He that is *willing* to be a slave, let him be a slave."

V

THE TRIALS OF GIRLHOOD

During the first years of my service in Dr. Flint's family, I was accustomed to share some indulgences with the children of my mistress. Though this seemed to me no more than right, I was grateful for it, and tried to merit the kindness by the faithful discharge of my duties. But I now entered on my fifteenth year—a sad epoch in the life of a slave girl. My master began to whisper foul words in my ear. Young as I was, I could not remain ignorant of their import. I tried to treat them with indifference or contempt. The master's age, my extreme youth, and the fear that his conduct would be reported to my grandmother, made him bear this treatment for many months. He was a crafty man, and resorted to many means to accomplish his purposes. Sometimes he had stormy, terrific ways, that made his victims tremble; sometimes he assumed a gentleness that he thought must surely subdue. Of the two, I preferred his stormy moods, although they left me trembling. He tried his utmost to corrupt the pure principles my grandmother had instilled. He peopled my young mind with unclean images, such as only a vile monster could think of. I turned from him with disgust and hatred. But he was my master. I was compelled to live under the same roof with him— where I saw a man forty years my senior daily violating the most sacred commandments of nature. He told me I was his property; that I must be subject to his will in all things. My soul revolted against the mean tyranny. But where could I turn for protection? No matter whether the slave girl be as black as ebony or as fair as her mistress. In either case, there is no shadow of law to protect her from insult, from violence, or even from death; all these are inflicted by fiends who bear the shape of men. The mistress, who ought to protect the helpless victim, has no other feelings towards her but those of jealousy and rage. The degradation, the wrongs, the vices, that grow out of slavery, are more than I can describe. They are greater than you would willingly believe. Surely, if you credited one half the truths that are told you concerning the helpless millions suffering in this cruel bondage, you at the north would not help to tighten the yoke. You surely would refuse to do for the master, on your own soil, the mean and cruel work which trained bloodhounds and the lowest class of whites do for him at the south. Every where the years bring to all enough of sin and sorrow; but in slavery the very dawn of life is darkened by these shadows. Even the little child, who is accustomed to wait on her mistress and her children, will learn, before she is twelve years old, why it is that her mistress hates such and such a one among the slaves. Perhaps the child's own mother is among those hated ones. She listens to violent outbreaks of jealous passion, and cannot help understanding what is the cause. She will become prematurely knowing in evil things. Soon she will learn to tremble when she hears her master's footfall. She will be compelled to realize that she is no longer a child. If God has bestowed beauty upon her, it will prove her greatest curse. That which commands admiration in the white woman only hastens the degradation of the female slave. I know that some are too much brutalized by slavery to feel the humiliation of their position; but many slaves feel it most acutely, and shrink from the memory of it. I cannot tell how much I suffered in the presence of these wrongs, nor how I am still pained by the retrospect. My master met me at every turn, reminding me that I belonged to him, and swearing by heaven and earth that he would compel me to submit to him. If I went out for a breath of fresh air, after a day of unwearied toil, his footsteps dogged me. If I knelt by my mother's grave, his dark shadow fell on me even there. The light heart which nature had given me became heavy with sad forebodings. The other slaves in my master's house noticed the change. Many of them pitied me; but none dared to ask the cause. They had no need to inquire. They knew too well the guilty practices under that roof; and they were aware that to speak of them was an offense that never went unpunished.

I longed for some one to confide in. I would have given the world to have laid my head on my grandmother's faithful bosom, and told her all my troubles. But Dr. Flint swore he would kill me, if I was not as silent as the grave. Then, although my grandmother was all in all to me, I feared her as well as loved her. I had been accustomed to look up to her with a respect bordering upon awe. I was very young, and felt shamefaced about telling her such impure things, especially as I knew her to be very strict on such subjects. Moreover, she was a woman of a high spirit. She was usually very quiet in her demeanor; but if her indignation was once roused, it was not very easily quelled. I had been told that she once chased a white gentleman with a loaded pistol, because he insulted one of her daughters. I dreaded the consequences of a violent outbreak; and both pride and fear kept me silent. But though I did not confide in my grandmother, and even evaded her vigilant watchfulness and inquiry, her presence in the neighborhood was some protection to me. Though she had been a slave, Dr. Flint was afraid of her. He dreaded her scorching rebukes. Moreover, she was known and patronized by many people; and he did not wish to have his villainy made public. It was lucky for me that I did not live on a distant plantation, but in a town not so large that the inhabitants were ignorant of each other's affairs. Bad as are the laws and customs in a slaveholding community, the doctor, as a professional man, deemed it prudent to keep up some outward show of decency.

O, what days and nights of fear and sorrow that man caused me! Reader, it is not to awaken sympathy for myself that I am telling you truthfully what I suffered in slavery. I do it to kindle a flame of compassion in your hearts for my sisters who are still in bondage, suffering as I once suffered.

I once saw two beautiful children playing together. One was a fair white child; the other was her slave, and also her sister. When I saw them embracing each other, and heard their joyous laughter, I turned sadly away from the lovely sight. I foresaw the inevitable blight that would fall on the little slave's heart. I knew how soon her laughter would be changed to sighs. The fair child grew up to be a still fairer woman. From childhood to womanhood her pathway was blooming with flowers, and overarched by a sunny sky. Scarcely one day of her life had been clouded when the sun rose on her happy bridal morning.

How had those years dealt with her slave sister, the little playmate of her childhood? She, also, was very beautiful; but the flowers and sunshine of love were not for her. She drank the cup of sin, and shame, and misery, whereof her persecuted race are compelled to drink.

In view of these things, why are ye silent, ye free men and women of the north? Why do your tongues falter in maintenance of the right? Would that I had more ability! But my heart is so full, and my pen is so weak! There are noble men and women who plead for us, striving to help those who cannot help themselves. God bless them! God give them strength and courage to go on! God bless those, every where, who are laboring to advance the cause of humanity!

VI

THE JEALOUS MISTRESS

I would ten thousand times rather that my children should be the half-starved paupers of Ireland than to be the most pampered among the slaves of America. I would rather drudge out my life on a cotton plantation, till the grave opened to give me rest, than to live with an unprincipled master and a jealous mistress. The felon's home in a penitentiary is preferable. He may repent, and turn from the error of his ways, and so find peace; but it is not so with a favorite slave. She is not allowed to have any pride of character. It is deemed a crime in her to wish to be virtuous.

Mrs. Flint possessed the key to her husband's character before I was born. She might have used this knowledge to counsel and to screen the young and the innocent among her slaves; but for them she had no sympathy. They were the objects of her constant suspicion and malevolence. She watched her husband with unceasing vigilance; but he was well practiced in means to evade it. What he could not find opportunity to say in words he manifested in signs. He invented more than were ever thought of in a deaf and dumb asylum. I let them pass, as if I did not understand what he meant; and many were the curses and threats bestowed on me for my stupidity. One day he caught me teaching myself to write. He frowned, as if he was not well pleased; but suppose he came to the conclusion that such an accomplishment might help to advance his favorite scheme. Before long, notes were often slipped into my hand. I would return them, saying, "I can't read them, sir." "Can't you?" he replied "then I must read them to you." He always finished the reading by asking, "Do you understand?" Sometimes he would complain of the heat of the tea room, and order his supper to be placed on a small table in the piazza. He would seat himself there with a well-satisfied smile, and tell me to stand by and brush away the flies. He would eat very slowly, pausing between the mouthfuls. These intervals were employed in describing the happiness I was so foolishly throwing away, and in threatening me with the penalty that finally awaited my stubborn disobedience. He boasted much of the forbearance he had exercised towards me, and reminded me that there was a limit to his patience. When I succeeded in avoiding opportunities for him to talk to me at home, I was ordered to come to his office, to do some errand. When there, I was obliged to stand and listen to such language as he saw fit to address to me. Sometimes I so openly expressed my contempt for him that he would become violently enraged, and I wondered why he did not strike me. Circumstanced as he was, he probably thought it was better policy to be forbearing. But the state of things grew worse and worse daily. In desperation I told him that I must and would apply to my grandmother for protection. He threatened me with death, and worse than death, if I made any complaint to her. Strange to say, I did not despair. I was naturally of a buoyant disposition, and always I had a hope of somehow getting out of his clutches. Like many a poor, simple slave before me, I trusted that some threads of joy would yet be woven into my dark destiny.

I had entered my sixteenth year, and every day it became more apparent that my presence was intolerable to Mrs. Flint. Angry words frequently passed between her and her husband. He had never punished me himself, and he would not allow any body else to punish me. In that respect, she was never satisfied; but, in her angry moods, no terms were too vile for her to bestow upon me. Yet I, whom she detested so bitterly, had far more pity for her than he had, whose duty it was to make her life happy. I never wronged her, or wished to wrong her; and one word of kindness from her would have brought me to her feet.

After repeated quarrels between the doctor and his wife, he announced his intention to take his youngest daughter, then four years old, to sleep in his apartment. It was necessary that a servant should sleep in the same room, to be on hand if the child stirred. I was selected for that office, and informed for what purpose that arrangement had been made. By managing to keep within sight of people, as much as possible, during the day time, I had hitherto succeeded in eluding my master, though a razor was often held to my throat to force me to change this line of policy. At night I slept by the side of my great aunt, where I felt safe. He was too prudent to come into her room. She was an old woman, and had been in the family many years. Moreover, as a married man, and a professional man, he deemed it necessary to save appearances in some degree. But he resolved to remove the obstacle in the way of his scheme; and he thought he had planned it so that he should evade suspicion. He was well aware how much I prized my refuge by the side of my old aunt, and he determined to dispossess me of it. The first night the doctor had the little child in his room alone. The next morning, I was ordered to take my station as nurse the following night. A kind Providence interposed in my favor. During the day Mrs. Flint heard of this new arrangement, and a storm followed. I rejoiced to hear it rage.

After a while my mistress sent for me to come to her room. Her first question was, "Did you know you were to sleep in the doctor's room?"

"Yes, ma'am."

"Who told you?"

"My master." "Will you answer truly all the questions I ask?"

"Yes, ma am."

"Tell me, then, as you hope to be forgiven, are you innocent of what I have accused you?"

"I am."

She handed me a Bible, and said, "Lay your hand on your heart, kiss this holy book, and swear before God that you tell me the truth."

I took the oath she required, and I did it with a clear conscience.

"You have taken God's holy word to testify your innocence," said she. "If you have deceived me, beware! Now take this stool, sit down, look me directly in the face, and tell me all that has passed between your master and you."

I did as she ordered. As I went on with my account her color changed frequently, she wept, and sometimes groaned. She spoke in tones so sad, that I was touched by her grief. The tears came to my eyes; but I was soon convinced that her emotions arose from anger and wounded pride. She felt that her marriage vows were desecrated, her dignity insulted; but she had no compassion for the poor victim of her husband's perfidy. She pitied herself as a martyr; but she was incapable of feeling for the condition of shame and misery in which her unfortunate, helpless slave was placed.

Yet perhaps she had some touch of feeling for me; for when the conference was ended, she spoke kindly, and promised to protect me. I should have been much comforted by this assurance if I could have had confidence in it; but my experiences in slavery had filled me with distrust. She was not a very refined woman, and had not much control over her passions. I was an object of her jealousy, and, consequently, of her hatred; and I knew I could not expect kindness or confidence from her under the circumstances in which I was placed. I could not blame her. Slaveholders' wives feel as other women would under similar circumstances. The fire of her temper kindled from small sparks, and now the flame became so intense that the doctor was obliged to give up his intended arrangement.

I knew I had ignited the torch, and I expected to suffer for it afterwards; but I felt too thankful to my mistress for the timely aid she rendered me to care much about that. She now took me to sleep in a room adjoining her own. There I was an object of her especial care, though not of her especial comfort, for she spent many a sleepless night to watch over me. Sometimes I woke up, and found her bending over me. At other times she whispered in my ear, as though it was her husband who was speaking to me, and listened to hear what I would answer. If she startled me, on such occasions, she would glide stealthily away; and the next morning she would tell me I had been talking in my sleep, and ask who I was talking to. At last, I began to be fearful for my life. It had been often threatened; and you can imagine, better than I can describe, what an unpleasant sensation it must produce to wake up in the dead of night and find a jealous woman bending over you. Terrible as this experience was, I had fears that it would give place to one more terrible.

My mistress grew weary of her vigils; they did not prove satisfactory. She changed her tactics. She now tried the trick of accusing my master of crime, in my presence, and gave my name as the author of the accusation. To my utter astonishment, he replied, "I don't believe it; but if she did acknowledge it, you tortured her into exposing me." Tortured into exposing him! Truly, Satan had no difficulty in distinguishing the color of his soul! I understood his object in making this false representation. It was to show me that I gained nothing by seeking the protection of my mistress; that the power was still all in his own hands. I pitied Mrs. Flint. She was a second wife, many years the junior of her husband; and the hoary-headed miscreant was enough to try the patience of a wiser and better woman. She was completely foiled, and knew not how to proceed. She would gladly have had me flogged for my supposed false oath; but, as I have already stated, the doctor never allowed any one to whip me. The old sinner was politic. The application of the lash might have led to remarks that would have exposed him in the eyes of his children and grandchildren. How often did I rejoice that I lived in a town where all the inhabitants knew each other! If I had been on a remote plantation, or lost among the multitude of a crowded city, I should not be a living woman at this day.

The secrets of slavery are concealed like those of the Inquisition. My master was, to my knowledge, the father of eleven slaves. But did the mothers dare to tell who was the father of their children? Did the other slaves dare to allude to it, except in whispers among themselves? No, indeed! They knew too well the terrible consequences.

My grandmother could not avoid seeing things which excited her suspicions. She was uneasy about me, and tried various ways to buy me; but the never-changing answer was always repeated: "Linda does not belong to me. She is my daughter's property, and I have no legal right to sell her." The conscientious man! He was too scrupulous to sell me; but he had no scruples whatever about committing a much greater wrong against the helpless young girl placed under his guardianship, as his daughter's property. Sometimes my persecutor would ask me whether I would like to be sold. I told him I would rather be sold to any body than to lead such a life as I did. On such occasions he would assume the air of a very injured individual, and reproach me for my ingratitude. "Did I not take you into the house, and make you the companion of my own children?" he would say. "Have I ever treated you like a negro? I have never allowed you to be punished, not even to please your mistress. And this is the recompense I get, you ungrateful girl!" I answered that he had reasons of his own for screening me from punishment, and that the course he pursued made my mistress hate me and persecute me. If I wept, he would say, "Poor child! Don't cry! don't cry! I will make peace for you with your mistress. Only let me arrange matters in my own way. Poor, foolish girl! you don't know what is for your own good. I would cherish you. I would make a lady of you. Now go, and think of all I have promised you."

I did think of it.

Reader, I draw no imaginary pictures of southern homes. I am telling you the plain truth. Yet when victims make their escape from this wild beast of Slavery, northerners consent to act the part of bloodhounds, and hunt the poor fugitive back into his den, "full of dead men's bones, and all uncleanness." Nay, more, they are not only willing, but proud, to give their daughters in marriage to slaveholders. The poor girls have romantic notions of a sunny clime, and of the flowering vines that all the year round shade a happy home. To what disappointments are they destined! The young wife soon learns that the husband in whose hands she has placed her happiness pays no regard to his marriage vows. Children of every shade of complexion play with her own fair babies, and too well she knows that they are born unto him of his own household. Jealousy and hatred enter the flowery home, and it is ravaged of its loveliness.

Southern women often marry a man knowing that he is the father of many little slaves. They do not trouble themselves about it. They regard such children as property, as marketable as the pigs on the plantation; and it is seldom that they do not make them aware of this by passing them into the slavetrader's hands as soon as possible, and thus getting them out of their sight. I am glad to say there are some honorable exceptions.

I have myself known two southern wives who exhorted their husbands to free those slaves towards whom they stood in a "parental relation;" and their request was granted. These husbands blushed before the superior nobleness of their wives' natures. Though they had only counseled them to do that which it was their duty to do, it commanded their respect, and rendered their conduct more exemplary. Concealment was at an end, and confidence took the place of distrust.

Though this bad institution deadens the moral sense, even in white women, to a fearful extent, it is not altogether extinct. I have heard southern ladies say of Mr. Such a one, "He not only thinks it no disgrace to be the father of those little niggers, but he is not ashamed to call himself their master. I declare, such things ought not to be tolerated in any decent society!"

VII
THE LOVER

Why does the slave ever love? Why allow the tendrils of the heart to twine around objects which may at any moment be wrenched away by the hand of violence? When separations come by the hand of death, the pious soul can bow in resignation, and say, "Not my will, but thine be done, O Lord!" But when the ruthless hand of man strikes the blow, regardless of the misery he causes, it is hard to be submissive. I did not reason thus when I was a young girl. Youth will be youth. I loved, and I indulged the hope that the dark clouds around me would turn out a bright lining. I forgot that in the land of my birth the shadows are too dense for light to penetrate. A land

"Where laughter is not mirth; nor thought the mind;

Nor words a language; nor e'en men mankind.
Where cries reply to curses, shrieks to blows,
And each is tortured in his separate hell."

There was in the neighborhood a young colored carpenter; a free-born man. We had been well acquainted in childhood, and frequently met together afterwards. We became mutually attached, and he proposed to marry me. I loved him with all the ardor of a young girl's first love. But when I reflected that I was a slave, and that the laws gave no sanction to the marriage of such, my heart sank within me. My lover wanted to buy me; but I knew that Dr. Flint was too willful and arbitrary a man to consent to that arrangement. From him, I was sure of experiencing all sorts of opposition, and I had nothing to hope from my mistress. She would have been delighted to have got rid of me, but not in that way. It would have relieved her mind of a burden if she could have seen me sold to some distant state, but if I was married near home I should be just as much in her husband's power as I had previously been,— for the husband of a slave has no power to protect her. Moreover, my mistress, like many others, seemed to think that slaves had no right to any family ties of their own; that they were created merely to wait upon the family of the mistress. I once heard her abuse a young slave girl, who told her that a colored man wanted to make her his wife. "I will have you peeled and pickled, my lady," said she, "if I ever hear you mention that subject again. Do you suppose that I will have you tending *my* children with the children of that nigger?" The girl to whom she said this had a mulatto child, of course not acknowledged by its father. The poor black man who loved her would have been proud to acknowledge his helpless offspring.

Many and anxious were the thoughts I revolved in my mind. I was at a loss what to do. Above all things, I was desirous to spare my lover the insults that had cut so deeply into my own soul. I talked with my grandmother about it, and partly told her my fears. I did not dare to tell her the worst. She had long suspected all was not right, and if I confirmed her suspicions I knew a storm would rise that would prove the overthrow of all my hopes.

This love-dream had been my support through many trials; and I could not bear to run the risk of having it suddenly dissipated. There was a lady in the neighborhood, a particular friend of Dr. Flint's, who often visited the house. I had a great respect for her, and she had always manifested a friendly interest in me.

Grandmother thought she would have great influence with the doctor. I went to this lady, and told her my story. I told her I was aware that my lover's being a free-born man would prove a great objection; but he wanted to buy me; and if Dr. Flint would consent to that arrangement, I felt sure he would be willing to pay any reasonable price. She knew that Mrs. Flint disliked me; therefore, I ventured to suggest that perhaps my mistress would approve of my being sold, as that would rid her of me. The lady listened with kindly sympathy, and promised to do her utmost to promote my wishes. She had an interview with the doctor, and I believe she pleaded my cause earnestly; but it was all to no purpose.

How I dreaded my master now! Every minute I expected to be summoned to his presence; but the day passed, and I heard nothing from him. The next morning, a message was brought to me: "Master wants you in his study." I found the door ajar, and I stood a moment gazing at the hateful man who claimed a right to rule me, body and soul. I entered, and tried to appear calm. I did not want him to know how my heart was bleeding. He looked fixedly at me, with an expression which seemed to say, "I have half a mind to kill you on the spot." At last he broke the silence, and that was a relief to both of us.

"So you want to be married, do you?" said he, "and to a free nigger."

"Yes, sir."

"Well, I'll soon convince you whether I am your master, or the nigger fellow you honor so highly. If you must have a husband, you may take up with one of my slaves."

What a situation I should be in, as the wife of one of his slaves, even if my heart had been interested!

I replied, "Don't you suppose, sir, that a slave can have some preference about marrying? Do you suppose that all men are alike to her?"

"Do you love this nigger?" said he, abruptly.

"Yes, sir."

"How dare you tell me so!" he exclaimed, in great wrath. After a slight pause, he added, "I supposed you thought more of yourself; that you felt above the insults of such puppies."

I replied, "If he is a puppy I am a puppy, for we are both of the negro race. It is right and honorable for us to love each other. The man you call a puppy never insulted me, sir; and he would not love me if he did not believe me to be a virtuous woman."

He sprang upon me like a tiger, and gave me a stunning blow. It was the first time he had ever struck me; and fear did not enable me to control my anger. When I had recovered a little from the effects, I exclaimed, "You have struck me for answering you honestly. How I despise you!"

There was silence for some minutes. Perhaps he was deciding what should be my punishment; or, perhaps, he wanted to give me time to reflect on what I had said, and to whom I had said it. Finally, he asked, "Do you know what you have said?"

"Yes, sir; but your treatment drove me to it."

"Do you know that I have a right to do as I like with you,—that I can kill you, if I please?"

"You have tried to kill me, and I wish you had; but you have no right to do as you like with me."

"Silence!" he exclaimed, in a thundering voice. "By heavens, girl, you forget yourself too far! Are you mad? If you are, I will soon bring you to your senses. Do you think any other master would bear what I have borne from you this morning? Many masters would have killed you on the spot. How would you like to be sent to jail for your insolence?"

"I know I have been disrespectful, sir," I replied; "but you drove me to it; I couldn't help it. As for the jail, there would be more peace for me there than there is here."

"You deserve to go there," said he, "and to be under such treatment, that you would forget the meaning of the word peace. It would do you good. It would take some of your high notions out of you. But I am not ready to send you there yet, notwithstanding your ingratitude for all my kindness and forbearance. You have been the plague of my life. I have wanted to make you happy, and I have been repaid with the basest ingratitude; but though you have proved yourself incapable of appreciating my kindness, I will be lenient towards you, Linda. I will give you one more chance to redeem your character. If you behave yourself and do as I require, I will forgive you and treat you as I always have done; but if you disobey me, I will punish you as I would the meanest slave on my plantation. Never let me hear that fellow's name mentioned again. If I ever know of your speaking to him, I will cowhide you both; and if I catch him lurking about my premises, I will shoot him as soon as I would a dog. Do you hear what I say? I'll teach you a lesson about marriage and free niggers! Now go, and let this be the last time I have occasion to speak to you on this subject."

Reader, did you ever hate? I hope not. I never did but once; and I trust I never shall again. Somebody has called it "the atmosphere of hell;" and I believe it is so.

For a fortnight the doctor did not speak to me. He thought to mortify me; to make me feel that I had disgraced myself by receiving the honorable addresses of a respectable colored man, in preference to the base proposals of a white man. But though his lips disdained to address me, his eyes were very loquacious No animal ever watched its prey more narrowly than he watched me. He knew that I could write, though he had failed to make me read his letters; and he was now troubled lest I should exchange letters with another man. After a while he became weary of silence; and I was sorry for it. One morning, as he passed through the hall, to leave the house, he contrived to thrust a note into my hand. I thought I had better read it, and spare myself the vexation of having him read it to me. It expressed regret for the blow he had given me, and reminded me that I myself was wholly to blame for it. He hoped I had become convinced of the injury I was doing myself by incurring his displeasure. He wrote that he had made up his mind to go to Louisiana; that he should take several slaves with him, and intended I should be one of the number. My mistress would remain where she was; therefore I should have nothing to fear from that quarter. If I merited kindness from him, he assured me that it would be lavishly bestowed. He begged me to think over the matter, and answer the following day.

The next morning I was called to carry a pair of scissors to his room. I laid them on the table, with the letter beside them. He thought it was my answer, and did not call me back. I went as usual to attend my young mistress to and from school. He met me in the street, and ordered me to stop at his office on my way back. When I entered, he showed me his letter, and asked me why I had not answered it. I replied, "I am your daughter's property, and it is in your power to send me, or take me, wherever you please." He said he was very glad to find me so willing to go, and that we should start early in the autumn. He had a large practice in the town, and I rather thought he had made up the story merely to frighten me.

However that might be, I was determined that I would never go to Louisiana with him.

Summer passed away, and early in the autumn Dr. Flint's eldest son was sent to Louisiana to examine the country, with a view to emigrating. That news did not disturb me. I knew very well that I should not be sent with *him*. That I had not been taken to the plantation before this time, was owing to the fact that his son was there. He was jealous of his son; and jealousy of the overseer had kept him from punishing me by sending me into the fields to work. Is it strange that I was not proud of these protectors? As for the overseer, he was a man for whom I had less respect than I had for a bloodhound.

Young Mr. Flint did not bring back a favorable report of Louisiana, and I heard no more of that scheme. Soon after this, my lover met me at the corner of the street, and I stopped to speak to him. Looking up, I saw my master watching us from his window. I hurried home, trembling with fear. I was sent for, immediately, to go to his room. He met me with a blow. "When is mistress to be married?" said he, in a sneering tone. A shower of oaths and imprecations followed. How thankful I was that my lover was a free man! that my tyrant had no power to flog him for speaking to me in the street!

Again and again I revolved in my mind how all this would end. There was no hope that the doctor would consent to sell me on any terms. He had an iron will, and was determined to keep me, and to conquer me. My lover was an intelligent and religious man. Even if he could have obtained permission to marry me while I was a slave, the marriage would give him no power to protect me from my master. It would have made him miserable to witness the insults I should have been subjected to. And then, if we had children, I knew they must "follow the condition of the mother." What a terrible blight that would be on the heart of a free, intelligent father! For his sake, I felt that I ought not to link his fate with my own unhappy destiny. He was going to Savannah to see about a little property left him by an uncle; and hard as it was to bring my feelings to it, I earnestly entreated him not to come back. I advised him to go to the Free States, where his tongue would not be tied, and where his intelligence would be of more avail to him. He left me, still hoping the day would come when I could be bought. With me the lamp of hope had gone out. The dream of my girlhood was over. I felt lonely and desolate.

Still I was not stripped of all. I still had my good grandmother, and my affectionate brother. When he put his arms round my neck, and looked into my eyes, as if to read there the troubles I dared not tell, I felt that I still had something to love. But even that pleasant emotion was chilled by the reflection that he might be torn from me at any moment, by some sudden freak of my master. If he had known how we loved each other, I think he would have exulted in separating us. We often planned together how we could get to the north. But, as William remarked, such things are easier said than done. My movements were very closely watched, and we had no means of getting any money to defray our expenses. As for grandmother, she was strongly opposed to her children's undertaking any such project. She had not forgotten poor Benjamin's sufferings, and she was afraid that if another child tried to escape, he would have a similar or a worse fate. To me, nothing seemed more dreadful than my present life. I said to myself, "William *must* be free. He shall go to the north, and I will follow him." Many a slave sister has formed the same plans.

VIII
WHAT SLAVES ARE TAUGHT TO THINK OF THE NORTH

Slaveholders pride themselves upon being honorable men; but if you were to hear the enormous lies they tell their slaves, you would have small respect for their veracity. I have spoken plain English. Pardon me. I cannot use a milder term. When they visit the north, and return home, they tell their slaves of the runaways they have seen, and describe them to be in the most deplorable condition. A slaveholder once told me that he had seen a runaway friend of mine in New York, and that she besought him to take her back to her master, for she was literally dying of starvation; that many days she had only one cold potato to eat, and at other times could get nothing at all. He said he refused to take her, because he knew her master would not thank him for bringing such a miserable wretch to his house. He ended by saying to me, "This is the punishment she brought on herself for running away from a kind master."

This whole story was false. I afterwards staid with that friend in New York, and found her in comfortable circumstances. She had never thought of such a thing as wishing to go back to slavery. Many of the slaves believe such stories, and think it is not worth while to exchange slavery for such a hard kind of freedom. It is difficult to persuade such that freedom could make them useful men, and enable them to protect their wives and children. If those heathens in our Christian land had as much teaching as some Hindus, they would think otherwise. They would know that liberty is more valuable than life. They would begin to understand their own capabilities, and exert themselves to become men and women.

But while the Free States sustain a law which hurls fugitives back into slavery, how can the slaves resolve to become men? There are some who strive to protect wives and daughters from the insults of their masters; but those who have such sentiments have had advantages above the general mass of slaves. They have been partially civilized and Christianized by favorable circumstances. Some are bold enough to *utter* such sentiments to their masters. O, that there were more of them!

Some poor creatures have been so brutalized by the lash that they will sneak out of the way to give their masters free access to their wives and daughters. Do you think this proves the black man to belong to an inferior order of beings? What would *you* be, if you had been born and brought up a slave, with generations of slaves for ancestors? I admit that the black man is inferior. But what is it that makes him so? It is the ignorance in which white men compel him to live; it is the torturing whip that lashes manhood out of him; it is the fierce bloodhounds of the south, and the scarcely less cruel human bloodhounds of the north, who enforce the Fugitive Slave Law.* *They* do the work.

Southern gentlemen indulge in the most contemptuous expressions about the Yankees, while they, on their part, consent to do the vilest work for them, such as the ferocious bloodhounds and the despised negro-hunters are employed to do at home. When southerners go to the north, they are proud to do them honor; but the northern man is not welcome south of Mason and Dixon's line,** unless he suppresses every thought and feeling at variance with their "peculiar institution." Nor is it enough to be silent. The masters are not pleased, unless they obtain a greater degree of subservience than that; and they are generally accommodated. Do they respect the northerner for this? I trow not. Even the slaves despise "a northern man with southern principles;" and that is the class they generally see. When northerners go to the south to reside, they prove very apt scholars. They soon imbibe the sentiments and disposition of their neighbors, and generally go beyond their teachers. Of the two, they are proverbially the hardest masters.

They seem to satisfy their consciences with the doctrine that God created the Africans to be slaves. What a libel upon the heavenly Father, who "made of one blood all nations of men!" And then who are Africans? Who can measure the amount of Anglo-Saxon blood coursing in the veins of American slaves?

I have spoken of the pains slaveholders take to give their slaves a bad opinion of the north; but, notwithstanding this, intelligent slaves are aware that they have many friends in the Free States. Even the most ignorant have some confused notions about it. They knew that I could read; and I was often asked if I had seen any thing in the newspapers about white folks over in the big north, who were trying to get their freedom for them. Some believe that the abolitionists have already made them free, and that it is established by law, but that their masters prevent the law from going into effect. One woman begged me to get a newspaper and read it over. She said her husband told her that the black people had sent word to the queen of 'Merica that they were all slaves; that she didn't believe it, and went to Washington city to see the president about it. They quarreled; she drew her sword upon him, and swore that he should help her to make them all free.

That poor, ignorant woman thought that America was governed by a Queen, to whom the President was subordinate. I wish the President was subordinate to Queen Justice.

There was a planter in the country, not far from us, whom I will call Mr. Fitch. He was an ill-bred, uneducated man, but very wealthy. He had six hundred slaves, many of whom he did not know by sight. His extensive plantation was managed by well-paid overseers. There was a jail and a whipping post on his grounds; and whatever cruelties were perpetrated there, they passed without comment. He was so effectually screened by his great wealth that he was called to no account for his crimes, not even for murder.

* Enacted in September 1850, the Fugitive Slave Law made it easy to seize legally and enslave any black man or woman at large. A white man had only to appear before a specially appointed United States commissioner, swear ownership of the black person, and request a certificate for arresting him. The commissioner received more money (ten dollars) for issuing such a certificate and less (five dollars) for refusing it. The alleged fugitive was not permitted to testify, nor, if he claimed to be a freeman, did he have the right to trial by jury. Citizens, if called on, had to assist United States marshals in making arrests. Anyone harboring or rescuing a fugitive could be fined, imprisoned, and sued for damages. The Fugitive Slave Law brought on an era of slave hunting and kidnapping in the North that forced hundreds of slaves who had escaped before 1850 to flee to Canada. It polarized opinions and helped set the stage for the Civil War. Linda Brent's editor, L. Maria Child, wrote a pamphlet entitled *Duty of Disobedience to the Fugitive Slave Act*, published by the American Anti-Slavery Society, Boston, in 1860. W. T.

Various were the punishments resorted to. A favorite one was to tie a rope round a man's body, and suspend him from the ground. A fire was kindled over him, from which was suspended a piece of fat pork. As this cooked, the scalding drops of fat continually fell on the bare flesh. On his own plantation, he required very strict obedience to the eighth commandment. But depredations on the neighbors were allowable, provided the culprit managed to evade detection or suspicion. If a neighbor brought a charge of theft against any of his slaves, he was browbeaten by the master, who assured him that his slaves had enough of every thing at home, and had no inducement to steal. No sooner was the neighbor's back turned, than the accused was sought out, and whipped for his lack of discretion. If a slave stole from him even a pound of meat or a peck of corn, if detection followed, he was put in chains and imprisoned, and so kept till his form was attenuated by hunger and suffering.

A freshet once bore his wine cellar and meat house miles away from the plantation. Some slaves followed, and secured bits of meat and bottles of wine. Two were detected; a ham and some liquor being found in their huts. They were summoned by their master. No words were used, but a club felled them to the ground. A rough box was their coffin, and their interment was a dog's burial. Nothing was said.

Murder was so common on his plantation that he feared to be alone after nightfall. He might have believed in ghosts.

His brother, if not equal in wealth, was at least equal in cruelty. His bloodhounds were well trained. Their pen was spacious, and a terror to the slaves. They were let loose on a runaway, and, if they tracked him, they literally tore the flesh from his bones. When this slaveholder died, his shrieks and groans were so frightful that they appalled his own friends. His last words were, "I am going to hell; bury my money with me."

After death his eyes remained open. To press the lids down, silver dollars were laid on them. These were buried with him. From this circumstance, a rumor went abroad that his coffin was filled

*Completed after four years of work by two eighteenth-century English surveyors, Charles Mason and Jeremiah Dixon, it established a line that formed the southern boundary of Pennsylvania and the northern boundary of Delaware, Maryland, and part of Virginia, now West Virginia. In the period before the Civil War, the Mason-Dixon line marked the division between slave states and free soil. W. T.

with money. Three times his grave was opened, and his coffin taken out. The last time, his body was found on the ground, and a flock of buzzards were pecking at it. He was again interred, and a sentinel set over his grave. The perpetrators were never discovered.

Cruelty is contagious in uncivilized communities. Mr. Conant, a neighbor of Mr. Litch, returned from town one evening in a partial state of intoxication. His body servant gave him some offense. He was divested of his clothes, except his shirt, whipped, and tied to a large tree in front of the house. It was a stormy night in winter. The wind blew bitterly cold, and the boughs of the old tree crackled under falling sleet. A member of the family, fearing he would freeze to death, begged that he might be taken down; but the master would not relent. He remained there three hours; and, when he was cut down, he was more dead than alive. Another slave, who stole a pig from this master, to appease his hunger, was terribly flogged. In desperation, he tried to run away. But at the end of two miles, he was so faint with loss of blood, he thought he was dying. He had a wife, and he longed to see her once more. Too sick to walk, he crept back that long distance on his hands and knees. When he reached his master's, it was night. He had not strength to rise and open the gate. He moaned, and tried to call for help. I had a friend living in the same family. At last his cry reached her. She went out and found the prostrate man at the gate. She ran back to the house for assistance, and two men returned with her. They carried him in, and laid him on the floor. The back of his shirt was one clot of blood. By means of lard, my friend loosened it from the raw flesh. She bandaged him, gave him cool drink, and left him to rest. The master said he deserved a hundred more lashes. When his own labor was stolen from him, he had stolen food to appease his hunger. This was his crime.

Another neighbor was a Mrs. Wade. At no hour of the day was there cessation of the lash on her premises. Her labors began with the dawn, and did not cease till long after nightfall. The barn was her particular place of torture. There she lashed the slaves with the might of a man. An old slave of hers once said to me, "It is hell in missis's house. 'Pears I can never get out. Day and night I prays to die."

The mistress died before the old woman, and, when dying, entreated her husband not to permit any one of her slaves to look on her after death. A slave who had nursed her children, and had still a child in her care, watched her chance, and stole with it in her arms to the room where lay her dead mistress. She gazed a while on her, then raised her hand and dealt two blows on her face, saying, as she did so, "The devil is got you *now*!" She forgot that the child was looking on. She had just begun to talk; and she said to her father, "I did see ma, and mammy did strike ma, so," striking her own face with her little hand. The master was startled. He could not imagine how the nurse could obtain access to the room where the corpse lay; for he kept the door locked. He questioned her. She confessed that what the child had said was true, and told how she had procured the key. She was sold to Georgia.

In my childhood I knew a valuable slave, named Charity, and loved her, as all children did. Her young mistress married, and took her to Louisiana. Her little boy, James, was sold to a good sort of master. He became involved in debt, and James was sold again to a wealthy slaveholder, noted for his cruelty. With this man he grew up to manhood, receiving the treatment of a dog. After a severe whipping, to save himself from further infliction of the lash, with which he was threatened, he took to the woods. He was in a most miserable condition, cut by the cowskin, half naked, half starved, and without the means of procuring a crust of bread.

Some weeks after his escape, he was captured, tied, and carried back to his master's plantation This man considered punishment in his jail, on bread and water, after receiving hundreds of lashes, too mild for the poor slave's offense. Therefore he decided, after the overseer should have whipped him to his satisfaction, to have him placed between the screws of the cotton gin, to stay as long as he had been in the woods. This wretched creature was cut with the whip from his head to his feet, then washed with strong brine, to prevent the flesh from mortifying, and make it heal sooner than it otherwise would. He was then put into the cotton gin, which was screwed down, only allowing him room to turn on his side when he could not lie on his back. Every morning a slave was sent with a piece of bread and bowl of water, which were placed within reach of the poor fellow. The slave was charged, under penalty of severe punishment, not to speak to him.

Four days passed, and the slave continued to carry the bread and water. On the second morning, he found the bread gone, but the water untouched. When he had been in the press four days and five nights, the slave informed his master that the water had not been used for four mornings, and that a horrible stench came from the gin house. The overseer was sent to examine into it. When the press was unscrewed, the dead body was found partly eaten by rats and vermin. Perhaps the rats that devoured his bread had gnawed him before life was extinct. Poor Charity! Grandmother and I often asked each other how her affectionate heart would bear the news, if she should ever hear of the murder of her son. We had known her husband, and knew that James was like him in manliness and intelligence. These were the qualities that made it so hard for him to be a plantation slave. They put him into a rough box, and buried him with less feeling than would have been manifested for an old house dog. Nobody asked any questions. He was a slave; and the feeling was that the master had a right to do what he pleased with his own property. And what did he care for the value of a slave? He had hundreds of them. When they had finished their daily toil, they must hurry to eat their little morsels, and be ready to extinguish their pine knots before nine o'clock, when the overseer went his patrol rounds. He entered every cabin, to see that men and their wives had gone to bed together, lest the men, from over fatigue, should fall asleep in the chimney corner, and remain there till the morning horn called them to their daily task. Women are considered of no value, unless they continually increase their owner's stock. They are put on a par with animals. This same master shot a woman through the head, who had run away and been brought back to him. No one called him to account for it. If a slave resisted being whipped, the bloodhounds were unpacked, and set upon him, to tear his flesh from his bones. The master who did these things was highly educated, and styled a perfect gentleman. He also boasted the name and standing of a Christian, though Satan never had a truer follower.

I could tell of more slaveholders as cruel as those I have described. They are not exceptions to the general rule. I do not say there are no humane slaveholders. Such characters do exist, notwithstanding the hardening influences around them. But they are "like angels' visits—few and far between."

I knew a young lady who was one of these rare specimens. She was an orphan, and inherited as slaves a woman and her six children. Their father was a free man. They had a comfortable home of their own, parents and children living together. The mother and eldest daughter served their mistress during the day, and at night returned to their dwelling, which was on the premises. The young lady was very pious, and there was some reality in her religion. She taught her slaves to lead pure lives, and wished them to enjoy the fruit of their own industry. *Her* religion was not a garb put on for Sunday, and laid aside till Sunday returned again. The eldest daughter of the slave mother was promised in marriage to a free man; and the day before the wedding this good mistress emancipated her, in order that her marriage might have the sanction of *law*.

Report said that this young lady cherished an unrequited affection for a man who had resolved to marry for wealth. In the course of time a rich uncle of hers died. He left six thousand dollars to his two sons by a colored woman, and the remainder of his property to this orphan niece. The metal soon attracted the magnet. The lady and her weighty purse became his. She offered to manumit her slaves—telling them that her marriage might make unexpected changes in their destiny, and she wished to insure their happiness. They refused to take their freedom, saying that she had always been their best friend, and they could not be so happy any where as with her. I was not surprised. I had often seen them in their comfortable home, and thought that the whole town did not contain a happier family. They had never felt slavery; and, when it was too late, they were convinced of its reality.

When the new master claimed this family as his property, the father became furious, and went to his mistress for protection. "I can do nothing for you now, Harry," said she. "I no longer have the power I had a week ago. I have succeeded in obtaining the freedom of your wife; but I cannot obtain it for your children." The unhappy father swore that nobody should take his children from him. He concealed them in the woods for some days; but they were discovered and taken. The father was put in jail, and the two oldest boys sold to Georgia. One little girl, too young to be of service to her master, was left with the wretched Mother. The other three were carried to their master's plantation. The eldest soon became a mother; and, when the slaveholder's wife looked at the babe, she wept bitterly. She knew that her own husband had violated the purity she had so carefully inculcated. She had a second child by her master, and then he sold her and his offspring to his brother. She bore two children to the brother, and was sold again. The next sister went crazy. The life she was compelled to lead drove her mad. The third one became the mother of five daughters. Before the birth of the fourth the pious mistress died. To the last, she rendered every kindness to the slaves that her unfortunate circumstances permitted. She passed away peacefully, glad to close her eyes on a life which had been made so wretched by the man she loved.

This man squandered the fortune he had received, and sought to retrieve his affairs by a second marriage; but, having retired after a night of drunken debauch, he was found dead in the morning. He was called a good master; for he fed and clothed his slaves better than most masters, and the lash was not heard on his plantation so frequently as on many others. Had it not been for slavery, he would have been a better man, and his wife a happier woman.

No pen can give an adequate description of the all-pervading corruption produced by slavery. The slave girl is reared in an atmosphere of licentiousness and fear. The lash and the foul talk of her master and his sons are her teachers. When she is fourteen or fifteen, her owner, or his sons, or the overseer, or perhaps all of them, begin to bribe her with presents. If these fail to accomplish their purpose, she is whipped or starved into submission to their will. She may have had religious principles inculcated by some pious mother or grandmother, or some good mistress; she may have a lover, whose good opinion and peace of mind are dear to her heart; or the profligate men who have power over her may be exceedingly odious to her. But resistance is hopeless.

> "The poor worm
> Shall prove her contest vain. Life's little day
> Shall pass, and she is gone!"

The slaveholder's sons are, of course, vitiated, even while boys, by the unclean influences everywhere around them. Nor do the master's daughters always escape. Severe retributions sometimes come upon him for the wrongs he does to the daughters of the slaves. The white daughters early hear their parents quarreling about some female slave. Their curiosity is excited, and they soon learn the cause. They are attended by the young slave girls whom their father has corrupted; and they hear such talk as should never meet youthful ears, or any other ears. They know that the women slaves are subject to their father's authority in all things; and in some cases they exercise the same authority over the men slaves. I have myself seen the master of such a household whose head was bowed down in shame; for it was known in the neighborhood that his daughter had selected one of the meanest slaves on his plantation to be the father of his first grandchild. She did not make her advances to her equals, nor even to her father's more intelligent servants. She selected the most brutalized, over whom her authority could be exercised with less fear of exposure. Her father, half frantic with rage, sought to revenge himself on the offending black man; but his daughter, foreseeing the storm that would arise, had given him free papers, and sent him out of the state.

In such cases the infant is smothered, or sent where it is never seen by any who know its history. But if the white parent is the *father,* instead of the mother, the offspring are unblushingly reared for the market. If they are girls, I have indicated plainly enough what will be their inevitable destiny.

You may believe what I say; for I write only that whereof I know. I was twenty-one years in that cage of obscene birds. I can testify, from my own experience and observation, that slavery is a curse to the whites as well as to the blacks. It makes the white fathers cruel and sensual; the sons violent and licentious; it contaminates the daughters, and makes the wives wretched. And as for the colored race, it needs an abler pen than mine to describe the extremity of their sufferings, the depth of their degradation.

Yet few slaveholders seem to be aware of the widespread moral ruin occasioned by this wicked system. Their talk is of blighted cotton crops—not of the blight on their children's souls.

If you want to be fully convinced of the abominations of slavery, go on a southern plantation, and call yourself a negro trader. Then there will be no concealment; and you will see and hear things that will seem to you impossible among human beings with immortal souls.

X

A Perilous Passage in the Slave Girl's Life

After my lover went away, Dr. Flint contrived a new plan. He seemed to have an idea that my fear of my mistress was his greatest obstacle. In the blandest tones, he told me that he was going to build a small house for me, in a secluded place, four miles away from the town. I shuddered; but I was constrained to listen, while he talked of his intention to give me a home of my own, and to make a lady of me. Hitherto, I had escaped my dreaded fate, by being in the midst of people. My grandmother had already had high words with my master about me. She had told him pretty plainly what she thought of his character, and there was considerable gossip in the neighborhood about our affairs, to which the open-mouthed jealousy of Mrs. Flint contributed not a little. When my master said he was going to build a house for me, and that he could do it with little trouble and expense, I was in hopes something would happen to frustrate his scheme; but I soon heard that the house was actually begun. I vowed before my Maker that I would never enter it. I had rather toil on the plantation from dawn till dark; I had rather live and die in jail, than drag on, from day to day, through such a living death. I was determined that the master, whom I so hated and loathed, who had blighted the prospects of my youth, and made my life a desert, should not, after my long struggle with him, succeed at last in trampling his victim under his feet. I would do any thing, every thing, for the sake of defeating him. What could I do? I thought and thought, till I became desperate, and made a plunge into the abyss.

And now, reader, I come to a period in my unhappy life, which I would gladly forget if I could. The remembrance fills me with sorrow and shame. It pains me to tell you of it; but I have promised to tell you the truth, and I will do it honestly, let it cost me what it may. I will not try to screen myself behind the plea of compulsion from a master; for it was not so. Neither can I plead ignorance or thoughtlessness. For years, my master had done his utmost to pollute my mind with foul images, and to destroy the pure principles inculcated by my grandmother, and the good mistress of my childhood. The influences of slavery had had the same effect on me that they had on other young girls; they had made me prematurely knowing, concerning the evil ways of the world. I knew what I did, and I did it with deliberate calculation.

But, O, ye happy women, whose purity has been sheltered from childhood, who have been free to choose the objects of your affection, whose homes are protected by law, do not judge the poor desolate slave girl too severely! If slavery had been abolished, I, also, could have married the man of my choice; I could have had a home shielded by the laws; and I should have been spared the painful task of confessing what I am now about to relate; but all my prospects had been blighted by slavery. I wanted to keep myself pure; and, under the most adverse circumstances, I tried hard to preserve my self-respect; but I was struggling alone in the powerful grasp of the demon Slavery; and the monster proved too strong for me. I felt as if I was forsaken by God and man; as if all my efforts must be frustrated; and I became reckless in my despair.

I have told you that Dr. Flint's persecutions and his wife's jealousy had given rise to some gossip in the neighborhood. Among others, it chanced that a white unmarried gentleman had obtained some knowledge of the circumstances in which I was placed. He knew my grandmother, and often spoke to me in the street. He became interested for me, and asked questions about my master, which I answered in part. He expressed a great deal of sympathy, and a wish to aid me. He constantly sought opportunities to see me, and wrote to me frequently. I was a poor slave girl, only fifteen years old.

So much attention from a superior person was, of course, flattering; for human nature is the same in all. I also felt grateful for his sympathy, and encouraged by his kind words. It seemed to me a great thing to have such a friend. By degrees, a more tender feeling crept into my heart. He was an educated and eloquent gentleman; too eloquent, alas, for the poor slave girl who trusted in him. Of course I saw whither all this was tending. I knew the impassable gulf between us; but to be an object of interest to a man who is not married, and who is not her master, is agreeable to the pride and feelings of a slave, if her miserable situation has left her any pride or sentiment. It seems less degrading to give one's self, than to submit to compulsion. There is something akin to freedom in having a lover who has no control over you, except that which he gains by kindness and attachment. A master may treat you as rudely as he pleases, and you dare not speak; moreover, the wrong does not seem so great with an unmarried man, as with one who has a wife to be made unhappy. There may be sophistry in all this; but the condition of a slave confuses all principles of morality, and, in fact, renders the practice of them impossible.

When I found that my master had actually begun to build the lonely cottage, other feelings mixed with those I have described. Revenge, and calculations of interest, were added to flattered vanity and sincere gratitude for kindness. I knew nothing would enrage Dr. Flint so much as to know that I favored another; and it was something to triumph over my tyrant even in that small way. I thought he would revenge himself by selling me, and I was sure my friend, Mr. Sands, would buy me. He was a man of more generosity and feeling than my master, and I thought my freedom could be easily obtained from him. The crisis of my fate now came so near that I was desperate. I shuddered to think of being the mother of children that should be owned by my old tyrant. I knew that as soon as a new fancy took him, his victims were sold far off to get rid of them; especially if they had children. I had seen several women sold, with his babies at the breast. He never allowed his offspring by slaves to remain long in sight of himself and his wife. Of a man who was not my master I could ask to have my children well supported; and in this case, I felt confident I should obtain the boon. I also felt quite sure that they would be made free. With all these thoughts revolving in my mind, and seeing no other way of escaping the doom I so much dreaded, I made a headlong plunge. Pity me, and pardon me, O virtuous reader! You never knew what it is to be a slave; to be entirely unprotected by law or custom; to have the laws reduce you to the condition of a chattel, entirely subject to the will of another. You never exhausted your ingenuity in avoiding the snares, and eluding the power of a hated tyrant; you never shuddered at the sound of his footsteps, and trembled within hearing of his voice. I know I did wrong. No one can feel it more sensibly than I do. The painful and humiliating memory will haunt me to my dying day. Still, in looking back, calmly, on the events of my life, I feel that the slave woman ought not to be judged by the same standard as others.

The months passed on. I had many unhappy hours. I secretly mourned over the sorrow I was bringing on my grandmother, who had so tried to shield me from harm. I knew that I was the greatest comfort of her old age, and that it was a source of pride to her that I had not degraded myself, like most of the slaves. I wanted to confess to her that I was no longer worthy of her love; but could not utter the dreaded words.

As for Dr. Flint, I had a feeling of satisfaction and triumph in the thought of telling him. From time to time he told me of his intended arrangements, and I was silent. At last, he came and told me the cottage was completed, and ordered me to go to it. I told him I would never enter it. He said, "I have heard enough of such talk as that. You shall go, if you are carried by force; and you shall remain there."

I replied, "I will never go there. In a few months I shall be a mother."

He stood and looked at me in dumb amazement, and left the house without a word. I thought I should be happy in my triumph over him. But now that the truth was out, and my relatives would hear of it, I felt wretched. Humble as were their circumstances, they had pride in my good character. Now, how could I look them in the face! My self-respect was gone! I had resolved that I would be virtuous, though I was a slave. I had said, "Let the storm beat! I will brave it till I die." And now, how humiliated I felt!

I went to my grandmother. My lips moved to make confession, but the words stuck in my throat. I sat down in the shade of a tree at her door and began to sew. I think she saw something unusual was the matter with me. The mother of slaves is very watchful. She knows there is no security for her children. After they have entered their teens she lives in daily expectation of trouble. This leads to many questions. If the girl is of a sensitive nature, timidity keeps her from answering truthfully, and this well-meant course has a tendency to drive her from maternal counsels. Presently, in came my mistress, like a mad woman, and accused me concerning her husband. My grandmother, whose suspicions had been previously awakened, believed what she said. She exclaimed, "O Linda! Has it come to this? I had rather see you dead than to see you as you now are. You are a disgrace to your dead mother." She tore from my fingers my mother's wedding ring and her silver thimble. "Go away!" she exclaimed, "and never come to my house, again." Her reproaches fell so hot and heavy, that they left me no chance to answer. Bitter tears, such as the eyes never shed but once, were my only answer. I rose from my seat, but fell back again, sobbing. She did not speak to me; but the tears were running down her furrowed cheeks, and they scorched me like fire. She had always been so kind to me! So kind! How I longed to throw myself at her feet, and tell her all the truth! But she had ordered me to go, and never to come there again. After a few minutes, I mustered strength, and started to obey her. With what feelings did I now close that little gate, which I used to open with such an eager hand in my childhood! It closed upon me with a sound I never heard before.

Where could I go? I was afraid to return to my master's. I walked on recklessly, not caring where I went, or what would become of me. When I had gone four or five miles, fatigue compelled me to stop. I sat down on the stump of an old tree. The stars were shining through the boughs above me. How they mocked me, with their bright, calm light! The hours passed by, and as I sat there alone a chilliness and deadly sickness came over me. I sank on the ground. My mind was full of horrid thoughts. I prayed to die; but the prayer was not answered. At last, with great effort I roused myself, and walked some distance further, to the house of a woman who had been a friend of my mother. When I told her why I was there, she spoke soothingly to me; but I could not be comforted. I thought I could bear my shame if I could only be reconciled to my grandmother. I longed to open my heart to her. I thought if she could know the real state of the case, and all I had been bearing for years, she would perhaps judge me less harshly. My friend advised me to send for her. I did so; but days of agonizing suspense passed before she came. Had she utterly forsaken me? No. She came at last. I knelt before her, and told her things that had poisoned my life; how long I had been persecuted; that I saw no way of escape; and in an hour of extremity I had become desperate. She listened in silence. I told her I would bear any thing and do any thing, if in time I had hopes of obtaining her forgiveness. I begged of her to pity me, for my dead mother's sake. And she did pity me. She did not say, "I forgive you;" but she looked at me lovingly, with her eyes full of tears. She laid her old hand gently on my head, and murmured, "Poor child! Poor child!"

XI
THE NEW TIE TO LIFE

I returned to my good grandmother's house. She had an interview with Mr. Sands. When she asked him why he could have left her one ewe lamb,—whether there were not plenty of slaves who did not care about character,—he made no answer; but he spoke kind and encouraging words. He promised to care for my child, and to buy me, be the conditions what they might.

I had not seen Dr. Flint for five days. I had never seen him since I made the avowal to him. He talked of the disgrace I had brought on myself; how I had sinned against my master, and mortified my old grandmother. He intimated that if I had accepted his proposals, he, as a physician, could have saved me from exposure. He even condescended to pity me. Could he have offered wormwood more bitter? He, whose persecutions had been the cause of my sin!

"Linda," said he, "though you have been criminal towards me, I feel for you, and I can pardon you if you obey my wishes. Tell me whether the fellow you wanted to marry is the father of your child. If you deceive me, you shall feel the fires of hell."

I did not feel as proud as I had done. My strongest weapon with him was gone. I was lowered in my own estimation, and had resolved to bear his abuse in silence. But when he spoke contemptuously of the lover who had always treated me honorably; when I remembered that but for him I might have been a virtuous, free, and happy wife, I lost my patience. "I have sinned against God and myself," I replied; "but not against you."

He clinched his teeth, and muttered, "Curse you!" He came towards me, with ill-suppressed rage, and exclaimed, "You obstinate girl! I could grind your bones to powder! You have thrown yourself away on some worthless rascal. You are weak-minded, and have been easily persuaded by those who don't care a straw for you. The future will settle accounts between us. You are blinded now; but hereafter you will be convinced that your master was your best friend. My lenity towards you is a proof of it. I might have punished you in many ways. I might have had you whipped till you fell dead under the lash. But I wanted you to live; I would have bettered your condition. Others cannot do it. You are my slave. Your mistress, disgusted by your conduct, forbids you to return to the house; therefore I leave you here for the present; but I shall see you often. I will call tomorrow."

He came with frowning brows, that showed a dissatisfied state of mind. After asking about my health, he inquired whether my board was paid, and who visited me. He then went on to say that he had neglected his duty; that as a physician there were certain things that he ought to have explained to me. Then followed talk such as would have made the most shameless blush. He ordered me to stand up before him. I obeyed. "I command you," said he, "to tell me whether the father of your child is white or black." I hesitated. "Answer me this instant!" he exclaimed. I did answer. He sprang upon me like a wolf, and grabbed my arm as if he would have broken it. "Do you love him?" said he, in a hissing tone.

"I am thankful that I do not despise him," I replied.

He raised his hand to strike me; but it fell again. I don't know what arrested the blow. He sat down, with lips tightly compressed. At last he spoke. "I came here," said he, "to make you a friendly proposition; but your ingratitude chafes me beyond endurance. You turn aside all my good intentions towards you. I don't know what it is that keeps me from killing you." Again he rose, as if he had a mind to strike me.

But he resumed. "On one condition I will forgive your insolence and crime. You must henceforth have no communication of any kind with the father of your child. You must not ask any thing from him, or receive any thing from him. I will take care of you and your child. You had better promise this at once, and not wait till you are deserted by him. This is the last act of mercy I shall show towards you."

I said something about being unwilling to have my child supported by a man who had cursed it and me also. He rejoined, that a woman who had sunk to my level had no right to expect any thing else. He asked, for the last time, would I accept his kindness? I answered that I would not.

"Very well," said he; "then take the consequences of your wayward course. Never look to me for help. You are my slave, and shall always be my slave. I will never sell you, that you may depend upon."

Hope died away in my heart as he closed the door after him. I had calculated that in his rage he would sell me to a slavetrader; and I knew the father of my child was on the watch to buy me.

About this time my uncle Phillip was expected to return from a voyage. The day before his departure I had officiated as bridesmaid to a young friend. My heart was then ill at ease, but my smiling countenance did not betray it. Only a year had passed; but what fearful changes it had wrought! My heart had grown gray in misery. Lives that flash in sunshine, and lives that are born in tears, receive their hue from circumstances. None of us know what a year may bring forth.

I felt no joy when they told me my uncle had come. He wanted to see me, though he knew what had happened. I shrank from him at first; but at last consented that he should come to my room. He received me as he always had done. O, how my heart smote me when I felt his tears on my burning cheeks! The words of my grandmother came to my mind,— "Perhaps your mother and father are taken from the evil days to come." My disappointed heart could now praise God that it was so. But why, thought I, did my relatives ever cherish hopes for me? What was there to save me from the usual fate of slave girls? Many more beautiful and more intelligent than I had experienced a similar fate, or a far worse one. How could they hope that I should escape?

My uncle's stay was short, and I was not sorry for it. I was too ill in mind and body to enjoy my friends as I had done.

For some weeks I was unable to leave my bed. I could not have any doctor but my master, and I would not have him sent for. At last, alarmed by my increasing illness, they sent for him. I was very weak and nervous; and as soon as he entered the room, I began to scream. They told him my state was very critical. He had no wish to hasten me out of the world, and he withdrew.

When my babe was born, they said it was premature. It weighed only four pounds; but God let it live. I heard the doctor say I could not survive till morning. I had often prayed for death; but now I did not want to die, unless my child could die too. Many weeks passed before I was able to leave my bed. I was a mere wreck of my former self. For a year there was scarcely a day when I was free from chills and fever. My babe also was sickly. His little limbs were often racked with pain. Dr. Flint continued his visits, to look after my health; and he did not fail to remind me that my child was an addition to his stock of slaves.

I felt too feeble to dispute with him, and listened to his remarks in silence. His visits were less frequent; but his busy spirit could not remain quiet. He employed my brother in his office, and he was made the medium of frequent notes and messages to me. William was a bright lad, and of much use to the doctor. He had learned to put up medicines, to leech, cup, and bleed. He had taught himself to read and spell. I was proud of my brother; and the old doctor suspected as much. One day, when I had not seen him for several weeks, I heard his steps approaching the door. I dreaded the encounter, and hid myself. He inquired for me, of course; but I was nowhere to be found. He went to his office, and despatched William with a note. The color mounted to my brother's face when he gave it to me; and he said, "Don't you hate me, Linda, for bringing you these things?" I told him I could not blame him; he was a slave, and obliged to obey his master's will. The note ordered me to come to his office. I went. He demanded to know where I was when he called. I told him I was at home. He flew into a passion, and said he knew better. Then he launched out upon his usual themes,—my crimes against him, and my ingratitude for his forbearance. The laws were laid down to me anew, and I was dismissed. I felt humiliated that my brother should stand by, and listen to such language as would be addressed only to a slave. Poor boy! He was powerless to defend me; but I saw the tears, which he vainly strove to keep back. This manifestation of feeling irritated the doctor. William could do nothing to please him. One morning he did not arrive at the office so early as usual; and that circumstance afforded his master an opportunity to vent his spleen. He was put in jail. The next day my brother sent a trader to the doctor, with a request to be sold. His master was greatly incensed at what he called his insolence. He said he had put him there to reflect upon his bad conduct, and he certainly was not giving any evidence of repentance. For two days he harassed himself to find somebody to do his office work; but every thing went wrong without William. He was released, and ordered to take his old stand, with many threats, if he was not careful about his future behavior.

As the months passed on, my boy improved in health. When he was a year old, they called him beautiful. The little vine was taking deep root in my existence, though its clinging fondness excited a mixture of love and pain. When I was most sorely oppressed I found a solace in his smiles. I loved to watch his infant slumbers; but always there was a dark cloud over my enjoyment. I could never forget that he was a slave. Sometimes I wished that he might die in infancy. God tried me. My darling became very ill. The bright eyes grew dull, and the little feet and hands were so icy cold that I thought death had already touched them. I had prayed for his death, but never so earnestly as I now prayed for his life; and my prayer was heard. Alas, what mockery it is for a slave mother to try to pray back her dying child to life! Death is better than slavery. It was a sad thought that I had no name to give my child. His father caressed him and treated him kindly, whenever he had a chance to see him. He was not unwilling that he should bear his name; but he had no legal claim to it; and if I had bestowed it upon him, my master would have regarded it as a new crime, a new piece of insolence, and would, perhaps, revenge it on the boy. O, the serpent of Slavery has many and poisonous fangs!

XII

FEAR OF INSURRECTION

Not far from this time Nat Turner's insurrection* broke out; and the news threw our town into great commotion. Strange that they should be alarmed, when their slaves were so "contented and happy!" But so it was.

It was always the custom to have a muster every year. On that occasion every white man shouldered his musket. The citizens and the so-called country gentlemen wore military uniforms. The poor whites took their places in the ranks in every-day dress, some without shoes, some without hats. This grand occasion had already passed; and when the slaves were told there was to be another muster, they were surprised and rejoiced. Poor creatures! They thought it was going to be a holiday. I was informed of the true state of affairs, and imparted it to the few I could trust. Most gladly would I have proclaimed it to every slave; but I dared not. All could not be relied on. Mighty is the power of the torturing lash.

By sunrise, people were pouring in from every quarter within twenty miles of the town. I knew the houses were to be searched; and I expected it would be done by country bullies and the poor whites. I knew nothing annoyed them so much as to see colored people living in comfort and respectability; so I made arrangements for them with especial care. I arranged everything in my grandmother's house as neatly as possible. I put white quilts on the beds, and decorated some of the rooms with flowers. When all was arranged, I sat down at the window to watch. Far as my eye could reach, it rested on a motley crowd of soldiers. Drums and fifes were discoursing martial music. The men were divided into companies of sixteen, each headed by a captain. Orders were given, and the wild scouts rushed in every direction, wherever a colored face was to be found.

It was a grand opportunity for the low whites, who had no negroes of their own to scourge. They exulted in such a chance to exercise a little brief authority, and show their subserviency to the slaveholders; not reflecting that the power which trampled on the colored people also kept themselves in poverty, ignorance, and moral degradation. Those who never witnessed such scenes can hardly believe what I know was inflicted at this time on innocent men, women, and children, against whom there was not the slightest ground for suspicion. Colored people and slaves who lived in remote parts of the town suffered in an especial manner. In some cases the searchers scattered powder and shot among their clothes, and then sent other parties to find them, and bring them forward as proof that they were plotting insurrection. Every where men, women, and children were whipped till the blood stood in puddles at their feet. Some received five hundred lashes; others were tied hands and feet, and tortured with a bucking paddle, which blisters the skin terribly. The dwellings of the colored people, unless they happened to be protected by some influential white person, who was nigh at hand, were robbed of clothing and every thing else the marauders thought worth carrying away. All day long these unfeeling wretches went round, like a troop of demons, terrifying and tormenting the helpless. At night, they formed themselves into patrol bands, and went wherever they chose among the colored people, acting out their brutal will. Many women hid themselves in woods and swamps, to keep out of their way. If any of the husbands or fathers told of these outrages, they were tied up to the public whipping post, and cruelly scourged for telling lies about white men. The consternation was universal. No two people that had the slightest tinge of color in their faces dared to be seen talking together.

I entertained no positive fears about our household, because we were in the midst of white families who would protect us. We were ready to receive the soldiers whenever they came. It was not long before we heard the tramp of feet and the sound of voices. The door was rudely pushed open; and in they tumbled, like a pack of hungry wolves. They snatched at every thing within their reach. Every box, trunk, closet, and corner underwent a thorough examination. A box in one of the drawers containing some silver change was eagerly pounced upon. When I stepped forward to take it from them, one of the soldiers turned and said angrily, "What d'ye foller us fur? D'ye s'pose white folks is come to steal?"

I replied, "You have come to search; but you have searched that box, and I will take it, if you please."

At that moment I saw a white gentleman who was friendly to us; and I called to him, and asked him to have the goodness to come in and stay till the search was over. He readily complied. His entrance into the house brought in the captain of the company, whose business it was to guard the outside of the house, and see that none of the inmates left it. This officer was Mr. Litch, the wealthy slaveholder whom I mentioned, in the account of neighboring planters, as being notorious for his cruelty. He felt above soiling his hands with the search. He merely gave orders; and, if a bit of writing was discovered, it was carried to him by his ignorant followers,

*The most famous American slave revolt, it broke out on August 21, 1831, in Southampton County in southeast Virginia. About sixty whites were killed in the uprising, and in the suppression that followed at least one hundred blacks died. The leader, Nat Turner, was captured October 30th and executed November 11, 1831. He was born on the plantation of Benjamin Turner in Southampton County in 1800 to a slave, Nancy, a native of Africa, and to an unknown father. Chapter 12 of Linda Brent's book gives a vivid account of the effects of the revolt on slave communities. W. T.

who were unable to read.

My grandmother had a large trunk of bedding and table cloths. When that was opened, there was a great shout of surprise; and one exclaimed, "Where'd the damned niggers git all dis sheet an' table clarf?"

My grandmother, emboldened by the presence of our white protector, said, "You may be sure we didn't pilfer'em from *your* houses."

"Look here, mammy," said a grim-looking fellow without any coat, "you seem to feel mighty gran' 'cause you got all them 'ere fixens. White folks oughter have 'em all."

His remarks were interrupted by a chorus of voices shouting, "We's got 'em! We's got 'em! Dis 'ere yaller gal's got letters!"

There was a general rush for the supposed letter, which, upon examination, proved to be some verses written to me by a friend. In packing away my things, I had overlooked them. When their captain informed them of their contents, they seemed much disappointed. He inquired of me who wrote them. I told him it was one of my friends. "Can you read them?" he asked. When I told him I could, he swore, and raved, and tore the paper into bits. "Bring me all your letters!" said he, in a commanding tone. I told him I had none. "Don't be afraid," he continued, in an insinuating way. "Bring them all to me. Nobody shall do you any harm." Seeing I did not move to obey him, his pleasant tone changed to oaths and threats. "Who writes to you? half free niggers?" inquired he. I replied, "O, no; most of my letters are from white people. Some request me to burn them after they are read, and some I destroy without reading."

An exclamation of surprise from some of the company put a stop to our conversation. Some silver spoons which ornamented an old-fashioned buffet had just been discovered. My grandmother was in the habit of preserving fruit for many ladies in the town, and of preparing suppers for parties; consequently she had many jars of preserves. The closet that contained these was next invaded, and the contents tasted. One of them, who was helping himself freely, tapped his neighbor on the shoulder, and said, "Wal done! Don't wonder de niggers want to kill all de white folks, when dey live on 'sarves" [meaning preserves]. I stretched out my hand to take the jar, saying, "You were not sent here to search for sweetmeats."

"And what *were* we sent for?" said the captain, bristling up to me. I evaded the question.

The search of the house was completed, and nothing found to condemn us. They next proceeded to the garden, and knocked about every bush and vine, with no better success. The captain called his men together, and, after a short consultation, the order to march was given. As they passed out of the gate, the captain turned back, and pronounced a malediction on the house. He said it ought to be burned to the ground, and each of its inmates receive thirty-nine lashes. We came out of this affair very fortunately; not losing any thing except some wearing apparel.

Towards evening the turbulence increased. The soldiers, stimulated by drink, committed still greater cruelties. Shrieks and shouts continually rent the air. Not daring to go to the door, I peeped under the window curtain. I saw a mob dragging along a number of colored people, each white man, with his musket upraised, threatening instant death if they did not stop their shrieks. Among the prisoners was a respectable old colored minister. They had found a few parcels of shot in his house, which his wife had for years used to balance her scales. For this they were going to shoot him on Court House Green. What a spectacle was that for a civilized country! A rabble, staggering under intoxication, assuming to be the administrators of justice!

The better class of the community exerted their influence to save the innocent, persecuted people; and in several instances they succeeded, by keeping them shut up in jail till the excitement abated. At last the white citizens found that their own property was not safe from the lawless rabble they had summoned to protect them. They rallied the drunken swarm, drove them back into the country, and set a guard over the town.

The next day, the town patrols were commissioned to search colored people that lived out of the city; and the most shocking outrages were committed with perfect impunity. Every day for a fortnight, if I looked out, I saw horsemen with some poor panting negro tied to their saddles, and compelled by the lash to keep up with their speed, till they arrived at the jail yard. Those who had been whipped too unmercifully to walk were washed with brine, tossed into a cart, and carried to jail. One black man, who had not fortitude to endure scourging, promised to give information about the conspiracy. But it turned out that he knew nothing at all. He had not even heard the name of Nat Turner. The poor fellow had, however, made up a story, which augmented his own sufferings and those of the colored people.

The day patrol continued for some weeks, and at sundown a night guard was substituted. Nothing at all was proved against the colored people, bond or free. The wrath of the slaveholders was somewhat appeased by the capture of Nat Turner. The imprisoned were released. The slaves were sent to their masters, and the free were permitted to return to their ravaged homes. Visiting was strictly forbidden on the plantations. The slaves begged the privilege of again meeting at their little church in the woods, with their burying ground around it. It was built by the colored people, and they had no higher happiness than to meet there and sing hymns together, and pour out their hearts in spontaneous prayer. Their request was denied, and the church was demolished. They were permitted to attend the white churches, a certain portion of the galleries being appropriated to their use. There, when everybody else had partaken of the communion, and the benediction had been pronounced, the minister said, "Come down, now, my colored friends." They obeyed the summons, and partook of the bread and wine, in commemoration of the meek and lowly Jesus, who said, "God is your Father, and all ye are brethren."

XIII

THE CHURCH AND SLAVERY

After the alarm caused by Nat Turner's insurrection had subsided, the slaveholders came to the conclusion that it would be well to give the slaves enough of religious instruction to keep them from murdering their masters. The Episcopal clergyman offered to hold a separate service on Sundays for their benefit. His colored members were very few, and also very respectable—a fact which I presume had some weight with him. The difficulty was to decide on a suitable place for them to worship. The Methodist and Baptist churches admitted them in the afternoon; but their carpets and cushions were not so costly as those at the Episcopal church. It was at last decided that they should meet at the house of a free colored man, who was a member.

I was invited to attend, because I could read. Sunday evening came, and, trusting to the cover of night, I ventured out. I rarely ventured out by daylight, for I always went with fear, expecting at every turn to encounter Dr. Flint, who was sure to turn me back, or order me to his office to inquire where I got my bonnet, or some other article of dress. When the Rev. Mr. Pike came, there were some twenty persons present. The reverend gentleman knelt in prayer, then seated himself, and requested all present, who could read, to open their books, while he gave out the portions he wished them to repeat or respond to.

His text was, "Servants, be obedient to them that are your masters according to the flesh, with fear and trembling, in singleness of your heart, as unto Christ."

Pious Mr. Pike brushed up his hair till it stood upright, and, in deep, solemn tones, began: "Hearken, ye servants! Give strict heed unto my words. You are rebellious sinners. Your hearts are filled with all manner of evil. 'Tis the devil who tempts you. God is angry with you, and will surely punish you, if you don't forsake your wicked ways. You that live in town are eye-servants behind your master's back. Instead of serving your masters faithfully, which is pleasing in the sight of your heavenly Master, you are idle, and shirk your work. God sees you. You tell lies. God hears you. Instead of being engaged in worshipping him, you are hidden away somewhere, feasting on your master's substance; tossing coffee-grounds with some wicked fortuneteller, or cutting cards with another old hag. Your masters may not find you out, but God sees you, and will punish you. O, the depravity of your hearts! When your master's work is done, are you quietly together, thinking of the goodness of God to such sinful creatures? No; you are quarreling, and tying up little bags of roots* to bury under the door-steps to poison each other with. God sees you. You men steal away to every grog shop to sell your master's corn, that you may buy rum to drink. God sees you. You sneak into the back streets, or among the bushes, to pitch coppers. Although your masters may not find you out, God sees you; and he will punish you. You must forsake your sinful ways, and be faithful servants. Obey your old master and your young master—your old mistress and your young mistress. If you disobey your earthly master, you offend your heavenly Master. You must obey God's commandments. When you go from here, don't stop at the corners of the streets to talk, but go directly home, and let your master and mistress see that you have come."

The benediction was pronounced. We went home, highly amused at brother Pike's gospel teaching, and we determined to hear him again. I went the next Sabbath evening, and heard pretty much a repetition of the last discourse. At the close of the meeting,

Mr. Pike informed us that he found it very inconvenient to meet at the friend's house, and he should be glad to see us, every Sunday evening, at his own kitchen.

I went home with the feeling that I had heard the Reverend Mr. Pike for the last time. Some of his members repaired to his house, and found that the kitchen sported two tallow candles; the first time, I am sure, since its present occupant owned it, for the servants never had any thing but pine knots. It was so long before the reverend gentleman descended from his comfortable parlor that the slaves left, and went to enjoy a Methodist shout. They never seem so happy as when shouting and singing at religious meetings. Many of them are sincere, and nearer to the gate of heaven than sanctimonious Mr. Pike, and other long-faced Christians, who see wounded Samaritans, and pass by on the other side.

The slaves generally compose their own songs and hymns; and they do not trouble their heads much about the measure. They often sing the following verses:

"Old Satan is one busy ole man;
He rolls dem blocks all in my way;
But Jesus is my bosom friend;
He rolls dem blocks away.

"If I had died when I was young,
Den how my stam'ring tongue would have sung;
But I am ole, and now I stand
A narrow chance for to tread dat heavenly land."

I well remember one occasion when I attended a Methodist class meeting. I went with a burdened spirit, and happened to sit next a poor, bereaved mother, whose heart was still heavier than mine. The class leader was the town constable—a man who bought and sold slaves, who whipped his brethren and sisters of the church at the public whipping post, in jail or out of jail. He was ready to perform that Christian office any where for fifty cents. This white-faced, black-hearted brother came near us, and said to the stricken

* This was the bag used by the conjure man, woman, or doctor (also called root man, woman, or doctor) in the practice of conjuring, or hoodooing, African magic. W. T.

woman, "Sister, can't you tell us how the Lord deals with your soul? Do you love him as you did formerly?"

She rose to her feet, and said, in piteous tones, "My Lord and Master, help me! My load is more than I can bear. God has hid himself from me, and I am left in darkness and misery." Then, striking her breast, she continued, "I can't tell you what is in here! They've got all my children. Last week they took the last one. God only knows where they've sold her. They let me have her sixteen years, and then — O! O! Pray for her brothers and sisters! I've got nothing to live for now. God make my time short!"

She sat down, quivering in every limb. I saw that constable class leader become crimson in the face with suppressed laughter, while he held up his handkerchief, that those who were weeping for the poor woman's calamity might not see his merriment. Then, with assumed gravity, he said to the bereaved mother, "Sister, pray to the Lord that every dispensation of his divine will may be sanctified to the good of your poor needy soul!"

The congregation struck up a hymn, and sung as though they were as free as the birds that warbled round us,—

"Ole Satan thought he had a mighty aim;
He missed my soul, and caught my sins.
Cry Amen, cry Amen, cry Amen to God!

"He took my sins upon his back;
Went muttering and grumbling down to hell.
Cry Amen, cry Amen, cry Amen to God!

"Ole Satan's church is here below.
Up to God's free church I hope to go.
Cry Amen, cry Amen, cry Amen to God!"

Precious are such moments to the poor slaves. If you were to hear them at such times, you might think they were happy. But can that hour of singing and shouting sustain them through the dreary week, toiling without wages, under constant dread of the lash?

The Episcopal clergyman, who, ever since my earliest recollection, had been a sort of god among the slaveholders, concluded, as his family was large, that he must go where money was more abundant. A very different clergyman took his place. The change was very agreeable to the colored people, who said, "God has sent us a good man this time." They loved him, and their children followed him for a smile or a kind word. Even the slaveholders felt his influence. He brought to the rectory five slaves. His wife taught them to read and write, and to be useful to her and themselves. As soon as he was settled, he turned his attention to the needy slaves around him. He urged upon his parishioners the duty of having a meeting expressly for them every Sunday, with a sermon adapted to their comprehension. After much argument and importunity, it was finally agreed that they might occupy the gallery of the church on Sunday evenings. Many colored people, hitherto unaccustomed to attend church, now gladly went to hear the gospel preached. The sermons were simple, and they understood them. Moreover, it was the first time they had ever been addressed as human beings. It was not long before his white parishioners began to be dissatisfied. He was accused of preaching better sermons to the negroes than he did to them. He honestly confessed that he bestowed more pains upon those sermons than upon any others; for the slaves were reared in such ignorance that it was a difficult task to adapt himself to their comprehension. Dissensions arose in the parish. Some wanted he should preach to them in the evening, and to the slaves in the afternoon. In the midst of these disputings his wife died, after a very short illness. Her slaves gathered round her dying bed in great sorrow. She said, "I have tried to do you good and promote your happiness; and if I have failed, it has not been for want of interest in your welfare. Do not weep for me; but prepare for the new duties that lie before you. I leave you all free. May we meet in a better world." Her liberated slaves were sent away, with funds to establish them comfortably. The colored people will long bless the memory of that truly Christian woman. Soon after her death her husband preached his farewell sermon, and many tears were shed at his departure.

Several years after, he passed through our town and preached to his former congregation. In his afternoon sermon he addressed the colored people. "My friends," said he, "it affords me great happiness to have an opportunity of speaking to you again. For two years I have been striving to do something for the colored people of my own parish; but nothing is yet accomplished. I have not even preached a sermon to them. Try to live according to the word of God, my friends. Your skin is darker than mine; but God judges men by their hearts, not by the color of their skins." This was strange doctrine from a southern pulpit. It was very offensive to slaveholders. They said he and his wife had made fools of their slaves, and that he preached like a fool to the negroes.

I knew an old black man, whose piety and childlike trust in God were beautiful to witness. At fifty-three years old he joined the Baptist church. He had a most earnest desire to learn to read. He thought he should know how to serve God better if he could only read the Bible. He came to me, and begged me to teach him. He said he could not pay me, for he had no money; but he would bring me nice fruit when the season for it came. I asked him if he didn't know it was contrary to law; and that slaves were whipped and imprisoned for teaching each other to read. This brought the tears into his eyes. "Don't be troubled, uncle Fred," said I. "I have no thoughts of refusing to teach you. I only told you of the law, that you might know the danger, and be on your guard." He thought he could plan to come three times a week without its being suspected. I selected a quiet nook, where no intruder was likely to penetrate, and there I taught him his A, B, C. Considering his age, his progress was astonishing. As soon as he could spell in two syllables he wanted to spell out words in the Bible. The happy smile that illuminated his face put joy into my heart. After spelling out a few words, he paused, and said, "Honey, it 'pears when I can read dis good book I shall be nearer to God. White man is got all de sense. He can larn easy. It ain't easy for ole black man like me. I only wants to read dis book, dat I may know how to live; den I hab no fear 'bout dying."

I tried to encourage him by speaking of the rapid progress he had made. "Hab patience, child," he replied. "I larns slow."

I had no need of patience. His gratitude, and the happiness I imparted, were more than a recompense for all my trouble.

At the end of six months he had read through the New Testament, and could find any text in it. One day, when he had recited unusually well, I said, "Uncle Fred, how do you manage to get your lessons so well?"

"Lord bless you, chile," he replied. "You nebber gibs me a lesson dat I don't pray to God to help me to understan' what I spells and what I reads. And he *does* help me, chile. Bless his holy name!"

There are thousands, who, like good uncle Fred, are thirsting for the water of life; but the law forbids it, and the churches withhold it. They send the Bible to heathen abroad, and neglect the heathen at home. I am glad that missionaries go out to the dark corners of the earth; but I ask them not to overlook the dark corners at home. Talk to American slaveholders as you talk to savages in Africa. Tell *them* it is wrong to traffic in men. Tell them it is sinful to sell their own children, and atrocious to violate their own daughters. Tell them that all men are brethren, and that man has no right to shut out the light of knowledge from his brother. Tell them they are answerable to God for sealing up the fountain of Life from souls that are thirsting for it.

There are men who would gladly undertake such missionary work as this; but, alas! their number is small. They are hated by the south, and would be driven from its soil, or dragged to prison to die, as others have been before them. The field is ripe for the harvest, and awaits the reapers. Perhaps the great grandchildren of uncle Fred may have freely imparted to them the divine treasures, which he sought by stealth, at the risk of the prison and the scourge.

Are doctors of divinity blind, or are they hypocrites? I suppose some are the one, and some the other; but I think if they felt the interest in the poor and the lowly, that they ought to feel, they would not be so *easily* blinded. A clergyman who goes to the south, for the first time, has usually some feeling, however vague, that slavery is wrong. The slaveholder suspects this, and plays his game accordingly. He makes himself as agreeable as possible; talks on theology, and other kindred topics. The reverend gentleman is asked to invoke a blessing on a table loaded with luxuries. After dinner he walks round the premises, and sees the beautiful groves and flowering vines, and the comfortable huts of favored household slaves. The southerner invites him to talk with these slaves. He asks them if they want to be free, and they say, "O, no, massa." This is sufficient to satisfy him. He comes home to publish a "South-Side View of Slavery," and to complain of the exaggerations of abolitionists. He assures people that he has been to the south, and seen slavery for himself; that it is a beautiful "patriarchal institution;" that the slaves don't want their freedom; that they have hallelujah meetings, and other religious privileges.

What does he know of the half-starved wretches toiling from dawn till dark on the plantations? of mothers shrieking for their children, torn from their arms by slave-traders? of young girls dragged down into moral filth? of pools of blood around the whipping post? of hounds trained to tear human flesh? of men screwed into cotton gins to die? The slaveholder showed him none of these things, and the slaves dared not tell of them if he had asked them.

318

There is a great difference between Christianity and religion at the south. If a man goes to the communion table, and pays money into the treasury of the church, no matter if it be the price of blood, he is called religious. If a pastor has offspring by a woman not his wife, the church dismiss him, if she is a white woman; but if she is colored, it does not hinder his continuing to be their good shepherd.

When I was told that Dr. Flint had joined the Episcopal church, I was much surprised. I supposed that religion had a purifying effect on the character of men; but the worst persecutions I endured from him were after he was a communicant. The conversation of the doctor, the day after he had been confirmed, certainly gave *me* no indication that he had "renounced the devil and all his works." In answer to some of his usual talk, I reminded him that he had just joined the church. "Yes, Linda," said he. "It was proper for me to do so. I am getting in years, and my position in society requires it, and it puts an end to all the damned slang. You would do well to join the church, too, Linda."

"There are sinners enough in it already," rejoined I. "If I could be allowed to live like a Christian, I should be glad."

"You can do what I require; and if you are faithful to me, you will be as virtuous as my wife," he replied.

I answered that the Bible didn't say so.

His voice became hoarse with rage. "How dare you preach to me about your infernal Bible!" he exclaimed. "What right have you, who are my negro, to talk to me about what you would like, and what you wouldn't like? I am your master, and you shall obey me."

No wonder the slaves sing,—

"Ole Satan's church is here below;
Up to God's free church I hope to go."

XIV

CONTINUED PERSECUTIONS

I had not returned to my master's house since the birth of my child. The old man raved to have me thus removed from his immediate power; but his wife vowed, by all that was good and great, she would

319

kill me if I came back; and he did not doubt her word. Sometimes he would stay away for a season. Then he would come and renew the old threadbare discourse about his forbearance and my ingratitude. He labored, most unnecessarily, to convince me that I had lowered myself. The venomous old reprobate had no need of descanting on that theme. I felt humiliated enough. My unconscious babe was the ever-present witness of my shame. I listened with silent contempt when he talked about my having forfeited his good opinion; but I shed bitter tears that I was no longer worthy of being respected by the good and pure. Alas! slavery still held me in its poisonous grasp. There was no chance for me to be respectable. There was no prospect of being able to lead a better life.

Sometimes, when my master found that I still refused to accept what he called his kind offers, he would threaten to sell my child. "Perhaps that will humble you," said he.

Humble *me*! Was I not already in the dust? But his threat lacerated my heart. I knew the law gave him power to fulfill it; for slaveholders have been cunning enough to enact that "the child shall follow the condition of the *mother*," not of the *father;* thus taking care that licentiousness shall not interfere with avarice. This reflection made me clasp my innocent babe all the more firmly to my heart. Horrid visions passed through my mind when I thought of his liability to fall into the slavetrader's hands. I wept over him, and said, "O my child! perhaps they will leave you in some cold cabin to die, and then throw you into a hole, as if you were a dog."

When Dr. Flint learned that I was again to be a mother, he was exasperated beyond measure. He rushed from the house, and returned with a pair of shears. I had a fine head of hair; and he often railed about my pride of arranging it nicely. He cut every hair close to my head, storming and swearing all the time. I replied to some of his abuse, and he struck me. Some months before, he had pitched me down stairs in a fit of passion; and the injury I received was so serious that I was unable to turn myself in bed for many days. He then said, "Linda, I swear by God I will never raise my hand against you again;" but I knew that he would forget his promise.

After he discovered my situation, he was like a restless spirit from the pit. He came every day; and I was subjected to such insults as no pen can describe. I would not describe them if I could; they were too low, too revolting. I tried to keep them from my grandmother's knowledge as much as I could. I knew she had enough to sadden her life, without having my troubles to bear. When she saw the doctor treat me with violence, and heard him utter oaths terrible enough to palsy a man's tongue, she could not always hold her peace. It was natural and motherlike that she should try to defend me; but it only made matters worse.

When they told me my new-born babe was a girl, my heart was heavier than it had ever been before. Slavery is terrible for men; but it is far more terrible for women. Superadded to the burden common to all, *they* have wrongs, and sufferings, and mortifications peculiarly their own.

Dr. Flint had sworn that he would make me suffer, to my last day, for this new crime against *him,* as he called it; and as long as he had me in his power he kept his word. On the fourth day after the birth of my babe, he entered my room suddenly, and commanded me to rise and bring my baby to him. The nurse who took care of me had gone out of the room to prepare some nourishment, and I was alone. There was no alternative. I rose, took up my babe, and crossed the room to where he sat. "Now stand there," said he, "till I tell you to go back!" My child bore a strong resemblance to her father, and to the deceased Mrs. Sands, her grandmother. He noticed this; and while I stood before him, trembling with weakness, he heaped upon me and my little one every vile epithet he could think of. Even the grandmother in her grave did not escape his curses. In the midst of his vituperations I fainted at his feet. This recalled him to his senses. He took the baby from my arms, laid it on the bed, dashed cold water in my face, took me up, and shook me violently, to restore my consciousness before any one entered the room. Just then my grandmother came in, and he hurried out of the house. I suffered in consequence of this treatment; but I begged my friends to let me die, rather than send for the doctor. There was nothing I dreaded so much as his presence. My life was spared; and I was glad for the sake of my little ones. Had it not been for these ties to life, I should have been glad to be released by death, though I had lived only nineteen years.

Always it gave me a pang that my children had no lawful claim to a name. Their father offered his; but, if I had wished to accept the offer, I dared not while my master lived. Moreover, I knew it would not be accepted at their baptism. A Christian name they were at least entitled to; and we resolved to call my boy for our dear good Benjamin, who had gone far away from us.

My grandmother belonged to the church; and she was very

desirous of having the children christened. I knew Dr. Flint would forbid it, and I did not venture to attempt it. But chance favored me. He was called to visit a patient out of town, and was obliged to be absent during Sunday. "Now is the time," said my grandmother; "we will take the children to church, and have them christened."

When I entered the church, recollections of my mother came over me, and I felt subdued in spirit. There she had presented me for baptism, without any reason to feel ashamed. She had been married, and had such legal rights as slavery allows to a slave. The vows had at least been sacred to *her*, and she had never violated them. I was glad she was not alive, to know under what different circumstances her grandchildren were presented for baptism. Why had my lot been so different from my mother's? *Her* master had died when she was a child; and she remained with her mistress till she married. She was never in the power of any master; and thus she escaped one class of the evil that generally falls slaves.

When my baby was about to be christened, the former mistress of my father stepped up to me, and proposed to give it her Christian name. To this I added the surname of my father, who had himself no legal right to it; for my grandfather on the paternal side was a white gentleman. What tangled skeins are the genealogies of slavery! I loved my father; but it mortified me to be obliged to bestow his name on my children.

When we left the church, my father's old mistress invited me to go home with her. She clasped a gold chain round my baby's neck. I thanked her for this kindness; but I did not like the emblem. I wanted no chain to be fastened on my daughter, not even if its links were of gold. How earnestly I prayed that she might never feel the weight of slavery's chain, whose iron entereth into the soul!

My children grew finely; and Dr. Flint would often say to me, with an exulting smile, "These brats will bring me a handsome sum of money one of these days."

I thought to myself that, God being my helper, they should never pass into his hands. It seemed to me I would rather see them killed than have them given up to his power. The money for the freedom of myself and my children could be obtained; but I derived no advantage from that circumstance. Dr. Flint loved money, but he loved power more. After much discussion, my friends resolved on making another trial. There was a slaveholder about to leave for Texas, and he was commissioned to buy me. He was to begin with nine hundred dollars, and go up to twelve. My master refused his offers. "Sir," said he, "she don't belong to me. She is my daughter's property, and I have no right to sell her. I mistrust that you come from her paramour. If so, you may tell him that he cannot buy her for any money; neither can he buy her children."

The doctor came to see me the next day, and my heart beat quicker as he entered. I never had seen the old man tread with so majestic a step. He seated himself and looked at me with withering scorn. My children had learned to be afraid of him. The little one would shut her eyes and hide her face on my shoulder whenever she saw him; and Benny, who was now nearly five years old, often inquired, "What makes that bad man come here so many times? Does he want to hurt us?" I would clasp the dear boy in my arms, trusting that he would be free before he was old enough to solve the problem. And now, as the doctor sat there so grim and silent, the child left his play and came and nestled up by me. At last my tormentor spoke. "So you are left in disgust, are you?" said he. "It is no more than I expected. You remember I told you years ago that you would be treated so. So he is tired of you? Ha! ha! ha! The virtuous madam don't like to hear about it, does she? Ha! ha! ha!" There was a sting in his calling me virtuous madam. I no longer had the power of answering him as I had formerly done. He continued: "So it seems you are trying to get up another intrigue. Your new paramour came to me, and offered to buy you; but you may be assured you will not succeed. You are mine; and you shall be mine for life. There lives no human being that can take you out of slavery. I would have done it; but you rejected my kind offer."

I told him I did not wish to get up any intrigue; that I had never seen the man who offered to buy me.

"Do you tell me I lie?" exclaimed he, dragging me from my chair. "Will you say again that you never saw that man?"

I answered, "I do say so."

He clinched my arm with a volley of oaths. Ben began to scream, and I told him to go to his grandmother.

"Don't you stir a step, you little wretch!" said he. The child drew nearer to me, and put his arms round me, as if he wanted to protect me. This was too much for my enraged master. He caught him up and hurled him across the room. I thought he was dead, and rushed towards him to take him up.

"Not yet!" exclaimed the doctor. "Let him lie there till he comes to."

"Let me go! Let me go!" I screamed, "or I will raise the whole house." I struggled and got away; but he clinched me again. Somebody opened the door, and he released me. I picked up my insensible child, and when I turned my tormentor was gone. Anxiously I bent over the little form, so pale and still; and when the brown eyes at last opened, I don't know whether I was very happy.

All the doctor's former persecutions were renewed. He came morning, noon, and night. No jealous lover ever watched a rival more closely than he watched me and the unknown slaveholder, with whom he accused me of wishing to get up an intrigue. When my grandmother was out of the way he searched every room to find him.

In one of his visits, he happened to find a young girl, whom he had sold to a trader a few days previous. His statement was, that he sold her because she had been too familiar with the overseer. She had had a bitter life with him, and was glad to be sold. She had no mother, and no near ties. She had been torn from all her family years before. A few friends had entered into bonds for her safety, if the trader would allow her to spend with them the time that intervened between her sale and the gathering up of his human stock. Such a favor was rarely granted. It saved the trader the expense of board and jail fees, and though the amount was small, it was a weighty consideration in a slave-trader's mind.

Dr. Flint always had an aversion to meeting slaves after he had sold them. He ordered Rose out of the house; but he was no longer her master, and she took no notice of him. For once the crushed Rose was the conqueror. His gray eyes flashed angrily upon her; but that was the extent of his power. "How came this girl here?" he exclaimed. "What right had you to allow it, when you knew I had sold her?"

I answered "This is my grandmother's house, and Rose came to see her. I have no right to turn any body out of doors, that comes here for honest purposes."

He gave me the blow that would have fallen upon Rose if she had still been his slave. My grandmother's attention had been attracted by loud voices, and she entered in time to see a second blow dealt. She was not a woman to let such an outrage, in her own house, go unrebuked. The doctor undertook to explain that I had been insolent. Her indignant feelings rose higher and higher, and finally boiled over in words. "Get out of my house!" she exclaimed. "Go home, and take care of your wife and children, and you will have enough to do, without watching my family."

He threw the birth of my children in her face, and accused her of sanctioning the life I was leading. She told him I was living with her by compulsion of his wife; that he needn't accuse her, for he was the one to blame; he was the one who had caused all the trouble. She grew more and more excited as she went on. "I tell you what, Dr. Flint," said she, "you ain't got many more years to live, and you'd better be saying your prayers. It will take 'em all, and more too, to wash the dirt off your soul."

"Do you know whom you are talking to?" he exclaimed.

She replied, "Yes, I know very well who I am talking to."

He left the house in a great rage. I looked at my grandmother. Our eyes met. Their angry expression had passed away, but she looked sorrowful and weary—weary of incessant strife. I wondered that it did not lessen her love for me; but if it did she never showed it. She was always kind, always ready to sympathize with my troubles. There might have been peace and contentment in that humble home if it had not been for the demon Slavery.

The winter passed undisturbed by the doctor. The beautiful spring came; and when Nature resumes her loveliness, the human soul is apt to revive also. My drooping hopes came to life again with the flowers. I was dreaming of freedom again; more for my children's sake than my own. I planned and I planned. Obstacles hit against plans. There seemed no way of overcoming them; and yet I hoped.

Back came the wily doctor. I was not at home when he called. A friend had invited me to a small party, and to gratify her I went. To my great consternation, a messenger came in haste to say that Dr. Flint was at my grandmother's, and insisted on seeing me. They did not tell him where I was, or he would have come and raised a disturbance in my friend's house. They sent me a dark wrapper; I threw it on and hurried home. My speed did not save me; the doctor had gone away in anger. I dreaded the morning, but I could not delay it; it came, warm and bright. At an early hour the doctor came and asked me where I had been last night. I told him. He did not believe me, and sent to my friend's house to ascertain the facts. He came in the afternoon to assure me he was satisfied that I had spoken the truth. He seemed to be in a facetious mood, and I expected some jeers were coming. "I suppose you need some recreation," said he, "but I am surprised at your being there, among those negroes. It was not the place for *you*. Are you *allowed* to visit such people?"

I understood this covert fling at the white gentleman who was my friend; but I merely replied, "I went to visit my friends, and any company they keep is good enough for me."

He went on to say, "I have seen very little of you of late, but my interest in you in unchanged. When I said I would have no more mercy on you I was rash. I recall my words. Linda, you desire freedom for yourself and your children, and you can obtain it only through me. If you agree to what I am about to propose, you and they shall be free. There must be no communication of any kind between you and their father. I will procure a cottage, where you and the children can live together. Your labor shall be light, such as sewing for my family. Think what is offered you, Linda—a home and freedom! Let the past be forgotten. If I have been harsh with you at times, your willfulness drove me to it. You know I enact obedience from my own children, and I consider you as yet a child."

He paused for an answer, but I remained silent.

"Why don't you speak?" said he. "What more do you wait for?"

"Nothing, sir."

"Then you accept my offer?"

"No, sir."

His anger was ready to break loose; but he succeeded in curbing it, and replied, "You have answered without thought.

But I must let you know there are two sides to my proposition; if you reject the bright side, you will be obliged to take the dark one. You must either accept my offer, or you and your children shall be sent to your young master's plantation, there to remain till your young mistress is married; and your children shall fare like the rest of the negro children. I give you a week to consider of it."

He was shrewd; but I knew he was not to be trusted. I told him I was ready to give my answer now.

"I will not receive it now," he replied. "You act too much from impulse. Remember that you and your children can be free a week from to-day if you choose."

On what a monstrous chance hung the destiny of my children! I knew that my master's offer was a snare, and that if I entered it escape would be impossible. As for his promise, I knew him so well that I was sure if he gave me free papers, they would be so managed as to have no legal value. The alternative was inevitable. I resolved to go to the plantation. But then I thought how completely I should be in his power, and the prospect was appalling. Even if I should kneel before him, and implore him to spare me, for the sake of my children, I knew he would spurn me with his foot, and my weakness would be his triumph.

Before the week expired, I heard that young Mr. Flint was about to be married to a lady of his own stamp. I foresaw the position I should occupy in his establishment. I had once been sent to the plantation for punishment, and fear of the son had induced the father to recall me very soon. My mind was made up; I was resolved that I would foil my master and save my children, or I would perish in the attempt. I kept my plans to myself; I knew that friends would try to dissuade me from them, and I would not wound their feelings by rejecting their advice.

On the decisive day the doctor came, and said he hoped I had made a wise choice.

"I am ready to go to the plantation, sir," I replied.

"Have you thought how important your decision is to your children?" said he.

I told him I had.

"Very well. Go to the plantation, and my curse go with you," he replied. "Your boy shall be put to work, and he shall soon be sold; and your girl shall be raised for the purpose of selling well. Go your own ways!" He left the room with curses, not to be repeated.

As I stood rooted to the spot, my grandmother came and said, "Linda, child, what did you tell him?"

I answered that I was going to the plantation.

"*Must* you go?" said she. "Can't something be done to stop it?"

I told her it was useless to try; but she begged me not to give up. She said she would go to the doctor, and remind him how long and how faithfully she had served in the family, and how she had taken her own baby from her breast to nourish his wife. She would tell him I had been out of the family so long they would not miss me; that she would pay them for my time, and the money would procure a woman who had more strength for the situation than I had. I begged her not to go; but she persisted in saying, "He will listen to me, Linda." She went, and was treated as I expected. He coolly listened to what she said, but denied her request. He told her that what he did was for my good, that my feelings were entirely above my situation, and that on the plantation I would receive treatment that was suitable to my behavior.

My grandmother was much cast down. I had my secret hopes; but I must fight my battle alone. I had a woman's pride, and a mother's love for my children; and I resolved that out of the darkness of this hour a brighter dawn should rise for them. My master had power and law on his side; I had a determined will. There is might in each.

XVI

Scenes at the Plantation

Early the next morning I left my grandmother's with my youngest child. My boy was ill, and I left him behind. I had many sad thoughts as the old wagon jolted on. Hitherto, I had suffered alone; now, my little one was to be treated as a slave. As we drew near the great house, I thought of the time when I was formerly sent there out of revenge. I wondered for what purpose I was now sent. I could not tell. I resolved to obey orders so far as duty required; but within myself, I determined to make my stay as short as possible. Mr. Flint was waiting to receive us, and told me to follow him up stairs to receive orders for the day. My little Ellen was left below in the kitchen. It was a change for her, who had always been so carefully tended. My young master said she might amuse herself in the yard. This was kind of him, since the child was hateful to his sight. My task was to fit up the house for the reception of the bride. In the midst of sheets, tablecloths, towels, drapery, and carpeting, my head was as busy planning, as were my fingers with the needle. At noon I was allowed to go to Ellen. She had sobbed herself to sleep. I heard Mr. Flint say to a neighbor, "I've got her down here, and I'll soon take the town notions out of her head. My father is partly to blame for her nonsense. He ought to have broke her in long ago." The remark was made within my hearing, and it would have been quite as manly to have made it to my face. He had said things to my face which might, or might not, have surprised his neighbor if he had known of them. He was "a chip of the old block."

I resolved to give him no cause to accuse me of being too much of a lady, so far as work was concerned. I worked day and night, with wretchedness before me. When I lay down beside my child, I felt how much easier it would be to see her die than to see her master beat her about, as I daily saw him beat other little ones. The spirit of the mothers was so crushed by the lash, that they stood by, without courage to remonstrate. How much more must I suffer, before I should be "broke in" to that degree?

I wished to appear as contented as possible. Sometimes I had

an opportunity to send a few lines home; and this brought up recollections that made it difficult, for a time, to seem calm and indifferent to my lot. Notwithstanding my efforts, I saw that Mr. Flint
regarded me with a suspicious eye. Ellen broke down under the trials of her new life. Separated from me, with no one to look after
her, she wandered about, and in a few days cried herself sick. One
day, she sat under the window where I was at work, crying that
weary cry which makes a mother's heart bleed. I was obliged to
steel myself to bear it. After a while it ceased. I looked out, and she
was gone. As it was near noon, I ventured to go down in search of
her. The great house was raised two feet above the ground. I looked
under it, and saw her about midway, fast asleep. I crept under and
drew her out. As I held her in my arms, I thought how well it would
be for her if she never waked up; and I uttered my thought aloud.
I was startled to hear someone say, "Did you speak to me?" I looked
up, and saw Mr. Flint standing beside me. He said nothing further,
but turned, frowning, away. That night he sent Ellen a biscuit and
a cup of sweetened milk. This generosity surprised me. I learned
afterwards, that in the afternoon he had killed a large snake, which
crept from under the house; and I supposed that incident had
prompted his unusual kindness.

The next morning the old cart was loaded with shingles for
town. I put Ellen into it, and sent her to her grandmother. Mr.
Flint said I ought to have asked his permission. I told him the child
was sick, and required attention which I had no time to give. He let
it pass; for he was aware that I had accomplished much work in a
little time.

I had been three weeks on the plantation, when I planned a
visit home. It must be at night, after every body was in bed. I was
six miles from town, and the road was very dreary. I was to go with
a young man, who, I knew, often stole to town to see his mother.
One night, when all was quiet, we started. Fear gave speed to our
steps, and we were not long in performing the journey. I arrived at
my grandmother's. Her bed room was on the first floor, and the
window was open, the weather being warm. I spoke to her and she
awoke. She let me in and closed the window, lest some late passer-
by should see me. A light was brought, and the whole household
gathered round me, some smiling and some crying. I went to look
at my children, and thanked God for their happy sleep. The tears
fell as I leaned over them. As I moved to leave, Benny stirred. I
turned back, and whispered, "Mother is here." After digging at his

eyes with his little fist, they opened, and he sat up in bed, looking at me curiously. Having satisfied himself that it was I, he exclaimed, "O mother! you ain't dead, are you? They didn't cut off your head at the plantation, did they?"

My time was up too soon, and my guide was waiting for me. I laid Benny back in his bed, and dried his tears by a promise to come again soon. Rapidly we retraced our steps back to the plantation. About half way we were met by a company of four patrols. Luckily we heard their horses' hoofs before they came in sight, and we had time to hide behind a large tree. They passed, hallooing and shouting in a manner that indicated a recent carousal. How thankful we were that they had not their dogs with them! We hastened our footsteps, and when we arrived on the plantation we heard the sound of the hand-mill. The slaves were grinding their corn. We were safely in the house before the horn summoned them to their labor. I divided my little parcel of food with my guide, knowing that he had lost the chance of grinding his corn, and must toil all day in the field.

Mr. Flint often took an inspection of the house, to see that no one was idle. The entire management of the work was trusted to me, because he knew nothing about it; and rather than hire a superintendent he contented himself with my arrangements. He had often urged upon his father the necessity of having me at the plantation to take charge of his affairs, and make clothes for the slaves; but the old man knew him too well to consent to that arrangement.

When I had been working a month at the plantation, the great aunt of Mr. Flint came to make him a visit. This was the good old lady who paid fifty dollars for my grandmother, for the purpose of making her free, when she stood on the auction block. My grandmother loved this old lady, whom we all called Miss Fanny. She often came to take tea with us. On such occasions the table was spread with a snow-white cloth, and the china cups and silver spoons were taken from the old-fashioned buffet. There were hot muffins, tea rusks, and delicious sweetmeats. My grandmother kept two cows, and the fresh cream was Miss Fanny's delight. She invariably declared that it was the best in town. The old ladies had cosy times together. They would work and chat and sometimes, while talking over old times, their spectacles would get dim with tears, and would have to be taken off and wiped. When Miss Fanny bade us good by, her bag was filled with grandmother's best cakes, and she was urged to come again soon.

There had been a time when Dr. Flint's wife came to take tea with us, and when her children were also sent to have a feast of "Aunt Marthy's" nice cooking. But after I became an object of her jealousy and spite, she was angry with grandmother for giving a shelter to me and my children. She would not even speak to her in the street. This wounded my grandmother's feelings, for she could not retain ill will against the woman whom she had nourished with her milk when a babe. The doctor's wife would gladly have prevented our intercourse with Miss Fanny if she could have done it, but fortunately she was not dependent on the bounty of the Flints. She had enough to be independent; and that is more than can ever be gained from charity, however lavish it may be.

Miss Fanny was endeared to me by many recollections, and I was rejoiced to see her at the plantation. The warmth of her large, loyal heart made the house seem pleasanter while she was in it. She staid a week, and I had many talks with her. She said her principal object in coming was to see how I was treated, and whether any thing could be done for me. She inquired whether she could help me in any way. I told her I believed not. She condoled with me in her own peculiar way; saying she wished that I and all my grandmother's family were at rest in our graves, for not until then should she feel any peace about us. The good old soul did not dream that I was planning to bestow peace upon her, with regard to myself and my children; not by death, but by securing our freedom.

Again and again I had traversed those dreary twelve miles, to and from the town; and all the way, I was meditating upon some means of escape for myself and my children. My friend had made every effort that ingenuity could devise to effect our purchase, but all their plans had proved abortive. Dr. Flint was suspicious, and determined not to loosen his grasp upon us. I could have made my escape alone; but it was more for my helpless children than for myself that I longed for freedom. Though the boon would have been precious to me, above all price, I would not have taken it at the expense of leaving them in slavery. Every trial I endured, every sacrifice I made for their sakes, drew them closer to my heart, and gave me fresh courage to beat back the dark waves that rolled and rolled over me in a seemingly endless night of storms.

The six weeks were nearly completed, when Mr. Flint's bride was expected to take possession of her new home. The arrangements were all completed, and Mr. Flint said I had done well. We expected to leave home on Saturday, and return with his bride the following Wednesday. After receiving various orders from him, I ventured to ask permission to spend Sunday in town. It was granted; for which favor I was thankful. It was the first I had ever asked of him, and I intended it should be the last. It needed more than one night to accomplish the project I had in view; but the whole of Sunday would give me an opportunity. I spent the Sabbath with my grandmother. A calmer, more beautiful day never came down out of heaven. To me it was a day of conflicting emotions. Perhaps it was the last day I should ever spend under that dear, old sheltering roof! Perhaps these were the last talks I should ever have with the faithful old friend of my whole life! Perhaps it was the last time I and my children should be together! Well, better so, I thought, than that they should be slaves. I knew the doom that awaited my fair baby in slavery, and I determined to save her from it, or perish in the attempt. I went to make this vow at the graves of my poor parents, in the burying-ground of the slaves. "There the wicked cease from troubling, and there the weary be at rest. There the prisoners rest together; they hear not the voice of the oppressor; the servant is free from his master." I knelt by the graves of my parents, and thanked God, as I had often done before, that they had not lived to witness my trials, or to mourn over my sins. I had received my mother's blessing when she died; and in many an hour of tribulation I had seemed to hear her voice, sometimes chiding me, sometimes whispering loving words into my wounded heart. I have shed many and bitter tears, to think that when I am gone from my children they cannot remember me with such entire satisfaction as I remembered my mother.

The graveyard was in the woods, and twilight was coming on. Nothing broke the death-like stillness except the occasional twitter of a bird. My spirit was overawed by the solemnity of the scene. For more than ten years I had frequented this spot, but never had it seemed to me so sacred as now. A black stump, at the head of my mother's grave, was all that remained of a tree my father had planted. His grave was marked by a small wooden board, bearing his name, the letters of which were nearly obliterated. I knelt down and kissed them, and poured forth a prayer to God for guidance and support in the perilous step I was about to take. As I passed the wreck of the old meeting house, where, before Nat Turner's time, the slaves had been allowed to meet for worship, I seemed to hear my father's voice come from it, bidding me not to tarry till I reached freedom or the grave. I rushed on with renovated hopes. My trust in God had been strengthened by that prayer among the graves.

My plan was to conceal myself at the house of a friend, and remain there a few weeks till the search was over. My hope was that the doctor would get discouraged, and, for fear of losing my value, and also of subsequently finding my children among the missing, he would consent to sell us; and I knew somebody would buy us. I had done all in my power to make my children comfortable during the time I expected to be separated from them. I was packing my things, when grandmother came into the room, and asked what I was doing. "I am putting my things in order," I replied. I tried to look and speak cheerfully; but her watchful eye detected something beneath the surface. She drew me towards her, and asked me to sit down. She looked earnestly at me, and said, "Linda, do you want to kill your old grandmother? Do you mean to leave your little, helpless children? I am old now, and cannot do for your babies as I once did for you."

I replied, that if I went away, perhaps their father would be able to secure their freedom.

"Ah, my child," said she, "don't trust too much to him. Stand by your own children, and suffer with them till death. Nobody respects a mother who forsakes her children; and if you leave them, you will never have a happy moment. If you go, you will make me miserable the short time I have to live. You would be taken and brought back, and your sufferings would be dreadful. Remember poor Benjamin. Do give it up, Linda. Try to bear a little longer. Things may turn out better than we expect."

My courage failed me, in view of the sorrow I should bring on that faithful, loving old heart. I promised that I would try longer, and that I would take nothing out of her house without her knowledge.

Whenever the children climbed on my knee, or laid their heads on my lap, she would say, "Poor little souls! what would you do without a mother? She don't love you as I do" And she would hug them to her own bosom, as if to reproach me for my want of affection; but she knew all the while that I loved them better than my life. I slept with her that night, and it was the last time. The memory of it haunted me for many a year.

On Monday I returned to the plantation, and busied myself with preparations for the important day. Wednesday came. It was a beautiful day, and the faces of the slaves were as bright as the sunshine. The poor creatures were merry. They were expecting little presents from the bride, and hoping for better times under her administration. I had no such hopes for them. I knew that the young wives of slaveholders often thought their authority and importance would be best established and maintained by cruelty; and what I had heard of young Mrs. Flint gave me no reason to expect that her rule over them would be less severe than that of the master and overseer. Truly, the colored race are the most cheerful and forgiving people on the face of the earth. That their masters sleep in safety is owing to their superabundance of heart; and yet they look upon their sufferings with less pity than they would bestow on those of a horse or a dog.

I stood at the door with others to receive the bridegroom and bride. She was a handsome, delicate-looking girl, and her face flushed with emotion at sight of her new home. I thought it likely that visions of a happy future were rising before her. It made me sad; for I knew how soon clouds would come over her sunshine. She examined every part of the house, and told me she was delighted with the arrangements I had made. I was afraid old Mrs. Flint had tried to prejudice her against me, and I did my best to please her.

It passed off smoothly for me until dinner time arrived. I did not mind the embarrassment of waiting on a dinner party, for the first time in my life, half so much as I did the meeting with Dr. Flint and his wife, who would be among the guests. It was a mystery to me why Mrs. Flint had not made her appearance at the plantation during all the time I was putting the house in order. I had not met her, face to face, for five years, and I had no wish to see her now. She was a praying woman, and, doubtless, considered my present position a special answer to her prayers. Nothing could please her better than to see me humbled and trampled upon. I was just where she would have me—in the power of a hard, unprincipled master. She did not speak to me when she took her seat at table; but her satisfied, triumphant smile, when I handed her plate, was more eloquent than words. The old doctor was not so quiet in his demonstrations. He ordered me here and there, and spoke with peculiar emphasis when he said "your *mistress.*" I was drilled like a disgraced soldier. When all was over, and the last key turned, I sought my pillow, thankful that God had appointed a season of rest for the weary.

The next day my new mistress began her housekeeping. I was not exactly appointed maid of all work; but I was to do whatever I was told. Monday evening came. It was always a busy time. On that night the slaves received their weekly allowance of food. Three pounds of meat, a peck of corn, and perhaps a dozen herring were allowed to each man. Women received a pound and a half of meat, a peck of corn, and the same number of herring. Children over twelve years old had half the allowance of the women. The meat was cut and weighed by the foreman of the field hands, and piled on planks before the meat house. Then the second foreman went behind the building, and when the first foreman called out, "Who takes this piece of meat?" he answered by calling somebody's name. This method was resorted to as means of preventing partiality in distributing the meat. The young mistress came out to see how things were done on her plantation, and she soon gave a specimen of her character. Among those in waiting for their allowance was a very old slave, who had faithfully served the Flint family through three generations. When he hobbled up to get his bit of meat, the mistress said he was too old to have any allowance; that when niggers were too old to work, they ought to be fed on grass. Poor old man! He suffered much before he found rest in the grave.

My mistress and I got along very well together. At the end of a week, old Mrs. Flint made us another visit, and was closeted a long time with her daughter-in-law. I had my suspicions what was the subject of the conference. The old doctor's wife had been informed that I could leave the plantation on one condition, and she was very desirous to keep me there. If she had trusted me, as I deserved to be trusted by her, she would have had no fears of my accepting that condition. When she entered her carriage to return home, she said to young Mrs. Flint, "Don't neglect to send for them as quick as possible." My heart was on the watch all the time, and I at once concluded that she spoke of my children. The doctor came the next day, and as I entered the room to spread the tea table, I heard him say, "Don't wait any longer. Send for them to-morrow." I saw through the plan. They thought my children's being there would fetter me to the spot, and that it was a good place to break us all in to abject submission to our lot as slaves. After the doctor left, a gentleman called, who had always manifested friendly feelings towards my grandmother and her family. Mr. Flint carried him over the plantation to show him the results of labor performed by men and women who were unpaid, miserably clothed, and half famished.

The cotton crop was all they thought of. It was duly admired, and the gentleman returned with specimens to show his friends. I was ordered to carry water to wash his hands. As I did so, he said, "Linda, how do you like your new home?" I told him I liked it as well as I expected. He replied, "They don't think you are contented, and to-morrow they are going to bring your children to be with you. I am sorry for you, Linda. I hope they will treat you kindly." I hurried from the room, unable to thank him. My suspicions were correct. My children were to be brought to the plantation to be "broke in."

To this day I feel grateful to the gentleman who gave me this timely information. It nerved me to immediate action.

XVII

THE FLIGHT

Mr. Flint was hard pushed for house servants, and rather than lose me he had restrained his malice. I did my work faithfully, though not, of course, with a willing mind. They were evidently afraid I should leave them. Mr. Flint wished that I should sleep in the great house instead of the servants' quarters. His wife agreed to the proposition, but said I mustn't bring my bed into the house, because it would scatter feathers on her carpet. I knew when I went there that they would never think of such a thing as furnishing a bed of any kind for me and my little one. I therefore carried my own bed, and now I was forbidden to use it. I did as I was ordered. But now that I was certain my children were to be put in their power, in order to give them a stronger hold on me, I resolved to leave them that night. I remembered the grief this step would bring upon my dear old grandmother; and nothing less than the freedom of my children would have induced me to disregard her advice. I went about my evening work with trembling steps. Mr. Flint twice called from his chamber door to inquire why the house was not locked up. I replied that I had not done my work. "You have had time enough to do it," said he. "Take care how you answer me!"

I shut all the windows, locked all the doors, and went up to the third story, to wait till midnight. How long those hours seemed, and how fervently I prayed that God would not forsake me in this hour of utmost need! I was about to risk every thing on the throw of a die; and if I failed, O what would become of me and my poor children? They would be made to suffer for my fault.

At half past twelve I stole softly down stairs. I stopped on the second floor, thinking I heard a noise. I felt my way down into the parlor, and looked out of the window. The night was so intensely dark that I could see nothing. I raised the window very softly and jumped out. Large drops of rain were falling, and the darkness bewildered me. I dropped on my knees, and breathed a short prayer to God for guidance and protection. I groped my way to the road, and rushed towards the town with almost lightning speed. I arrived at my grandmother's house, but dared not see her. She would say, "Linda, you are killing me;" and I knew that would unnerve me. I tapped softly at the window of a room, occupied by a woman, who had lived in the house several years. I knew she was a faithful friend, and could be trusted with my secret. I tapped several times before she heard me. At last she raised the window, and I whispered, "Sally, I have run away. Let me in, quick." She opened the door softly, and said in low tones, "For God's sake, don't. Your grandmother is trying to buy you and de chillern. Mr. Sands was here last week. He tole her he was going away on business, but he wanted her to go ahead about buying you and de chillern, and he would help her all he could. Don't run away, Linda. Your grandmother is all bowed down wid trouble now."

I replied, "Sally, they are going to carry my children to the plantation to-morrow; and they will never sell them to any body so long as they have me in their power. Now, would you advise me to go back?"

"No, chile, no," answered she. "When dey finds you is gone, dey won't want de plague ob de chillern; but where is you going to hide? Dey knows ebery inch ob dis house."

I told her I had a hiding-place, and that was all it was best for her to know. I asked her to go into my room as soon as it was light, and take all my clothes out of my trunk, and pack them in hers; for I knew Mr. Flint and the constable would be there early to search my room. I feared the sight of my children would be too much for my full heart; but I could not go out into the uncertain future without one last look. I bent over the bed where lay my little Benny and baby Ellen. Poor little ones! fatherless and motherless! Memories of their father came over me. He wanted to be kind to them; but they were not all to him, as they were to my womanly heart. I knelt and prayed for the innocent little sleepers. I kissed them lightly, and turned away.

As I was about to open the street door, Sally laid her hand on my shoulder, and said, "Linda, is you gwine all alone? Let me call your uncle."

"No, Sally," I replied, "I want no one to be brought into trouble on my account."

I went forth into the darkness and rain. I ran on till I came to the house of the friend who was to conceal me.

Early the next morning Mr. Flint was at my grandmother's inquiring for me. She told him she had not seen me, and supposed I was at the plantation. He watched her face narrowly, and said, "Don't you know any thing about her running off?" She assured him that she did not. He went on to say, "Last night she ran off without the least provocation. We had treated her very kindly. My wife liked her. She will soon be found and brought back. Are her children with you?" When told that they were, he said, "I am very glad to hear that. If they are here, she cannot be far off. If I find out that any of my niggers have had any thing to do with this damned business, I'll give 'em five hundred lashes." As he started to go to his father's, he turned round and added, persuasively, "Let her be brought back, and she shall have her children to live with her."

The tidings made the old doctor rave and storm at a furious rate. It was a busy day for them. My grandmother's house was searched from top to bottom. As my trunk was empty, they concluded I had taken my clothes with me. Before ten o'clock every vessel northward bound was thoroughly examined, and the law against harboring fugitives was read to all on board. At night a watch was set over the town. Knowing how distressed my grandmother would be, I wanted to send her a message; but it could not be done. Every one who went in or out of her house was closely watched. The doctor said he would take my children, unless she became responsible for them; which of course she willingly did. The next day was spent in searching. Before night, the following advertisement was posted at every corner, and in every public place for miles round:—

"$300 REWARD! Ran away from the subscriber, an intelligent, bright, mulatto girl, named Linda, 21 years of age. Five feet four inches high. Dark eyes, and black hair inclined to curl; but it can be made straight. Has a decayed spot on a front tooth. She can read and write, and in all probability will try to get to the Free States. All persons are

338

forbidden, under penalty of the law, to harbor or employ said slave. $150 will be given to whoever takes her in the state, and $300 if taken out of the state and delivered to me, or lodged in jail. — DR. FLINT

XVIII

Months of Peril

The search for me was kept up with more perseverance than I had anticipated. I began to think that escape was impossible. I was in great anxiety lest I should implicate the friend who harbored me. I knew the consequences would be frightful; and much as I dreaded being caught, even that seemed better than causing an innocent person to suffer for kindness to me. A week had passed in terrible suspense, when my pursuers came into such close vicinity that I concluded they had tracked me to my hiding-place. I flew out of the house, and concealed myself in a thicket of bushes. There I remained in an agony of fear for two hours. Suddenly, a reptile of some kind seized my leg. In my fright, I struck a blow which loosened its hold, but I could not tell whether I had killed it; it was so dark, I could not see what it was; I only knew it was something cold and slimy. The pain I felt soon indicated that the bite was poisonous. I was compelled to leave my place of concealment, and I groped my way back into the house. The pain had become intense, and my friend was startled by my look of anguish. I asked her to prepare a poultice of warm ashes and vinegar, and I applied it to my leg, which was already much swollen. The application gave me some relief, but the swelling did not abate. The dread of being disabled was greater than the physical pain I endured. My friend asked an old woman, who doctored among the slaves, what was good for the bite of a snake or a lizard. She told her to steep a dozen coppers in vinegar, over night, and apply the cankered vinegar to the inflamed part.

I had succeeded in cautiously conveying some messages to my relatives. They were harshly threatened, and despairing of my having a chance to escape, they advised me to return to my master, ask his forgiveness, and let him make an example of me. But such counsel had no influence with me. When I started upon this hazardous undertaking, I had resolved that, come what would, there should be no turning back. "Give me liberty, or give me death," was my motto. When my friend contrived to make known to my relatives the painful situation I had been in for twenty-four hours, they said no more about my going back to my master. Something must be done, and that speedily; but where to turn for help, they knew not. God in his mercy raised up "a friend in need."

Among the ladies who were acquainted with my grandmother, was one who had known her from childhood, and always been very friendly to her. She had also known my mother and her children, and felt interested for them. At this crisis of affairs she called to see my grandmother, as she not infrequently did. She observed the sad and troubled expression of her face, and asked if she knew where Linda was, and whether she was safe. My grandmother shook her head, without answering. "Come, Aunt Martha," said the kind lady, "tell me all about it. Perhaps I can do something to help you." The husband of this lady held many slaves, and bought and sold slaves. She also held a number in her own name; but she treated them kindly, and would never allow any of them to be sold. She was unlike the majority of slaveholders' wives. My grandmother looked earnestly at her. Something in the expression of her face said "Trust me!" and she did trust her. She listened attentively to the details of my story, and sat thinking for a while. At last she said, "Aunt Martha, I pity you both. If you think there is any chance of Linda's getting to the Free States, I will conceal her for a time. But first you must solemnly promise that my name shall never be mentioned. If such a thing should become known, it would ruin me and my family. No one in my house must know of it, except the cook. She is so faithful that I would trust my own life with her; and I know she likes Linda. It is a great risk; but I trust no harm will come of it. Get word to Linda to be ready as soon as it is dark, before the patrols are out. I will send the housemaids on errands, and Betty shall go to meet Linda." The place where we were to meet was designated and agreed upon. My grandmother was unable to thank the lady for this noble deed; overcome by her emotions, she sank on her knees and sobbed like a child.

* The poison of a snake has a powerful acid, and is counteracted by powerful alkalies, such as potash, ammonia, &c. The Indians are accustomed to apply wet ashes, or plunge the limb into strong lie. White men, employed to lay out railroads in snaky places often carry ammonia with them as an antidote. L. M. C.

I received a message to leave my friend's house at such an hour, and go to a certain place where a friend would be waiting for me. As a matter of prudence no names were mentioned. I had no means of conjecturing who I was to meet, or where I was going. I did not like to move thus blindfolded, but I had no choice. It would not do for me to remain where I was. I disguised myself, summoned up courage to meet the worst, and went to the appointed place. My friend Betty was there; she was the last person I expected to see. We hurried along in silence. The pain in my leg was so intense that it seemed as if I should drop; but fear gave me strength. We reached the house and entered unobserved. Her first words were: "Honey, now you is safe. Dem devils ain't coming to search dis house. When I get you into missis' safe place, I will bring some nice hot supper. I specs you need it after all dis skeering." Betty's vocation led her to think eating the most important thing in life. She did not realize that my heart was too full for me to care much about supper.

The mistress came to meet us, and led me up stairs to a small room over her own sleeping apartment. "You will be safe here, Linda," said she; "I keep this room to store away things that are out of use. The girls are not accustomed to be sent to it, and they will not suspect any thing unless they hear some noise. I always keep it locked, and Betty shall take care of the key. But you must be very careful, for my sake as well as your own; and you must never tell my secret; for it would ruin me and my family. I will keep the girls busy in the morning, that Betty may have a chance to bring your breakfast; but it will not do for her to come to you again till night. I will come to see you sometimes. Keep up your courage. I hope this state of things will not last long." Betty came with the "nice hot supper," and the mistress hastened down stairs to keep things straight till she returned. How my heart overflowed with gratitude! Words choked in my throat; but I could have kissed the feet of my benefactress. For that deed of Christian womanhood, may God forever bless her!

I went to sleep that night with the feeling that I was for the present the most fortunate slave in town. Morning came and filled my little cell with light. I thanked the heavenly Father for this safe retreat. Opposite my window was a pile of feather beds. On the top of these I could lie perfectly concealed, and command a view of the street through which Dr. Flint passed to his office. Anxious as I was, I felt a gleam of satisfaction when I saw him. Thus far I had outwitted him, and I triumphed over it. Who can blame slaves for being cunning? They are constantly compelled to resort to it. It is the only weapon of the weak and oppressed against the strength of their tyrants.

I was daily hoping to hear that my master had sold my children; for I knew who was on the watch to buy them. But Dr. Flint cared even more for revenge than he did for money. My brother William, and the good aunt who had served in his family twenty years, and my little Benny, and Ellen, who was a little over two years old, were thrust into jail, as a means of compelling my relatives to give some information about me. He swore my grandmother should never see one of them again till I was brought back. They kept these facts from me for several days. When I heard that my little ones were in a loathsome jail, my first impulse was to go to them. I was encountering dangers for the sake of freeing them, and must I be the cause of their death? The thought was agonizing. My benefactress tried to soothe me by telling me that my aunt would take good care of the children while they remained in jail. But it added to my pain to think that the good old aunt, who had always been so kind to her sister's orphan children, should be shut up in prison for no other crime than loving them. I suppose my friends feared a reckless movement on my part, knowing, as they did, that my life was bound up in my children. I received a note from my brother William. It was scarcely legible, and ran thus: "Wherever you are, dear sister, I beg of you not to come here. We are all much better off than you are. If you come, you will ruin us all. They would force you to tell where you had been, or they would kill you. Take the advice of your friends; if not for the sake of me and your children, at least for the sake of those you would ruin."

Poor William! He also must suffer for being my brother. I took his advice and kept quiet. My aunt was taken out of jail at the end of a month, because Mrs. Flint could not spare her any longer. She was tired of being her own housekeeper. It was quite too fatiguing to order her dinner and eat it too. My children remained in jail, where brother William did all he could for their comfort. Betty went to see them sometimes, and brought me tidings. She was not permitted to enter the jail; but William would hold them up to the grated window while she chatted with them. When she repeated their prattle, and told me how they wanted to see their ma, my tears would flow. Old Betty would exclaim, "Lors, chile! what's you crying 'bout? Dem young uns will kill you dead. Don't be so chick'n hearted! If you does, you vil nebber git thro' dis world."

Good old soul! She had gone through the world childless. She had never had little ones to clasp their arms round her neck; she had never seen their soft eyes looking into hers; no sweet little voices had called her mother; she had never pressed her own infants to her heart, with the feeling that even in fetters there was something to live for. How could she realize my feelings? Betty's husband loved children dearly, and wondered why God had denied them to him. He expressed great sorrow when he came to Betty with the tidings that Ellen had been taken out of jail and carried to Dr. Flint's. She had the measles a short time before they carried her to jail, and the disease had left her eyes affected. The doctor had taken her home to attend to them. My children had always been afraid of the doctor and his wife. They had never been inside of their house. Poor little Ellen cried all day to be carried back to prison. The instincts of childhood are true. She knew she was loved in the jail. Her screams and sobs annoyed Mrs. Flint. Before night she called one of the slaves, and said, "Here, Bill, carry this brat back to the jail. I can't stand her noise. If she would be quiet I should like to keep the little minx. She would make a handy waiting-maid for my daughter by and by. But if she staid here, with her white face, I suppose I should either kill her or spoil her. I hope the doctor will sell them as far as wind and water can carry them. As for their mother, her ladyship will find out yet what she gets by running away. She hasn't so much feeling for her children as a cow has for its calf. If she had, she would have come back long ago, to get them out of jail, and save all this expense and trouble. The good-for-nothing hussy! When she is caught, she shall stay in jail, in irons, for one six months, and then be sold to a sugar plantation. I shall see her broke in yet. What do you stand there for, Bill? Why don't you go off with the brat? Mind, now, that you don't let any of the niggers speak to her in the street!"

When these remarks were reported to me, I smiled at Mrs. Flint's saying that she should either kill my child or spoil her. I thought to myself there was very little danger of the latter. I have always considered it as one of God's special providences that Ellen screamed till she was carried back to jail.

That same night Dr. Flint was called to a patient, and did not return till near morning. Passing my grandmother's, he saw a light in the house, and thought to himself, "Perhaps this has something to do with Linda." He knocked, and the door was opened. "What calls you up so early?" said he. "I saw your light, and I thought I would just stop and tell you that I have found out where Linda is. I know where to put my hands on her, and I shall have her before twelve o'clock.'

When he had turned away, my grandmother and my uncle looked anxiously at each other. They did not know whether or not it was merely one of the doctor's tricks to frighten them. In their uncertainty, they thought it was best to have a message conveyed to my friend Betty. Unwilling to alarm her mistress, Betty resolved to dispose of me herself. She came to me, and told me to rise and dress quickly. We hurried down stairs, and across the yard, into the kitchen. She locked the door, and lifted up a plank in the floor. A buffalo skin and a bit of carpet were spread for me to lie on, and a quilt thrown over me. "Stay dar," said she, "till I sees if dey know 'bout you. Dey say dey vil put thar hans on you afore twelve o'clock. If dey *did* know whar you are, dey won't know *now*. Dey'll be disapinted dis time. Dat's all I got to say. If dey comes rummagin 'mong *my* tings, dey'll get one bressed sarssin from dis 'ere nigger." In my shallow bed I had but just room enough to bring my hands to my face to keep the dust out of my eyes; for Betty walked over me twenty times in an hour, passing from the dresser to the fireplace. When she was alone, I could hear her pronouncing anathemas over Dr. Flint and all his tribe, every now and then saying, with a chuckling laugh, "Dis nigger's too cute for 'em dis time." When the housemaids were about, she had sly ways of drawing them out, that I might hear what they would say. She would repeat stories she had heard about my being in this, or that, or the other place. To which they would answer, that I was not fool enough to be staying round there; that I was in Philadelphia or New York before this time. When all were abed and asleep, Betty raised the plank, and said, "Come out, chile; come out. Dey don't know nottin 'bout you. 'Twas only white folks' lies, to skeer de niggers."

Some days after this adventure I had a much worse fright. As I sat very still in my retreat above stairs, cheerful visions floated through my mind. I thought Dr. Flint would soon get discouraged, and would be willing to sell my children, when he lost all hopes of making them the means of my discovery. I knew who was ready to buy them. Suddenly I heard a voice that chilled my blood. The sound was too familiar to me, it had been too dreadful, for me not to recognize at once my old master. He was in the house, and I at once concluded he had come to seize me. I looked round in terror: There was no way of escape. The voice receded. I supposed the constable was with him, and they were searching the house. In my alarm I did not forget the trouble I was bringing on my generous benefactress. It seemed as if I were born to bring sorrow on all who befriended me, and that was the bitterest drop in the bitter cup of my life. After a while I heard approaching footsteps; the key was turned in my door. I braced myself against the wall to keep from falling. I ventured to look up, and there stood my kind benefactress alone. I was too much overcome to speak, and sunk down upon the floor.

"I thought you would hear your master's voice," she said; "and knowing you would be terrified, I came to tell you there is nothing to fear. You may even indulge in a laugh at the old gentleman's expense. He is so sure you are in New York, that he came to borrow five hundred dollars to go in pursuit of you. My sister had some money to loan on interest. He has obtained it, and proposes to start for New York to-night. So, for the present, you see you are safe. The doctor will merely lighten his pocket hunting after the bird he has left behind."

XIX

THE CHILDREN SOLD

The doctor came back from New York, of course without accomplishing his purpose. He had expended considerable money, and was rather disheartened. My brother and the children had now been in jail two months, and that also was some expense. My friends thought it was a favorable time to work on his discouraged feelings. Mr. Sands sent a speculator to offer him nine hundred dollars for my brother William, and eight hundred for the two children. These were high prices, as slaves were then selling; but the offer was rejected. If it had been merely a question of money, the doctor would have sold any boy of Benny's age for two hundred dollars; but he could not bear to give up the power of revenge. But he was hard pressed for money, and he revolved the matter in his mind. He knew that if he could keep Ellen till she was fifteen, he could sell her for a high price; but I presume he reflected that she might die, or might be stolen away. At all events, he came to the conclusion that he had better accept the slave-trader's offer. Meeting him in the street, he inquired when he would leave town. "To-day, at ten o'clock," he replied. "Ah, do you go so soon?" said the doctor; "I have been reflecting upon your proposition, and I have concluded to let you have the three negroes if you will say nineteen hundred dollars." After some parley, the trader agreed to his terms. He wanted the bill of sale drawn up and signed immediately, as he had a great deal to attend to during the short time he remained in town. The doctor went to the jail and told William he would take him back into his service if he would promise to behave himself; but he replied that he would rather be sold. "And you *shall* be sold, you ungrateful rascal!" exclaimed the doctor. In less than an hour the money was paid, the papers were signed, sealed, and delivered, and my brother and children were in the hands of the trader.

It was a hurried transaction; and after it was over, the doctor's characteristic caution returned. He went back to the speculator, and said, "Sir, I have come to lay you under obligations of a thousand dollars not to sell any of those negroes in this state." "You come too late," replied the trader; "our bargain is closed." He had, in fact, already sold them to Mr. Sands, but he did not mention it. The doctor required him to put irons on "that rascal, Bill," and to pass through the back streets when he took his gang out of town. The trader was privately instructed to concede to his wishes. My good old aunt went to the jail to bid the children good by, supposing them to be the speculator's property, and that she should never see them again. As she held Benny in her lap, he said, "Aunt Nancy, I want to show you something." He led her to the door and showed her a long row of marks, saying, "Uncle Will taught me to count. I have made a mark for every day I have been here, and it is sixty days. It is a long time; and the speculator is going to take me and Ellen away. He's a bad man. It's wrong for him to take grandmother's children. I want to go to my mother."

My grandmother was told that the children would be restored to her, but she was requested to act as if they were really to be sent away. Accordingly, she made up a bundle of clothes and went to the jail. When she arrived, she found William handcuffed among the gang, and the children in the trader's cart. The scene seemed too much like reality. She was afraid there might have been some deception or mistake. She fainted, and was carried home.

When the wagon stopped at the hotel, several gentlemen came out and proposed to purchase William, but the trader refused their offers, without stating that he was already sold. And now came the trying hour for that drove of human beings, driven away like cattle, to be sold they knew not where. Husbands were torn from wives,

346

parents from children, never to look upon each other again this side the grave. There was wringing of hands and cries of despair.

Dr. Flint had the supreme satisfaction of seeing the wagon leave town, and Mrs. Flint had the gratification of supposing that my children were going "as far as wind and water would carry them." According to agreement, my uncle followed the wagon some miles, until they came to an old farm house. There the trader took the irons from William, and as he did so, he said, "You are a damned clever fellow. I should like to own you myself. Them gentlemen that wanted to buy you said you was a bright, honest chap, and I must git you a good home. I guess your old master will swear to-morrow, and call himself an old fool for selling the children. I reckon he'll never git their mammy back agin. I expect she's made tracks for the north. Good by, old boy. Remember, I have done you a good turn. You must thank me by coaxing all the pretty gals to go with me next fall. That's going to be my last trip. This trading in niggers is a bad business for a fellow that's got any heart. Move on, you fellows!" And the gang went on, God alone knows where.

Much as I despise and detest the class of slave-traders, whom I regard as the vilest wretches on earth, I must do this man the justice to say that he seemed to have some feeling. He took a fancy to William in the jail, and wanted to buy him. When he heard the story of my children, he was willing to aid them in getting out of Dr. Flint's power, even without charging the customary fee.

My uncle procured a wagon and carried William and the children back to town. Great was the joy in my grandmother's house! The curtains were closed, and the candles lighted. The happy grandmother cuddled the little ones to her bosom. They hugged her, and kissed her, and clapped their hands, and shouted. She knelt down and poured forth one of her heartfelt prayers of thanksgiving to God. The father was present for a while; and though such a "parental relation" as existed between him and my children takes slight hold of the hearts or consciences of slaveholders, it must be that he experienced some moments of pure joy in witnessing the happiness he had imparted.

I had no share in the rejoicings of that evening. The events of the day had not come to my knowledge. And now I will tell you something that happened to me; though you will, perhaps, think it illustrates the superstition of slaves. I sat in my usual place on the floor near the window, where I could hear much that was said in the street without being seen. The family had retired for the night, and all was still. I sat there thinking of my children, when I heard a low strain of music. A band of serenaders were under the window, playing "Home, sweet home." I listened till the sounds did not seem like music, but like the moaning of children. It seemed as if my heart would burst. I rose from my sitting posture, and knelt. A streak of moonlight was on the floor before me, and in the midst of it appeared the forms of my two children. They vanished; but I had seen them distinctly. Some will call it a dream, others a vision. I know not how to account for it, but it made a strong impression on my mind, and I felt certain something had happened to my little ones.

I had not seen Betty since morning. Now I heard her softly turning the key. As soon as she entered, I clung to her, and begged her to let me know whether my children were dead, or whether they were sold; for I had seen their spirits in my room, and I was sure something had happened to them. "Lor, chile," said she, putting her arms round me, "you's got de highsterics. I'll sleep wid you to-night, 'cause you'll make a noise, and ruin missis. Something has stirred you up mightily. When you is done cryin, I'll talk wid you. De chillern is well, and mighty happy. I seed 'em myself. Does dat satisfy you? Dar, chile, be still! somebody will hear you." I tried to obey her. She lay down, and was soon sound asleep; but no sleep would come to my eyelids.

At dawn, Betty was up and off to the kitchen. The hours passed on, and the vision of the night kept constantly recurring to my thoughts. After a while I heard the voices of two women in the entry. In one of them I recognized the housemaid. The other said to her, "Did you know Linda Brent's children was sold to the speculator yesterday. They say ole massa Flint was mighty glad to see 'em drove out of town; but they say they've come back agin. I'spect it's all their daddy's doings. They say he's bought William too. Lor! how it will take hold of old massa Flint! I'm going roun' to aunt Marthy's to see 'bout it."

I bit my lips till the blood came to keep from crying out. Were my children with their grandmother, or had the speculator carried them off? The suspense was dreadful. Would Betty *never* come, and tell me the truth about it? At last she came, and I eagerly repeated what I had overheard. Her face was one broad, bright smile. "Lor, you foolish ting!" said she. "I'se gwine to tell you all 'bout it. De gals is eating thar breakfast, and missus tole me to let her tell you; but, poor creeter! T'aint right to keep you waitin', and

I'se gwine to tell you. Brudder, chillern, all is bought by de daddy! I'se laugh more dan nuff, tinking 'bout ole massa Flint. Lor, how he *vill* swar! He's got ketched dis time, any how; but I must be getting out o 'dis, or dem gals vill come and ketch *me.* "

Betty went off laughing; and I said to myself, "Can it be true that my children are free? I have not suffered for them in vain. Thank God!"

Great surprise was expressed when it was known that my children had returned to their grandmother's. The news spread through the town, and many a kind word was bestowed on the little ones.

Dr. Flint went to my grandmother's to ascertain who was the owner of my children, and she informed him. "I expected as much," said he. "I am glad to hear it. I have had news from Linda lately, and I shall soon have her. You need never expect to see *her* free. She shall be my slave as long as I live, and when I am dead she shall be the slave of my children. If I ever find out that you or Phillip had any thing to do with her running off I'll kill him. And if I meet William in the street, and he presumes to look at me, I'll flog him within an inch of his life. Keep those brats out of my sight!"

As he turned to leave, my grandmother said something to remind him of his own doings. He looked back upon her, as if he would have been glad to strike her to the ground. I had my season of joy and thanksgiving. It was the first time since my childhood that I had experienced any real happiness. I heard of the old doctor's threats, but they no longer had the same power to trouble me. The darkest cloud that hung over my life had rolled away. Whatever slavery might do to me, it could not shackle my children. If I fell a sacrifice, my little ones were saved. It was well for me that my simple heart believed all that had been promised for their welfare. It is always better to trust than to doubt.

XX

NEW PERILS

The doctor, more exasperated than ever, again tried to revenge himself on my relatives. He arrested uncle Phillip on the charge of having aided my flight. He was carried before a court, and swore truly that he knew nothing of my intention to escape, and that he had not seen me since I left my master's plantation. The doctor then demanded that he should give bail for five hundred dollars that he would have nothing to do with me. Several gentlemen offered to be security for him; but Mr. Sands told him he had better go back to jail, and he would see that he came out without giving bail.

The news of his arrest was carried to my grandmother, who conveyed it to Betty. In the kindness of her heart, she again stowed me away under the floor; and as she walked back and forth, in the performance of her culinary duties, she talked apparently to herself, but with the intention that I should hear what was going on. I hoped that my uncle's imprisonment would last but few days; still I was anxious. I thought it likely Dr. Flint would do his utmost to taunt and insult him, and I was afraid my uncle might lose control of himself, and retort in some way that would be construed into a punishable offense; and I was well aware that in court his word would not be taken against any white man's. The search for me was renewed. Something had excited suspicions that I was in the vicinity. They searched the house I was in. I heard their steps and their voices. At night, when all were asleep, Betty came to release me from my place of confinement. The fright I had undergone, the constrained posture, and the dampness of the ground, made me ill for several days. My uncle was soon after taken out of prison; but the movements of all my relatives, and of all our friends, were very closely watched.

We all saw that I could not remain where I was much longer. I had already staid longer than was intended, and I knew my presence must be a source of perpetual anxiety to my kind benefactress. During this time, my friends had laid many plans for my escape, but the extreme vigilance of my persecutors made it impossible to carry them into effect.

One morning I was much startled by hearing somebody trying to get into my room. Several keys were tried, but none fitted. I instantly conjectured it was one of the housemaids; and I concluded she must either have heard some noise in the room, or have noticed the entrance of Betty. When my friend came, at her usual time, I told her what had happened. "I knows who it was," said she. "Pend upon it, 'twas dat Jenny. Dat nigger allers got de debble in her." I suggested that she might have seen or heard something that excited her curiosity.

"Tut! tut! chile!" exclaimed Betty, "she ain't seen notin, nor hearn notin'. She only 'spects someting. Dat's all. She wants to fine out who hab cut and make my gowns. But she won't nebber know. Dat's sartin. I'll git missis to fix her."

I reflected a moment, and said, "Betty, I must leave here tonight."

"Do as you tink best, poor chile," she replied. "I'se mighty 'fraid dat 'ere nigger vill pop on you some time."

She reported the incident to her mistress, and received orders to keep Jenny busy in the kitchen till she could see my uncle Phillip. He told her he would send a friend for me that very evening. She told him she hoped I was going to the north, for it was very dangerous for me to remain any where in the vicinity. Alas, it was not an easy thing, for one in my situation, to go to the north. In order to leave the coast quite clear for me, she went into the country to spend the day with her brother, and took Jenny with her. She was afraid to come and bid me good by, but she left a kind message with Betty. I heard her carriage roll from the door, and I never again saw her who had so generously befriended the poor, trembling fugitive! Though she was a slaveholder, to this day my heart blesses her!

I had not the slightest idea where I was going. Betty brought me a suit of sailor's clothes,—jacket, trowsers, and tarpaulin hat. She gave me a small bundle, saying I might need it where I was going. In cheery tones, she exclaimed, "I'se *so* glad you is gwine to free parts! Don't forget ole Betty. P'raps I'll come 'long by and by."

I tried to tell her how grateful I felt for all her kindness, but she interrupted me. "I don't want no tanks, honey. I'se glad I could help you, and I hope de good Lord vill open de path for you. I'se gwine wid you to de lower gate. Put your hands in your pockets, and walk ricketty, like de sailors."

I performed to her satisfaction. At the gate I found Peter, a young colored man, waitng for me. I had known him for years. He had been an apprentice to my father, and had always borne a good character. I was not afraid to trust to him. Betty bade me a hurried good by, and we walked off. "Take courage, Linda," said my friend Peter. "I've got a dagger, and no man shall take you from me, unless he passes over my dead body."

It was a long time since I had taken a walk out of doors, and the fresh air revived me. It was also pleasant to hear a human voice speaking to me above a whisper. I passed several people whom I knew, but they did not recognize me in my disguise. I prayed internally that, for Peter's sake, as well as my own, nothing might occur to bring out his dagger. We walked on till we came to the wharf. My aunt Nancy's husband was a seafaring man, and it had been deemed necessary to let him into our secret. He took me into his boat, rowed out to a vessel not far distant, and hoisted me on board. We three were the only occupants of the vessel. I now ventured to ask what they proposed to do with me. They said I was to remain on board till near dawn, and then they would hide me in Snaky Swamp, till my uncle Phillip had prepared a place of concealment for me. If the vessel had been bound north, it would have been of no avail to me, for it would certainly have been searched. About four o'clock, we were again seated in the boat, and rowed three miles to the swamp. My fear of snakes had been increased by the venomous bite I had received, and I dreaded to enter this hiding-place. But I was in no situation to choose, and I gratefully accepted the best that my poor, persecuted friends could do for me.

Peter landed first, and with a large knife cut a path through bamboos and briers of all descriptions. He came back, took me in his arms, and carried me to a seat made among the bamboos. Before we reached it, we were covered with hundreds of mosquitoes. In an hour's time they had so poisoned my flesh that I was a pitiful sight to behold. As the light increased, I saw snake after snake crawling round us. I had been accustomed to the sight of snakes all my life, but these were larger than any I had ever seen. To this day I shudder when I remember that morning. As evening approached, the number of snakes increased so much that we were continually obliged to thrash them with sticks to keep them from crawling over us.

The bamboos were so high and so thick that it was impossible to see beyond a very short distance. Just before it became dark we procured a seat nearer to the entrance of the swamp, being fearful of losing our way back to the boat. It was not long before we heard the paddle of oars, and the low whistle, which had been agreed upon as a signal. We made haste to enter the boat, and were rowed back to the vessel. I passed a wretched night; for the heat of the swamp, the mosquitoes, and the constant terror of snakes, had brought on a burning fever. I had just dropped asleep, when they came and told me it was time to go back to that horrid swamp. I could scarcely summon courage to rise. But even those large, venomous snakes were less dreadful to my imagination than the white men in that community called civilized. This time Peter took a quantity of tobacco to burn, to keep off the mosquitos. It produced the desired effect on them, but gave me nausea and severe headache. At dark we returned to the vessel. I had been so sick during the day, that Peter declared I should go home that night, if the devil himself was on patrol. They told me a place of concealment had been provided for me at my grandmother's. I could not imagine how it was possible to hide me in her house, every nook and corner of which was known to the Flint family. They told me to wait and see. We were rowed ashore, and went boldly through the streets, to my grandmother's. I wore my sailor's clothes, and had blackened my face with charcoal. I passed several people whom I knew. The father of my children came so near that I brushed against his arm; but he had no idea who it was.

"You must make the most of this walk," said my friend Peter, "for you may not have another very soon."

I thought his voice sounded sad. It was kind of him to conceal from me what a dismal hole was to be my home for a long, long time.

XXI

THE LOOPHOLE OF RETREAT

A small shed had been added to my grandmother's house years ago. Some boards were laid across the joists at the top, and between these boards and the roof was a very small garret, never occupied by any thing but rats and mice. It was a pent roof, covered with nothing but shingles, according to the southern custom for such buildings. The garret was only nine feet long and seven wide. The highest part was three feet high, and sloped down abruptly to the loose board floor. There was no admission for either light or air. My uncle Phillip, who was a carpenter, had very skillfully made a concealed trap-door, which communicated with the storeroom. He had been doing this while I was waiting in the swamp. The storeroom opened upon a piazza. To this hole I was conveyed as soon as I entered the house. The air was stifling; the darkness total. A bed had been spread on the floor. I could sleep quite comfortably on one side; but the slope was so sudden that I could not turn on the other without hitting the roof. The rats and mice ran over my bed; but I was weary, and I slept such sleep as the wretched may, when a tempest has passed over them. Morning came. I knew it only by the noises I heard; for in my small den day and night were all the same. I suffered for air even more than for light. But I was not comfortless. I heard the voices of my children. There was joy and there was sadness in the sound. It made my tears flow. How I longed to speak to them! I was eager to look on their faces; but there was no hole, no crack, through which I could peep. This continued darkness was oppressive. It seemed horrible to sit or lie in a cramped position day after day, without one gleam of light. Yet I would have chosen this, rather than my lot as a slave, though white people considered it an easy one; and it was so compared with the fate of others. I was never cruelly overworked; I was never lacerated with the whip from head to foot; I was never so beaten and bruised that I could not turn from one side to the other; I never had my heel-strings cut to prevent my running away; I was never chained to a log and forced to drag it about, while I toiled in the fields from morning till night; I was never branded with hot iron, or torn by bloodhounds. On the contrary, I had always been kindly treated, and tenderly cared for, until I came into the hands of Dr. Flint. I had never wished for freedom till then. But though my life in slavery was comparatively devoid of hardships, God pity the woman who is compelled to lead such a life!

My food was passed up to me through the trap-door my uncle had contrived; and my grandmother, my uncle Phillip, and aunt Nancy would seize such opportunities as they could, to mount up there and chat with me at the opening. But of course this was not safe in the daytime. It must all be done in darkness. It was impossible for me to move in an erect position, but I crawled about my den for exercise. One day I hit my head against something, and found it was a gimlet. My uncle had left it sticking there when he made the trap-door. I was as rejoiced as Robinson Crusoe could have been at finding such a treasure. It put a lucky thought into my head. I said to myself, "Now I will have some light. Now I will see my children." I did not dare to begin my work during the daytime, for fear of attracting attention. But I groped round; and having found the side next the street, where I could frequently see my children, I stuck the gimlet in and waited for evening. I bored three rows of holes, one above another; then I bored out the interstices between. I thus succeeded in making one hole about an inch long and an inch broad. I sat by it till late into the night, to enjoy the little whiff of air that floated in. In the morning I watched for my children. The first person I saw in the street was Dr. Flint. I had a shuddering, superstitious feeling that it was a bad omen. Several familiar faces passed by. At last I heard the merry laugh of children, and presently two sweet little faces were looking up at me, as though they knew I was there, and were conscious of the joy they imparted. How I longed to *tell* them I was there!

My condition was now a little improved. But for weeks I was tormented by hundreds of little red insects, fine as a needle's point, that pierced through my skin, and produced an intolerable burning. The good grandmother gave me herb teas and cooling medicines, and finally I got rid of them. The heat of my den was intense, for nothing but thin shingles protected me from the scorching summer's sun. But I had my consolations. Through my peeping-hole I could watch the children, and when they were near enough, I could hear their talk. Aunt Nancy brought me all the news she could hear at Dr. Flint's. From her I learned that the doctor had written to New York to a colored woman, who had been born and raised in our neighborhood, and had breathed his contaminating atmosphere. He offered her a reward if she could find out any thing about me. I know not what was the nature of her reply; but he soon after started for New York in haste, saying to his family that he had business of importance to transact. I peeped at him as he passed on his way to the steamboat. It was a satisfaction to have miles of land and water between us, even for a little while; and it was a still greater satisfaction to know that he believed me to be in the Free States. My little den seemed less dreary than it had done. He returned, as he did from his former journey to New York, without obtaining any satisfactory information. When he passed our house next morning, Benny was standing at the gate. He had heard them say that he had gone to find me, and he called out, "Dr. Flint, did you bring my mother home? I want to see her." The doctor stamped his foot at him in a rage, and exclaimed, "Get out of the way, you little damned rascal! If you don't, I'll cut off your head."

Benny ran terrified into the house, saying, "You can't put me in jail again. I don't belong to you now." It was well that the wind carried the words away from the doctor's ear. I told my grandmother of it, when we had our next conference at the trap-door; and begged of her not to allow the children to be impertinent to the irascible old man.

Autumn came, with a pleasant abatement of heat. My eyes had become accustomed to the dim light, and by holding my book or work in a certain position near the aperture I contrived to read and sew. That was a great relief to the tedious monotony of my life. But when winter came, the cold penetrated through the thin shingle roof, and I was dreadfully chilled. The winters there are not so long, or so severe, as in northern latitudes; but the houses are not built to shelter from cold, and my little den was peculiarly comfortless. The kind grandmother brought me bed-clothes and warm drinks. Often I was obliged to lie in bed all day to keep comfortable; but with all my precautions, my shoulders and feet were frostbitten. O, those long, gloomy days, with no object for my eye to rest upon, and no thoughts to occupy my mind, except the dreary past and the uncertain future! I was thankful when there came a day sufficiently mild for me to wrap myself up and sit at the loophole to watch the passers by. Southerners have the habit of stopping and talking in the streets, and I heard many conversations not intended to meet my ears. I heard slave-hunters planning how to catch some poor fugitive. Several times I heard allusions to Dr. Flint, myself, and the history of my children, who, perhaps, were playing near the gate. One would say, "I wouldn't move my little finger to catch her, as old Flint's property," Another would say, "I'll catch *any* nigger for the reward. A man ought to have what belongs to him, if he *is* a damned brute." The opinion was often expressed that I was in the Free States. Very rarely did any one suggest that I might be in the vicinity. Had the least suspicion rested on my grandmother's house, it would have been burned to the ground. But it was the last place they thought of. Yet there was no place, where slavery existed, that could have afforded me so good a place of concealment.

Dr. Flint and his family repeatedly tried to coax and bribe my children to tell something they had heard said about me. One day the doctor took them into a shop, and offered them some bright little silver pieces and gay handkerchiefs if they would tell where their mother was. Ellen shrank away from him, and would not speak; but Benny spoke up, and said, "Dr. Flint, I don't know where my mother is. I guess she's in New York; and when you go there again, I wish you'd ask her to come home, for I want to see her; but if you put her in jail, or tell her you'll cut her head off, I'll tell her to go right back."

XXII

Christmas Festivities

Christmas was approaching. Grandmother brought me materials, and I busied myself making some new garments and little playthings for my children. Were it not that hiring day is near at hand, and many families are fearfully looking forward to the probability of separation in a few days, Christmas might be a happy season for the poor slaves. Even slave mothers try to gladden the hearts of their little ones on that occasion. Benny and Ellen had their Christmas stockings filled. Their imprisoned mother could not have the privilege of witnessing their surprise and joy. But I had the pleasure of peeping at them as they went into the street with their new suits on. I heard Benny ask a little playmate whether Santa Claus brought him any thing. "Yes," replied the boy; "but Santa Claus ain't a real man. It's the children's mothers that put things into the stockings." "No, that can't be," replied Benny, "for Santa Claus brought Ellen and me these new clothes, and my mother has been gone this long time."

How I longed to tell him that his mother made those garments, and that many a tear fell on them while she worked!

Every child rises early on Christmas morning to see the Johnkannaus.* Without them, Christmas would be shorn of its greatest attraction. They consist of companies of slaves from the plantations, generally of the lower class. Two athletic men, in calico wrappers, have a net thrown over them, covered with all manner of bright-colored stripes. Cows' tails are fastened to their backs, and their heads are decorated with horns. A box, covered with sheepskin, is called the gumbo box. A dozen beat on this, while others strike triangles and jawbones, to which bands of dancers keep time. For a month previous they are composing songs, which are sung on this occasion. These companies, of a hundred each, turn out early in the morning, and are allowed to go round till twelve o'clock, begging for contributions. Not a door is left unvisited where there is the least chance of obtaining a penny or a glass of rum. They do not drink while they are out, but carry the rum home in jugs, to have a carousal. These Christmas donations frequently amount to twenty or thirty dollars. It is seldom that any white man or child refuses to give them a trifle. If he does, they regale his ears with the following song:—

"Poor massa, so dey say;
Down in de heel, so dey say;
got no money, so dey say;
Not one shillin,* so dey say;
God A'mighty bress you, so dey say."

Christmas is a day of feasting, both with white and colored people. Slaves, who are lucky enough to have a few shillings, are sure to spend them for good eating; and many a turkey and pig is captured, without saying, "By your leave, sir." Those who cannot obtain these, cook a 'possum, or a raccoon, from which savory dishes can be made. My grandmother raised poultry and pigs for sale; and it was her established custom to have both a turkey and a pig roasted for Christmas dinner.

On this occasion, I was warned to keep extremely quiet, because two guests had been invited. One was the town constable, and the other was a free colored man, who tried to pass himself off for white, and who was always ready to do any mean work for the sake of currying favor with white people. My grandmother had a motive for inviting them. She managed to take them all over the house. All the rooms on the lower floor were thrown open for them to pass in and out; and after dinner, they were invited up stairs to look at a fine mocking bird my uncle had just brought home. There, too, the rooms were all thrown open, that they might look in. When I heard them talking on the piazza, my heart almost stood still. I knew this colored man had spent many nights hunting for me. Every body knew he had the blood of a slave father in his veins; but for the sake of passing himself off for white, he was ready to kiss the slaveholders' feet. How I despised him! As for the constable, he wore no false colors. The duties of his office were despicable, but he was superior to his companion, inasmuch as he did not pretend to be what he was not. Any white man, who could raise money enough to buy a slave, would have considered himself degraded by being a constable; but the office enabled its possessor to exercise authority. If he found any slave out after nine o'clock, he could whip him as much as he liked; and that was a privilege to be coveted. When the guests were ready to depart, my grandmother gave each of them some of her nice pud-

* Apparently derived from an African word meaning an orphan. W. T.

ding, as a present for their wives. Through my peep-hole I saw them go out of the gate, and I was glad when it closed after them. So passed the first Christmas in my den.

XXIII
Still In Prison

When spring returned, and I took in the little patch of green the aperture commanded, I asked myself how many more summers and winters I must be condemned to spend thus. I longed to draw in a plentiful draught of fresh air, to stretch my cramped limbs, to have room to stand erect, to feel the earth under my feet again. My relatives were constantly on the lookout for a chance of escape; but none offered that seemed practicable, and even tolerably safe. The hot summer came again, and made the turpentine drop from the thin roof over my head.

During the long nights I was restless for want of air, and I had no room to toss and turn. There was but one compensation; the atmosphere was so stifled that even mosquitos would not condescend to buzz in it. With all my detestation of Dr. Flint, I could hardly wish him a worse punishment, either in this world or that which is to come, than to suffer what I suffered in one single summer. Yet the laws allowed him to be out in the free air, while I, guiltless of crime, was pent up here, as the only means of avoiding the cruelties the laws allowed him to inflict upon me! I don't know what kept life within me. Again and again, I thought I should die before long; but I saw the leaves of another autumn whirl through the air, and felt the touch of another winter. In summer the most terrible thunder storms were acceptable, for the rain came through the roof, and I rolled up my bed that it might cool the hot boards under it. Later in the season, storms sometimes wet my clothes through and through, and that was not comfortable when the air grew chilly. Moderate storms I could keep out by filling the chinks with oakum.

But uncomfortable as my situation was, I had glimpses of things out of doors, which made me thankful for my wretched hiding-

---

* This is a shilling—any of several early American coins. W. T.

place. One day I saw a slave pass our gate, muttering, "It's his own, and he can kill it if he will." My grandmother told me that woman's history. Her mistress had that day seen her baby for the first time, and in the lineaments of its fair face she saw a likeness to her husband. She turned the bondwoman and her child out of doors, and forbade her ever to return. The slave went to her master, and told him what had happened. He promised to talk with her mistress, and make it all right. The next day she and her baby were sold to a Georgia trader.

Another time I saw a woman rush wildly by, pursued by two men. She was a slave, the wet nurse of her mistress's children. For some trifling offense her mistress ordered her to be stripped and whipped. To escape the degradation and the torture, she rushed to the river, jumped in, and ended her wrongs in death.

Senator Brown,* of Mississippi, could not be ignorant of many such facts as these, for they are of frequent occurrence in every Southern State. Yet he stood up in the Congress of the United States, and declared that slavery was "a great moral, social, and political blessing; a blessing to the master, and a blessing to the slave!"

I suffered much more during the second winter than I did during the first. My limbs were benumbed by inaction, and the cold filled them with cramp. I had a very painful sensation of coldness in my head; even my face and tongue stiffened, and I lost the power of speech. Of course it was impossible, under the circumstances, to summon any physician. My brother William came and did all he could for me. Uncle Phillip also watched tenderly over me; and poor grandmother crept up and down to inquire whether there were any signs of returning life. I was restored to consciousness by the dashing of cold water in my face, and found myself leaning against my brother's arm, while he bent over me with streaming eyes. He afterwards told me he thought I was dying, for I had been in an unconscious state sixteen hours. I next became delirious, and was in great danger of betraying myself and my friends. To prevent this, they stupefied me with drugs. I remained in bed six weeks, weary in body and sick at heart. How to get medical advice was the question. William finally went to a Thompsonian doctor,* and described himself as having all my pains and aches. He returned with herbs, roots, and ointment. He was especially charged to rub on the ointment by a fire; but how could a fire be made in my little den? Charcoal in a furnace was tried, but there was no outlet for the gas, and it nearly cost me my life. Afterwards coals, already kindled, were brought up in an iron pan, and placed on bricks. I was so weak, and it was so long since I had enjoyed the warmth of a fire, that those few coals actually made me weep. I think the medicines did me some good; but my recovery was very slow.

Dark thoughts passed through my mind as I lay there day after day. I tried to be thankful for my little cell, dismal as it was, and even to love it, as part of the price I had paid for the redemption of my children. Sometimes I thought God was a compassionate Father, who would forgive my sins for the sake of my sufferings. At other times, it seemed to me there was no justice or mercy in the divine government. I asked why the curse of slavery was permitted to exist, and why I had been so persecuted and wronged from youth upward. These things took the shape of mystery, which is to this day not so clear to my soul as I trust it will be hereafter.

In the midst of my illness, grandmother broke down under the weight of anxiety and toil. The idea of losing her, who had always been my best friend and a mother to my children, was the sorest trial I had yet had. O, how earnestly I prayed that she might recover! How hard it seemed, that I could not tend upon her, who had so long and so tenderly watched over me!

One day the screams of a child nerved me with strength to crawl to my peeping-hole, and I saw my son covered with blood. A fierce dog, usually kept chained, had seized and bitten him. A doctor was sent for, and I heard the groans and screams of my child while the wounds were being sewed up. O, what torture to a mother's heart, to listen to this and be unable to go to him!

But childhood is like a day in spring, alternately shower and sunshine. Before night Benny was bright and lively, threatening the destruction of the dog; and great was his delight when the doctor told him the next day that the dog had bitten another boy and been shot. Benny recovered from his wounds; but it was long before he could walk.

When my grandmother's illness became known, many ladies, who were her customers, called to bring her some little comforts, and to inquire whether she had every thing she wanted. Aunt

---

* Allbert Gallatin Brown (1813-1880), congressman, governor of Mississippi, and senator, was a vigorous, articulate, and popular proponent of states' rights, slavery, and in general, all policies advocated by his small farmer constituents. See M. W. Cluskey, ed., *Speeches, Messages and Other Writings of the Hon. Albert G. Brown*, Philadelphia, 1859. W. T.

Nancy one night asked permission to watch with her sick mother, and Mrs. Flint replied, "I don't see any need of your going. I can't spare you." But when she found other ladies in the neighborhood were so attentive, not wishing to be outdone in Christian charity, she also sallied forth, in magnificent condescension, and stood by the bedside of her who had loved her in her infancy, and who had been repaid by such grievous wrongs. She seemed surprised to find her so ill, and scolded uncle Phillip for not sending for Dr. Flint. She herself sent for him immediately, and he came. Secure as I was in my retreat, I should have been terrified if I had known he was so near me. He pronounced my grandmother in a very critical situation, and said if her attending physician wished it, he would visit her. Nobody wished to have him coming to the house at all hours, and we were not disposed to give him a chance to make out a long bill.

As Mrs. Flint went out, Sally told her the reason Benny was lame was, that a dog had bitten him. "I'm glad of it," replied she. "I wish he had killed him. It would be good news to send to his mother. *Her* day will come. The dogs will grab *her* yet." With these Christian words she and her husband departed, and, to my great satisfaction, returned no more.

I heard from uncle Phillip, with feelings of unspeakable joy and gratitude, that the crisis was passed and grandmother would live. I could now say from my heart, "God is merciful. He has spared me the anguish of feeling that I caused her death."

XXIV
THE CANDIDATE FOR CONGRESS

The summer had nearly ended, when Dr. Flint made a third visit to New York, in search of me. Two candidates were running for Congress, and he returned in season to vote. The father of my children was the Whig candidate. The doctor had hitherto been a stanch Whig; but now he exerted all his energies for the defeat of Mr. Sands. He invited large parties of men to dine in the shade of his trees, and supplied them with plenty of rum and brandy. If any

---

* This was a doctor licensed to practice the Thomsonian System patented by Samuel Thomson (1769-1843), botanic physician and author. His name was often misspelled—the letter *p* added, as above. W. T.

poor fellow drowned his wits in the bowl, and, in the openness of his convivial heart, proclaimed that he did not mean to vote the Democratic ticket, he was shoved into the street without ceremony.

The doctor expended his liquor in vain. Mr. Sands was elected; an event which occasioned me some anxious thoughts.

He had not emancipated my children, and if he should die they would be at the mercy of his heirs. Two little voices, that frequently met my ear, seemed to plead with me not to let their father depart without striving to make their freedom secure. Years had passed since I had spoken to him. I had not even seen him since the night I passed him, unrecognized, in my disguise of a sailor. I supposed he would call before he left, to say something to my grandmother concerning the children, and I resolved what course to take.

The day before his departure for Washington I made arrangements, towards evening, to get from my hiding-place into the storeroom below. I found myself so stiff and clumsy that it was with great difficulty I could hitch from one resting place to another. When I reached the storeroom my ankles gave way under me, and I sank exhausted on the floor. It seemed as if I could never use my limbs again. But the purpose I had in view roused all the strength I had. I crawled on my hands and knees to the window, and, screened behind a barrel, I waited for his coming. The clock struck nine, and I knew the steamboat would leave between ten and eleven. My hopes were failing. But presently I heard his voice, saying to some one, "Wait for me a moment. I wish to see aunt Martha." When he came out, as he passed the window, I said, "Stop one moment, and let me speak for my children." He started, hesitated, and then passed on, and went out of the gate. I closed the shutter I had partially opened, and sank down behind the barrel. I had suffered much; but seldom had I experienced a keener pang than I then felt. Had my children, then, become of so little consequence to him? And had he so little feeling for their wretched mother that he would not listen a moment while she pleaded for them? Painful memories were so busy within me, that I forgot I had not hooked the shutter, till I heard some one opening it. I looked up. He had come back. "Who called me?" said he, in a low tone. "I did," I replied. "Oh, Linda," said he, "I knew your voice; but I was afraid to answer, lest my friend should hear me. Why do you come here? Is it possible you risk yourself in this house? They are mad to allow it. I shall expect to hear that you are all ruined." I did not wish to implicate him, by letting him know my place of concealment; so I merely said, "I thought you would come to bid grandmother good by, and so I came here to speak a few words to you about emancipating my children. Many changes may take place during the six months you are gone to Washington, and it does not seem right for you to expose them to the risk of such changes. I want nothing for myself; all I ask is, that you will free my children, or authorize some friend to do it, before you go."

He promised he would do it, and also expressed a readiness to make any arrangements whereby I could be purchased.

I heard footsteps approaching, and closed the shutter hastily. I wanted to crawl back to my den, without letting the family know what I had done; for I knew they would deem it very imprudent. But he stepped back into the house, to tell my grandmother that he had spoken with me at the storeroom window, and to beg of her not to allow me to remain in the house over night. He said it was the height of madness for me to be there; that we should certainly all be ruined. Luckily, he was in too much of a hurry to wait for a reply, or the dear old woman would surely have told him all.

I tried to go back to my den, but found it more difficult to go up than I had to come down. Now that my mission was fulfilled, the little strength that had supported me through it was gone, and I sank helpless on the floor. My grandmother, alarmed at the risk I had run, came into the storeroom in the dark, and locked the door behind her. "Linda," she whispered, "where are you?"

"I am here by the window," I replied. "I couldn't have him go away without emancipating the children. Who knows what may happen?"

"Come, come, child," said she, "it won't do for you to stay here another minute. You've done wrong; but I can't blame you, poor thing!"

I told her I could not return without assistance, and she must call my uncle. Uncle Phillip came, and pity prevented him from scolding me. He carried me back to my dungeon, laid me tenderly on the bed, gave me some medicine, and asked me if there was any thing more he could do. Then he went away, and I was left with my own thoughts—starless as the midnight darkness around me.

My friends feared I should become a cripple for life; and I was so weary of my long imprisonment that, had it not been for the hope of serving my children, I should have been thankful to die; but, for their sakes, I was willing to bear on.

XXV

COMPETITION IN CUNNING

Dr. Flint had not given me up. Every now and then he would say to my grandmother that I would yet come back, and voluntarily surrender myself, and that when I did, I could be purchased by my relatives, or any one who wished to buy me. I knew his cunning nature too well not to perceive that this was a trap laid for me; and so all my friends understood it. I resolved to match my cunning against his cunning. In order to make him believe that I was in New York, I resolved to write him a letter dated from that place. I sent for my friend Peter, and asked him if he knew any trustworthy seafaring person, who would carry such a letter to New York, and put it in the post office there. He said he knew one that he would trust with his own life to the ends of the world. I reminded him that it was a hazardous thing for him to undertake. He said he knew it, but he was willing to do any thing to help me. I expressed a wish for a New York paper, to ascertain the names of some of the streets. He ran his hand into his pocket, and said, "Here is half a one, that was round a cap I bought of a peddler yesterday." I told him the letter would be ready the next evening. He bade me good by, adding, "Keep up your spirits, Linda; brighter days will come by and by."

My uncle Phillip kept watch over the gate until our brief interview was over. Early the next morning, I seated myself near the little aperture to examine the newspaper. It was a piece of the New York Herald;* and, for once, the paper that systematically abuses the colored people, was made to render them a service. Having obtained what information I wanted concerning streets and numbers, I wrote two letters, one to my grandmother, the other to Dr. Flint. I reminded him how he, a gray-headed man, had treated a helpless child, who had been placed in his power, and what years of misery he had brought upon her. To my grandmother, I expressed a wish to have my children sent to me at the north, where I could teach them to respect themselves, and set them a virtuous example; which a slave mother was not allowed to do at the south. I asked her to direct her answer to a certain street in Boston, as I did not live in New York, though I went there sometimes. I dated these letters ahead, to allow for the time it would take to carry them, and sent a memorandum of the date to the messenger. When my friend came for the letters, I said, "God bless and reward you, Peter, for this disinterested kindness. Pray be careful. If you are detected, both you and I will have to suffer dreadfully. I have not a relative who would dare to do it for me." He replied, "You may trust to me, Linda. I don't forget that your father was my best friend, and I will be a friend to his children so long as God lets me live."

It was necessary to tell my grandmother what I had done, in order that she might be ready for the letter, and prepared to hear what Dr. Flint might say about my being at the north. She was sadly troubled. She felt sure mischief would come of it. I also told my plan to aunt Nancy, in order that she might report to us what was said at Dr. Flint's house. I whispered it to her through a crack, and she whispered back, "I hope it will succeed. I shan't mind being a slave all *my* life, if I can only see you and the children free."

I had directed that my letters should be put into the New York post office on the 20th of the month. On the evening of the 24th my aunt came to say that Dr. Flint and his wife had been talking in a low voice about a letter he had received, and that when he went to his office he promised to bring it when he came to tea. So I concluded I should hear my letter read the next morning. I told my grandmother Dr. Flint would be sure to come, and asked her to have him sit near a certain door, and leave it open, that I might hear what he said. The next morning I took my station within sound of that door, and remained motionless as a statue. It was not long before I heard the gate slam, and the well-known footsteps enter the house. He seated himself in the chair that was placed for him, and said, "Well, Martha, I've brought you a letter from Linda. She has sent me a letter, also. I know exactly where to find her; but I don't choose to go to Boston for her. I had rather she would come back of her own accord, in a respectable manner. Her uncle Phillip is the best person to go for her. With *him*, she would feel perfectly free to act. I am willing to pay his expenses going and returning. She shall be sold to her friends. Her children are free; at least I suppose they are; and when you obtain her freedom, you'll make a happy family. I suppose, Martha, you have no objection to my reading to you the letter Linda has written to you."

He broke the seal, and I heard him read it. The old villain! He had suppressed the letter I wrote to grandmother, and prepared a substitute of his own, the purport of which was as follows:—

*Founded in 1833 by James Gordon Bennett (1796–1872), this newspaper was proslavery until the Civil War, then switched and became pro-Union. W.T.

"Dear Grandmother: I have long wanted to write to you; but the disgraceful manner in which I left you and my children made me ashamed to do it. If you knew how much I have suffered since I ran away, you would pity and forgive me. I have purchased freedom at a dear rate. If any arrangement could be made for me to return to the south without being a slave, I would gladly come. If not, I beg of you to send my children to the north. I cannot live any longer without them. Let me know in time, and I will meet them in New York or Philadelphia, whichever place best suits my uncle's convenience. Write as soon as possible to your unhappy daughter,
LINDA.

"It is very much as I expected it would be," said the old hypocrite, rising to go. "You see the foolish girl has repented of her rashness, and wants to return. We must help her to do it, Martha. Talk with Phillip about it. If he will go for her, she will trust to him, and come back. I should like an answer tomorrow. Good morning, Martha."

As he stepped out on the piazza, he stumbled over my little girl. "Ah, Ellen, is that you?" he said, in his most gracious manner. "I didn't see you. How do you do?"

"Pretty well, sir," she replied. "I heard you tell grandmother that my mother is coming home. I want to see her."

"Yes, Ellen, I am going to bring her home very soon," rejoined he; "and you shall see her as much as you like, you little curly-headed nigger."

This was as good as a comedy to me, who had heard it all; but grandmother was frightened and distressed, because the doctor wanted my uncle to go for me.

The next evening Dr. Flint called to talk the matter over. My uncle told him that from what he had heard of Massachusetts, he judged he should be mobbed if he went there after a runaway slave. "All stuff and nonsense, Phillip!" replied the doctor. "Do you suppose I want you to kick up a row in Boston? The business can all be done quietly. Linda writes that she wants to come back. You are her relative, and she would trust *you*. The case would be different if I went. She might object to coming with *me;* and the damned abolitionists, if they knew I was her master, would not believe me, if I told them she had begged to go back. They would get up a row; and I should not like to see Linda dragged through the streets like a common negro. She has been very ungrateful to me for all my kindness; but I forgive her, and want to act the part of a friend towards her. I have no wish to hold her as my slave. Her friends can buy her as soon as she arrives here."

Finding that his arguments failed to convince my uncle, the doctor "let the cat out of the bag," by saying that he had written to the mayor of Boston, to ascertain whether there was a person of my description at the street and number from which my letter was dated. He had omitted this date in the letter he had made up to read to my grandmother. If I had dated from New York, the old man would probably have made another journey to that city. But even in that dark region, where knowledge is so carefully excluded from the slave, I had heard enough about Massachusetts to come to the conclusion that slaveholders did not consider it a comfortable place to go to in search of a runaway. That was before the Fugitive Slave Law was passed; before Massachusetts had consented to become a "nigger hunter" for the south.

My grandmother, who had become skittish by seeing her family always in danger, came to me with a very distressed countenance, and said, "What will you do if the mayor of Boston sends him word that you haven't been there? Then he will suspect the letter was a trick; and maybe he'll find out something about it, and we shall all get into trouble. O Linda, I wish you had never sent the letters."

"Don't worry yourself, grandmother," said I. "The mayor of Boston won't trouble himself to hunt niggers for Dr. Flint. The letters will do good in the end. I shall get out of this dark hole some time or other."

"I hope you will, child," replied the good, patient old friend. "You have been here a long time; almost five years; but whenever you do go, it will break your old grandmother's heart. I should be expecting every day to hear that you were brought back in irons and put in jail. God help you, poor child! Let us be thankful that some time or other we shall go where the wicked cease from troubling, and the weary are at rest." My heart responded, Amen.

The fact that Dr. Flint had written to the mayor of Boston convinced me that he believed my letter to be genuine, and of course that he had no suspicion of my being any where in the vicinity. It was a great object to keep up this delusion, for it made me and my friends feel less anxious, and it would be very convenient whenever there was a chance to escape. I resolved, therefore, to continue to write letters from the north from time to time.

Two or three weeks passed, and as no news came from the mayor of Boston, grandmother began to listen to my entreaty to be allowed to leave my cell, sometimes, and exercise my limbs to prevent my becoming a cripple. I was allowed to slip down into the small storeroom, early in the morning, and remain there a little while. The room was all filled up with barrels, except a small open space under my trap-door. This faced the door, the upper part of which was of glass, and purposely left uncurtained, that the curious might look in. The air of this place was close; but it was so much better than the atmosphere of my cell, that I dreaded to return. I came down as soon as it was light, and remained till eight o'clock, when people began to be about, and there was danger that some one might come on the piazza. I had tried various applications to bring warmth and feeling into my limbs, but without avail. They were so numb and stiff that it was a painful effort to move; and had my enemies come upon me during the first mornings I tried to exercise them a little in the small unoccupied space of the storeroom, it would have been impossible for me to have escaped.

XXVI

AN IMPORTANT ERA
IN MY BROTHER'S LIFE

I missed the company and kind attentions of my brother William, who had gone to Washington with his master, Mr. Sands. We received several letters from him, written without any allusion to me, but expressed in such a manner that I knew he did not forget me. I disguised my hand, and wrote to him in the same manner. It was a long session; and when it closed, William wrote to inform us the Mr. Sands was going to the north, to be gone some time, and that he was to accompany him. I knew that his master had promised to give him his freedom, but no time had been specified. Would William trust to a slave's chances? I remembered how we used to talk together, in our young days, about obtaining our freedom, and I thought it very doubtful whether he would come back to us.

Grandmother received a letter from Mr. Sands, saying that William had proved a most faithful servant, and he would also say a valued friend; that no mother had ever trained a better boy. He said he had traveled through the Northern States and Canada; and though the abolitionists had tried to decoy him away, they had never succeeded. He ended by saying they should be at home shortly.

We expected letters from William, describing the novelties of his journey, but none came. In time, it was reported that Mr. Sands would return late in the autumn, accompanied by a bride. Still no letters from William. I felt almost sure I should never see him again on southern soil; but had he no word of comfort to send to his friends at home "to the poor captive in her dungeon." My thoughts wandered through the dark past, and over the uncertain future. Alone in my cell, where no eye but God's could see me, I wept bitter tears. How earnestly I prayed to him to restore me to my children, and enable me to be a useful woman and a good mother!

At last the day arrived for the return of the travelers. Grandmother had made loving preparations to welcome her absent boy back to the old hearthstone. When the dinner table was laid, William's plate occupied its old place. The stage coach went by empty. My grandmother waited dinner. She thought perhaps he was necessarily detained by his master. In my prison I listened anxiously, expecting every moment to hear my dear brother's voice and step. In the course of the afternoon a lad was sent by Mr. Sands to tell grandmother that William did not return with him; that the abolitionists had decoyed him away. But he begged her not to feel troubled about it, for he felt confident she would see William in a few days. As soon as he had time to reflect he would come back, for he could never expect to be so well off at the north as he had been with him.

If you had seen the tears, and heard the sobs, you would have thought the messenger had brought tidings of death instead of freedom. Poor old grandmother felt that she should never see her darling boy again. And I was selfish. I thought more of what I had lost, than of what my brother had gained. A new anxiety began to trouble me. Mr. Sands had expended a good deal of money, and would naturally feel irritated by the loss he had incurred. I greatly feared this might injure the prospects of my children, who were now becoming valuable property. I longed to have their emancipation made certain.

The more so, because their master and father was now married. I was too familiar with slavery not to know that promises made to slaves, though with kind intentions, and sincere at the time, depend upon many contingencies for their fulfillment.

Much as I wished William to be free, the step he had taken made me sad and anxious. The following Sabbath was calm and clear; so beautiful that it seemed like a Sabbath in the eternal world. My grandmother brought the children out on the piazza, that I might hear their voices. She thought it would comfort me in my despondency; and it did. They chatted merrily, as only children can. Benny said, "Grandmother, do you think uncle Will has gone for good? Won't he ever come back again? May be he'll find mother. If he does, *won't* she be glad to see him! Why don't you and uncle Phillip, and all of us, go and live where mother is? I should like it; wouldn't you, Ellen?"

"Yes, I should like it," replied Ellen; "but how could we find her? Do you know the place, grandmother? I don't remember how mother looked—do you, Benny?"

Benny was just beginning to describe me when they were interrupted by an old slave woman, a near neighbor, named Aggie. This poor creature had witnessed the sale of her children, and seen them carried off to parts unknown, without any hopes of ever hearing from them again. She saw that my grandmother had been weeping, and she said, in a sympathizing tone, "What's the matter, aunt Marthy?"

"O Aggie," she replied, "it seems as if I shouldn't have any of my children or grandchildren left to hand me a drink when I'm dying, and lay my old body in the ground. My boy didn't come back with Mr. Sands. He staid at the north."

Poor old Aggie clapped her hands for joy. "*Is dat* what you's crying fur?" she exclaimed. "Git down on your knees and bress de Lord! I don't know whar my poor children is, and I nebber 'spect to know. You don't know whar poor Linda's gone to; but you *do* know whar her brudder is. He's in free parts; and dat's de right place. Don't murmur at de Lord's doings, but git down on your knees and tank him for his goodness."

My selfishness was rebuked by what poor Aggie said. She rejoiced over the escape of one who was merely her fellowbondman, while his own sister was only thinking what his good fortune might cost her children. I knelt and prayed God to forgive me; and I thanked him from my heart, that one of my family was saved from the grasp of slavery.

It was not long before we received a letter from William. He wrote that Mr. Sands had always treated him kindly, and that he had tried to do his duty to him faithfully. But ever since he was a boy, he had longed to be free; and he had already gone through enough to convince him he had better not lose the chance that offered. He concluded by saying, "Don't worry about me, dear grandmother. I shall think of you always; and it will spur me on to work hard and try to do right. When I have earned money enough to give you a home, perhaps you will come to the north, and we can all live happy together."

Mr. Sands told my uncle Phillip the particulars about William's leaving him. He said, "I trusted him as if he were my own brother, and treated him as kindly. The abolitionists talked to him in several places; but I had no idea they could tempt him. However, I don't blame William. He's young and inconsiderate, and those Northern rascals decoyed him. I must confess the scamp was very bold about it. I met him coming down the steps of the Astor House with his trunk on his shoulder, and I asked him where he was going. He said he was going to change his old trunk. I told him it was rather shabby, and asked if he didn't need some money. He said, No, thanked me, and went off. He did not return so soon as I expected; but I waited patiently. At last I went to see if our trunks were packed, ready for our journey. I found them locked, and a sealed note on the table informed me where I could find the keys. The fellow even tried to be religious. He wrote that he hoped God would always bless me, and reward me for my kindness; that he was not unwilling to serve me; but he wanted to be a free man; and that if I thought he did wrong, he hoped I would forgive him. I intended to give him his freedom in five years. He might have trusted me. He has shown himself ungrateful; but I shall not go for him, or send for him. I feel confident that he will soon return to me."

I afterwards heard an account of the affair from William himself. He had not been urged away by abolitionists. He needed no information they could give him about slavery to stimulate his desire for freedom. He looked at his hands, and remembered that they were once in irons. What security had he that they would not be so again? Mr. Sands was kind to him; but he might indefinitely postpone the promise he had made to give him his freedom. He might come under pecuniary embarrassments, and his property be seized by creditors; or he might die, without making any arrangements in his favor. He had too often known such accidents to happen to slaves who had kind masters, and he wisely resolved to make sure of the present opportunity to own himself. He was scrupulous about taking any money from his master on false pretenses; so he sold his best clothes to pay for his passage to Boston. The slaveholders pronounced him a base, ungrateful wretch, for thus requiting his master's indulgence. What would *they* have done under similar circumstances?

When Dr Flint's family heard that William had deserted Mr. Sands, they chuckled greatly over the news. Mrs. Flint made her usual manifestations of Christian feeling, by saying, "I'm glad of it. I hope he'll never get him again. I like to see people paid back in their own coin. I reckon Linda's children will have to pay for it. I should be glad to see them in the speculator's hands again, for I'm tired of seeing those little niggers march about the streets."

XXVII

New Destination for the Children

Mrs. Flint proclaimed her intention of informing Mrs. Sands who was the father of my children. She likewise proposed to tell her what an artful devil I was; that I had made a great deal of trouble in her family; that when Mr. Sands was at the north, she didn't doubt that I had followed him in disguise and persuaded William to run away. She had some reason to entertain such an idea; for I had written from the north, from time to time, and I dated my letters from various places. Many of them fell into Dr. Flint's hands, as I expected they would; and he must have come to the conclusion that I traveled about a good deal. He kept a close watch over my children, thinking they would eventually lead to my detection.

A new and unexpected trial was in store for me. One day, when Mr. Sands and his wife were walking in the street, they met Benny. The lady took a fancy to him, and exclaimed, "What a pretty little negro! Whom does he belong to?"

Benny did not hear the answer; but he came home very indignant with the stranger lady, because she had called him a negro. A few days afterwards, Mr. Sands called on my grandmother and told her he wanted her to take the children to his house. He said he had informed his wife of his relation to them, and told her they were motherless; and she wanted to see them.

373

When he had gone, my grandmother came and asked what I would do. The question seemed a mockery. What could I do? They were Mr. Sands's slaves, and their mother was a slave, whom he had represented to be dead. Perhaps he thought I was. I was too much pained and puzzled to come to any decision; and the children were carried without my knowledge.

Mrs. Sands had a sister from Illinois staying with her. This lady, who had no children of her own, was so much pleased with Ellen, that she offered to adopt her, and bring her up as she would a daughter. Mrs. Sands wanted to take Benjamin. When grandmother reported this to me, I was tried almost beyond endurance. Was this all I was to gain by what I had suffered for the sake of having my children free? True, the prospect *seemed* fair; but I know too well how lightly slaveholders held such "parental relations." If pecuniary troubles should come, or if the new wife required more money than could conveniently be spared, my children might be thought of as a convenient means of raising funds. I had no trust in that, O Slavery! Never should I know peace till my children were emancipated with all due formalities of law.

I was too proud to ask Mr. Sands to do any thing for my own benefit; but I could bring myself to become a suppliant for my children. I resolved to remind him of the promise he had made me, and to throw myself upon his honor for the performance of it. I persuaded my grandmother to go to him, and tell him I was not dead, and that I earnestly entreated him to keep the promise he had made me; that I had heard of the recent proposals concerning my children, and did not feel easy to accept them; that he had promised to emancipate them, and it was time for him to redeem his pledge. I knew there was some risk in thus betraying that I was in the vicinity; but what will not a mother do for her children? He received the message with surprise, and said, "The children are free. I have never intended to claim them as slaves. Linda may decide their fate. In my opinion, they had better be sent to the north. I don't think they are quite safe here. Dr. Flint boasts that they are still in his power. He says they were his daughter's property, and as she was not of age when they were sold, the contract is not legally binding."

So, then, after all I had endured for their sakes, my poor children were between two fires; between my old master and their new master! And I was powerless. There was no protecting arm of the law for me to invoke. Mr. Sands proposed that Ellen should go, for the present, to some of his relatives, who had removed to Brooklyn, Long Island. It was promised that she should be well taken care of, and sent to school. I consented to it, as the best arrangement I could make for her. My grandmother, of course, negotiated it all; and Mrs. Sands knew of no other person in the transaction. She proposed that they should take Ellen with them to Washington, and keep her till they had a good chance of sending her, with friends, to Brooklyn. She had an infant daughter. I had had a glimpse of it, as the nurse passed with it in her arms. It was not a pleasant thought to me, that the bond-woman's child should tend her free-born sister; but there was no alternative. Ellen was made ready for the journey. O, how it tried my heart to send her away, so young, alone, among strangers! Without a mother's love to shelter her from the storms of life; almost without memory of a mother! I doubted whether she and Benny would have for me the natural affection that children feel for a parent. I thought to myself that I might perhaps never see my daughter again, and I had a great desire that she should look upon me, before she went, that she might take my image with her in her memory. It seemed to me cruel to have her brought to my dungeon. It was sorrow enough for her young heart to know that her mother was a victim of slavery, without seeing the wretched hiding-place to which it had driven her. I begged permission to pass the last night in one of the open chambers, with my little girl. They thought I was crazy to think of trusting such a young child with my perilous secret. I told them I had watched her character, and I felt sure she would not betray me; that I was determined to have an interview, and if they would not facilitate it, I would take my own way to obtain it. They remonstrated against the rashness of such a proceeding; but finding they could not change my purpose, they yielded. I slipped through the trap-door into the storeroom, and my uncle kept watch at the gate, while I passed into the piazza and went up stairs, to the room I used to occupy. It was more than five years since I had seen it; and how the memories eroded on me! There I had taken shelter when my mistress drove me from her house; there came my old tyrant, to mock, insult, and curse me; there my children were first laid in my arms; there I had watched over them, each day with a deeper and sadder love; there I had knelt to God, in anguish of heart, to forgive the wrong I had done. How vividly it all came back! And after this long, gloomy interval, I stood there such a wreck!

In the midst of these meditations, I heard footsteps on the

stairs. The door opened, and my uncle Phillip came in, leading Ellen by the hand. I put my arms round her, and said, "Ellen, my dear child, I am your mother." She drew back a little, and looked at me; then, with sweet confidence, she laid her cheek against mine, and I folded her to the heart that had been so long desolated. She was the first to speak. Raising her head, she said, inquiringly, "You really *are* my mother? I told her I really was; that during all the long time she had not seen me, I had loved her most tenderly; and that now she was going away, I wanted to see her and talk with her, that she might remember me. With a sob in her voice, she said, "I'm glad you've come to see me; but why didn't you ever come before? Benny and I have wanted so much to see you! He remembers you, and sometimes he tells me about you. Why didn't you come home when Dr. Flint went to bring you?"

I answered, "I couldn't come before, dear. But now that I am with you, tell me whether you like to go away." "I don't know," said she, crying. "Grandmother says I ought not to cry; that I am going to a good place, where I can learn to read and write, and that by and by I can write her a letter. But I shan't have Benny, or grandmother, or uncle Phillip, or any body to love me. Can't you go with me? O, do go, dear mother!"

I told her I couldn't go now; but sometimes I would come to her, and then she and Benny and I would live together, and have happy times. She wanted to run and bring Benny to see me now. I told her he was going to the north, before long, with uncle Phillip, and then I would come to see him before he went away. I asked if she would like to have me stay all night and sleep with her. "O, yes," she replied. Then, turning to her uncle, she said, pleadingly, "*May* I stay? Please, uncle! She is my own mother." He laid his hand on her head, and said, solemnly, "Ellen, this is the secret you have promised grandmother never to tell. If you ever speak of it to any body, they will never let you see your grandmother again, and your mother can never come to Brooklyn." "Uncle," she replied, "I will never tell." He told her she might stay with me; and when he had gone, I took her in my arms and told her I was a slave, and that was the reason she must never say she had seen me. I exhorted her to be a good child, to try to please the people where she was going, and that God would raise her up friends. I told her to say her prayers, and remember always to pray for her poor mother, and that God would permit us to meet again. She wept, and I did not check her tears. Perhaps she would never again have a chance to pour her tears into a mother's bosom. All night she nestled in my arms, and I had no inclination to slumber. The moments were too precious to lose any of them. Once, when I thought she was asleep, I kissed her forehead softly, and she said, "I am not asleep, dear mother."

Before dawn they came to take me back to my den. I drew aside the window curtain, to take a last look of my child. The moonlight shone on her face, and I bent over her, as I had done years before, that wretched night when I ran away. I hugged her close to my throbbing heart; and tears, too sad for such young eyes to shed, flowed down her cheeks, as she gave her last kiss, and whispered in my ear, "Mother, I will never tell." And she never did.

When I got back to my den, I threw myself on the bed and wept there alone in the darkness. It seemed as if my heart would burst. When the time for Ellen's departure drew nigh, I could hear neighbors and friends saying to her, "Good by, Ellen. I hope your poor mother will find you out. Won't you be glad to see her!" She replied, "Yes, ma'am;" and they little dreamed of the weighty secret that weighed down her young heart. She was an affectionate child, but naturally very reserved, except with those she loved, and I felt secure that my secret would be safe with her. I heard the gate close after her, with such feelings as only a slave mother can experience. During the day my meditations were very sad. Sometimes I feared I had been very selfish not to give up all claim to her, and let her go to Illinois, to be adopted by Mrs. Sands's sister. It was my experience of slavery that decided me against it. I feared that circumstances might arise that would cause her to be sent back. I felt confident that I should go to New York myself; and then I should be able to watch over her, and in some degree protect her.

Dr. Flint's family knew nothing of the proposed arrangement till after Ellen was gone, and the news displeased them greatly. Mrs. Flint called on Mrs. Sands's sister to inquire into the matter. She expressed her opinion very freely as to the respect Mr. Sands showed for his wife, and for his own character, in acknowledging those "young niggers." And as for sending Ellen away, she pronounced it to be just as much stealing as it would be for him to come and take a piece of furniture out of her parlor. She said her daughter was not of age to sign the bill of sale, and the children were her property; and when she became of age, or was married, she could take them, wherever she could lay hands on them.

Miss Emily Flint, the little girl to whom I had bequeathed, was now in her sixteenth year. Her mother considered it all right and honorable for her, or her future husband, to steal my children; but she did not understand how any body could hold up their heads in respectable society, after they had purchased their own children, as Mr. Sands had done. Dr. Flint said very little. Perhaps he thought that Benny would be less likely to be sent away if he kept quiet. One of my letters, that fell into his hands, was dated from Canada; and he seldom spoke of me now. This state of things enabled me to slip down into the storeroom more frequently, where I could stand upright, and move my limbs more freely.

Days, weeks, and months passed, and there came no news of Ellen. I sent a letter to Brooklyn, written in my grandmother's name, to inquire whether she had arrived there. Answer was returned that she had not. I wrote to her in Washington; but no notice was taken of it. There was one person there, who ought to have had some sympathy with the anxiety of the child's friends at home; but the links of such relations as he had formed with me, are easily broken and cast away as rubbish. Yet how protectingly and persuasively he once talked to the poor, helpless slave girl! And how entirely I trusted him! But now suspicions darkened my mind. Was my child dead, or had they deceived me, and sold her?

If the secret memoirs of many members of Congress should be published, curious details would be unfolded. I once saw a letter from a member of Congress to a slave, who was the mother of six of his children. He wrote to request that she would send her children away from the great house before his return, as he expected to be accompanied by friends. The woman could not read, and was obliged to employ another to read the letter. The existence of the colored children did not trouble this gentleman, it was only the fear that friends might recognize in their features a resemblance to him.

At the end of six months, a letter came to my grandmother, from Brooklyn. It was written by a young lady in the family, and announced that Ellen had just arrived. It contained the following message from her: "I do try to do just as you told me to, and I pray for you every night and morning." I understood that these words were meant for me; and they were a balsam to my heart. The writer closed her letter by saying, "Ellen is a nice little girl, and we shall like to have her with us. My cousin, Mr. Sands, has given her to me, to be my little waiting maid. I shall send her to school, and I hope some day she will write to you herself." This letter perplexed and troubled me. Had my child's father merely placed her there till she was old enough to support herself? Or had he given her to his cousin, as a piece of property? If the last idea was correct, his cousin might return to the south at any time, and hold Ellen as a slave. I tried to put away from me the painful thought that such a foul wrong would have been done to us. I said to myself, "Surely there must be *some* justice in man;" then I remembered, with a sigh, how slavery perverted all the natural feelings of the human heart. It gave me a pang to look on my light-hearted boy. He believed himself free; and to have him brought under the yoke of slavery, would be more than I could bear. How I longed to have him safely out of the reach of its power!

XXVIII

AUNT NANCY

I have mentioned my great-aunt, who was a slave in Dr. Flint's family, and who had been my refuge during the shameful persecutions I suffered from him. This aunt had been married at twenty years of age; that is, as far as slaves can marry. She had the consent of her master and mistress, and a clergyman performed the ceremony. But it was a mere form, without any legal value.* Her master or mistress could annul it any day they pleased. She had always slept on the floor in the entry, near Mrs. Flint's chamber door, that she might be within call. When she was married, she was told she might have the use of a small room in an out-house. Her mother and her husband furnished it. He was a seafaring man, and was allowed to sleep there when he was at home. But on the wedding evening, the bride was ordered to her old post on the entry floor.

Mrs. Flint, at that time, had no children; but she was expecting to be a mother, and if she should want a drink of water in the night, what could she do without her slave to bring it? So my aunt was compelled to lie at her door, until one midnight she was forced to leave, to give premature birth to a child. In a fortnight she was required to resume her place on the entry floor, because Mrs. Flint's babe needed her attentions. She kept her station there through summer and winter, until she had given premature birth to six children; and all the while she was employed as night-nurse to Mrs. Flint's children. Finally, toiling all day, and being deprived of rest at night, completely broke down her constitution, and Dr. Flint declared it was impossible she could ever become the mother of a living child. The fear of losing so valuable a servant by death, now induced them to allow her to sleep in her little room in the out-house, except when there was sickness in the family. She afterwards had two feeble babes, one of whom died in a few days, and the other in four weeks. I well remember her patient sorrow as she held the last dead baby in her arms. "I wish it could have lived," she said; "it is not the will of God that any of my children should live. But I will try to be fit to meet their little spirits in heaven."

Aunt Nancy was housekeeper and waiting-maid in Dr. Flint's family. Indeed, she was the *factotum* of the household. Nothing went on well without her. She was my mother's twin sister, and, as far as was in her power, she supplied a mother's place to us orphans. I slept with her all the time I lived in my old master's house, and the bond between us was very strong. When my friends tried to discourage me from running away, she always encouraged me. When they thought I had better return and ask my master's pardon, because there was no possibility of eseape, she sent me word never to yield. She said if I persevered I might, perhaps, gain the freedom of my children; and even if I perished in doing it, that was better than to leave them to groan under the same persecutions that had blighted my own life. After I was shut up in my dark cell, she stole away, whenever she could, to bring me the news and say something cheering. How often did I kneel down to listen to her words of consolation, whispered through a crack! "I am old, and have not long to live," she used to say; "and I could die happy if I could only see you and the children free. You must pray to God, Linda, as I do for you, that he will lead you out of this darkness." I would beg her not to worry herself on my account; that there was an end of all suffering sooner or later, and that whether I lived in chains or in freedom, I should always remember her as the good friend who had been the comfort of my life. A word from her always strengthened me; and not me only. The whole family relied upon her judgment, and were guided by her advice.

* The slave had no civil or political rights. He could not contract marriage (or enter into any other contract), exercise authority over his family, or assume responsibility for his children. He could not hold property, testify in court except against another slave, or assemble with other slaves without a white person present. There were laws against teaching him to read or write. W. T.

I had been in my cell six years when my grandmother was summoned to the bedside of this, her last remaining daughter. She was very ill, and they said she would die. Grandmother had not entered Dr. Flint's house for several years. They had treated her cruelly, but she thought nothing of that now. She was grateful for permission to watch by the death-bed of her child. They had always been devoted to each other; and now they sat looking into each other's eyes, longing to speak of the secret that had weighed so much on the hearts of both. My aunt had been stricken with paralysis. She lived but two days, and the last day she was speechless. Before she lost the power of utterance, she told her mother not to grieve if she could not speak to her; that she would try to hold up her hand, to let her know that all was well with her. Even the hard-hearted doctor was a little softened when he saw the dying woman try to smile on the aged mother, who was kneeling by her side. His eyes moistened for a moment, as he said she had always been a faithful servant, and they should never be able to supply her place. Mrs. Flint took to her bed, quite overcome by the shock. While my grandmother sat alone with the dead, the doctor came in, leading his youngest son, who had always been a great pet with aunt Nancy, and was much attached to her. "Martha," said he, "aunt Nancy loved this child, and when he comes where you are, I hope you will be kind to him, for her sake." She replied, "Your wife was my foster-child, Dr. Flint, the foster-sister of my poor Nancy, and you little know me if you think I can feel any thing but good will for her children."

"I wish the past could be forgotten, and that we might never think of it," said he; "and that Linda would come to supply her aunt's place. She would be worth more to us than all the money that could be paid for her. I wish it for your sake also, Martha. Now that Nancy is taken away from you, she would be a great comfort to your old age."

He knew he was touching a tender chord. Almost choking with grief, my grandmother replied, "It was not I that drove Linda away. My grandchildren are gone; and of my nine children only one is left. God help me!"

To me, the death of this kind relative was an inexpressible sorrow. I knew that she had been slowly murdered; and I felt that my troubles had helped to finish the work. After I heard of her illness, I listened constantly to hear what news was brought from the great house; and the thought that I could not go to her made me utterly miserable. At last, as uncle Phillip came into the house, I heard some one inquire, "How is she?" and he answered, "She is dead." My little cell seemed whirling round, and I knew nothing more till I opened my eyes and found uncle Phillip bending over me. I had no need to ask any questions. He whispered, "Linda, she died happy." I could not weep. My fixed gaze troubled him. "Don't look so," he said. "Don't add to my poor mother's trouble. Remember how much she had to bear, and that we ought to do all we can to comfort her." Ah, yes, that blessed old grandmother, who for seventy-three years had borne the pelting storms of a slave-mother's life. She did indeed need consolation!

Mrs. Flint had rendered her poor foster-sister childless, apparently without any compunction; and with cruel selfishness had ruined her health by years of incessant, unrequited toil, and broken rest. But now she became very sentimental. I suppose she thought it would be a beautiful illustration of the attachment existing between slaveholder and slave, if the body of her old worn-out servant was buried at her feet. She sent for the clergyman and asked if he had any objection to burying aunt Nancy in the doctor's family burial-place. No colored person had ever been allowed interment in the white people's burying-ground, and the minister knew that all the deceased of our family reposed together in the old graveyard of the slaves. He therefore replied, "I have no objection to complying with your wish; but perhaps aunt Nancy's *mother* may have some choice as to where her remains shall be deposited."

It had never occurred to Mrs. Flint that slaves could have any feelings. When my grandmother was consulted, she at once said she wanted Nancy to lie with all the rest of her family, and where her own old body would be buried. Mrs. Flint graciously complied with her wish, though she said it was painful to her to have Nancy buried away from her. She might have added with touching pathos, "I was so long used to sleep with her lying near me, on the entry floor."

My uncle Phillip asked permission to bury his sister at his own expense; and slaveholders are always ready to grant such favors to slaves and their relatives. The arrangements were very plain, but perfectly respectable. She was buried on the Sabbath, and Mrs. Flint's minister read the funeral service. There was a large concourse of colored people, bond and free, and a few white persons who had always been friendly to our family. Dr. Flint's carriage was in the procession; and when the body was deposited in its humble resting place, the mistress dropped a tear, and returned to her carriage, probably thinking she had performed her duty nobly.

It was talked of by the slaves as a mighty grand funeral. Northern travelers, passing through the place, might have described this tribute of respect to the humble dead as a beautiful feature in the "patriarchal institution;" a touching proof of the attachment between slaveholders and their servants; and tender-hearted Mrs. Flint would have confirmed this impression, with handkerchief at her eyes. We could have told them a different story. We could have given them a chapter of wrongs and sufferings, that would have touched their hearts, if they *had* any hearts to feel for the colored people. We could have told them how the poor old slavemother had toiled, year after year, to earn eight hundred dollars to buy her son Phillip's right to his own earnings; and how that same Phillip paid the expenses of the funeral, which they regarded as doing so much credit to the master. We could also have told them of a poor, blighted young creature, shut up in a living grave for years, to avoid the tortures that would be inflicted on her, if she ventured to come out and look on the face of her departed friend.

All this, and much more, I thought of, as I sat at my loophole, waiting for the family to return from the grave; sometimes weeping, sometimes falling asleep, dreaming strange dreams of the dead and the living.

It was sad to witness the grief of my bereaved grandmother. She had always been strong to bear, and now, as ever, religious faith supported her. But her dark life had become still darker, and age and trouble were leaving deep traces on her withered face. She had four places to knock for me to come to the trap-door, and each place had a different meaning. She now came oftener than she had done, and talked to me of her dead daughter, while tears trickled slowly down her furrowed cheeks. I said all I could to comfort her; but it was a sad reflection, that instead of being able to help her, I was a constant source of anxiety and trouble. The poor old back was fitted to its burden. It bent under it, but did not break.

XXIX

Preparations for Escape

I hardly expect that the reader will credit me, when I affirm that I lived in that little dismal hole, almost deprived of light and air, and with no space to move my limbs, for nearly seven years. But it is a fact; and to me a sad one, even now; for my body still suffers from the effects of that long imprisonment, to say nothing of my soul. Members of my family, now living in New York and Boston, can testify to the truth of what I say.

Countless were the nights that I sat late at the little loophole scarcely large enough to give me a glimpse of one twinkling star. There, I heard the patrols and slave-hunters conferring together about the capture of runaways, well knowing how rejoiced they would be to catch me.

Season after season, year after year, I peeped at my children's faces, and heard their sweet voices, with a heart yearning all the while to say, "Your mother is here." Sometimes it appeared to me as if ages had rolled away since I entered upon that gloomy, monotonous existence. At times, I was stupefied and listless; at other times I became very impatient to know when these dark years would end, and I should again be allowed to feel the sunshine, and breathe the pure air.

After Ellen left us, this feeling increased. Mr. Sands had agreed that Benny might go to the north whenever his uncle Phillip could go with him; and I was anxious to be there also, to watch over my children, and protect them so far as I was able. Moreover, I was likely to be drowned out of my den, if I remained much longer; for the slight roof was getting badly out of repair, and uncle Phillip was afraid to remove the shingles, lest some one should get a glimpse of me. When storms occurred in the night, they spread mats and bits of carpet, which in the morning appeared to have been laid out to dry; but to cover the roof in the daytime might have attracted attention. Consequently, my clothes and bedding were often drenched; a process by which the pains and aches in my cramped and stiffened limbs were greatly increased. I revolved various plans of escape in my mind, which I sometimes imparted to my grandmother, when she came to whisper with me at the trap-door. The kind-hearted old woman had an intense sympathy for runaways. She had known too much of the cruelties inflicted on those who were captured. Her memory always flew back at once to the sufferings of her bright and handsome son, Benjamin, the youngest and dearest of her flock. So, whenever I alluded to the subject, she would groan out, "O, don't think of it, child. You'll break my heart." I had no good old aunt Nancy now to encourage me; but my brother William and my children were continually beckoning me to the north.

And now I must go back a few months in my story. I have stated that the first of January was the time for selling slaves, or leasing them out to new masters. If time were counted by heart-throbs, the poor slaves might reckon years of suffering during that festival so joyous to the free. On the New Year's day preceding my aunt's death, one of my friends, named Fanny, was to be sold at auction, to pay her master's debts. My thoughts were with her during all the day, and at night I anxiously inquired what had been her fate. I was told that she had been sold to one master, and her four little girls to another master, far distant; that she had escaped from her purchaser, and was not to be found. Her mother was the old Aggie I have spoken of. She lived in a small tenement belonging to my grandmother, and built on the same lot with her own house. Her dwelling was searched and watched, and that brought the patrols so near me that I was obliged to keep very close in my den. The hunters were somehow eluded; and not long afterwards Benny accidentally caught sight of Fanny in her mother's hut. He told his grandmother, who charged him never to speak of it, explaining to him the frightful consequences; and he never betrayed the trust. Aggie little dreamed that my grandmother knew where her daughter was concealed, and that the stooping form of her old neighbor was bending under a similar burden of anxiety and fear; but these dangerous secrets deepened the sympathy between the two old persecuted mothers.

My friend Fanny and I remained many weeks hidden within call of each other; but she was unconscious of the fact. I longed to have her share my den, which seemed a more secure retreat than her own; but I had brought so much trouble on my grandmother, that it seemed wrong to ask her to incur greater risks. My restlessness increased. I had lived too long in bodily pain and anguish of spirit. Always I was in dread that by some accident, or some contrivance, slavery would succeed in snatching my children from me. This thought drove me nearly frantic, and I determined to steer for the North Star* at all hazards. At this crisis, Providence opened an unexpected way for me to escape. My friend Peter came one evening, and asked to speak with me. "Your day has come, Linda," said he. "I have found a chance for you to go to the Free States. You have a fortnight to decide." The news seemed too good to be true; but Peter explained his arrangements, and told me all that was necessary was for me to say I would go. I was going to answer him with a joyful yes, when the thought of Benny came to my mind. I told him the temptation was exceedingly strong, but I was terribly afraid of Dr. Flint's alleged power over my child, and that I could not go and leave him behind. Peter remonstrated earnestly. He said such a good chance might never occur again; that Benny was free, and could be sent to me; and that for the sake of my children's welfare I ought not to hesitate a moment. I told him I would consult with uncle Phillip. My uncle rejoiced in the plan, and bade me go by all means. He promised, if his life was spared, that he would either bring or send my son to me as soon as I reached a place of safety. I resolved to go, but thought nothing had better be said to my grandmother till very near the time of departure. But my uncle thought she would feel it more keenly if I left her so suddenly. "I will reason with her," said he, "and convince her how necessary it is, not only for your sake, but for hers also. You cannot be blind to the fact that she is sinking under her burdens." I was not blind to it. I knew that my concealment was an ever-present source of anxiety, and that the older she grew the more nervously fearful she was of discovery. My uncle talked with her, and finally succeeded in persuading her that it was absolutely necessary for me to seize the chance so unexpectedly offered.

The anticipation of being a free woman proved almost too much for my weak frame. The excitement stimulated me, and at the same time bewildered me. I made busy preparations for my journey, and for my son to follow me. I resolved to have an interview with him before I went, that I might give him cautions and advice, and tell him how anxiously I should be waiting for him at the north. Grandmother stole up to me as often as possible to whisper words of counsel. She insisted upon my writing to Dr. Flint, as soon as I arrived in the Free States, and asking him to sell me to her. She said she would sacrifice her house, and all she had in the world, for the sake of having me safe with my children in any part of the world. If she could only live to know *that* she could die in peace. I promised the dear old faithful friend that I would write to her as soon as I arrived, and put the letter in a safe way to reach her; but in my own mind I resolved that not another cent of her hard earnings should be spent to pay rapacious slaveholders for what they called their property. And even if I had not been unwilling to buy what I had already a right to possess, common humanity would have prevented

* This was the only guide of many a fleeing slave, hiding by day and running by night. W. T.

386

me from accepting the generous offer, at the expense of turning my aged relative out of house and home, when she was trembling on the brink of the grave.

I was to escape in a vessel; but I forbear to mention any further particulars. I was in readiness, but the vessel was unexpectedly detained several days. Meantime, news came to town of a most horrible murder committed on a fugitive slave, named James. Charity, the mother of this unfortunate young man, had been an old acquaintance of ours. I have told the shocking particulars of his death, in my description of some of the neighboring slaveholders. My grandmother, always nervously sensitive about runaways, was terribly frightened. She felt sure that a similar fate awaited me, if I did not desist from my enterprise. She sobbed, and groaned, and entreated me not to go. Her excessive fear was somewhat contagious, and my heart was not proof against her extreme agony. I was grievously disappointed, but I promised to relinquish my project.

When my friend Peter was apprised of this, he was both disappointed and vexed. He said, that judging from our past experience, it would be a long time before I had such another chance to throw away. I told him it need not be thrown away; that I had a friend concealed near by, who would be glad enough to take the place that had been provided for me. I told him about poor Fanny, and the kind-hearted, noble fellow, who never turned his back upon any body in distress, white or black, expressed his readiness to help her. Aggie was much surprised when she found that we knew her secret. She was rejoiced to hear of such a chance for Fanny, and arrangements were made for her to go on board the vessel the next night. They both supposed that I had long been at the north, therefore my name was not mentioned in the transaction. Fanny was carried on board at the appointed time, and stowed away in a very small cabin. This accommodation had been purchased at a price that would pay for a voyage to England. But when one proposes to go to fine old England, they stop to calculate whether they can afford the cost of the pleasure; while in making a bargain to escape from slavery, the trembling victim is ready to say, "Take all I have, only don't betray me!"

The next morning I peeped through my loophole, and saw that it was dark and cloudy. At night I received news that the wind was ahead, and the vessel had not sailed. I was exceedingly anxious about Fanny, and Peter too, who was running a tremendous risk at my instigation. Next day the wind and weather remained the same.

Poor Fanny had been half dead with fright when they carried her on board, and I could readily imagine how she must be suffering now. Grandmother came often to my den, to say how thankful she was I did not go. On the third morning she rapped for me to come down to the storeroom. The poor old sufferer was breaking down under her weight of trouble. She was easily flurried now. I found her in a nervous, excited state, but I was not aware that she had forgotten to lock the door behind her, as usual. She was exceedingly worried about the detention of the vessel. She was afraid all would be discovered, and then Fanny, and Peter, and I, would all be tortured to death, and Phillip would be utterly ruined, and her house would be torn down. Poor Peter! If he should die such a horrible death as the poor slave James had lately done, and all for his kindness in trying to help me, how dreadful it would be for us all! Alas, the thought was familiar to me, and had sent many a sharp pang through my heart. I tried to suppress my own anxiety, and speak soothingly to her. She brought in some allusion to aunt Nancy, the dear daughter she had recently buried, and then she lost all control of herself. As she stood there, trembling and sobbing, a voice from the piazza called out, "Whar is you, aunt Marthy?" Grandmother was startled, and in her agitation opened the door, without thinking of me. In stepped Jenny, the mischievous housemaid, who had tried to enter my room, when I was concealed in the house of my white benefactress. "I's bin huntin ebery whar for you, aunt Marthy," said she. "My missis wants you to send her some crackers." I had slunk down behind a barrel, which entirely screened me, but I imagined that Jenny was looking directly at the spot, and my heart beat violently. My grandmother immediately thought what she had done, and went out quickly with Jenny to count the crackers locking the door after her. She returned to me, in a few minutes, the perfect picture of despair. "Poor child!" she exclaimed, "my carelessness has ruined you. The boat ain't gone yet. Get ready immediately, and go with Fanny. I ain't got another word to say against it now; for there's no telling what may happen this day."

Uncle Phillip was sent for, and he agreed with his mother in thinking that Jenny would inform Dr. Flint in less than twenty-four hours. He advised getting me on board the boat, if possible; if not, I had better keep very still in my den, where they could not find me without tearing the house down. He said it would not do for him to move in the matter, because suspicion would be immediately excited; but he promised to communicate with Peter. I felt reluctant to apply to him again, having implicated him too much already; but there seemed to be no alternative. Vexed as Peter had been by my indecision, he was true to his generous nature, and said at once that he would do his best to help me, trusting I should show myself a stronger woman this time.

He immediately proceeded to the wharf, and found that the wind had shifted, and the vessel was slowly beating down stream. On some pretext of urgent necessity, he offered two boatmen a dollar apiece to catch up with her. He was of lighter complexion than the boatmen he hired, and when the captain saw them coming so rapidly, he thought officers were pursuing his vessel in search of the runaway slave he had on board. They hoisted sails, but the boat gained upon them, and the indefatigable Peter sprang on board.

The captain at once recognized him. Peter asked him to go below, to speak about a bad bill he had given him. When he told his errand, the captain replied, "Why, the woman's here already; and I've put her where you or the devil would have a tough job to find her."

"But it is another woman I want to bring," said Peter. *"She* is in great distress, too, and you shall be paid any thing within reason, if you'll stop and take her."

"What's her name?" inquired the captain.

"Linda," he replied.

"That's the name of the woman already here," rejoined the captain." By George! I believe you mean to betray me."

"O!" exclaimed Peter, "God knows I wouldn't harm a hair of your head. I am too grateful to you. But there really is another woman in great danger. Do have the humanity to stop and take her!"

After a while they came to an understanding. Fanny, not dreaming I was any where about in that region, had assumed my name, though she called herself Johnson. "Linda is a common name," said Peter, "and the woman I want to bring is Linda Brent."

The captain agreed to wait at a certain place till evening, being handsomely paid for his detention.

Of course, the day was an anxious one for us all. But we concluded that if Jenny had seen me, she would be too wise to let her mistress know of it; and that she probably would not get a chance to see Dr. Flint's family till evening, for I knew very well what were the rules in that household. I afterwards believed that she did not see me; for nothing ever came of it, and she was one of those base characters that would have jumped to betray a suffering fellow being for the sake of thirty pieces of silver.

I made all my arrangements to go on board as soon as it was dusk. The intervening time I resolved to spend with my son. I had not spoken to him for seven years, though I had been under the same roof, and seen him every day, when I was well enough to sit at the loophole. I did not dare to venture beyond the storeroom; so they brought him there, and locked us up together, in a place concealed from the piazza door. It was an agitating interview for both of us. After we had talked and wept together for a little while, he said, "Mother, I'm glad you're going away. I wish I could go with you. I knew you was here; and I have been so afraid they would come and catch you!"

I was greatly surprised, and asked him how he had found it out.

He replied," I was standing under the eaves, one day, before Ellen went away, and I heard somebody cough up over the wood shed. I don't know what made me think it was you, but I did think so. I missed Ellen, the night before she went away; and grandmother brought her back into the room in the night; and I thought maybe she'd been to see you, before she went, for I heard grandmother whisper to her, 'Now go to sleep; and remember never to tell.'"

I asked him if he ever mentioned his suspicions to his sister. He said he never did; but after he heard the cough, if he saw her playing with other children on that side of the house, he always tried to coax her round to the other side, for fear they would hear me cough, too. He said he had kept a close lookout for Dr. Flint, and if he saw him speak to a constable, or a patrol, he always told grandmother. I now recollected that I had seen him manifest uneasiness, when people were on that side of the house, and I had at the time been puzzled to conjecture a motive for his actions. Such prudence may seem extraordinary in a boy of twelve years, but slaves, being surrounded by mysteries, deceptions, and dangers, early learn to be suspicious and watchful, and prematurely cautious and cunning. He had never asked a question of grandmother, or uncle Phillip, and I had often heard him chime in with other children, when they spoke of my being at the north.

I told him I was now really going to the Free States, and if he was a good, honest boy, and a loving child to his dear old grandmother, the Lord would bless him, and bring him to me, and we and Ellen would live together. He began to tell me that grandmother had not eaten any thing all day. While he was speaking, the door was unlocked, and she came in with small bag of money, which she wanted me to take. I begged her to keep a part of it, at least, to pay for Benny's being sent to the north; but she insisted, while her tears were falling fast, that I should take the whole. "You may be sick among strangers," she said, "and they would send you to the poor house to die." Ah, that good grandmother!

For the last time I went up to my nook. Its desolate appearance no longer chilled me, for the light of hope had risen in my soul. Yet, even with the blessed prospect of freedom before me, I felt very sad at leaving forever that old homestead, where I had been sheltered so long by the dear old grandmother; where I had dreamed my first young dream of love; and where, after that had faded away, my children came to twine themselves so closely round my desolate heart. As the hour approached for me to leave, I again descended to the storeroom. My grandmother and Benny were there. She took me by the hand, and said, "Linda, let us pray." We knelt down together, with my child pressed to my heart, and my other arm round the faithful, loving old friend I was about to leave forever. On no other occasion has it ever been my lot to listen to so fervent a supplication for mercy and protection. It thrilled through my heart, and inspired me with trust in God.

Peter was waiting for me in the street. I was soon by his side, faint in body, but strong of purpose. I did not look back upon the old place, though I felt that I should never see it again.

XXX

NORTHWARD BOUND

I never could tell how we reached the wharf. My brain was all of a whirl, and my limbs tottered under me. At an appointed place we met my uncle Phillip, who had started before us on a different route, that he might reach the wharf first, and give us timely warning if there was any danger. A rowboat was in readiness. As I was about to step in, I felt something pull me gently, and turning round I saw Benny, looking pale and anxious. He whispered in my ear, "I've been peeping into the doctor's window, and he's at home.

Good by, mother. Don't cry; I'll come." He hastened away. I clasped the hand of my good uncle, to whom I owed so much, and of Peter, the brave, generous friend who had volunteered to run such terrible risks to secure my safety. To this day I remember how his bright face beamed with joy, when he told me he had discovered a safe method for me to escape. Yet that intelligent, enterprising, noble-hearted man was a chattel! liable, by the laws of a country that calls itself civilized, to be sold with horses and pigs! We parted in silence. Our hearts were all too full for words!

Swiftly the boat glided over the water. After a while, one of the sailors said, "Don't be down-hearted madam. We will take you safely to your husband, in ——." At first I could not imagine what he meant; but I had presence of mind to think that it probably referred to something the captain had told him; so I thanked him, and said I hoped we should have pleasant weather.

When I entered the vessel the captain came forward to meet me. He was an elderly man, with a pleasant countenance. He showed me to a little box of a cabin, where sat my friend Fanny. She started as if she had seen a specter. She gazed on me in utter astonishment, and exclaimed, "Linda, can this be you, or is it your ghost?" When we were locked in each other's arms, my overwrought feelings could no longer be restrained. My sobs reached the ears of the captain, who came and very kindly reminded us, that for his safety, as well as our own, it would be prudent for us not to attract any attention. He said that when there was a sail in sight he wished us to keep below; but at other times, he had no objection to our being on deck. He assured us that he would keep a good lookout, and if we acted prudently, he thought we should be in no danger. He had represented us as women going to meet our husbands in ——. We thanked him, and promised to observe carefully all the directions he gave us.

Fanny and I now talked by ourselves, low and quietly, in our little cabin. She told me of the sufferings she had gone through in making her escape, and of her terrors while she was concealed in her mother's house. Above all, she dwelt on the agony of separation from all her children on that dreadful auction day. She could scarcely credit me, when I told her of the place where I had passed nearly seven years. "We have the same sorrows," said I. "No," replied she, "you are going to see your children soon, and there is no hope that I shall ever even hear from mine."

The vessel was soon under way, but we made slow progress.

The wind was against us. I should not have cared for this, if we had been out of sight of the town; but until there were miles of water between us and our enemies, we were filled with constant apprehensions that the constables would come on board. Neither could I feel quite at ease with the captain and his men. I was an entire stranger to that class of people, and I had heard that sailors were rough, and sometimes cruel. We were so completely in their power, that if they were bad men, our situation would be dreadful. Now that the captain was paid for our passage, might he not be tempted to make more money by giving us up to those who claimed us as property ? I was naturally of a confiding disposition, but slavery had made me suspicious of every body. Fanny did not share my distrust of the captain or his men. She said she was afraid at first, but she had been on board three days while the vessel lay in the dock, and nobody had betrayed her, or treated her otherwise than kindly.

The captain soon came to advise us to go on deck for fresh air. His friendly and respectful manner, combined with Fanny's testimony, reassured me, and we went with him. He placed us in a comfortable seat, and occasionally entered into conversation. He told us he was a southerner by birth, and had spent the greater part of his life in the slave states, and that he had recently lost a brother who traded in slaves. "But," said he, "it is a pitiable and degrading business, and I always felt ashamed to acknowledge my brother in connection with it." As we passed Snaky Swamp he pointed to it, and said "There is a slave territory that defies all the laws." I thought of the terrible days I had spent there, and though it was not called Dismal Swamp,* it made me feel very dismal as I looked at it.

I shall never forget that night. The balmy air of spring was so refreshing! And how shall I describe my sensations when we were fairly sailing on Chesapeake Bay. O, the beautiful sunshine! the exhilarating breeze! and I could enjoy them without fear or restraint. I had never realized what grand things air and sunlight are till I had been deprived of them.

Ten days after we left land we were approaching Philadelphia. The captain said we should arrive there in the night, but he thought we had better wait till morning, and go on shore in broad daylight, as the best way to avoid suspicion.

I replied, "You know best. But will you stay on board and protect us?"

He saw that I was suspicious, and he said he was sorry, now that he had brought us to the end of our voyage, to find I had so little confidence in him. Ah, if he had ever been a slave he would have known how difficult it was to trust a white man. He assured us that we might sleep through the night without fear; that he would take care we were not left unprotected. Be it said to the honor of this captain, Southerner as he was, that if Fanny and I had been white ladies, and our passage lawfully engaged, he could not have treated us more respectfully. My intelligent friend, Peter, had rightly estimated the character of the man to whose honor he had entrusted us.

The next morning I was on deck as soon as the day dawned. I called Fanny to see the sun rise, for the first time in our lives, on free soil; for such I *then* believed it to be. We watched the reddening sky, and saw the great orb come up slowly out of the water, as it seemed. Soon the waves began to sparkle, and every thing caught the beautiful glow. Before us lay the city of strangers. We looked at each other, and the eyes of both were moistened with tears. We had escaped from slavery, and we supposed ourselves to be safe from the hunters. But we were alone in the world, and we had left dear ties behind us; ties cruelly sundered by the demon Slavery.

XXXI

INCIDENTS IN PHILADELPHIA

I had heard that the poor slave had many friends at the north. I trusted we should find some of them. Meantime, we would take for granted that all were friends, till they proved to the contrary. I sought out the kind captain, thanked him for his attentions, and told him I should never cease to be grateful for the service he had rendered us. I gave him a message to the friends I had left at home, and he promised to deliver it. We were placed in a rowboat, and in about fifteen minutes were landed on a wood wharf in Philadelphia. As I stood looking round, the friendly captain touched me on the shoulder, and said, "There is a respectable-looking colored man behind you. I will speak to him about the New York trains, and tell him you wish to go directly on." I thanked him, and asked him to direct me to some shops where I

---

* About thirty miles long and ten wide, lying in southeast Virginia and northeast North Carolina, it is perhaps the best known of many extensive tracts of swampland in the coastal plain of Virginia and the Carolina. W. T.

could buy gloves and veils. He did so, and said he would talk with the colored man till I returned. I made what haste I could. Constant exercise on board the vessel, and frequent rubbing with salt water, had nearly restored the use of my limbs. The noise of the great city confused me, but I found the shops, and bought some double veils and gloves for Fanny and myself. The shopman told me they were so many levies.* I had never heard the word before, but I did not tell him so. I thought if he knew I was a stranger he might ask me where I came from. I gave him a gold piece, and when he returned the change, I counted it, and found out how much a levy was. I made my way back to the wharf, where the captain introduced me to the colored man, as the Rev. Jeremiah Durham, minister of Bethel church. He took me by the hand, as if I had been an old friend. He told us we were too late for the morning cars to New York, and must wait until the evening, or the next morning. He invited me to go home with him, assuring me that his wife would give me a cordial welcome; and for my friend he would provide a home with one of his neighbors. I thanked him for so much kindness to strangers, and told him if I must be detained, I should like to hunt up some people who formerly went from our part of the country. Mr. Durham insisted that I should dine with him, and then he would assist me in finding my friends. The sailors came to bid us good by. I shook their hardy hands, with tears in my eyes. They had all been kind to us, and they had rendered us a greater service than they could possibly conceive of.

I had never seen so large a city, or been in contact with so many people in the streets. It seemed as if those who passed looked at us with an expression of curiosity. My face was so blistered and peeled, by sitting on deck, in wind and sunshine, that I thought they could not easily decide to what nation I belonged.

Mrs. Durham met me with a kindly welcome, without asking any questions. I was tired, and her friendly manner was a sweet refreshment. God bless her! I was sure that she had comforted other weary hearts, before I received her sympathy. She was surrounded by her husband and children, in a home made sacred by protecting laws. I thought of my own children, and sighed.

After dinner Mr. Durham went with me in quest of the friends I had spoken of. They went from my native town, and I anticipated much pleasure in looking on familiar faces. They were not at home, and we retraced our steps through streets delightfully clean. On the way, Mr. Durham observed that I had spoken to him of a daughter I expected to meet; that he was surprised, for I looked so young he had taken me for a single woman. He was approaching a subject on which I was extremely sensitive. He would ask about my husband next, I thought, and if I answered him truly what would he think of me? I told him I had two children, one in New York the other at the south. He asked some further questions, and I frankly told him some of the most important events of my life. It was painful for me to do it; but I would not deceive him. If he was desirous of being my friend, I thought he ought to know how far I was worthy of it. "Excuse me, if I have tried your feelings," said he. "I did not question you from idle curiosity. I wanted to understand your situation, in order to know whether I could be of any service to you, or your little girl. Your straightforward answers do you credit; but don't answer every body so openly. It might give some heartless people a pretext for treating you with contempt."

That word *contempt* burned me like coals of fire. I replied, "God alone knows how I have suffered; and He, I trust, will forgive me. If I am permitted to have my children, I intend to be a good mother, and to live in such a manner that people cannot treat me with contempt."

"I respect your sentiments," said he. "Place your trust in God, and be governed by good principles, and you will not fail to find friends."

When we reached home, I went to my room, glad to shut out the world for a while. The words he had spoken made an indelible impression upon me. They brought up great shadows from the mournful past. In the midst of my meditations I was startled by a knock at the door. Mrs. Durham entered, her face all beaming with kindness, to say that there was an antislavery friend down stairs, who would like to see me. I overcame my dread of encountering strangers, and went with her. Many questions were asked concerning my experiences, and my escape from slavery; but I observed how careful they all were not to say any thing that might wound my feelings. How gratifying this was, can be fully understood only by those who have been accustomed to be treated as if they were not included within the pale of human beings. The anti-slavery friend had come to inquire into my plans, and to offer assistance, if

* The coin that farther north was called a shilling and in the South, a bit, was in Pennsylvania, Maryland, and Delaware known as a levy, a contraction for eleven pence. It was worth about twelve-and-a-half cents. W. T.

needed. Fanny was comfortably established, for the present, with a friend of Mr. Durham. The Anti-Slavery Society* agreed to pay her expenses to New York. The same was offered to me, but I declined to accept it; telling them that my grandmother had given me sufficient to pay for my expenses to the end of my journey. We were urged to remain in Philadelphia a few days, until some suitable escort could be found for us. I gladly accepted the proposition, for I had a dread of meeting slaveholders, and some dread also of railroads. I had never entered a railroad car in my life, and it seemed to me quite an important event.

That night I sought my pillow with feelings I had never carried to it before. I verily believed myself to be a free woman. I was wakeful for a long time, and I had no sooner fallen asleep, than I was roused by fire-bells. I jumped up, and hurried on my clothes. Where I came from, every body hastened to dress themselves on such occasions. The white people thought a great fire might be used as a good opportunity for insurrection, and that it was best to be in readiness; and the colored people were ordered out to labor in extinguishing the flames. There was but one engine in our town, and colored women and children were often required to drag it to the river's edge and fill it. Mrs. Durham's daughter slept in the same room with me, and seeing that she slept through all the din, I thought it was my duty to wake her. "What's the matter?" said she, rubbing her eyes.

"They're screaming fire in the streets, and the bells are ringing," I replied.

"What of that?" said she, drowsily. "We are used to it. We never get up, without the fire is very near. What good would it do?"

I was quite surprised that it was not necessary for us to go and help fill the engine. I was an ignorant child, just beginning to learn how things went on in great cities.

At daylight, I heard women crying fresh fish, berries, radishes, and various other things. All this was new to me. I dressed myself at an early hour, and sat at the window to watch that unknown tide of life. Philadelphia seemed to me a wonderfully great place. At the breakfast table, my idea of going out to drag the engine was laughed over, and I joined in the mirth.

I went to see Fanny, and found her so well contented among her new friends that she was in no haste to leave. I was also very happy with my kind hostess. She had had advantages for education, and was vastly my superior. Every day, almost every hour, I was adding to my little stock of knowledge. She took me out to see the city as much as she deemed prudent. One day she took me to an artist's room, and showed me the portraits of some of her children. I had never seen any paintings of colored people before, and they seemed to me beautiful.

At the end of five days, one of Mrs. Durham's friends offered to accompany us to New York the following morning. As I held the hand of my good hostess in a parting clasp, I longed to know whether her husband had repeated to her what I had told him. I supposed he had, but she never made any allusion to it. I presume it was the delicate silence of womanly sympathy.

When Mr. Durham handed us our tickets, he said, "I am afraid you will have a disagreeable ride; but I could not procure tickets for the first-class cars."

Supposing I had not given him money enough, I offered more. "O, no," said he, "They could not be had for any money. They don't allow colored people to go in the first-class cars."

This was the first chill to my enthusiasm about the Free States. Colored people were allowed to ride in a filthy box, behind white people, at the south, but there they were not required to pay for the privilege. It made me sad to find how the north aped the customs of slavery.

We were stowed away in a large, rough car, with windows on each side, too high for us to look out without standing up. It was crowded with people, apparently of all nations. There were plenty of beds and cradles, containing screaming and kicking babies. Every other man had a cigar or pipe in his mouth, and jugs of whiskey were handed round freely. The fumes of the whiskey and the dense tobacco smoke were sickening to my senses, and my mind was equally nauseated by the coarse jokes and ribald songs around me. It was a very disagreeable ride. Since that time there has been some improvement in these matters.

---

*There were many antislavery organizations in the North in the thirty years preceding the Civil War, often with hundreds of members. W. T.

XXXII

THE MEETING OF
MOTHER AND DAUGHTER

When we arrived in New York, I was half crazed by the crowd of coachmen calling out, "Carriage, ma'am?" We bargained with one to take us to Sullivan Street for twelve shillings. A burly Irishman stepped up and said, "I'll tak' ye for sax shillings." The reduction of half the price was an object to us, and we asked if he could take us right away. "Troth an I will, ladies," he replied. I noticed that the hackmen smiled at each other, and I inquired whether his conveyance was decent. "Yes, it's decent it is, marm. Devil a bit would I be after takin' ladies in a cab that was not decent." We gave him our checks. He went for the baggage, and soon reappeared, saying, "This way, if you please, ladies." We followed, and found our trunks on a truck, and we were invited to take our seats on them. We told him that was not what we bargained for, and he must take the trunks off. He swore they should not be touched till we had paid him six shillings. In our situation it was not prudent to attract attention, and I was about to pay him what he required, when a man near by shook his head for me not to do it. After a great ado we got rid of the Irishman, and had our trunks fastened on a hack. We had been recommended to a boarding-house in Sullivan Street, and thither we drove. There Fanny and I separated. The Anti-Slavery Society provided a home for her, and I afterwards heard of her in prosperous circumstances. I sent for an old friend from my part of the country, who had for some time been doing business in New York. He came immediately. I told him I wanted to go to my daughter, and asked him to aid me in procuring an interview.

I cautioned him not to let it be known to the family that I had just arrived from the south, because they supposed I had been at the north seven years. He told me there was a colored woman in Brooklyn who came from the same town I did, and I had better go to her house, and have my daughter meet me there. I accepted the proposition thankfully, and he agreed to escort me to Brooklyn. We crossed Fulton ferry, went up Myrtle Avenue, and stopped at the house he designated. I was just about to enter, when two girls passed. My friend called my attention to them. I turned, and recognized in the eldest, Sarah, the daughter of a woman who used to live with my grandmother, but who had left the south years ago.

Surprised and rejoiced at this unexpected meeting, I threw my arms round her, and inquired concerning her mother.

"You take no notice of the other girl," said my friend. I turned, and there stood my Ellen! I pressed her to my heart, then held her away from me to take a look at her. She had changed a good deal in the two years since I parted from her. Signs of neglect could be discerned by eyes less observing than a mother's. My friend invited us all to go into the house; but Ellen said she had been sent of an errand, which she would do as quickly as possible, and go home and ask Mrs. Hobbs to let her come and see me. It was agreed that I should send for her the next day. Her companion, Sarah, hastened to tell her mother of my arrival. When I entered the house, I found the mistress of it absent, and I waited for her return. Before I saw her, I heard her saying, "Where is Linda Brent? I used to know her father and mother." Soon Sarah came with her mother. So there was quite a company of us, all from my grandmother's neighborhood. These friends gathered round me and questioned me eagerly. They laughed, they cried, and they shouted. They thanked God that I had got away from my persecutors and was safe on Long Island. It was a day of great excitement. How different from the silent days I had passed in my dreary den!

The next morning was Sunday. My first waking thoughts were occupied with the note I was to send to Mrs. Hobbs, the lady with whom Ellen lived. That I had recently come into that vicinity was evident; otherwise I should have sooner inquired for my daughter. It would not do to let them know I had just arrived from the south, for that would involve the suspicion of my having been harbored there, and might bring trouble, if not ruin, on several people.

I like a straightforward course, and am always reluctant to resort to subterfuges. So far as my ways have been crooked, I charge them all upon slavery. It was that system of violence and wrong which now left me no alternative but to enact a falsehood. I began my note by stating that I had recently arrived from Canada, and was very desirous to have my daughter come to see me. She came and brought a message from Mrs. Hobbs, inviting me to her house, and assuring me that I need not have any fears. The conversation I had with my child did not leave my mind at ease. When I asked if she was well treated, she answered yes; but there was no heartiness in the tone, and it seemed to me that she said it from an unwillingness to have me troubled on her account. Before she left me, she asked very earnestly, "Mother, when will you take me to live with you?" It made me sad to think that I could not give her a home till I went to work and earned the means; and that might take me a long time. When she was placed with Mrs. Hobbs, the agreement was that she should be sent to school. She had been there two years, and was now nine years old, and she scarcely knew her letters. There was no excuse for this, for there were good public schools in Brooklyn, to which she could have been sent without expense.

She staid with me till dark, and I went home with her. I was received in a friendly manner by the family, and all agreed in saying that Ellen was a useful, good girl. Mrs. Hobbs looked me coolly in the face, and said, "I suppose you know that my cousin, Mr. Sands, has *given* her to my eldest daughter. She will make a nice waiting-maid for her when she grows up." I did not answer a word. How *could* she, who knew by experience the strength of a mother's love, and who was perfectly aware of the relation Mr. Sands bore to my children,—how *could* she look me in the face, while she thrust such a dagger into my heart?

I was no longer surprised that they had kept her in such a state of ignorance. Mr. Hobbs had formerly been wealthy, but he had failed, and afterwards obtained a subordinate situation in the Custom House. Perhaps they expected to return to the south some day; and Ellen's knowledge was quite sufficient for a slave's condition. I was impatient to go to work and earn money, that I might change the uncertain position of my children. Mr. Sands had not kept his promise to emancipate them. I had also been deceived about Ellen. What security had I with regard to Benjamin? I felt that I had none.

I returned to my friend's house in an uneasy state of mind. In order to protect my children, it was necessary that I should own myself. I called myself free, and sometimes felt so; but I knew I was insecure. I sat down that night and wrote a civil letter to Dr. Flint, asking him to state the lowest terms on which he would sell me; and as I belonged by law to his daughter, I wrote to her also, making a similar request.

Since my arrival at the north I had not been unmindful of my dear brother William. I had made diligent inquiries for him, and having heard of him in Boston, I went thither. When I arrived there, I found he had gone to New Bedford. I wrote to that place, and was informed he had gone on a whaling voyage, and would not return for some months. I went back to New York to get employment near Ellen. I received an answer from Dr. Flint, which gave me no encouragement. He advised me to return and submit myself to my rightful owners, and then any request I might make would be granted. I lent this letter to a friend, who lost it; otherwise I would present a copy to my readers.

XXXIII

A HOME FOUND

My greatest anxiety now was to obtain employment. My health was greatly improved, though my limbs continued to trouble me with swelling whenever I walked much. The greatest difficulty in my way was, that those who employed strangers required a recommendation; and in my peculiar position, I could, of course, obtain no certificates from the families I had so faithfully served.

One day an acquaintance told me of a lady who wanted a nurse for her babe, and I immediately applied for the situation. The lady told me she preferred to have one who had been a mother, and accustomed to the care of infants. I told her I had nursed two babes of my own. She asked me many questions, but, to my great relief, did not require a recommendation from my former employers. She told me she was an English woman, and that was a pleasant circumstance to me, because I had heard they had less prejudice against color than Americans entertained. It was agreed that we should try each other for a week. The trial proved satisfactory to both parties, and I was engaged for a month.

The heavenly Father had been most merciful to me in leading me to this place. Mrs. Bruce was a kind and gentle lady, and proved a true and sympathizing friend. Before the stipulated month expired, the necessity of passing up and down stairs frequently, caused my limbs to swell so painfully, that I became unable to perform my duties. Many ladies would have thoughtlessly discharged me; but Mrs. Bruce made arrangements to save me steps, and employed a physician to attend upon me. I had not yet told her that I was a fugitive slave. She noticed that I was often sad, and kindly inquired the cause. I spoke of being separated from my children, and from relatives who were dear to me; but I did not mention the constant feeling of insecurity which oppressed my spirits. I longed for some one to confide in; but I had been so deceived by white people, that I had lost all confidence in them. If they spoke kind words to me, I thought it was for some selfish purpose. I had entered this family with the distrustful feelings I had brought with me out of slavery; but ere six months had passed, I found that the gentle deportment of Mrs. Bruce and the smiles of her lovely babe were thawing my chilled heart. My narrow mind also began to expand under the influences of her intelligent conversation, and the opportunities for reading, which were gladly allowed me whenever I had leisure from my duties. I gradually became more energetic and more cheerful.

The old feeling of insecurity, especially with regard to my children, often threw its dark shadow across my sunshine. Mrs. Bruce offered me a home for Ellen; but pleasant as it would have been, I did not dare to accept it, for fear of offending the Hobbs family. Their knowledge of my precarious situation placed me in their power; and I felt that it was important for me to keep on the right side of them, till, by dint of labor and economy, I could make a home for my children. I was far from feeling satisfied with Ellen's situation. She was not well cared for. She sometimes came to New York to visit me; but she generally brought a request from Mrs. Hobbs that I would buy her a pair of shoes, or some article of clothing. This was accompanied by a promise of payment when Mr. Hobbs's salary at the Custom House became due; but some how or other the pay-day never came. Thus many dollars of my earnings were expended to keep my child comfortably clothed. That, however, was a slight trouble, compared with the fear that their pecuniary embarrassments might induce them to sell my precious young daughter. I knew they were in constant communication with Southerners, and had frequent opportunities to do it. I have stated that when Dr. Flint put Ellen in jail, at two years old, she had an inflammation of the eyes, occasioned by measles. This disease still troubled her; and kind Mrs. Bruce proposed that she should come to New York for a while, to be under the care of Dr. Elliott, a well known oculist. It did not occur to me that there was any thing improper in a mother's making such a request; but Mrs. Hobbs was very angry, and refused to let her go. Situated as I was, it was not politic to insist upon it. I made no complaint, but I longed to be entirely free to act a mother's part towards my children. The next time I went over to Brooklyn, Mrs. Hobbs, as if to apologize for her anger, told me she had employed her own physician to attend to Ellen's eyes, and that she had refused my request because she did not consider it safe to trust her in New York. I accepted the explanation in silence; but she had told me that my child *belonged* to her daughter, and I suspected that her real motive was a fear of my conveying her property away from her. Perhaps I did her injustice; but my knowledge of Southerners made it difficult for me to feel otherwise.

Sweet and bitter were mixed in the cup of my life, and I was thankful that it had ceased to be entirely bitter. I loved Mrs. Bruce's babe. When it laughed and crowed in my face, and twined its little tender arms confidingly about my neck, it made me think of the time when Benny and Ellen were babies, and my wounded heart was soothed. One bright morning, as I stood at the window, tossing baby in my arms, my attention was attracted by a young man in sailor's dress, who was closely observing every house as he passed. I looked at him earnestly. Could it be my brother William? It *must* be he—and yet, how changed! I placed the baby safely, flew down stairs, opened the front door, beckoned to the sailor, and in less than a minute I was clasped in my brother's arms. How much we had to tell each other! How we laughed, and how we cried, over each other's adventures! I took him to Brooklyn, and again saw him with Ellen, the dear child whom he had loved and tended so carefully, while I was shut up in my miserable den. He staid in New York a week. His old feelings of affection for me and Ellen were as lively as ever. There are no bonds so strong as those which are formed by suffering together.

XXXIV

THE OLD ENEMY AGAIN

My young mistress, Miss Emily Flint, did not return any answer to my letter requesting her to consent to my being sold. But after a while, I received a reply, which purported to be written by her younger brother. In order rightly to enjoy the contents of this letter, the reader must bear in mind that the Flint family supposed I had been at the north many years. They had no idea that I knew of the doctor's three excursions to New York in search of me; that I had heard his voice, when he came to borrow five hundred dollars for that purpose; and that I had seen him pass on his way to the steamboat. Neither were they aware that all the particulars of aunt Nancy's death and burial were conveyed to me at the time they occurred. I have kept the letter, of which I herewith subjoin a copy:—

"Your letter to sister was received a few days ago. I gather from it that you are desirous of returning to your native place, among your friends and relatives. We were all gratified with the contents of your letter; and let me assure you that if any members of the family have had any feeling of resentment towards you, they feel it no longer. We all sympathize with you in your unfortunate condition, and are ready to do all in our power to make you contented and happy. It is difficult for you to return home as a free person. If you were purchased by your grandmother, it is doubtful whether you would be permitted to remain, although it would be lawful for you to do so. If a servant should be allowed to purchase herself, after absenting herself so long from her owners, and return free, it would have an injurious effect. From your letter, I think your situation must be hard and uncomfortable. Come home. You have it in your power to be reinstated in our affections. We would receive you with open arms and tears of joy. You need not apprehend any unkind treatment, as we have not put ourselves to any trouble or expense to get you. Had we done so, perhaps we should feel otherwise. You know my sister was always attached to you, and that you were never treated as a slave. You were never put to hard work, nor exposed to field labor. On the contrary, you were taken into the house, and treated as one of us, and almost as free; and we, at least, felt that you were above disgracing yourself by running away. Believing you may be induced to come home voluntarily has induced me to write for my sister. The family will be rejoiced to see you; and your poor old grandmother expressed a great desire to have you come, when she heard your letter read. In her old age she needs the consolation of having her children round her. Doubtless you have heard of the death of your aunt. She was a faithful servant, and a faithful member of the Episcopal church. In her Christian life she taught us how to live—and, O, too high the price of knowledge, she taught us how to die! Could you have seen us round her death bed, with her mother, all mingling our tears in one common stream, you would have thought the same heart-felt tie existed between a master and his servant, as between a mother and her child. But this subject is too painful to dwell upon. I must bring my letter to a close. If you are contented to stay away from your old grandmother, your child, and the friends who love you, stay where you are. We shall never trouble ourselves to apprehend you. But should you prefer to come home, we will do all that we can to make you happy. If you do not wish to remain in the family, I know that father, by our persuasion, will be induced to let you be purchased by any person you may choose in our community. You will please answer this as soon as possible, and let us know your decision. Sister sends much love to you. In the mean time believe me your sincere friend and well wisher."

This letter was signed by Emily's brother, who was as yet a mere lad. I knew, by the style, that it was not written by a person of his age, and though the writing was disguised, I had been made too unhappy by it, in former years, not to recognize at once the hand of Dr. Flint. O, the hypocrisy of slaveholders! Did the old fox suppose I was goose enough to go into such a trap? Verily, he relied too much on "the stupidity of the African race." I did not return the family of Flints any thanks for their cordial invitation—a remissness for which I was, no doubt, charged with base ingratitude.

Not long afterwards I received a letter from one of my friends at the south, informing me that Dr. Flint was about to visit the north. The letter had been delayed, and I supposed he might be already on the way. Mrs. Bruce did not know I was a fugitive. I told her that important business called me to Boston, where my brother then was, and asked permission to bring a friend to supply my place as nurse, for a fortnight. I started on my journey immediately; and as soon as I arrived, I wrote to my grandmother that if Benny came, he must be sent to Boston. I knew she was only waiting for a good chance to send him north, and, fortunately, she had the legal power to do so, without asking leave of any body. She was a free woman; and when my children were purchased, Mr. Sands preferred to have the bill of sale drawn up in her name. It was conjectured that he advanced the money, but it was not known. At the south, a gentleman may have a shoal of colored children without any disgrace; but if he is known to purchase them, with the view of setting them free, the example is thought to be dangerous to their "peculiar institution," and he becomes unpopular.

There was a good opportunity to send Benny in a vessel coming directly to New York. He was put on board with a letter to a friend, who was requested to see him off to Boston. Early one morning, there was a loud rap at my door, and in rushed Benjamin, all out of breath. "O mother!" he exclaimed, "here I am! I run all the way; and I come all alone. How d'you do?"

O reader, can you imagine my joy? No, you cannot, unless you have been a slave mother. Benjamin rattled away as fast as his tongue could go. "Mother, why don't you bring Ellen here? I went over to Brooklyn to see her, and she felt very bad when I bid her good by. She said, 'O Ben, I wish I was going too.' I thought she'd know ever so much; but she don't know so much as I do; for I can read, and she can't. And, mother, I lost all my clothes coming. What can I do to get some more? I'spose free boys can get along here at the north as well as white boys."

I did not like to tell the sanguine, happy little fellow how much he was mistaken. I took him to a tailor, and procured a change of clothes. The rest of the day was spent in mutual asking and answering of questions, with the wish constantly repeated that the good old grandmother was with us, and frequent injunctions from Benny to write to her immediately, and be sure to tell her every thing about his voyage, and his journey to Boston.

Dr. Flint made his visit to New York, and made every exertion to call upon me, and invite me to return with him; but not being able to ascertain where I was, his hospitable intentions were frustrated, and the affectionate family, who were waiting for me with "open arms," were doomed to disappointment.

As soon as I knew he was safely at home, I placed Benjamin in the care of my brother William, and returned to Mrs. Bruce. There I remained through the winter and spring, endeavoring to perform my duties faithfully, and finding a good degree of happiness in the attractions of baby Mary, the considerate kindness of her excellent mother, and occasional interviews with my darling daughter.

But when summer came, the old feeling of insecurity haunted me. It was necessary for me to take little Mary out daily, for exercise and fresh air, and the city was swarming with Southerners, some of whom might recognize me. Hot weather brings out snakes and slaveholders, and I like one class of the venomous creatures as little as I do the other. What a comfort it is, to be free to *say* so!

XXXV

PREJUDICE AGAINST COLOR

It was a relief to my mind to see preparations for leaving the city. We went to Albany in the steamboat Knickerbocker. When the gong sounded for tea, Mrs. Bruce said, "Linda, it is late, and you and baby had better come to the table with me." I replied, "I know it is time baby had her supper, but I had rather not go with you, if you please. I am afraid of being insulted." "O no, not if you are with me," she said. I saw several white nurses go with their ladies, and I ventured to do the same. We were at the extreme end of the table. I was no sooner seated, than a gruff voice said, "Get up! You know you are not allowed to sit here." I looked up, and, to my astonishment and indignation, saw that the speaker was a colored man. If his office required him to enforce the by-laws of the boat, he might, at least, have done it politely. I replied, "I shall not get up, unless the captain comes and takes me up." No cup of tea was offered me, but Mrs. Bruce handed me hers and called for another. I looked to see whether the other nurses were treated in a similar manner. They were all properly waited on.

Next morning, when we stopped at Troy for breakfast, every body was making a rush for the table. Mrs. Bruce said, "Take my arm, Linda, and we'll go in together." The landlord heard her, and said, "Madam, will you allow your nurse and baby to take breakfast with my family?" I knew this was to be attributed to my complexion; but he spoke courteously, and therefore I did not mind it.

At Saratoga we found the United States Hotel crowded, and Mr. Bruce took one of the cottages belonging to the hotel. I had thought, with gladness, of going to the quiet of the country, where I should meet few people, but here I found myself in the midst of a swarm of Southerners. I looked round me with fear and trembling, dreading to see some one who would recognize me. I was rejoiced to find that we were to stay but a short time.

We soon returned to New York, to make arrangements for spending the remainder of the summer at Rockaway. While the laundress was putting the clothes in order, I took an opportunity to go over to Brooklyn to see Ellen. I met her going to a grocery store, and the first words she said, were, "O, mother, don't go to Mrs. Hobbs's. Her brother, Mr. Thorne, has come from the south, and may be he'll tell where you are." I accepted the warning. I told her I was going away with Mrs. Bruce the next day, and would try to see her when I came back.

Being in servitude to the Anglo-Saxon race, I was not put into a "Jim Crow car,"* on our way to Rockaway, neither was I invited to ride through the streets on the top of trunks in a truck; but everywhere I found the same manifestations of that cruel prejudice, which so discourages the feelings, and represses the energies of the colored people. We reached Rockaway before dark, and put up at the Pavilion—a large hotel, beautifully situated by the sea-side—a great resort of the fashionable world. Thirty or forty nurses were there, of a great variety of nations. Some of the ladies had colored waiting-maids and coachmen, but I was the only nurse tinged with the blood of Africa. When the tea bell rang, I took little Mary and followed the other nurses. Supper was served in a long hall. A young man, who had the ordering of things, took the circuit of the table two or three times, and finally pointed me to a seat at the lower end of it. As there was but one chair, I sat down and took the child in my lap. Whereupon the young man came to me and said, in the blandest manner possible, "Will you please to seat the little girl in the chair, and stand behind it and feed her? After they have done, you will be shown to the kitchen, where you will have a good supper."

This was the climax! I found it hard to preserve my self-control, when I looked round, and saw women who were nurses, as I was, and only one shade lighter in complexion, eyeing me with a defiant look, as if my presence were a contamination. However, I said nothing. I quietly took the child in my arms, went to our room, and refused to go to the table again. Mr. Bruce ordered meals to be sent to the room for little Mary and I. This answered for a few days; but the waiters of the establishment were white, and they soon began to complain, saying they were not hired to wait on negroes. The landlord requested Mr. Bruce to send me down to my meals, because his servants rebelled against bringing them up, and the colored servants of other boarders were dissatisfied because all were not treated alike.

My answer was that the colored servants ought to be dissatisfied with *themselves,* for not having too much self-respect to submit to such treatment; that there was no difference in the price of board for colored and white servants, and there was no justification for difference of treatment. I stayed a month after this, and finding I was resolved to stand up for my rights, they concluded to treat me well. Let every colored man and woman do this, and eventually we shall cease to be trampled under foot by our oppressors.

XXXVI

THE HAIRBREADTH ESCAPE

After we returned to New York, I took the earliest opportunity to go and see Ellen. I asked to have her called down stairs; for I supposed Mrs. Hobbs's southern brother might still be there, and I was desirous to avoid seeing him, if possible. But Mrs. Hobbs came to the kitchen, and insisted on my going up stairs. "My brother wants to see you," said she, "and he is sorry you seem to shun him. He knows you are living in New York. He told me to say to you that he owes thanks to good old aunt Martha for too many little acts of kindness for him to be base enough to betray her grandchild."

This Mr. Thorne had become poor and reckless long before he left the south, and such persons had much rather go to one of the faithful old slaves to borrow a dollar, or get a good dinner, than to go to one whom they consider an equal. It was such acts of kindness as these for which he professed to feel grateful to my grandmother. I wished he had kept at a distance, but as he was here, and knew where I was, I concluded there was nothing to be gained by trying to avoid him; on the contrary, it might be the means of exciting his ill will. I followed his sister up stairs. He met me in a very friendly manner, congratulated me on my escape from slavery, and hoped I had a good place, where I felt happy.

I continued to visit Ellen as often as I could. She, good thoughtful child, never forgot my hazardous situation, but always kept a vigilant lookout for my safety. She never made any complaint about her own inconveniences and troubles; but a mother's observing eye easily perceived that she was not happy. On the occasion of one of my visits I found her unusually serious. When I asked her what was the matter, she said nothing was the matter. But I insisted upon knowing what made her look so very grave. Finally, I ascertained that she felt troubled about the dissipation that was continually going on in the house. She was sent to the store very often for rum and brandy, and she felt ashamed to ask for it so often; and Mr. Hobbs and Mr. Thorne drank a good deal, and their hands trembled so that they

* This was a place for blacks only—a common and widespread form of discrimination. W. T.

had to call her to pour out the liquor for them. "But for all that," said she, "Mr. Hobbs is good to me, and I can't help liking him. I feel sorry for him " I tried to comfort her, by telling her that I had laid up a hundred dollars, and that before long I hoped to be able to give her and Benjamin a home, and send them to school. She was always desirous not to add to my troubles more than she could help, and I did not discover till years afterwards that Mr. Thorne's intemperance was not the only annoyance she suffered from him. Though he professed too much gratitude to my grandmother to injure any of her descendants, he had poured vile language into the ears of her innocent great-grandchild.

I usually went to Brooklyn to spend Sunday afternoon. One Sunday, I found Ellen anxiously waiting for me near the house. "O, mother," said she, "I've been waiting for you this long time. I'm afraid Mr. Thorne has written to tell Dr. Flint where you are. Make haste and come in. Mrs. Hobbs will tell you all about it!"

The story was soon told. While the children were playing in the grape-vine arbor, the day before, Mr. Thorne came out with a letter in his hand, which he tore up and scattered about. Ellen was sweeping the yard at the time, and having her mind full of suspicions of him, she picked up the pieces and carried them to the children, saying, "I wonder who Mr. Thorne has been writing to."

"I'm sure I don't know, and don't care," replied the oldest of the children; "and I don't see how it concerns you."

"But it does concern me," replied Ellen; "for I'm afraid he's been writing to the south about my mother."

They laughed at her, and called her a silly thing, but good-naturedly put the fragments of writing together, in order to read them to her. They were no sooner arranged, than the little girl exclaimed, "I declare, Ellen, I believe you are right."

The contents of Mr. Thorne's letter, as nearly as I can remember, were as follows: "I have seen your slave, Linda, and conversed with her. She can be taken very easily, if you manage prudently. There are enough of us here to swear to her identity as your property. I am a patriot, a lover of my country, and I do this as an act of justice to the laws." He concluded by informing the doctor of the street and number where I lived. The children carried the pieces to Mrs. Hobbs, who immediately went to her brother's room for an explanation. He was not to be found. The servant said they saw him go out with a letter in his hand, and they supposed he had gone to the post office. The natural inference was, that he had sent to Dr. Flint a copy of those fragments. When he returned, his sister accused him of it, and he did not deny the charge. He went immediately to his room, and the next morning he was missing. He had gone over to New York, before any of the family were astir.

It was evident that I had no time to lose; and I hastened back to the city with a heavy heart. Again I was to be torn from a comfortable home, and all my plans for the welfare of my children were to be frustrated by that demon Slavery! I now regretted that I never told Mrs. Bruce my story. I had not concealed it merely on account of being a fugitive; that would have made her anxious, but it would have excited sympathy in her kind heart. I valued her good opinion, and I was afraid of losing it, if I told her all the particulars of my sad story. But now I felt that it was necessary for her to know how I was situated. I had once left her abruptly, without explaining the reason, and it would not be proper to do it again. I went home resolved to tell her in the morning. But the sadness of my face attracted her attention, and, in answer to her kind inquiries, I poured out my full heart to her, before bed time. She listened with true womanly sympathy, and told me she would do all she could to protect me. How my heart blessed her!

Early the next morning, Judge Vanderpool and Lawyer Hopper were consulted. They said I had better leave the city at once, as the risk would be great if the case came to trial. Mrs. Bruce took me in a carriage to the house of one of her friends, where she assured me I should be safe until my brother could arrive, which would be in a few days. In the interval my thoughts were much occupied with Ellen. She was mine by birth, and she was also mine by Southern law, since my grandmother held the bill of sale that made her so. I did not feel that she was safe unless I had her with me. Mrs. Hobbs, who felt badly about her brother's treachery, yielded to my entreaties, on condition that she should return in ten days. I avoided making any promise. She came to me clad in very thin garments, all outgrown, and with a school satchel on her arm, containing a few articles. It was late in October, and I knew the child must suffer; and not daring to go out in the streets to purchase any thing, I took off my own flannel skirt and converted it into one for her. Kind Mrs. Bruce came to bid me good by, and when she saw that I had taken off my clothing for my child, the tears came to her eyes. She said, "Wait for me, Linda," and went out. She soon returned with a nice warm shawl and hood for Ellen. Truly, of such souls as hers are the kingdom of heaven.

My brother reached New York on Wednesday. Lawyer Hopper advised us to go to Boston by the Stonington route, as there was less Southern travel in that direction. Mrs. Bruce directed her servants to tell all inquirers that I formerly lived there, but had gone from the city.

We reached the steamboat Rhode Island in safety. That boat employed colored hands, but I knew that colored passengers were not admitted to the cabin. I was very desirous for the seclusion of the cabin, not only on account of exposure to the night air, but also to avoid observation. Lawyer Hopper was waiting on board for us. He spoke to the stewardess, and asked, as a particular favor, that she would treat us well. He said to me, "Go and speak to the captain yourself by and by. Take your little girl with you, and I am sure that he will not let her sleep on deck." With these kind words and a shake of the hand he departed.

The boat was soon on her way, bearing me rapidly from the friendly home where I had hoped to find security and rest. My brother had left me to purchase the tickets, thinking that I might have better success than he would. When the stewardess came to me, I paid what she asked, and she gave me three tickets with clipped corners. In the most unsophisticated manner I said, "You have made a mistake; I asked you for cabin tickets. I cannot possibly consent to sleep on deck with my little daughter." She assured me there was no mistake. She said on some of the routes colored people were allowed to sleep in the cabin, but not on this route, which was much traveled by the wealthy. I asked her to show me to the captain's office, and she said she would after tea. When the time came, I took Ellen by the hand and went to the captain, politely requesting him to change our tickets, as we should be very uncomfortable on deck. He said it was contrary to their custom, but he would see that we had berths below; he would also try to obtain comfortable seats for us in the cars; of that he was not certain, but he would speak to the conductor about it, when the boat arrived. I thanked him, and returned to the ladies' cabin. He came afterwards and told me that the conductor of the cars was on board, that he had spoken to him, and he had promised to take care of us. I was very much surprised at receiving so much kindness. I don't know whether the pleasing face of my little girl had won his heart, or whether the stewardess inferred from Lawyer Hopper's manner that I was a fugitive, and had pleaded with him

413

in my behalf.

When the boat arrived at Stonington, the conductor kept his promise, and showed us to seats in the first car, nearest the engine. He asked us to take seats next the door, but as he passed through, we ventured to move on toward the other end of the car. No incivility was offered us, and we reached Boston in safety.

The day after my arrival was one of the happiest of my life. I felt as if I was beyond the reach of the bloodhounds; and, for the first time during many years, I had both my children together with me. They greatly enjoyed their reunion, and laughed and chatted merrily. I watched them with a swelling heart. Their every motion delighted me.

I could not feel safe in New York, and I accepted the offer of a friend, that we should share expenses and keep house together. I represented to Mrs. Hobbs that Ellen must have some schooling, and must remain with me for that purpose. She felt ashamed of being unable to read or spell at her age, so instead of sending her to school with Benny, I instructed her myself till she was fitted to enter an intermediate school. The winter passed pleasantly, while I was busy with my needle, and my children with their books.

XXXVII

A Visit to England

In the spring, sad news came to me. Mrs. Bruce was dead. Never again, in this world, should I see her gentle face, or hear her sympathizing voice. I had lost an excellent friend, and little Mary had lost a tender mother. Mr. Bruce wished the child to visit some of her mother's relatives in England, and he was desirous that I should take charge of her. The little motherless one was accustomed to me, and attached to me, and I thought she would be happier in my care than in that of a stranger. I could also earn more in this way than I could by my needle. So I put Benny to a trade, and left Ellen to remain in the house with my friend and go to school.

We sailed from New York, and arrived in Liverpool after a pleasant voyage of twelve days. We proceeded directly to London, and took lodgings at the Adelaide Hotel. The supper seemed to me less luxurious than those I had seen in American hotels; but my situation was indescribably more pleasant. For the first time in my life I was in a place where I was treated according to my deportment, without reference to my complexion. I felt as if a great millstone had been lifted from my breast. Ensconced in a pleasant room, with my dear little charge, I laid my head on my pillow, for the first time, with the delightful consciousness of pure, unadulterated freedom.

As I had constant care of the child, I had little opportunity to see the wonders of that great city; but I watched the tide of life that flowed through the streets, and found it a strange contrast to the stagnation in our Southern towns. Mr. Bruce took his little daughter to spend some days with friends in Oxford Crescent, and of course it was necessary for me to accompany her. I had heard much of the systematic method of English education, and I was very desirous that my dear Mary should steer straight in the midst of so much propriety. I closely observed her little playmates and their nurses, being ready to take any lessons in the science of good management. The children were more rosy than American children, but I did not see that they differed materially in other respects. They were like all children—sometimes docile and sometimes wayward.

We next went to Steventon, in Berkshire. It was a small town, said to be the poorest in the county. I saw men working in the fields for six shillings, and seven shillings, a week, and women for sixpence, and sevenpence, a day, out of which they boarded themselves. Of course they lived in the most primitive manner; it could not be otherwise, where a woman's wages for an entire day were not sufficient to buy a pound of meat. They paid very low rents, and their clothes were made of the cheapest fabrics, though much better than could have been procured in the United States for the same money. I had heard much about the oppression of the poor in Europe. The people I saw around me were, many of them, among the poorest poor. But when I visited them in their little thatched cottages, I felt that the condition of even the meanest and most ignorant among them was vastly superior to the condition of the most favored slaves in America. They labored hard; but they were not ordered out to toil while the stars were in the sky, and driven and slashed by an overseer, through heat and cold, till the stars shone out again. Their homes were very humble; but they were protected by law. No insolent patrols could come, in the dead of night, and flog them at their pleasure. The father, when he closed his cottage door, felt safe with his family around him. No master or overseer could come and take from him his wife, or his daughter. They must separate to earn their living; but the parents knew where their children were going, and could communicate with them by letters. The relations of husband and wife, parent and child, were too sacred for the richest noble in the land to violate with impunity. Much was being done to enlighten these poor people. Schools were established among them, and benevolent societies were active in efforts to ameliorate their condition. There was no law forbidding them to learn to read and write; and if they helped each other in spelling out the Bible, they were in no danger of thirty-nine lashes, as was the case with myself and poor, pious, old uncle Fred. I repeat that the most ignorant and the most destitute of these peasants was a thousand fold better off than the most pampered American slave.

I do not deny that the poor are oppressed in Europe. I am not disposed to paint their condition so rose-colored as the Hon. Miss Murray* paints the condition of the slaves in the United States. A small portion of *my* experience would enable her to read her own pages with anointed eyes. If she were to lay aside her title, and, instead of visiting among the fashionable, become domesticated, as a poor governess, on some plantation in Louisiana or Alabama, she would see and hear things that would make her tell quite a different story.

My visit to England is a memorable event in my life, from the fact of my having there received strong religious impressions. The contemptuous manner in which the communion had been administered to colored people, in my native place; the church membership of Dr. Flint, and others like him; and the buying and selling of slaves, by professed ministers of the gospel, had given me a prejudice against the Episcopal church. The whole service seemed to me a mockery and a sham. But my home in Steventon was in the family of a clergyman, who was a true disciple of Jesus. The beauty of his daily life inspired me with faith in the genuineness of Christian professions. Grace entered my heart, and I knelt at the communion table, I trust, in true humility of soul.

I remained abroad ten months, which was much longer than I had anticipated. During all that time, I never saw the slightest symptom of prejudice against color. Indeed, I entirely forgot it, till the time came for us to return to America.

XXXVIII

RENEWED INVITATIONS TO GO SOUTH

We had a tedious winter passage, and from the distance specters seemed to rise up on the shores of the United States. It is a sad feeling to be afraid of one's native country. We arrived in New York safely, and I hastened to Boston to look after my children. I found Ellen well, and improving at her school; but Benny was not there to welcome me. He had been left at a good place to learn a trade, and for several months every thing worked well. He was liked by the master, and was a favorite with his fellow-apprentices; but one day they accidentally discovered a fact they had never before suspected—that he was colored! This at once transformed him into a different being. Some of the apprentices were Americans, others American-born Irish; and it was offensive to their dignity to have a "nigger" among them, after they had been told that he was a "nigger." They began by treating him with silent scorn, and finding that he returned the same, they resorted to insults and abuse. He was too spirited a boy to stand that, and he went off. Being desirous to do something to support himself, and having no one to advise him, he shipped for a whaling voyage. When I received these tidings I shed many tears, and bitterly reproached myself for having left him so long. But I had done it for the best, and now all I could do was to pray to the heavenly Father to guide and protect him.

Not long after my return, I received the following letter from Miss Emily Flint, now Mrs. Dodge:—

"In this you will recognize the hand of your friend and mistress. Having heard that you had gone with a family to Europe, I have waited to hear of your return to write to you. I should have answered the letter you wrote to me long since, but as I could not then act independently of my father, I knew there could be nothing done satisfactory to

*Hon. Amelia Matilda Murray (1795-1884) was an English visitor and author of *Letters from the United States, Cuba and Canada,* published in London and New York in 1856. The closing words of her book exemplified her proslavery attitudes. "It is my belief, you may as well attempt to improve the morals, and add to the happiness of idiots by turning them out of asylums, as to imagine you can benefit the 'darkies' by abolitionism. Yours affectionately, A. M. M." W. T.

you. There were persons here who were willing to buy you and run the risk of getting you. To this I would not consent. I have always been attached to you, and would not like to see you the slave of another, or have unkind treatment. I am married now, and can protect you. My husband expects to move to Virginia this spring, where we think of settling. I am very anxious that you should come and live with me. If you are not willing to come, you may purchase yourself; but I should prefer having you live with me. If you come, you may, if you like, spend a month with your grandmother and friends, then come to me in Norfolk, Virginia. Think this over, and write as soon as possible, and let me know the conclusion. Hoping that your children are well, I remain your friend and mistress."

Of course I did not write to return thanks for this cordial invitation. I felt insulted to be thought stupid enough to be caught by such professions.

" 'Come up into my parlor,' said the spider to the fly;
' 'Tis the prettiest little parlor that ever you did spy.'"

It was plain that Dr. Flint's family were apprised of my movements, since they knew of my voyage to Europe. I expected to have further trouble from them; but having eluded them thus far, I hoped to be as successful in future. The money I had earned, I was desirous to devote to the education of my children, and to secure a home for them. It seemed not only hard, but unjust, to pay for myself. I could not possibly regard myself as a piece of property. Moreover, I had worked many years without wages, and during that time had been obliged to depend on my grandmother for many comforts in food and clothing. My children certainly belonged to me; but though Dr. Flint had incurred no expense for their support, he had received a large sum of money for them. I knew the law would decide that I was his property, and would probably still give his daughter a claim to my children; but I regarded such laws as the regulations of robbers, who had no rights that I was bound to respect.

The fugitive Slave Law had not then passed. The judges of Massachusetts had not then stooped under chains to enter her courts of justice, so called. I knew my old master was rather skittish of Massachusetts. I relied on her love of freedom, and felt safe on her soil. I am now aware that I honored the old Commonwealth beyond her deserts.

XXXIX

THE CONFESSION

For two years my daughter and I supported ourselves comfortably in Boston At the end of that time, my brother William offered to send Ellen to a boarding school. It required a great effort for me to consent to part with her, for I had few near ties, and it was her presence that made my two little rooms seem home-like. But my judgment prevailed over my selfish feelings. I made preparations for her departure. During the two years we had lived together I had often resolved to tell her something about her father; but I had never been able to muster sufficient courage. I had a shrinking dread of diminishing my child's love. I knew she must have curiosity on the subject, but she had never asked a question. She was always very careful not to say any thing to remind me of my troubles. Now that she was going from me, I thought if I should die before she returned, she might hear my story from some one who did not understand the palliating circumstances; and that if she were entirely ignorant on the subject, her sensitive nature might receive a rude shock.

When we retired for the night, she said, "Mother, it is very hard to leave you alone. I am almost sorry I am going, though I do want to improve myself. But you will write to me often; won't you, mother?"

I did not throw my arms round her. I did not answer her. But in a calm, solemn way, for it cost me great effort, I said, "Listen to me, Ellen; I have something to tell you!" I recounted my early sufferings in slavery, and told her how nearly they had crushed me. I began to tell her how they had driven me into a great sin, when she clasped me in her arms, and exclaimed, "O, don't, mother! Please don't tell me any more."

I said, "But, my child, I want you to know about your father."

"I know all about it, mother," she replied; "I am nothing to my father, and he is nothing to me. All my love is for you. I was with him five months in Washington, and he never cared for me. He never spoke to me as he did to his little Fanny. I knew all the time he was my father, for Fanny's nurse told me so; but she said I must never tell any body, and I never did. I used to wish he would take me in his arms and kiss me, as he did Fanny; or that he would sometimes smile at me, as he did at her. I thought if he was my own father, he ought to love me. I was a little girl then, and didn't know any better. But now I never think any thing about my father. All my love is for you." She hugged me closer as she spoke, and I thanked God that the knowledge I had so much dreaded to impart had not diminished the affection of my child. I had not the slightest idea she knew that portion of my history. If I had, I should have spoken to her long before; for my pent-up feelings had often longed to pour themselves out to some one I could trust. But I loved the dear girl better for the delicacy she had manifested towards her unfortunate mother.

The next morning, she and her uncle started on their journey to the village in New York, where she was to be placed at school. It seemed as if all the sunshine had gone away. My little room was dreadfully lonely. I was thankful when a message came from a lady, accustomed to employ me, requesting me to come and sew in her family for several weeks. On my return, I found a letter from brother William. He thought of opening an anti-slavery reading room in Rochester, and combining with it the sale of some books and stationery; and he wanted me to unite with him. We tried it, but it was not successful. We found warm anti-slavery friends there, but the feeling was not general enough to support such an establishment. I passed nearly a year in the family of Isaac and Amy Post,* practical believers in the Christian doctrine of human brotherhood. They measured a man's worth by his character, not by his complexion. The memory of those beloved and honored friends will remain with me to my latest hour.

XL

THE FUGITIVE SLAVE LAW

My brother, being disappointed in his project, concluded to go to California; and it was agreed that Benjamin should go with him. Ellen liked her school, and was a great favorite there. They did not know her history, and she did not tell it, because she had no desire to make capital out of their sympathy. But when it was accidentally discovered that her mother was a fugitive slave, every method was used to increase her advantages and diminish her expenses.

I was alone again. It was necessary for me to be earning money, and I preferred that it should be among those who knew me. On my return from Rochester, I called at the house of Mr. Bruce, to see Mary, the darling little babe that had thawed my heart, when it was freezing into a cheerless distrust of all my fellow-beings. She was growing a tall girl now, but I loved her always. Mr. Bruce had married again, and it was proposed that I should become nurse to a new infant. I had but one hesitation, and that was my feeling of insecurity in New York, now greatly increased by the passage of the Fugitive Slave Law. However, I resolved to try the experiment. I was again fortunate in my employer. The new Mrs. Bruce was an American, brought up under aristocratic influences, and still living in the midst of them; but if she had any prejudice against color, I was never made aware of it; and as for the system of slavery, she had a most hearty dislike of it. No sophistry of Southerners could blind her to its enormity. She was a person of excellent principles and a noble heart. To me, from that hour to the present, she has been a true and sympathizing friend. Blessings be with her and hers!

About the time that I reentered the Bruce family, an event occurred of disastrous import to the colored people. The slave Hamlin,* the first fugitive that came under the new law, was given up by the bloodhounds of the north to the bloodhounds of the south. It was the beginning of a reign of terror to the colored population. The great city rushed on in its whirl of excitement, taking no note of the "short and simple annals of the poor." But while fashionables were listening to the thrilling voice of Jenny Lind in Metropolitan Hall, the thrilling voices of poor hunted colored people went up, in an agony of supplication, to the Lord, from Zion's church. Many families, who had lived in the city for twenty years, fled from it now.

Many a poor washerwoman, who, by hard labor, had made her-

---

* Hundreds of blacks, it is said, owed their liberation to Isaac Post (1813-1880) and his wife Amy, pioneers in antislavery, woman suffrage, and other reforms. Their house in Rochester, New York, was a well-known station on the Underground Railroad, the system of cooperation among active antislavery people for helping fugitive slaves reach the North, or Canada. (See also the Appendix.) W. T.

self a comfortable home, was obliged to sacrifice her furniture, bid a hurried farewell to friends, and seek her fortune among strangers in Canada. Many a wife discovered a secret she had never known before—that her husband was a fugitive, and must leave her to insure his own safety. Worse still, many a husband discovered that his wife had fled from slavery years ago, and as "the child follows the condition of its mother," the children of his love were liable to be seized and carried into slavery. Every where, in those humble homes, there was consternation and anguish. But what cared the legislators of the "dominant race" for the blood they were crushing out of trampled hearts?

When my brother William spent his last evening with me, before he went to California, we talked nearly all the time of the distress brought on our oppressed people by the passage of this iniquitous law; and never had I seen him manifest such bitterness of spirit, such stern hostility to our oppressors. He was himself free from the operation of the law; for he did not run from any Slaveholding State, being brought into the Free States by his master. But I was subject to it; and so were hundreds of intelligent and industrious people all around us. I seldom ventured into the streets; and when it was necessary to do an errand for Mrs. Bruce, or any of the family, I went as much as possible through back streets and by-ways. What a disgrace to a city calling itself free, that inhabitants, guiltless of offense, and seeking to perform their duties conscientiously, should be condemned to live in such incessant fear, and have nowhere to turn for protection! This state of things, of course, gave rise to many impromptu vigilance committees. Every colored person, and every friend of their persecuted race, kept their eyes wide open. Every evening I examined the newspapers carefully, to see what Southerners had put up at the hotels. I did this for my own sake, thinking my young mistress and her husband might be among the list; I wished also to give information to others, if necessary; for if many were "running to and fro," I resolved that "knowledge should be increased."

This brings up one of my Southern reminiscences, which I will here briefly relate. I was somewhat acquainted with a slave named Luke, who belonged to a wealthy man in our vicinity. His master

*This may be a reference to James Hamlet, who is said to have been the first person arrested under the Fugitive Slave Law of 1850. A free black of New York, he was taken into slavery in Baltimore but later ransomed for eight hundred dollars put up by private individuals. W. T.

died, leaving a son and daughter heirs to his large fortune. In the division of the slaves, Luke was included in the son's portion. This young man became a prey to the vices growing out of the "patriarchal institution," and when he went to the north, to complete his education, he carried his vices with him. He was brought home, deprived of the use of his limbs, by excessive dissipation. Luke was appointed to wait upon his bed-ridden master, whose despotic habits were greatly increased by exasperation at his own helplessness. He kept a cowhide beside him, and, for the most trivial occurrence, he would order his attendant to bare his back, and kneel beside the couch, while he whipped him till his strength was exhausted. Some days he was not allowed to wear any thing but his shirt, in order to be in readiness to be flogged. A day seldom passed without his receiving more or less blows. If the slightest resistance was offered, the town constable was sent for to execute the punishment, and Luke learned from experience how much more the constable's strong arm was to be dreaded than the comparatively feeble one of his master. The arm of his tyrant grew weaker, and was finally palsied; and then the constable's services were in constant requisition. The fact that he was entirely dependent on Luke's care, and was obliged to be tended like an infant, instead of inspiring any gratitude or compassion towards his poor slave, seemed only to increase his irritability and cruelty. As he lay there on his bed, a mere degraded wreck of manhood, he took into his head the strangest freaks of despotism; and if Luke hesitated to submit to his orders, the constable was immediately sent for. Some of these freaks were of a nature too filthy to be repeated. When I fled from the house of bondage, I left poor Luke still chained to the bedside of this cruel and disgusting wretch.

One day, when I had been requested to do an errand for Mrs. Bruce, I was hurrying through back streets, as usual, when I saw a young man approaching, whose face was familiar to me. As he came nearer, I recognized Luke. I always rejoiced to see or hear of any one who had escaped from the black pit; but, remembering this poor fellow's extreme hardships, I was peculiarly glad to see him on Northern soil, though I no longer called it free soil. I well remembered what a desolate feeling it was to be alone among strangers, and I went up to him and greeted him cordially. At first, he did not know me; but when I mentioned my name, he remembered all about me. I told him of the Fugitive Slave Law, and asked him if he did not know that New York was a city of kidnappers.

He replied, "De risk ain't so bad for me, as 'tis fur you. 'Cause I runned away from de speculator, and you runned away from de massa. Dem speculators vont spen dar money to come here fur a runaway, if dey ain't sartin sure to put dar hans right on him. An I tell you I's tuk good car 'bout dat. I had too hard times down dar, to let 'em ketch dis nigger."

He then told me of the advice he had received, and the plans he had laid. I asked if he had money enough to take him to Canada. " 'Pend upon it, I hab," he replied. "I tuk car fur dat. I'd bin workin all my days fur dem cussed whites, an got no pay but kicks and cuffs. So I tought dis nigger had a right to money nuff to bring him to de Free States. Massa Henry he lib till ebery body vish him dead; an ven he did die, I knowed de debbil would hab him, an vouldn't vant him to bring his money 'long too. So I tuk some of his bills, and put 'em in de pocket of his ole trousers. An ven he was buried, dis nigger ask fur dem ole trousers, an dey gub 'em to me." With a low, chuckling laugh, he added, "You see I didn't *steal* it; dey *gub* it to me. I tell you, I had mighty hard time to keep de speculator from findin it; but he didn't git it."

This is a fair specimen of how the moral sense is educated by slavery. When a man has his wages stolen from him, year after year, and the laws sanction and enforce the theft, how can he be expected to have more regard to honesty than has the man who robs him? I have become somewhat enlightened, but I confess that I agree with poor, ignorant, much-abused Luke, in thinking he had a right to that money, as a portion of his unpaid wages. He went to Canada forthwith, and I have not since heard from him.

All that winter I lived in a state of anxiety. When I took the children out to breathe the air, I closely observed the countenances of all I met. I dreaded the approach of summer, when snakes and slaveholders make their appearance. I was, in fact, a slave in New York, as subject to slave laws as I had been in a Slave State. Strange incongruity in a State called free!

Spring returned, and I received warning from the south that Dr. Flint knew of my return to my old place, and was making preparations to have me caught. I learned afterwards that my dress, and that of Mrs. Bruce's children, had been described to him by some of the Northern tools, which slaveholders employ for their base purposes, and then indulge in sneers at their cupidity and mean servility.

I immediately informed Mrs. Bruce of my danger, and she took prompt measures for my safety. My place as nurse could not be supplied immediately, and this generous, sympathizing lady proposed that I should carry her baby away. It was a comfort to me to have the child with me; for the heart is reluctant to be torn away from every object it loves. But how few mothers would have consented to have one of their own babes become a fugitive, for the sake of a poor, hunted nurse, on whom the legislators of the country had let loose the bloodhounds! When I spoke of the sacrifice she was making, in depriving herself of her dear baby, she replied, "It is better for you to have baby with you, Linda; for if they get on your track, they will be obliged to bring the child to me; and then, if there is a possibility of saving you, you shall be saved."

This lady had a very wealthy relative, a benevolent gentleman in many respects, but aristocratic and pro-slavery. He remonstrated with her for harboring a fugitive slave; told her she was violating the laws of her country; and asked her if she was aware of the penalty. She replied, "I am very well aware of it. It is imprisonment and one thousand dollars fine. Shame on my country that it is so! I am ready to incur the penalty. I will go to the state's prison, rather than have any poor victim torn from *my* house, to be carried back to slavery."

The noble heart! The brave heart! The tears are in my eyes while I write of her. May the God of the helpless reward her for her sympathy with my persecuted people!

I was sent into New England, where I was sheltered by the wife of a senator, whom I shall always hold in grateful remembrance. This honorable gentleman would not have voted for the Fugitive Slave Law, as did the senator in "Uncle Tom's Cabin;" on the contrary, he was strongly opposed to it; but he was enough under its influence to be afraid of having me remain in his house many hours. So I was sent into the country, where I remained a month with the baby. When it was supposed that Dr. Flint's emissaries had lost track of me, and given up the pursuit for the present, I returned to New York.

XLI

FREE AT LAST

Mrs. Bruce, and every member of her family, were exceedingly kind to me. I was thankful for the blessings of my lot, yet I could not always wear a cheerful countenance. I was doing harm to no one; on the contrary, I was doing all the good I could in my small way; yet I could never go out to breathe God's free air without trepidation at my heart. This seemed hard; and I could not think it was a right state of things in any civilized country.

From time to time I received news from my good old grandmother. She could not write; but she employed others to write for her. The following is an extract from one of her last letters:—

"Dear Daughter: I cannot hope to see you again on earth; but I pray to God to unite us above, where pain will no more rack this feeble body of mine; where sorrow and parting from my children will be no more. God has promised these things if we are faithful unto the end. My age and feeble health deprive me of going to church now; but God is with me here at home. Thank your brother for his kindness. Give much love to him, and tell him to remember the Creator in the days of his youth, and strive to meet me in the Father's kingdom. Love to Ellen and Benjamin. Don't neglect him. Tell him for me, to be a good boy. Strive, my child, to train them for God's children. May he protect and provide for you, is the prayer of your loving old mother."

These letters both cheered and saddened me. I was always glad to have tidings from the kind, faithful old friend of my unhappy youth; but her messages of love made my heart yearn to see her before she died, and I mourned over the fact that it was impossible. Some months after I returned from my flight to New England, I received a letter from her, in which she wrote, "Dr. Flint is dead. He has left a distressed family. Poor old man! I hope he made his peace with God."

I remembered how he had defrauded my grandmother of the hard earnings she had loaned; how he had tried to cheat her out of the freedom her mistress had promised her, and how he had persecuted her children; and I thought to myself that she was a better Christian than I was, if she could entirely forgive him. I cannot say, with truth, that the news of my old master's death softened my feelings towards him. There are wrongs which even the grave does not bury. The man was odious to me while he lived, and his memory is odious now.

His departure from this world did not diminish my danger. He had threatened my grandmother that his heirs should hold me in slavery after he was gone; that I never should be free so long as a child of his survived. As for Mrs. Flint, I had seen her in deeper afflictions than I supposed the loss of her husband would be, for she had buried several children; yet I never saw any signs of softening in her heart. The doctor had died in embarrassed circumstances, and had little to will to his heirs, except such property as he was unable to grasp. I was well aware what I had to expect from the family of Flints; and my fears were confirmed by a letter from the south, warning me to be on my guard, because Mrs. Flint openly declared that her daughter could not afford to lose so valuable a slave as I was.

I kept close watch of the newspapers for arrivals; but one Saturday night, being much occupied, I forgot to examine the Evening Express as usual. I went down into the parlor for it, early in the morning, and found the boy about to kindle a fire with it. I took it from him and examined the list of arrivals. Reader, if you have never been a slave, you cannot imagine the acute sensation of suffering at my heart, when I read the names of Mr. and Mrs. Dodge, at a hotel in Courtland Street. It was a third-rate hotel, and that circumstance convinced me of the truth of what I had heard, that they were short of funds and had need of my value, as *they* valued me; and that was by dollars and cents. I hastened with the paper to Mrs. Bruce. Her heart and hand were always open to every one in distress, and she always warmly sympathized with mine. It was impossible to tell how near the enemy was. He might have passed and repassed the house while we were sleeping. He might at that moment be waiting to pounce upon me if I ventured out of doors. I had never seen the husband of my young mistress, and therefore I could not distinguish him from any other stranger. A carriage was hastily ordered; and, closely veiled, I followed Mrs. Bruce, taking the baby again with me into exile. After various turnings and crossings, and returnings, the carriage stopped at the house of one of Mrs. Bruce's friends, where I was kindly received. Mrs. Bruce returned immediately, to instruct the domestics what to say if any one came to inquire for me.

It was lucky for me that the evening paper was not burned up before I had a chance to examine the list of arrivals. It was not long after Mrs. Bruce's return to her house, before several people came to inquire for me. One inquired for me, another asked for my daughter Ellen, and another said he had a letter from my grand-mother, which he was requested to deliver in person.

They were told, "She *has* lived here, but she has left."

"How long ago?"

"I don't know, sir."

"Do you know where she went?"

"I do not, sir." And the door was closed.

This Mr. Dodge, who claimed me as his property, was origi-nally a Yankee pedler in the south; then he became a merchant, and finally a slaveholder. He managed to get introduced into what was called the first society, and married Miss Emily Flint. A quarrel arose between him and her brother, and the brother cowhided him. This led to a family feud, and he proposed to remove to Virginia. Dr. Flint left him no property, and his own means had become circumscribed, while a wife and children depended upon him for support. Under these circumstances, it was very natural that he should make an effort to put me into his pocket.

I had a colored friend, a man from my native place, in whom I had the most implicit confidence. I sent for him, and told him that Mr. and Mrs. Dodge had arrived in New York. I proposed that he should call upon them to make inquiries about his friends at the south, with whom Dr. Flint's family were well acquainted. He thought there was no impropriety in his doing so, and he con-sented. He went to the hotel, and knocked at the door of Mr. Dodge's room, which was opened by the gentleman himself, who gruffly inquired, "What brought you here? How came you to know I was in the city?"

"Your arrival was published in the evening papers, sir; and I called to ask Mrs. Dodge about my friends at home. I didn't sup-pose it would give any offense. "

"Where's that negro girl, that belongs to my wife?"

"What girl, sir?"

"You know well enough. I mean Linda, that ran away from Dr. Flint's plantation, some years ago. I dare say you've seen her, and know where she is."

"Yes, sir, I've seen her, and know where she is. She is out of your reach, sir."

"Tell me where she is, or bring her to me, and I will give her a chance to buy her freedom."

"I don't think it would be of any use, sir. I have heard her say she would go to the ends of the earth, rather than pay any man or woman for her freedom, because she thinks she has a right to it. Besides, she couldn't do it, if she would, for she has spent her earnings to educate her children."

This made Mr. Dodge very angry, and some high words passed between them. My friend was afraid to come where I was; but in the course of the day I received a note from him. I supposed they had not come from the south, in the winter, for a pleasure excursion; and now the nature of their business was very plain.

Mrs. Bruce came to me and entreated me to leave the city the next morning. She said her house was watched, and it was possible that some clew to me might be obtained. I refused to take her advice. She pleaded with an earnest tenderness, that ought to have moved me; but I was in a bitter, disheartened mood. I was weary of flying from pillar to post. I had been chased during half my life, and it seemed as if the chase was never to end. There I sat, in that great city, guiltless of crime, yet not daring to worship God in any of the churches. I heard the bells ringing for afternoon service, and, with contemptuous sarcasm, I said, "Will the preachers take for their text, 'Proclaim liberty to the captive, and the opening of prison doors to them that are bound'? or will they preach from the text, 'Do unto others as ye would they should do unto you'?" Oppressed Poles and Hungarians could find a safe refuge in that city; John Mitchell* was free to proclaim in the City Hall his desire for "a plantation well stocked with slaves;" but there I sat, an oppressed American, not daring to show my face. God forgive the black and bitter thoughts I indulged on that Sabbath day! The Scripture says, "Oppression makes even a wise man mad;" and I was not wise.

I had been told that Mr. Dodge said his wife had never signed away her right to my children, and if he could not get me, he would take them. This it was, more than any thing else, that roused such a tempest in my soul. Benjamin was with his uncle William in

---

*John Mitchell (1815-1875)—the name is spelled with a single *l*—Irish nationalist and advocate of armed resistance to England, was transported from Ireland to Van Dieman's Land (Tasmania) but escaped. In New York in 1853 he established a paper dedicated to the cause of Irish freedom, yet he opposed the abolitionists and came out in favor of slavery. He then moved to Knoxville, where he published a paper serving slavery interests. His sons fought in the Confederate army. "His intense nationalism," wrote a biographer in *Dictionary of American Biography,* "prevented his feeling any spirit of kinship with other men working in similar causes; for liberty in the abstract and humanity at large he cared nothing...." W. T.

California, but my innocent young daughter had come to spend a vacation with me. I thought of what I had suffered in slavery at her age, and my heart was like a tiger's when a hunter tries to seize her young.

Dear Mrs. Bruce! I seem to see the expression of her face, as she turned away discouraged by my obstinate mood. Finding her expostulations unavailing, she sent Ellen to entreat me. When ten o'clock in the evening arrived and Ellen had not returned, this watchful and unwearied friend became anxious. She came to us in a carriage, bringing a well-filled trunk for my journey—trusting that by this time I would listen to reason. I yielded to her, as I ought to have done before.

The next day, baby and I set out in a heavy snow storm, bound for New England again. I received letters from the City of Iniquity, addressed to me under an assumed name. In a few days one came from Mrs. Bruce, informing me that my new master was still searching for me, and that she intended to put an end to this persecution by buying my freedom. I felt grateful for the kindness that prompted this offer, but the idea was not so pleasant to me as might have been expected. The more my mind had become enlightened, the more difficult it was for me to consider myself an article of property; and to pay money to those who had so grievously oppressed me seemed like taking from my sufferings the glory of triumph. I wrote to Mrs. Bruce, thanking her, but saying that being sold from one owner to another seemed too much like slavery; that such a great obligation could not be easily canceled; and that I preferred to go to my brother in California.

Without my knowledge, Mrs. Bruce employed a gentleman in New York to enter into negotiations with Mr. Dodge. He proposed to pay three hundred dollars down, if Mr. Dodge would sell me, and enter into obligations to relinquish all claim to me or my children forever after. He who called himself my master said he scorned so small an offer for such a valuable servant. The gentleman replied, "You can do as you choose, sir. If you reject this offer you will never get any thing; for the woman has friends who will convey her and her children out of the country."

Mr. Dodge concluded that "half a loaf was better than no bread," and he agreed to the proffered terms. By the next mail I received this brief letter from Mrs. Bruce: "I am rejoiced to tell you that the money for your freedom has been paid to Mr. Dodge. Come home to-morrow. I long to see you and my sweet babe."

My brain reeled as I read these lines. A gentleman near me said, "It's true; I have seen the bill of sale." "The bill of sale!" Those words struck me like a blow. So I was sold at last! A human being *sold* in the free city of New York! The bill of sale is on record, and future generations will learn from it that women were articles of traffic in New York, late in the nineteenth century of the Christian religion. It may hereafter prove a useful document to antiquaries, who are seeking to measure the progress of civilization in the United States. I well know the value of that bit of paper; but much as I love freedom, I do not like to look upon it. I am deeply grateful to the generous friend who procured it, but I despise the miscreant who demanded payment for what never rightfully belonged to him or his.

I had objected to having my freedom bought, yet I must confess that when it was done I felt as if a heavy load had been lifted from my weary shoulders. When I rode home in the cars I was no longer afraid to unveil my face and look at people as they passed. I should have been glad to have met Daniel Dodge himself; to have had him seen me and known me, that he might have mourned over the untoward circumstances which compelled him to sell me for three hundred dollars.

When I reached home, the arms of my benefactress were thrown round me, and our tears mingled. As soon as she could speak, she said, "O Linda, I'm *so* glad it's all over! You wrote to me as if you thought you were going to be transferred from one owner to another. But I did not buy you for your services. I should have done just the same, if you had been going to sail for California to-morrow. I should, at least, have the satisfaction of knowing that you left me a free woman."

My heart was exceedingly full. I remembered how my poor father had tried to buy me, when I was a small child, and how he had been disappointed. I hoped his spirit was rejoicing over me now. I remembered how my good old grandmother had laid up her earnings to purchase me in later years, and how often her plans had been frustrated. Now that faithful, loving old heart would leap for joy, if she could look on me and my children now that we were free! My relatives had been foiled in all their efforts, but God had raised me up a friend among strangers, who had bestowed on me the precious, long-desired boon. Friend! It is a common word, often lightly used. Like other good and beautiful things, it may be tarnished by careless handling; but when I speak of Mrs. Bruce as my friend, the word is sacred.

My grandmother lived to rejoice in my freedom; but not long after, a letter came with a black seal. She had gone "where the wicked cease from troubling, and the weary are at rest."

Time passed on, and a paper came to me from the south, containing an obituary notice of my uncle Phillip. It was the only case I ever knew of such an honor conferred upon a colored person. It was written by one of his friends, and contained these words: "Now that death has laid him low, they call him a good man and a useful citizen; but what are eulogies to the black man, when the world has faded from his vision? It does not require man's praise to obtain rest in God's kingdom." So they called a colored man a citizen? Strange words to be uttered in that region!

Reader, my story ends with freedom; not in the usual way, with marriage. I and my children are now free! We are as free from the power of slaveholders as are the white people of the north; and though that, according to my ideas, is not saying a great deal, it is a vast improvement in my condition. The dream of my life is not yet realized. I do not sit with my children in a home of my own. I still long for a hearthstone of my own, however humble. I wish it for my children's sake far more than for my own. But God so orders circumstances as to keep me with my friend Mrs. Bruce. Love, duty, gratitude, also bind me to her side. It is a privilege to serve her who pities my oppressed people, and who has bestowed the inestimable boon of freedom on me and my children.

It has been painful to me, in many ways, to recall the dreary years I passed in bondage. I would gladly forget them if I could. Yet the retrospection is not altogether without solace; for with those gloomy recollections come tender memories of my good old grandmother, like light, fleecy clouds floating over a dark and troubled sea.

APPENDIX

The following statement is from Amy Post, a member of the Society of Friends in the State of New York, well known and highly respected by friends of the poor and the oppressed. As has been already stated, in the preceding pages, the author of this volume spent some time under her hospitable roof. L.M.C.

"The author of this book is my highly-esteemed friend. If its readers knew her as I know her, they could not fail to be deeply interested in her story. She was a beloved inmate of our family nearly the whole of the year 1849. She was introduced to us by her affectionate and conscientious brother, who had previously related to us some of the almost incredible events in his sister's life. I immediately became much interested in Linda; for her appearance was prepossessing, and her deportment indicated remarkable delicacy of feeling and purity of thought.

"As we became acquainted, she related to me, from time to time, some of the incidents in her bitter experiences as a slave-woman. Though impelled by a natural craving for human sympathy, she passed through a baptism of suffering, even in recounting her trials to me, in private confidential conversations. The burden of these memories lay heavily upon her spirit—naturally virtuous and refined. I repeatedly urged her to consent to the publication of her narrative; for I felt that it would arouse people to a more earnest work for the disinthralment of millions still remaining in that soul crushing condition, which was so unendurable to her. But her sensitive spirit shrank from publicity. She said, 'You know a woman can whisper her cruel wrongs in the ear of a dear friend much easier than she can record them for the world to read.' Even in talking with me, she wept so much, and seemed to suffer such mental agony, that I felt her story was too scared to be drawn from her by inquisitive questions, and I left her free to tell as much, or as little, as she chose. Still, I urged upon her the duty of publishing her experience, for the sake of the good it might do; and, at last, she undertook the task.

"Having been a slave so large a portion of her life, she is unlearned; she is obliged to earn her living by her own labor, and she has worked untiringly to procure education for her children; several times she has been obliged to leave her employments, in order to fly from the man-hunters and woman-hunters of our land; but she pressed through all these obstacles and overcame them. After the labors of the day were over, she traced secretly and wearily, by the midnight lamp, a truthful record of her eventful life.

"This Empire State is a shabby place of refuge for the oppressed; but here, through anxiety, turmoil, and despair, the freedom of Linda and her children was finally secured, by the exertions of a generous friend. She was grateful for the boon; but the idea of having been *bought* was always galling to a spirit that could never acknowledge itself to be a chattel. She wrote to us thus, soon after the event: 'I thank you for your kind expressions in regard to my freedom; but the freedom I had before the money was paid was dearer to me. God gave me that freedom; but man put God's image in the seals with the paltry sum of three hundred dollars. I served for my liberty as faithfully as Jacob served for Rachel. At the end, he had large possessions; but I was robbed of my victory; I was obliged to resign my crown, to rid myself of a tyrant.'

"Her story, as written by herself, cannot fail to interest the reader. It is a sad illustration of the condition of this country, which boasts of its civilization, while it sanctions laws and customs which make the experiences of the present more strange than any fictions of the past. AMY POST.
"ROCHESTER, N.Y., Oct. 30th, 1859."

The following testimonial is from a man who is now a highly respectable colored citizen of Boston. L. M. C.

"This narrative contains some incidents so extraordinary, that, doubtless, many persons, under whose eyes it may chance to fall, will be ready to believe that it is colored highly, to serve a special purpose. But, however it may be regarded by the incredulous, I know that it is full of living truths. I have been well acquainted with the author from my boyhood. The circumstances recounted in her history are perfectly familiar to me. I knew of her treatment from her master; of the imprisonment of her children; of their sale and redemption; of her seven years' concealment; and of her subsequent escape to the North. I am now a resident of Boston, and am a living witness to the truth of this interesting narrative.
George W. Lowther."